*Poverty, Charity, and Motherhood*

# Poverty, Charity, and Motherhood

## Maternal Societies in Nineteenth-Century France

CHRISTINE ADAMS

*University of Illinois Press*

URBANA, CHICAGO, AND SPRINGFIELD

Library of Congress Cataloging-in-Publication Data
Adams, Christine, 1962–
Poverty, charity, and motherhood : maternal societies
in nineteenth-century France / Christine Adams.
   p.   cm.
Includes bibliographical references and index.
ISBN 978-0-252-03547-0 (cloth : alk. paper)
1. Child welfare—France—History.
2. Mothers—Services for—France—History.
3. Children—Services for—France—History.
4. Poor—Services for—France—History.
I. Title.
HV761.A6A33      2010
362.7—dc22      2010002140

*To Paul, Sylvie, and Julia*

# Contents

# Acknowledgments

I first came across the Society for Maternal Charity when I was working on my dissertation, the story of a family in eighteenth-century Bordeaux. Fascinated by the documents, I vowed to come back to them. I got my first chance in 1995 when, thanks to a summer stipend from the National Endowment for the Humanities, I was able to spend two months researching in Bordeaux and Marseille. I was forced to put the Society for Maternal Charity aside for the next several years while I turned my dissertation into my first book, helped to edit a volume of essays, gave birth to my second child, and made tenure. It was during my first sabbatical, in 1999–2000, that I was able to turn my attention fully to maternal societies once again, deciding to expand my study to encompass the seven cities it now includes.

A book project requires the assistance of many people and institutions. I was very lucky to work with the University of Illinois Press. Since the beginning, Laurie Matheson has been supportive and encouraging, the ideal editor; the comments of the readers were crucial in making this a stronger book. I am also grateful for the assistance of project editor Jennifer Clark and copyeditor Angela Buckley. In addition to the NEH grant that launched this study, I received a Mellon Foreign Area Fellowship from the Library of Congress in 1999–2000, which allowed me to work there during my sabbatical. My place of employment, St. Mary's College of Maryland, helped to fund research trips with Faculty Development Grants in 1995, 1999, 2004, and 2005. In 2002 I received a fellowship to attend an NEH Summer Seminar on Motherhood and the Nation-State at Stanford University, organized by Karen M. Offen and Marilyn J. Boxer. The seminar was a fabulous experience that offered me new ways to think about the relationship between mothers and the state; both Karen and Marilyn have remained mentors and valued friends and helped immeasurably with this project. Chapter 4 of this book appeared in an earlier form as "In the Public Interest: Charitable Association, The State, and the Status of Utilité Publique in Nineteenth-Century France," in *Law and History Review* 25:2 (Summer 2007). I have also drawn on material published in two earlier articles: "Maternal Societies in France: Private Charity before the Welfare State," *Journal of Women's History* 17:1 (Spring 2005); and "Constructing Mothers and Families: The Society for Maternal Charity of Bordeaux, 1805–1860," *French Historical Studies* 22 (Winter 1999).

Working in France is always a pleasure. In Paris, the personnel at the Archives Nationales, the Bibliothèque Nationale, and especially the Archives de l'Assistance Publique were unfailingly professional and helpful. In Bordeaux, a city I knew well, colleagues at the Archives Départementales de la Gironde, Archives Municipales, and Bibliothèque Municipale were a joy; I was thrilled to work with my old friends Jean-Pierre Bériac and Jean-Paul Avisseau once again, and the woman in charge of microfilm at the Archives Départementales was amazingly helpful and generous. In Marseille, Claude and Claude Bayle (husband and wife) kindly showed me around the city and oriented me at the Archives Départementales des Bouches-du-Rhône, the Archives Municipales, and the Bibliothèque Municipale. In Rouen I was able to locate the necessary documents in a very quick trip to the Archives Départementales de la Seine-Maritime; the staff efficiently photocopied large numbers of documents, and my colleague Jeff Horn (who also shared a number of citations he came across in his own research) generously retrieved them for me. My trip to Limoges, where I worked at the Archives Départementales de la Haute-Vienne and the Bibliothèque Municipale, was a delight, as Marie-Ange Huon and Jonathan Bass opened their home to me. I arrived at Lyon and Dijon relatively late in this project, but I fell in love with both cities. The staff of the Archives Départementales du Rhône politely looked the other way as I spent several afternoons making photocopies; the Archives Municipales and Bibliothèque Municipale were equally obliging. I also have happy memories of the Archives Départementales de la Côte-d'Or, with its plaque commemorating Mozart's appearance there, and the Bibliothèque Municipale of Dijon.

Friends and colleagues have generously shared their time and expertise to read parts of this book, to offer suggestions, and to endlessly discuss it with me over coffee and drinks. Robert Forster, my graduate school mentor, has continued to be interested in my work; he was the first person to read the manuscript, and his criticisms were, as always, on target. Julie Hardwick and Denise Z. Davidson also both read the entire manuscript in draft; Denise has provided me with documents and citations over the years, as our work overlaps in some important ways. Carol E. Harrison offered thoughtful advice, especially on Chapter 4, and I have profited from the friendship of Sarah A. Curtis, who also works on charitable ladies. At a conference many years ago, Jo Burr Margadant offered a comment on a panel that Sarah and I collaborated on, and it pointed my work in a particularly promising direction; I never had the chance to tell Joby how important her words were, and I am happy to recognize her now. Sharon Kettering and Jack R. Censer have been unfailingly supportive, as have other members of the Ancien Régime and Modern French History reading groups in the D.C. area; I have appreciated their colleagueship. I don't know what I would have done without my sister Tracy Adams over the years; her careful reading of my work and her willingness to mull it over during our long walks and emails have been invaluable. Rachel G. Fuchs, whom I met at the Bibliothèque Nationale nearly fifteen years ago, has been key to getting this project out the door. Rachel has been a colleague, mentor, and friend and has read nearly everything I've written over the years. I hope that she realizes how much I have appreciated her advice and support.

While I am the only French historian at my small liberal arts college, I have wonderful students and colleagues who have helped me in many ways over the years. Steve Swisdak helped to sort through and organize endless microfilms and photocopies. Tom Barrett and Gail Savage, both of whom served as chair during the genesis of this book, have read chunks of it in various forms and have supported my work in many ways. My colleagues who meet regularly for afternoon coffees have offered encouragement and moral support over the years; Alan Dillingham, in particular, has cheered all my milestones. I especially want to thank Chuck Holden, my colleague in American history, who has been there for me every step of the way, in good times and in bad, and surely knows how much his friendship has meant to me.

My family has borne the brunt of the years I have devoted to this book. While I have researched and written it, I have watched my daughters, Sylvie and Julia, grow from small children to young women. Along the way I have missed dances, graduations, and award ceremonies; they have tried not to make me feel too guilty. My husband, Paul DeLaHunt, has been a loving single parent during my many visits to France and has more than once traveled with two young girls to meet up with me during a research trip. He helped me out with the organization of data and number crunching for this book; I'm not sure how I would have managed without his technical and emotional support. I am so grateful that we are able to give our daughters a life of love and privilege so different from that of the struggling mothers and children I have studied and written about in this book. It is dedicated to the three of them.

# Introduction

## *Maternal Societies in the Nineteenth Century*

At the general assembly of Lyon's Society for Maternal Charity in March 1847, Madame Delahante, *présidente,* celebrated the positive social influence of her charitable organization: "Some of these Ladies have also prevented several mothers from placing their children at the Foundling Hospice [Hospice des Enfants-Trouvés]; one of them gave the Maternal Charity's aid to a wretched woman who had already left two of these children at the Enfants-Trouvés and was prepared to do the same with the third; through her advice [*conseils*] and through her assistance these three children escaped the unhappy fate of abandoned children and were returned to their family and the dignity of legitimate children."[1] Emphasizing the personal ministrations of the *dames administrantes*[2] whose assistance and "conseils" persuaded the poor mother to keep her newborn and to retrieve two other children from the foundling hospice, Madame Delahante took credit for the happy outcome.

And certainly the outcome seemed happy. Still, the impression left by the vignette of a poor woman nonchalantly abandoning two children and ready to leave a third bears considerable nuancing. The account does not linger on the particulars; however, we can assume that this mother lived in one of the poorest sections of Lyon, perhaps in the center of town, between the right bank of the Saône and the left bank of the Rhône rivers. The *dame administrante* would not have had to travel far with her servant; the elegant Place Bellecour, home to many of the city's elite families, also lay between the two rivers. We can imagine the scenario. Despite the proximity to her neighborhood, she seems far from her elegant home as she mounts the crooked steps of the dark, dank lodging. The smell from the latrine on the landing is overwhelming. Entering the small attic room, she finds the object of her visit lying on a mattress on the floor, covered in thin, dirty bedclothes, attended by a neighbor who had helped her through childbirth. Her husband, a *canut,* a weaver, is not present; a victim of the "dead season" in the silk industry, he has left the city in search of temporary employment, or even alms, although proud silk workers were reluctant to beg. The silent loom rises in the corner of the bare room, as clean as an exhausted pregnant woman who had to carry in water could make it. The air is fetid in the closed space; it had been impossible to clean away all the remnants of the recent birth.

Our visiting lady had heard about this poor mother from the local *bureau de bienfaisance* (municipal relief agency). She has already climbed these stairs once before, to encourage the expectant mother to apply to her organization for assistance, giving her the subscription card to present to the society's secretary-treasurer. Consequently, the poor mother had gone to the home of M. Perret-Lagrive in the ninth month of her pregnancy to give him her registration card, carrying her proof of marriage, along with a certificate of indigence and good behavior issued by the *bureau de bienfaisance* and her parish priest. She confirmed that she had two living children, omitting the detail that she had been forced to abandon them at the Hospice de la Charité, which receives Lyon's abandoned children and foundlings, when her husband left town. She had hoped that the 100 francs and other assistance that Lyon's maternal charity promised would allow her to keep this baby, rather than abandoning it, as well; the 10 francs she received from M. Perret-Lagrive paid the midwife. However, reality set in, then despair. She realized that she could no more support this child than she could the other two, especially in the absence of her husband. With so little food in the cupboard, she was certain that she would not produce the milk necessary to breast-feed her new baby, as she had promised when requesting aid from the Society for Maternal Charity. She has already confided in her neighbor that she plans to abandon this child, as well.

The *dame administrante* has been visiting the homes of the poor since she was a girl accompanying her mother on her charitable rounds; she has been in many garrets like these. Her Catholic faith taught her that she must overcome her repugnance at the odor, the filth, and the poverty she confronts each time she makes a home visit; she has read *Le visiteur du pauvre* by her fellow Lyonnais, the Baron de Gérando, and knows the importance of face-to-face contact with the poor she serves. Her genuine compassion for these poor mothers helps her to mask the discomfort she feels in this hovel.

She kneels beside the woman holding her baby and motions to her servant to set down the bundle containing the layette, the food, and the first month's stipend. "How are you? Where are your other children?" she asks. The mother begins to weep and confesses that she has taken them to the foundling hospice and will be forced to do the same with this child. The *dame visiteuse* listens sympathetically. While social economists and others decried the immorality of a woman who abandoned her children to the care of the state, and while the regulations of her charitable organization decreed that this mother's actions should cause her to forfeit the society's assistance, her many years of charitable visits have made this *dame administrante* familiar with the harsh choices that poor mothers faced. In soothing tones, she promises that the society will provide assistance until the return of her husband; she will herself contact the director of the Hospice de la Charité to arrange for the return of her other children.[3] Realizing the delicacy of her mission, she shows much tact, but also a certain authority, indispensable qualities in a "visitor of the poor."[4] The miserable mother, exhausted but grieving at the thought of losing yet another child, agrees.

But surely her life did not become any easier with the return of two small children, and an infant to nurse, even with the pecuniary assistance and visits of her *patronnesse,* who continued to visit each week, to pray with her, to check discreetly for any evidence of poor use of the society's funds, and to offer advice that sometimes irritated its recipient, however well intended it may have been. The records of the Society for Maternal Charity offer moving insight into a society in which women of the bourgeoisie urged maternal identities upon women of the working class who had abandoned theirs, more often through necessity than neglect. The efforts of the members of this organization to spread their ideals of motherhood among their unfortunate compatriots merit integration into the narrative of the development of the welfare state in France.

Charitable associations were the key source of assistance for poor individuals before the advent of the welfare state. But this does not mean that these associations survived on private funding alone; indeed, the distinction between the private and public provision of social services was, and continues to be, less clear than we might think. In the United States, the second Bush administration's support of "faith-based" organizations, subsidized by federal dollars, to alleviate social problems is only the most recent manifestation of this blurring of the lines. Historians—particularly gender historians—have long questioned the stark division between public and private;[5] that binary opposition is particularly problematic in the case of charity and social services before the welfare state, and even after the state began to expand its public-assistance programs.[6] The Society for Maternal Charity was a private organization but received strong support from national, departmental, and municipal governments. In fact, the list of revenues from that same *compte rendu* of Lyon's society indicates that assorted governmental sources provided it with 7,790 FF in 1846, nearly 40 percent of its total income for that year.[7] Without state subsidies, the Society for Maternal Charity would have found it difficult to carry out its mission.

State intervention to deal with the problem of poverty and its effects on the family is not a product of our times. Rather, governments throughout history have sought the most effective ways to mitigate poverty and its effects on their most vulnerable citizens, always balancing societal needs with cultural and fiscal constraints, and often working through religious or other voluntary associations. This book focuses on one of the most serious sustained efforts in eighteenth- and nineteenth-century France to assist poor mothers and their children, the Société de Charité Maternelle (Society for Maternal Charity).[8] The best-known female-controlled charity in post-Revolutionary France, the Society for Maternal Charity was dedicated to providing assistance to poor women and their infant children. It was organized and run by middle-class and elite women and drew support from powerful families throughout France, as well as French regimes as diverse as that of Louis XVI, the Revolutionary and Napoleonic governments, subsequent monarchies, the Second Empire, and the early Third Republic. While the Paris maternal society was the largest and the best funded, provincial branches were organized throughout France. By 1813 there were sixty-two societies in addition to that of Paris; in 1831 the number had dropped to only thirty-two; but by 1853 there were forty-three, and sixty-seven by 1862. By the end of the nineteenth century, at least eighty-one maternal societies existed in France.[9]

The goal of the society was to provide financial assistance and moral guidance to women in childbirth and through the first two years of that child's life, in hopes that the mother would bond with, rather than abandon, the child. To that end, the society also championed contemporary ideas of good mothering, family solidarity, and legitimate marriages. This study, then, deals not only with the philosophy and goals of the society, which foreshadowed a variety of actions taken by the French government in the last quarter of the nineteenth century when laying the groundwork for the welfare state, but it also examines constructions of family and maternity that structured official, elite, and popular attitudes concerning gender and poverty. Indeed, maternal societies constitute the crucial link in the transition from a system in which the care of poor families was largely left in the hands of charitable volunteers promoting their own social vision, to a modern French state in which paid social-welfare workers took the lead in providing assistance and advice to indigent mothers and their children in the service of secular goals, including population growth, social hygiene, and strong, patriotic families.

Seth Koven and Sonya Michel have noted that in the United States and Europe since the nineteenth century, women have usually been the first to identify and respond to the social-welfare needs of mothers and children with various charitable organizations.[10] Anne Firor Scott goes further, noting that "it is possible to argue that since the late eighteenth century, women's organizations have provided a kind of early warning system, identifying emergent social needs and trying to deal with them."[11] The Society for Maternal Charity was a European pioneer in this regard. French governments, whether royal or imperial, provided considerable financial and institutional backing for maternal societies, which supplied material and moral assistance to poor parturient women of good character who were already the mothers of large families.[12] The type of assistance provided to indigent mothers by the Society for Maternal Charity—*secours à domicile* (home assistance, sometimes referred to as "outdoor assistance"), delivered in person and accompanied by moral advice and surveillance—would serve as a model for future public assistance to poor mothers and families. As early as 1837, Agénor-Étienne de Gasparin, former prefect of the Rhône and future minister of the interior, in his *Rapport au roi sur les hôpitaux, les hospices, et les services de bienfaisance* (Report to the King Concerning Hospitals, Hospices, and Charitable Services), suggested that a "fine system of home assistance for mothers," along the lines of the Society for Maternal Charity, could replace the nation's foundling hospices. "The Societies for Maternal Charity, whose activities are so *bienfaisantes* [charitable], provide an example of imposing authority, and it would perhaps suffice to organize these societies on a wider scale."[13] Two years later, noted philanthropist Baron Joseph-Marie de Gérando concurred that the assistance offered by the Society for Maternal Charity could easily be expanded, and taken over, in part, by the public sector.[14] The appearance of numerous charities, following a model similar to that of the Society for Maternal Charity, suggests the popularity of this type of voluntary association, with its emphasis on home assistance.[15] When the provision of state-funded services to children and families increased under the Third Republic, government agencies frequently followed the society's model.[16]

However, it was also under the government of the Third Republic that official support for the Society for Maternal Charity began to wane, as the moralistic and religious underpinnings of the societies came into conflict with the secular purposes of the government, especially as the state's welfare provisions were expanded under the leadership of philanthropists such as Théophile Roussel and Paul Strauss.[17] But even so, the Interior Ministry continued to look upon these societies as allies in its efforts to combat infant mortality and child abandonment, and to promote good mothering and strong families.[18]

My analysis of this charitable organization highlights a number of issues that preoccupied politicians and others in nineteenth-century France and that continued to be relevant in the twentieth century and beyond. Most importantly, the spread of this particular charitable organization reflected the growing concern for children's health and welfare. When the Society for Maternal Charity was first founded in 1788, its primary goal was to prevent the abandonment of legitimate children at the overburdened foundling hospices. Commentators decried the horrific mortality rates of abandoned children, but state administrators were at least as concerned about the cost of caring for abandoned children.[19] The issue of child abandonment continued to resonate with the French government and public throughout much of the nineteenth century and remained a serious problem until the 1860s. By the fall of the Second Empire in 1870, the problem of abandonment had declined significantly.[20] However, infant health, welfare, and hygiene achieved increasing importance. By the third quarter of the century, these new preoccupations would be reflected in legislation regulating the wet-nursing industry, maternity leave, and child protection. Maternal breast feeding, which the society championed vigorously, was of increasing interest to legislators, especially after the French defeat at the hands of the Prussians in 1871 against a backdrop of fears over depopulation and infant mortality.[21]

While the approach to mothering became increasingly "scientific" over the course of the nineteenth century, the promotion of maternal breast feeding, the core of the Society for Maternal Charity's program, had its roots in the eighteenth century, in the Age of Enlightenment, and especially in *philosophe* Jean-Jacques Rousseau's sentimental view of motherhood and the crucial role of breast feeding and maternal care in creating a permanent bond between mother and child.[22] The emotional resonance of this imagery, and its potential for ameliorating the effects of poverty, led the founders and later members of maternal societies to emphasize the development and nurturing of these positive emotions to carry out their work.

This new understanding of emotional response and its benefits shaped the program of the Society for Maternal Charity in its formative years and beyond. In his book on the navigation of emotions in pre- and post-Revolutionary France, William M. Reddy argued that many of the practices associated with the Enlightenment were predicated on "the novel view of emotions as a force for good in human affairs," and underlined the new "enthusiasm for emotional expression and intimacy."[23] Historians emphasize the pervasiveness of this "cult of sensibility" in France and in Europe more generally.[24] In the eighteenth century, moral philosophers increasingly valorized the warm sentiments that human beings feel for one another as natural, powerful, and crucial to the humane functioning of society. Rousseau in particular was associated with this school of thought, emphasizing the importance of sentiment in governing human relations.[25] Recognizing the moral value of emotions is a short step from stimulating those emotions for the purpose of accomplishing societal goals, as elite women and the French state sought to do through maternal societies.

While most historians interested in "emotionology" have focused primarily on the disciplining of emotions that accompanied "the civilizing process" in the early modern era, they have paid less attention the process of deliberately provoking, shaping, and making use of emotions considered desirable and socially beneficial.[26] Reddy's work on emotional style, and his exploration of "emotives," in contrast, focuses on conscious efforts by social and political actors to foster and make use of a particular emotional style.[27] In his work, Reddy applied his theoretical framework postulating the interdependence of emotion and emotional expression to eighteenth- and nineteenth-century France to highlight the evolving nature of emotional regimes.

But while the term *emotive* may be new, individuals have long understood this dynamic interplay among word, deed, and emotion. Social actors have long sought to cultivate—or, in Reddy's words, "to manage"—certain emotions beneficial to society. In the sentimental era of the late eighteenth century, the French valued and promoted the emotions of mother love and sympathy. And while the celebration of these emotions originated among the elite and middle classes, those same individuals made concerted efforts to nurture their expression among the poor, as well.[28] In the vignette that opened this chapter, the *dame administrante* urged the poor mother to give way to a maternal love that would impel her to bring her abandoned children home.

The question of mother love has been a thorny issue for scholars interested in the history of emotions. Is maternal love innate, natural, unchanging through time and space? Or was maternal love an emotion "invented," in a sense?[29] Élisabeth Badinter, in her sweeping and controversial book, argued that maternal instinct is a myth and that "At the end of the eighteenth century the idea of mother love resurged with the force and appeal of a brand-new concept . . . What was new . . . was the elevation of the idea of mother love to a natural and social good, favorable to the species and to society." She suggested that the imperative behind this new emphasis was the survival of children, and that the country's terrifying mortality rate could be arrested only if mothers were persuaded to "harness themselves to formerly neglected duties."[30]

The ideal of maternal love undergirded the philosophy of the Society for Maternal Charity. The women who staffed maternal societies believed strongly in the reality of a mother's love but also understood that it could be dulled by poverty and must be nurtured through loving practices, such as breast feeding. But women were also thought be more compassionate in general and more likely to understand the plight of other mothers; hence the emphasis on the development of sympathetic bonds between poor mothers and the women who assisted them and who could model appropriate maternal behavior for them.

And yet charitable organizations and society at large were acutely ambivalent about the proper role of mothers. A high percentage of French married women worked for pay in the nineteenth century, especially in comparison with their English and American counterparts.[31] Despite the growing ideology of domesticity—especially among elite women—throughout the nineteenth century, politicians demonstrated little enthusiasm for pushing women out of the labor force, reflecting economic realities. In some cases, even the *dames administrantes* who staffed the maternal societies were uneasy about poor women leaving the workforce to care for their children. This ambivalence played out in treatises on charity (which often stressed the need to provide working-class women with home-based employment), in government policies on assistance and maternal employment, and in the efforts of some maternal societies to sponsor day cares (crèches) to care for children while their mothers worked in factories.[32]

This uncertainty about the appropriate economic and public behavior of women extended to the charitable work of middle-class and elite women. While some philanthropists lauded the good works of women, especially in assisting poor mothers and infants, others derided what they perceived as the overly religious and moral preoccupations of charitable ladies, especially under the secular Third Republic.[33] In addition, some men objected to the public role that these women assumed, even if their good works could be defended as an extension of appropriate domestic concerns. The Society for Maternal Charity provided a unique and empowering opportunity for elite women to shape not only the nature of their charitable activities, and consequently, to pursue their social agenda, but also to influence government policy decisions concerning women, children, and welfare assistance. This potential power undoubtedly unnerved some policy makers.[34] And yet, despite this uneasiness and concerns about gender roles and behavior, these charities, staffed primarily by women, became an essential tool of state social policy. French regimes, whether royal, imperial, or republican, were never able to settle in a satisfactory manner the question: What is the appropriate role of the state in providing subsistence to its citizens? The issue was first highlighted in the work of the Comité de Mendicité in the early years of the French Revolution of 1789.[35] On the heels of the Revolutionary government's failure to cope with the problem of poverty, economists, philanthropists, and politicians wrote didactic tracts discussing the benefits and pitfalls of various forms of poor assistance in terms that mirror current debates—indication of the intractability of the problem.[36] French governments manifested their concern over poverty in a number of immense statistical reports on foundlings and assisted children, on public assistance, and on charitable associations.[37] In addition, a series of national and international conferences in the second half of the nineteenth century discussed and collaborated on the issues of public assistance and private charity, especially the problem of poor women and infants.[38] By the 1870s, worries about depopulation hammered home by defeat at the hands of the Germans led the French state to provide more meaningful care for at-risk children. The extensive legislation of the Revolutionary, Napoleonic, and subsequent governments grappled with these issues in a variety of ways, but until the last decades of the nineteenth century, private charitable organizations picked up much of the slack.

Since these charitable associations provided important services, services that the government could not or would not provide, their existence raised an important question: What should be the role of the government in subsidizing and controlling voluntary associations like the Society for Maternal Charity? Indeed, prior to 1871 and even beyond, the Society for Maternal Charity operated almost as a branch of government, although local sections tried to maintain independent control of their regulations and procedures. While historians have argued that women's charitable organizations generally possessed more influence in decentralized rather than strong states, recent research suggests that close relations between private-sector charities and governments were common in both weak and strong states; women, in fact, were key in influencing French family policy, even if they did not play a formal political role.[39] Scholars consider France's strongly centralized government exemplary of the strong-state model, but this did not preclude it from relying heavily on private-sector charities to carry out necessary social services—services that the government wished to control, but not necessarily to provide. While Alisa Klaus suggests that private agencies found themselves under increasingly strict government regulation as they were used to carry out public policy over the course of the nineteenth century, I would argue that, from the time of its establishment as an "imperial society" in 1811, the Society for Maternal Charity and its various branches operated under intense government scrutiny and control, and that its apparatus was used explicitly to carry out government initiatives.[40]

This interest in maternal societies suggests that French governments, even under the Ancien Régime, but certainly by the time of the First Empire, found it prudent, indeed necessary, to persuade their wealthy citizens to provide various services to the state, in many cases free of charge or at reduced cost. Robert Forster has examined Napoleon's efforts to administer the empire through the landed notability, which possessed sufficient wealth, leisure, and education to provide certain services. Napoleon and his successors relied upon the patriotism and pride of these notables to bring them into governmental service.[41] Frances Gouda sees a continuation of this process under the July Monarchy, arguing that the central government in Paris cleverly tied the political influence of regional elites to its own agenda and thus was able to use them to govern the country.[42] In a similar way, state officials encouraged elite women throughout France to join charitable organizations like the Society for Maternal Charity, which brought them status and social access while providing the state with a volunteer labor force.[43] Officials recognized the key role that maternal societies played; the permanent secretary of the Interior Ministry referred to Lyon's Society for Maternal Charity as a "useful auxiliary of public assistance in that city."[44] And these women agreed to perform these services, for charitable activities provided them with benefits, as well, both tangible and intangible. Philanthropic work offered status, power, and a public voice to the women who performed it.

But the civic importance of voluntary associations like the Society for Maternal Charity went beyond their role in debates over the best means of managing poverty and bolstering families. Voluntary associations play an important role in structuring civil society more generally, and they both reflect and shape the interests and sympathies of citizens. In the nineteenth century, Alexis de Tocqueville examined not only what he perceived as the centralizing tendencies of the French government, but also the difficulties that the French experienced in trying to create a viable and flourishing civil society, buttressed by a vibrant associational life. These associations act as intermediary (or buffer) between the state and individuals and allow people to learn the habits of citizenship.[45] Therein lay both the possibilities and the limitations of civil society. The French state recognized the benefits of associational life, which fostered the mobilization of charitable resources, cultural assets, and other public goods. But it feared the political and fiscal implications of allowing individuals to join together to work toward a common goal and thus regulated associational activity with a heavy hand. We should not assume that this legal and political control of associational activity is unique to strongly centralized states like France. William J. Novak has demonstrated that public coercive power underlay much of the theoretically private activity of voluntary associations even in the United States, the archetype of the independent civil society with a lively associational life.[46]

While, in general, the state worried about male associational activity far more than that of women, female-led organizations that achieved local or national—and thus political—importance also invited governmental scrutiny of their bylaws, fiscal activities, and charitable practices.[47] This was certainly the case for the Society for Maternal Charity; the Interior Ministry, local prefects, and departmental and municipal authorities kept close watch over the operations of local branches and regularly attempted to direct their actions in conformity with state policies. In part this was because even women's charitable activities could have a civic and political component, especially in a political terrain as contested and unstable as that of nineteenth-century France.[48] Participation in a charitable organization offered women potential access to status and claims to state consideration—not only for themselves, but on behalf of those they represented. And their particular status as women—mothers, wives, and sisters—could legitimize those claims.[49] Gender constrained women's ability to fully participate in the sociopolitical sphere. Still, shifting perceptions of citizenship, *bienfaisance,* and service shaped the ways in which women sought civic status and influence, beginning in the late eighteenth century and continuing through the Revolution and beyond. This new commitment to public service and utility—in addition to the traditional commitment to Christian charitable activity and, in some cases, a practical desire for enhanced social recognition—shaped the way in which women articulated and pursued their good works in tandem with like-minded women and men. The *dames administrantes* promoted their own vision of moral and religious family life as they distributed assistance to poor mothers. This vision could foster conflict between maternal societies and state representatives in some cases, as both sought to foster their own version of the "public good," especially over time as the increasingly secular bent of the French state conflicted with the Society for Maternal Charity's more spiritual mode of action.

## Scope, Methodology, Sources, and Organization

This study examines the Society for Maternal Charity in six provincial cities of France, as well as in Paris, site of the most important and best-funded of the maternal charities. The Paris society, the model for other maternal societies, obviously merited inclusion. But given that there were between 30 and 80 maternal societies in France in any year over the course of the nineteenth century, I chose carefully which others to explore. Certainly, the availability of sources was a key consideration; the archives of the maternal societies in Bordeaux, Lyon, and Rouen were particularly rich. But I also wanted to consider cities and towns that differed in their economic, social, cultural, and demographic profiles, which would allow a profitable comparison of charitable assistance and associational activity in different urban contexts. Local economies, as well as the patterns of employment and unemployment in various locations, created dissimilar cultures of poverty (although poverty was an immense problem in all large cities). The texture of class relations structured interactions between the *dames visiteuses* of the maternal societies and the recipients of their assistance. The history of political dealings between municipal notables and Paris authorities affected the ongoing dialogue between the administrators of local maternal societies, the prefects, and the Interior Ministry. Timothy B. Smith, who analyzed the creation of France's national welfare system by closely examining public assistance for the unemployed in nineteenth-century Lyon, argues that local studies can "highlight how relief systems tended to operate before the advent of the concept of a *national, citizenship-based* right to assistance. Prior to World War I, no such concept existed; assistance was dispensed for practical reasons geared to the needs of the locality in question."[50] Since France lacked a comprehensive national program of poor relief or social insurance prior to the 1920s, care of the poor was a local matter—cities and communes were forced to develop their own solutions to the problem of poverty.[51] Consequently, the nature of both public and private assistance looks very different depending upon the specific region. The end result was great disparity in relief spending between cities; some were comparatively more generous than others, a situation inevitable as long as municipalities were left to make these decisions on their own.[52] These considerations influenced which cities and towns I chose to examine for the purposes of this study.

*  *  *

The second-largest city in France throughout most of its history, Lyon was the capital of the department of the Rhône, a commercial, manufacturing and financial center situated at the confluence of two important rivers. Lyon had suffered enormously during the French Revolution; a center of federalist revolt in 1793, the Jacobin-dominated Committee for Public Safety had vowed to wipe the city off the map, executing nearly two thousand men, women, and children, burning many of its buildings, and renaming Lyon "Ville-Affranchie" (Liberated City). Demographics tell the story: the population of Lyon, which rose to 150,000 inhabitants before the Revolution, was reduced to 102,167 following the siege of Lyon in 1793.[53] The White Terror exacted a terrible revenge on the Jacobin supporters, nearly destroying the city's silk industry, but by 1815, Lyon's economy was well on its way to recovery.[54] The economy of Lyon throughout the eighteenth and much of the nineteenth centuries was dominated by the silk industry, an industry that suffered great instability despite the fact that the city as a whole enjoyed prosperity and economic growth.[55] As a result, Lyon experienced considerable unrest and social conflict over the course of the century, including major upheavals in 1831 and 1834.[56]

In the 1830s, about a quarter of Lyon's inhabitants were employed by the *fabrique,* the silk industry—silk and silk-related products made up about half the city's total commercial income and a third of the value of France's total exports.[57] Because Lyon's silk merchants and individual silk employers relied heavily on immigrant workers to serve as an expansible labor force, the system of public assistance was relatively generous throughout most of the nineteenth century. Not wanting to lose their labor force in good times, and hoping to quell the specter of class unrest, Lyon's elite subsidized workers in lean times, through both public assistance and private charity.[58] Lyon offered a wide array of charitable associations that its bourgeoisie supported. In fact, in response to a particularly severe economic crisis in 1825–26, the city of Lyon created a special committee to stimulate private giving;[59] around that same time, the Society for Maternal Charity began to publish its *comptes rendus.* Many of Lyon's charitable institutions were religious in inspiration; Lyon was a strongly Catholic city.[60] The Society for Maternal Charity was among the most important of its religiously inspired charities but perhaps drew less support than it might have in a city with fewer resources to offer its poor.[61] Still, the members of the society confidently called upon the support of their fellow citizens: "No charity has a goal more useful and more moral; and it is good to make the observation that it entails no kind of costs, and that all our means go directly to the poor. It is easy to understand that it is open to expansion among a population like that of the city of Lyon, which counts more than 80,000 workers of all types, often put at risk of destitution by the suspension of work. But the Lyonnais's spirit of charity has always risen to the level of needs that press around it."[62] Lyon laid claim to founding the first maternal society in France. In response to an appeal from Caron de Beaumarchais, published in the *Journal de Paris* on August 15, 1784, calling on the French to "take an interest in infants and in nursing mothers," the Lyonnais opened a public subscription on January 17, 1785, asking for donations to its Institut de Bienfaisance Maternelle. Its funds dried up during the economic crisis of 1788–89; the maternal society founded as a branch of the Imperial Society in 1811 was not a continuation of the old Institut, although it shared the same goals.[63] The high rate of child abandonment in the city of Lyon—its foundling population was second only to that of Paris throughout the nineteenth century—fostered continued interest in this problem and sympathy for any organization that sought to ameliorate its impact.[64]

This charitable assistance spread into the suburbs, which experienced the bulk of Lyon's growth in the first half of the nineteenth century. The population of Croix-Rousse (Lyon's closest suburb, and the center of fancy silk production, woven on Jacquard looms) quadrupled to 28,711, while the population of la Guillotière increased by a factor of seven, to 41,528.[65] The Society for Maternal Charity delivered assistance to the suburbs of Croix-Rousse, la Guillotière, and Vaise, assigning a *dame administrante* to each of them, but frequently complained about the lack of support from those *faubourgs'* municipal governments.[66]

Perhaps permanently scarred by its treatment during the Reign of Terror, Lyon maintained a strong desire for independence from Paris and the centralizing impulses of France's rulers. While the various regimes were usually able to keep Lyon docile prior to 1868, the Lyonnais's memory of municipal freedom led to discontent under the Second Empire, especially because Lyon had long been a cultural and economic center in its own right and had a tradition of resistance to Paris's attempts at political domination.[67]

Both the economy and the economic trajectory of Bordeaux were very different from those of Lyon. Located on the Garonne River, and capital of the department of the Gironde, Bordeaux was a port city and a key trading partner of England and Holland under the Ancien Régime, both of which valued its fine wines made from grapes grown in the premier vineyards of France. Bordeaux's commercial ties with the French West Indies and its role in the lucrative sugar and slave trade had enhanced the city's economic and demographic importance; between 1750 and 1790, Bordeaux's population nearly doubled, from 60,000 to around 111,000, making it the third-largest city in France. Its wealth underwrote extensive urban renewal, especially under the Marquis of Tourny (intendant of the Guyenne, 1743–58), and intensified local pride. In fact, the city's commercial expansion and prosperity crested during the eighteenth century. Forty-one percent of all French colonial trade went through the Garonne in 1789. But the Revolutionary and subsequent Napoleonic wars were disastrous for Bordeaux's maritime and commercial economy, and the city never fully recovered its economic glory.[68] From about 1795, the city turned monarchist in reaction against the excesses of the Jacobins, and later against the isolationist policies of Napoleon, which cut them off from international trade.[69] However, the bourgeoisie of Bordeaux was not necessarily Legitimist. The policies of the Restoration government rapidly disillusioned many Bordelais; their trade and financial interests would coincide with those of the July monarchy.[70]

While the Revolution damaged the fortunes of Bordeaux's powerful commercial elite, they emerged from the Revolution with a tight hold on municipal power—*négociants* (merchants) and businessmen controlled the municipal government.[71] Their wives would control the Society for Maternal Charity
over the course of the century; Madame Pierre-François Guestier, née Anna
Jonston, daughter of a wealthy wholesale merchant of Scotch-Irish descent,
and the maternal society's longest-serving *présidente* (1832–72), was the wife
of one of the founders of the famous wine house Maison Barton et Guestier.
For the most part, the city's economy continued to revolve around shipping
and wine commerce. The city was religiously diverse; while Bordeaux was
dominated by Catholics, as was the rest of France, Protestants and Jews were
very visible among the *négociant* families and coexisted in harmony by the
nineteenth century. This was true for the patronage and membership of the
Society for Maternal Charity, which was vocally committed to assisting poor
women of all religious faiths and notable for the "perfect harmony which
exists between the members of the different [religious] sects for the good of
the Charity."[72] The Gradis, a wealthy Jewish mercantile family, were strong
supporters of and made a substantial contribution to Bordeaux's maternal
society in 1857.[73]

Despite the traditional economy, Bordeaux's population grew tremendously over the course of the nineteenth century, from 90,992 in 1801 to
261,678 in 1911 (if the suburbs are included, the population grew from 103,000
to 340,360). As in Lyon, much of the increase was from immigrants, coming
to the city in search of jobs—mainly port jobs. The city was slow to industri-
alize, in large part because of the traditional conservatism of the Bordelais
elite. For the most part, outsiders invested in Bordeaux's new chemical and
food industries, which developed late in the century. Bordeaux's commercial
elite was, in fact, quite hostile toward industrial development, preferring
commerce and small family-owned businesses.

The economic trends in the city affected the class structure of Bordeaux;
industrial workers (most of whom were artisans rather than factory workers)
were a minority of the working-class population. The majority of the *classe
ouvrière* worked in small stores and workshops, not in factories, the bulk of
them in commerce, and many were connected to the shipping industry. Given
the vagaries of the commercial market, poverty was an ever-present specter
for workers and the *petite bourgeoisie*. The rich and middling bourgeoisie who
controlled the city made up a relatively small percentage of the population.[74]
Not surprisingly, given the class structure of the city, the wives and daughters
of wholesale merchants dominated the conseil d'administration of Bordeaux's
maternal society, along with a fair number of the professional bourgeoisie

and *hauts fonctionnaires* of the state or the city.[75] It was a popular association, one of the four largest maternal societies in the country, both in money spent and the number of families it assisted each year.[76] More than most maternal charities, it sought to maintain its independence from Paris, an attitude perhaps influenced more generally by the atmosphere of the city; in the words of André Jardin and André-Jean Tudesq, "The pervasive individualism of the region—not a theoretical postulate but an actual experience—marked by greater concern for liberty than for equality, was as hostile to constraints as to disturbances; and a greater tolerance, for example in the relations among Catholics, Protestants, and Jews, went hand in hand with distrust for everything that came from Paris and was too brazenly new."[77]

Marseille was also a port city but was in other ways very different from Bordeaux. While Bordeaux experienced economic stagnation, presided over by a conservative elite, Marseille, located on the Mediterranean, grew into France's most important shipping center. Like Lyon, Marseille was a city of the Rhône valley—located in the department "Bouches-du-Rhône"—and a dynamic metropolis; by the 1860s, Marseille had more than 300,000 inhabitants and was France's third largest city. This represented considerable growth over the population of 90,000 in the year 1811.[78] Much of that growth came during the Second Empire, when the city grew from 195,138 inhabitants in 1851 to 312,864 in 1870;[79] the opening of the Suez Canal enhanced the importance of this port city dramatically.[80] This was a spectacular turnaround from the Revolutionary period, which had damaged Marseille's economy much like Bordeaux's.[81] Raoul Busquet notes that of the 90,000 people living in Marseille under the First Empire, 30,000 received public assistance. Although Marseille had shown enthusiastic support for the Revolution in its early phases, its *fédérés* (militiamen) bringing the anthem "The Marseillaise" to Paris, many turned against the Jacobins; and by the time of Napoleon's fall from power, Busquet argues, "Economic distress had completely alienated Marseille from the empire."[82]

But the economic turnaround was at first slow for the Marseillais. The Restoration monarchy had acquiesced to the demand of Marseille's *commerçants* (shopkeepers) to open the ports for trade, but it took time for Marseille's economy to make the necessary adjustments to the economic changes that had taken place since 1792. The city had lost its continental and colonial markets but had begun to develop other industries, which took a hit with the Restoration. However, the economic future of Marseille over the long term of the nineteenth century was bright.[83] Already under the late Restoration government, and the July Monarchy, Marseille did very well; the conquest of Algeria and the maintenance of a French army in North Africa was extremely beneficial to commerce given its position on the Mediterranean, although the city was also susceptible to outbreaks of disease.[84] Legitimists, Orléanists, and Republicans all continued to play a role in Marseille's political life, and by the late 1860s, Marseille's working class was active in the radical opposition to the Second Empire.[85]

Marseille's location and its reputation even in the nineteenth century as a city open to foreigners led to concerns on the part of its *dames visiteuses* that other maternal societies did not articulate. Marseille's Society for Maternal Charity provided assistance only to "mothers of French families," a distinction the other maternal societies did not make.[86] This meant that poor Italian families, already subject to systematic discrimination and low rates of social mobility, were ineligible for assistance.[87] In addition, the vagaries of maritime commerce meant that the women who staffed Marseille's maternal society were particularly sensitive to the fate of families who had once been comfortably well-off but who, due to the reverses of fortune, were suddenly left in dire financial straits. As a result, the society's 1844 bylaws specified that these "shamefaced families [*familles honteuses*], composed of the nobility, wholesale merchants, seafaring captains [*capitaines au long cours*], and the bourgeoisie [*les bons bourgeois*]" were to be awarded preference in the distribution of assistance.[88]

Rouen, the old capital of Normandy and *chef-lieu* of the Seine-Inférieure (today the Seine-Maritime), was an industrial city by the nineteenth century, although the structure of its economy differed from that of Lyon. Rouen under the Ancien Régime had been an important textile center, although much of the cloth production took place in the surrounding countryside, typical of proto-industrialization.[89] Its location on the Seine River made it easy to ship textiles and other goods and contributed to the development of the city's industries. By 1830, the "*grande bourgeoisie industrielle*" had achieved political as well as economic power. While the wives of *hauts fonctionnaires* and the old landowning nobility that lived within the city controlled the Society for Maternal Charity under the empire and the Restoration, the wives of the industrial bourgeoisie became far more visible after the July Revolution and the advent of Louis-Philippe's bourgeois monarchy. Still, by the end of the July Monarchy, a quarter of the *dames administrantes* were still noblewomen, and they continued to monopolize the presidency of the maternal society until 1860. Madame Pouyer-Quertier, whose husband represented the *nouveaux riche* made wealthy by the cotton industry, was not admitted to membership until 1858.[90]

By midcentury, Rouen was a large city of 100,265 inhabitants.[91] As in other industrial cities, Rouen's working population was vulnerable to periodic downturns in production—for example in 1837, when Rouen's 50,000 workers were hit hard—and never lived particularly well. Already in May 1832 (the year that the cholera epidemic struck), the Commission Administrative des Hospices of Rouen "estimated at 30,000 souls those who, poorly nourished, poorly clothed, and with poor lodgings . . . are sustained by the hospitals of the city." In 1843, more than 7,300 individuals were assisted by the city's fourteen *bureaux de bienfaisance*. By 1848, the number had grown to more than 10,000, a number that still underestimates the true extent of poverty in the city.[92] But not only the textile workers were subject to periods of extreme poverty; artisans and *petits commerçants* also lived close to the margins, often swelling the ranks of the *pauvres honteux* when their businesses suffered a setback.

Like the rest of the French, the Rouennais had suffered during the Napoleonic wars, although mass conscription had improved salaries for some of the skilled laborers left behind. The Restoration improved the city's economic situation until the mid-1820s, when an economic downturn and dip in prices struck the weavers in particular, a trend that continued over the course of the century. The years 1853–57 would be especially difficult; between 1853 and 1855, the number of families assisted by the *bureaux de bienfaisance* of Rouen increased by 17 percent and the number of individuals by 24 percent. The early years of the 1860s were even worse for textile workers, as a free-trade treaty with the British increased competition, while the American Civil War cut off raw-cotton supplies. By the end of 1862, only two-fifths of the cotton textile factories in the Seine-Inférieure were still operating. This downturn was compounded by the fact that workers in the cotton industry, and especially women, were among the worst paid.[93] Poverty led to a high rate of child abandonment in the city, between 650 and 900 per year under the governments of the Restoration and the July Monarchy, which heightened the appeal of the Society for Maternal Charity.[94]

In a city with so much poverty, and the crime that is often the result, the elite feared the working classes as much as they pitied them: "The fear of the beggar and the vagabond turn into social fear in a city where so many individuals employed in industry gather."[95] It did not mean that the Rouen bourgeoisie rejected the benefits of charity—in fact, public assistance and private and confessional charities worked closely together—but they differentiated harshly between the "deserving" and "nondeserving" poor. Poor mothers and children, the targets of the Society for Maternal Charity, figured among the most innocent and deserving of the poor. On the other side, impoverished workers resented and sometimes hated the wealthy industrial bourgeoisie. An 1836 book by Charles Noiret, *Mémoires d'un ouvrier rouen-*

*nais,* described the terrible working conditions of weavers in the 1830s and demonstrated bourgeois responsibility for their deplorable poverty. Rouen's Chamber of Commerce consequently blamed Noiret's work for "the spirit of defiance and lack of submission which reigns among the spinners."[96] Charity was not enough to bridge the gap between rich and poor in Rouen; strikes and other forms of political unrest were common throughout most of the century.[97] The Revolution of 1848, coming at the tail of economic crisis, led to particular ferment in the city.

Dijon, located southeast of Paris in east-central France, was not a port city but, like Bordeaux, was located in an important wine-growing region, in this case, Burgundy. The emphasis on wine is not the city's only similarity to Bordeaux; while the population was significantly smaller (Dijon is the smallest of the seven cities I examine), Dijon, like Bordeaux, experienced "modernization without industrialization."[98] From 1789 until the 1850s, the city remained economically and demographically stagnant, its elite eschewing both the rewards and risks of large-scale industrialization, content to live on the revenues of their vineyards and other agricultural produce. Landowners with extensive properties in the countryside, who often served as functionaries or in the liberal professions, as well, topped the social hierarchy. Change finally came with the building of the railroads; with the construction of a railway line linking Dijon to Paris, the city began to grow significantly, and farmers started to migrate from the rural areas to the town.[99] The earliest immigrants were the *cheminots,* railway workers; but soon they began to move into industrial and commercial establishments whose construction was a by-product of the rail terminal. With the Franco-Prussian War in 1870–71 and the German annexation of Alsace-Lorraine, Burgundy became the French frontier, and Dijon home to refugees and soldiers.

Politically, Dijon and the entire region of the Côte-d'Or enjoyed a reputation for political liberalism. These liberal tendencies contrast with the political leanings of the women who dominated Dijon's Society for Maternal Charity, whose families tended to be conservative, usually Legitimist, in their political inclinations.[100] Perhaps this political disconnect kept Dijon's maternal society from gaining as much support as it did in other cities. Dijon's was one of the few maternal societies that did not receive a subsidy from either the city or the department, despite frequent requests. They also assisted a proportionally smaller number of mothers each year than maternal societies in larger cities.[101] But the generally liberal political attitudes of the town's elite did not lead to economic risk taking on their part; they were not interested in taking the chance that industrialization would lead to the kind of upheaval experienced by their larger neighbor to the south, Lyon.

Still, the lack of industrial development did not mean that there was less poverty in Dijon, although it might have been less striking than in larger industrial cities. Begging was visible in the streets, and between 1826 and 1853, about five hundred infants were abandoned in the city each year, approximately 20 percent of all births. Public authorities strictly limited and controlled assistance, especially under the July Monarchy, and in general believed that poverty was the result of immoral behavior.[102] This hands-off approach on the part of the government provided space for the development of charitable associations sponsored by religious and politically conservative women—in fact, between 1790 and 1911, "the most efficacious charities in Dijon were the result of private initiative."[103]

Limoges, whose maternal society appears to have been less proactive than the others in this study, was a highly industrialized city of factories by the mid-nineteenth century and was the *chef-lieu* of the Haute-Vienne in central France. According to John Merriman, "Limoges, not Paris, was *la ville rouge* in nineteenth-century France."[104] While Limoges had been celebrated for its enamels and silverwork during the Renaissance, by the nineteenth century its most important product was porcelain. The production of textiles was actually the largest industry in Limoges in the 1820s but was overshadowed by cloth production in the cities of the Nord and could not compete for markets nationally. The porcelain industry represented Limoges's future; while the Revolutionary period had not been favorable to the production of luxury goods, in its aftermath, and in particular during the Restoration, a number of individuals founded porcelain factories. In 1830 there were 2,300 porcelain factory workers in Limoges; in 1848, 5,000; and in 1880, 7,000.[105]

The wives of both the commercial bourgeoisie and factory owners (a small group which controlled the city's political and economic life) were among the members of the Society for Maternal Charity of Limoges; they saw their charitable work as a means of quelling labor unrest in the city and of shoring up the labor force for their husbands' factories.[106] As in other industrial towns, the bourgeoisie was actively involved in providing charitable assistance; Limoges was considered a refuge for the poverty-stricken. "Go to Limoges," beggars were still told in the final years of the Ancien Régime; "You will lack for nothing."[107] While that slogan was undoubtedly an exaggeration, Limoges did boast numerous charitable associations; in the words of Louise Mallevergne, one of the *présidentes* of Limoges's maternal society, there was an "infinite number of charitable associations, which, under diverse names, already exist in Limoges."[108] Still, poverty created despair and misery for many. Despite the efforts of the Society for Maternal Charity, a striking number of parents in the Haute-Vienne abandoned their children. Between

1816 and 1842, the proportion of *enfants trouvés* as compared to births was the highest of any department in France: one out of every twenty-four births, as compared to one out of thirty for the rest of the country.[109]

Limoges's growth, the fourth-greatest rate of increase in France during the first half of the nineteenth century, was most striking within the city limits; in 1831, the population reached over 27,000. By 1871, it had risen to 55,300.[110] Unlike Lyon, where much of the demographic growth took place in the surrounding suburbs, Limoges's industrial *faubourgs* remained within the city's limits. The city was overcrowded and dirty; houses were decrepit, sewage ran down ditches in the middle of roads, and butchers still slaughtered animals and left the carcasses on the narrow rue de la Boucherie. Overall, most French had an unfavorable impression of Limoges.

While French factory workers, in particular skilled porcelain workers, were relatively well paid in the first half of the nineteenth century, like silk workers, they frequently faced unemployment during the "dead season" and were subject to fluctuations in demand. Limoges's industries and its workers were extremely vulnerable to periods of crisis. Unemployment was a particularly serious problem in Limoges in 1812, 1817 (the year its maternal society was founded), 1830–31, and 1847, years that were also difficult for other French cities.[111] Any economic crisis that affected the porcelain workers trickled down rapidly to the rest of the city's workforce.[112] The concentration of workers within the city limits created a politically conscious class that sprang into action during the periods of revolutionary crisis, most notably 1830 and 1848. The efforts of charitable ladies were far from sufficient to quell the dissatisfaction of Limoges's suffering working classes.

While these six cities—seven when Paris is included—were very different, all saw the need for a maternal society to help alleviate the poverty so common throughout France. Consider that *bureaux de bienfaisance,* local public-assistance agencies that provided home assistance (as opposed to hospitals that housed people), were available only in about one-third of French communes as late as 1871. They provided very basic assistance (such as bread, coal, and clothing), but nationally, they helped only about 5 percent of the population.[113] Private charities helped to fill the gap, although certainly not adequately, and while, as we will see, the amounts provided by maternal societies were not large, they could play an important role in tiding over poor families during the difficult year following the birth of a child.

Of course, the Society for Maternal Charity envisioned a role for itself that went beyond the simple provision of assistance. Its local archives in these diverse cities offer insight to the encouragement of maternal duty and promotion of the family in cities throughout France, as well as charity in action at the grassroots level. The most useful documents are the *comptes rendus,* accounts issued by maternal societies each year. In addition to receipts and expenses, these reports frequently included commentary on various relevant issues, including the benefits of breast feeding, the difficult lives of poor mothers and their children, and the government's responsibility to provide funding to charities such as their own that assisted the deserving poor. The maternal societies' archives more generally, including correspondence and other records, illustrate elite concerns about poor women and children, as well as interactions between wealthy and poor women (mainly, of course, from the perspective of elite women), as the *dames patronnesses* tried both to alleviate misery and to shape the behavior of the lower classes to fit their vision of a moral society.

This study traces interactions between national and regional organizations in pursuit of these goals and suggests that local efforts were crucial in the promotion of the state's agenda of strong and legitimate families and in ameliorating the worst effects of poverty. Provincial archives, as well as the Archives Nationales in Paris, maintain detailed correspondence among the Interior Ministry (which provided oversight and funds to the maternal societies), the prefects, and the local maternal societies. In addition, the minutes of municipal and departmental council meetings occasionally illuminate the interactions between maternal societies and local governments, especially when they were deputized to carry out functions ordinarily assigned to the city public-assistance offices.

* * *

This narrative of the Society for Maternal Charity is organized thematically, but also in a loosely chronological manner. Chapter 1 examines the history of the society from the time of its origins in 1788, the Revolutionary Era, and its reconstitution during the period of the Consulate. It provides the context for its establishment: the growing problem of child abandonment; the intellectual climate of the Age of Enlightenment, which favored the creation of philanthropic organizations; and the willingness of the royal government to subsidize an organization working to keep families together. The chaos of the Revolution of 1789 led the society to change its tactics and rhetoric, but like other charitable organizations, it disappeared during the Reign of Terror. However, by 1801, the Paris society reassembled; in addition, similar maternal societies began to flourish in several provincial towns. By 1810, the Society for Maternal Charity was a respected and reputedly effective organization that drew Napoleon's attention. Chapter 2 explores Napoleon's appropriation of maternal societies, and the implications of this legacy of imperial control.

Napoleon believed that the society could both bolster the status of his new wife and bring prestige to his court. On a practical level, he made use of the labor and financial resources of France's notables to assist poor families and to deal with the pressing problem of child abandonment, but he also used the infrastructure of maternal societies to carry out some of his more ambitious social programs, such as universal vaccination. The members resented this takeover by Napoleon's ministers and tried to resist "mission creep," but even the Bourbon Restoration government and subsequent regimes considered the society and its provincial branches a useful adjunct to state services.

Chapter 3 shifts focus to the vital interactions between poor and elite women, and the maternal societies' efforts to shape poor women into caring mothers. Poor mothers, especially those married and virtuous, were sympathetic charitable objects and were considered susceptible to lessons in domesticity and good mothering from their elite counterparts. The Society for Maternal Charity promoted mother love as the key to social improvement, and the glorification of married motherhood underlay the society's mode of operation. Through maternal societies, the French elite and the state promoted their shared conception of motherhood on the national and provincial levels and shaped the modern celebration of domesticity and civic motherhood. Because of sources available, this chapter focuses primarily on the 1820s and 1830s, but these were also key years in which, according to Denise Davidson, "Middle-class women's lives . . . began to reflect the 'domestic ideology' prescribed by moralists and novelists since at least the time of Rousseau,"[114] which makes an emphasis on these decades particularly fruitful.

This close nexus between the French state and maternal societies sets the stage for Chapter 4, which examines how the sometimes tense relationship between maternal societies and the state played out in a specific context; during the 1840s, the Interior Ministry began to insist that provincial branches of the Society for Maternal Charity obtain recognition of their status as a public utility. The representatives of the ministry saw this as a reasonable demand; any voluntary association that claimed the right to accept donations and legacies was legally bound to obtain formal recognition as an *établissement reconnue d'utilité publique*. However, the administrative councils of a number of maternal societies were unhappy with the demand that they bring their bylaws into conformity with national regulations; they believed that their statutes and bylaws were suited to their local circumstances. This contested terrain highlights the efforts of local actors to resist the centralizing tendencies of the French state at a time when the reach of the government was expanding; but it also emphasizes the important civic role of these women's associations.

Ultimately, women's charitable organizations exercised enormous influence on the development of the welfare state, especially those policies geared to the assistance of women and children. This contribution is the focus of Chapter 5. The society would serve as a model for the provision of social services to poor mothers and their children under the Third Republic and beyond. The visibility of the *dames visiteuses* in providing assistance, advice, and surveillance to poor mothers and their families made it easier for administrators under the Third Republic—and even earlier—to accept women as inspectors in situations where their maternal and domestic skills were valued, paving the way for a new profession for women as social workers. While sometimes dismissed as elitist or overly moralistic, charitable women carried out their tasks with seriousness, and local and national officials respected their authority and effectiveness. Their spirited activity on behalf of the poor women they served brought them into conflict at times with changing governmental priorities as they fought to maintain autonomy for their organization in the face of an ever-encroaching state. Because of the dramatic shifts in policies concerning the provision of assistance to mothers and children after the Franco-Prussian War and the fall of the Second Empire, my quantitative analysis of the work of maternal societies ends with the year 1870.[115]

## Historiographical Context

Drawing on the interdisciplinary tools of gender studies and sociological analysis, this book feeds into several historiographical debates. First, it expands on the work already published by historians of gender and the family concerning domesticity and maternalism. The work of scholars such as Bonnie G. Smith centers on the creation of a domestic culture among middle-class and elite women. Smith identified elite women as key in both shaping notions of feminine and maternal duties and in communicating these ideas not only to their own daughters, but to women of other social classes.[116] However, she was less interested in the reception of those ideas. In her research, Rachel G. Fuchs considered the efforts of the state, through its welfare policies aimed primarily at single mothers, to foster maternal responsibility and to discourage child abandonment. But she focused on the strategies of these women to support themselves and their babies, rather than on their internalization of maternal values.[117] Neither examined the close collaboration between elite women and the state in both helping suffering families and inculcating the desired values in poor mothers, as I do. My approach may suggest the influence of Michel Foucault, who outlined the escalating intervention of the state into private matters with the increasing "tutelage" of the family, and Jacques

Donzelot, who keyed in on the alliance between the state and the family that emerged in the nineteenth century, with its different repercussions for rich and poor.[118] However, while the element of social control was certainly present, it was significantly more nuanced than those more critical of the work of "benevolent ladies" have sometimes acknowledged.[119]

An investigation of these interactions between maternal societies and the state challenges current historiography concerning the influence of women's charitable organizations on the development of the welfare state, especially those policies geared to the assistance of women and children. Alisa Klaus argued that in France, as in other Western countries, women's voluntary associations were a key force in the transition from private charity to a public welfare system, while Catherine Rollet-Echalier saw a direct link between maternal charities and future laws on assistance to large families. However, most historians, such as Seth Koven and Sonya Michel, have asserted that women's charitable organizations did more to shape family welfare policies in decentralized states than in "strong states," like France. This is clearly not the case. The influence of the Society for Maternal Charity demonstrates that we need to reassess this weak state/strong state dichotomy and to give full credit to maternal societies for their role in forging the nature of future assistance to women and children.

This study also suggests that we need to reconsider the political influence of women in the nineteenth century, even women who did not perceive or label their activities as explicitly "political." Elite women devoted considerable time and energy to charitable work, for these female-run organizations offered power and prestige to the women staffing them and gave them a voice in national debates concerning the social claims of poor mothers and their children.[120] The motives of these elite women were complex, and they acted both in concert with and in opposition to official state policies. Alisa Klaus and Evelyne Lejeune-Resnick suggest that, despite official and generous support for the Society for Maternal Charity, it was not a politically important organization.[121] However, this argument depends on a very narrow definition of the term *political*. For example, Jennifer J. Popiel's recent book makes a strong case that the prescribed gender distinctions associated with domesticity allowed women to claim new forms of civic power and influence.[122] While not "public" actors in the same sense that men could be political agents, women, as members of maternal societies, were participants in civil society, the "sphere of social interaction between economy and state, composed above all of the intimate sphere (especially the family), the sphere of associations (especially voluntary associations), social movements, and forms of public communications."[123] Not all political activity need be formalized, and women, as active agents in civil society, exercised political influence through their unofficial—or perhaps more accurately, semiofficial—charitable activities.[124] Bonnie Smith, in her seminal study of bourgeois women in northern France, effectively demonstrated that secular male politicians and industrialists saw women's charitable work as highly political and very problematic, especially when they "attempted to convert their domestic vision to social policy."[125] More generally, individuals linked with philanthropic associations during the Revolutionary era and beyond played a key role in formulating a new image of citizenship and enlightened concern for fellow human beings. This philanthropic agenda—shared by men and women—shaped a wide range of educational, judicial, and economic reforms, and the humanitarian ideals of philanthropists undergirded a number of political discourses of the late eighteenth and nineteenth centuries.[126] Shifting perceptions of citizenship, *bienfaisance,* and service during the period of the French Revolution influenced the ways in which women sought a civic identity through association with others. It is true that for women, the issues of citizenship, associational activity, utility, and service were problematized by the reality of gender constraints on their ability to fully participate in the sociopolitical sphere. However, in the case of the Society for Maternal Charity, elite connections, substantial resources, and a public voice on issues concerning motherhood, the protection of infants, and social policy made it an important, if sometimes muted, influence in debates over family politics and child welfare.[127]

These often polarizing debates would influence the nature of the welfare state as it developed in France. While Catherine Duprat's comprehensive study of philanthropic action in Paris from the late eighteenth century through the July Monarchy provides useful insight to controversies over the nature and delivery of charitable activities, she is less interested in how these disputes played out over the course of the nineteenth century and shaped the social-legislative agenda by the 1870s.[128] The development of the welfare state in Western Europe and the United States, and in particular, the important role played by women both as reformers and recipients of assistance, is a topic of great interest to historians in recent years. However, most of these studies have addressed the late nineteenth and twentieth centuries, when state services for mothers and children became more widespread.[129] In the case of France, historians have focused on the post-1871 period, when the French defeat in the Franco-Prussian War raised fears of depopulation and led to more generous subsidies for mothers and infants.[130] While Koven and Michel argue that the power of French women to shape social policy was more restricted than that of British and American women, as evidenced by the dominance of male politicians in the initiation of social-welfare policies for women and children,[131] I want to insist that the female members—whether *dames administrantes, dames distributrices, dames visiteuses,* or *dames associées,* depending on the structure of and the terminology used by the particular society—played a role both in shaping the language and policies of maternalism and in providing a future model for the provision of social services. Maternalism—the notion that their familial experiences and special moral sensibilities made women particularly well-suited to help improve the lives of poor mothers and their children—was a potent ideology by the late nineteenth century and provided the key link between women's private family roles and public activities.[132]

But the focus and discourse of women's charitable associations also contributed to what Jane Jenson calls the "doubly bifurcated identity of specialized motherhood," which highlighted maternal nurturing as the crux of women's claim to both citizenship and assistance. Long before the French defeat at the hand of the Prussian army in 1871 directed the attention of politicians and demographers to the specter of depopulation in France, the supporters of the Society for Maternal Charity asserted that poor mothers and their infants had a special claim on assistance, if not the absolute right to support. By demanding subsidies from the government for their charitable organization on behalf of the women they represented, members of the Society for Maternal Charity conveyed to the state a compelling claim to assistance on behalf of the poor mothers and children they represented and showed solidarity with their less fortunate sisters.[133] While it would fall to women of stronger feminist inclination to translate these maternalist claims into demands for citizenship rights, like suffrage, this discourse of the particular rights and needs of mothers would eventually become embedded in the French system of welfare, and undergird "l'État providence" under the Third Republic and beyond.[134]

# 1. "Moses Saved from the Waters"

## The Origins of the Society
## for Maternal Charity

When the members of the Society for Maternal Charity met in assembly on February 13, 1789, they set lofty goals for their organization, notably to "Save the life and *l'état* for a multitude of citizens sacrificed to extreme poverty; restore morality in indigent families; spare them from a crime; attach a prize to the observation of their duties."[1] The society thus took on one of the most pressing problems in Ancien Régime France: the ever-growing number of foundlings, abandoned due to poverty.

The problem of foundlings and abandoned children was an old one in France. Since the twelfth century, various charitable individuals had taken steps to care for abandoned children. Saint Vincent de Paul took up the cause in the seventeenth century and focused attention on the Hôpital des Enfants Trouvés (Foundling Hospital) in Paris. In 1670 the Hôpital des Enfants Trouvés was incorporated into the central organization of the Hôpital Général de Paris, which brought the problem of foundlings and abandoned children under the control of the state, although the Foundling Hospital was still administered with the help of private charity.[2] The state assumption of control over the Enfants Trouvés coincided with a dramatic increase in the number of admissions to the Maison de la Couche, the facility of the hospital that accepted infants not yet weaned. In fact, over the next century, the number of children admitted increased almost twenty-five-fold, from 312 admissions in 1670 to a high of 7,676 in 1772, although the number admitted per year stabilized at approximately 5,800 for the remainder of the Ancien Régime.[3]

The sheer numbers, as well as the expense of these abandoned children, excited concern over the course of the eighteenth century, especially among those who recognized the high death rates among those infants admitted.[4]

The difficulty in procuring wet nurses for foundlings contributed to their catastrophic mortality rate. In the last six months of 1781, 85.7 percent of newborns admitted to the foundling hospice died before their first birthday and 92.1 percent died before they turned eight years old.[5] However, even more shocking to many was the high proportion of legitimate children abandoned by their parents at the Foundling Hospital, which had been conceived as a place for unwed mothers to abandon the unwanted fruit of their sin. This fact was brought to public attention in the treatise *L'administration des finances,* written by Louis XVI's director general of finances, Jacques Necker, in 1784. In it, he deplored the high number of children exposed each year and suggested that "One cannot but feel distress in observing that the increase in care by the government diminishes the remorse of the parents and increases each day the number of abandoned children." He noted further that "His Majesty has noticed . . . with regret that the majority come from legitimate relationships."[6]

Both the king and Necker were mistaken. While it appears that the proportion of legitimate children left at the Foundling Hospital was on the rise in the eighteenth century, most historians agree that it was no more than one-third.[7] Still, to most observers, even this proportion was unacceptable, since the abandoned child faced not only a high risk of death in infancy, but also lost his or her *état,* knowledge of parents and status. Foundlings and abandoned children were presumed illegitimate; the traditional antipathy toward "bastards" as both depraved and a burden led some to consider this loss of status to be as damaging as the loss of a loving mother and father.[8]

But those worried about child abandonment increasingly emphasized the loss of a mother's nurture, as well as her milk. Yvonne Knibiehler and Catherine Fouquet point out that while "Maternal love has always existed," philosophers, doctors, and statesman increasingly focused their attention on the function of mothers after 1750.[9] Among the *philosophes,* Jean-Jacques Rousseau in particular idealized the image of the loving mother in his two best-sellers, the popular novel *La nouvelle Héloïse* and his treatise on education, *Émile.* As the mother's care was deemed essential to the well-being of the child, the behavior of the mother and the nature of true motherhood came under increasing scrutiny.[10]

The poor mother and her nursling aroused the interest of a sympathetic public. According to Stuart Woolf, art and literature frequently represented the poor mother and child as "innocent victims of a corrupt society," with the frugality and simplicity of hardworking poor mothers a salutary corrective to the ostentatious luxury of the idle rich.[11] However, these two romanticized visions—the loving mother and the poor but virtuous family—could crumble when poverty was too real and too intense. While some commentators pointed to debauchery and indifference as the reason that so many mothers abandoned their children, most gave at least equal weight to the problem of poverty.[12] Poverty was a crushing problem for a significant proportion of the population.[13] Surely, only terrifying indigence could persuade a mother to abandon her baby. In his *Tableau de Paris,* Louis-Sebastien Mercier, noting that somewhere between six and seven thousand children were abandoned each year at the Foundling Hospital, reflected on "What a terrible and striking picture of the poverty of the people and the degradation of the species" these figures presented.[14] It was this emphasis on the role of poverty in dulling, even extinguishing, maternal love and leading women to forget their maternal duties that led Madame de Fougeret to found the Society for Maternal Charity.

Born in Paris in 1745 or 1746, Anne-Françoise d'Outremont was exposed to the problem of foundlings at an early age.[15] Her father, a distinguished jurisconsultant, was a member of the council of notables who administered the hospitals of Paris under the authority of the Archbishop. Monsieur d'Outremont was responsible for the administration of the foundling hospice. His daughter apparently accompanied him on his visits there and undoubtedly heard him lament the growing number of foundlings, their appalling mortality, and the difficulty of procuring wet nurses for them.[16]

In 1762, Anne d'Outremont married Jean Fougeret de Château-Renard, *receveur général des finances.* In addition to giving birth to four daughters and three sons (the three sons died at an early age), Madame de Fougeret took part in Paris's elite society. While raising and educating her own children, she continued to ponder the problem of Paris's growing population of foundlings and the difficulty of finding suitable wet nurses for them at the Hôpital des Enfants Trouvés.

Fougeret first tried to ameliorate the problem in 1784. She proposed to the administration of the foundling hospice that she take charge of a certain number of babies, who would be consigned to the care of older, unemployed women from Monsieur de Fougeret's country properties. These women would come fetch the infants and remove them to the countryside in a vehicle that Madame de Fougeret designed herself, fitted with twenty suspended cradles that would provide a more comfortable voyage for the babies than the usual crowded ride in a wagon or on the back of a *meneur* (the man responsible for recruiting wet nurses and who served as a liaison between parents and nurses).[17] Once in the countryside, the women would care for the babies and feed them either cow's milk or goat's milk.

The experiment was not a success. The babies tolerated both the trip to the countryside (even in their individual cradles) and the "artificial nursing" with

difficulty (modern bottles with rubber nipples did not yet exist), reinforcing the experience of physicians who had attempted to replace breast milk
with other sources.[18] While the wagon made four trips from the Foundling
Hospital to the countryside, three-quarters of the babies died within the first
year. While the mortality was comparable to that of the general population
of foundlings, Fougeret decided to find another solution.

She concluded that the most desirable option was to prevent their abandonment in the first place—to persuade poor mothers to keep and nurse
their children themselves. In formulating her plan, Fougeret drew on the
philosophical currents of her time and social milieu: If poor mothers received
the financial means to care for their babies through that first difficult year of
life, they would no longer abandon their children. In the words of Madame
de Maussion, Fougeret's daughter, the need for wet nurses would disappear:
"To retrieve for them the milk of their mothers was to return them to life
and to society, and to recall their parents to the first obligations of nature."[19]
Rousseau's image of the devoted mother convinced Fougeret that the natural
bond forged between the nursing mother and her child would be strong
enough to overcome any future thoughts of abandonment. This belief was
the philosophical basis of the Society for Maternal Charity.

The intellectual climate of the *siècle des Lumières* (Age of Enlightenment)
favored the creation of organizations devoted to ameliorating the human
condition; in fact, Catherine Duprat has labeled the eighteenth century "the
age of philanthropists."[20] Poor married women and children had been objects
of social concern and pity since time immemorial. Consequently, it would not
be difficult to persuade charitable individuals, many of whom were already
involved in philanthropic activities, that poor mothers who wished to keep
and care for their infants deserved assistance.

In fact, other charitable organizations had already made a point of offering
assistance to poor mothers and their children. The Société Philanthropique
(Philanthropic Society), founded in 1780, which counted among its members
both the father and husband of Madame de Fougeret, considered women
and their newborn babies particular objects of concern, allocating money to
this class of individuals beginning in 1784.[21] In its *compte rendu* for 1787, the
Philanthropic Society proposed the sum of 7,200 *livres* to care for parturient
women, an increase from the 4,800 *livres* that had been accorded in previous years. It also made mention of "several respectable women who, having
privately adopted this group [of mothers], for the entire year devote the work
of their hands to fashioning the layettes that they send to us." Anticipating
the future requirements of the Society for Maternal Charity, the layettes—
clothing and other essentials for newborns—were reserved for women who
nursed their babies themselves as "a kind of *Préciput*" (preferential allotment)

to encourage the mothers "in that first obligation of Nature."[22] Not surprisingly, the founding and core members of the Society for Maternal Charity came from the wives of Philanthropic Society members.[23] The two organizations would continue to work together.[24]

Some of the influences of the Philanthropic Society are evident in the organization of the new maternal society—the administrative organization and the rules for admission were similar.[25] However, Fougeret drew up the *règlement*—the bylaws—of the new society, whose language reflected not only a careful blend of Enlightenment sensibility, but a strong commitment to religious principles, perhaps more deeply felt among the female administrators of the maternal society than by their often skeptical spouses. This cautious mix would continue to shape the language and attitude of the society's members. Both contemporaries and historians have perceived the Society for Maternal Charity as a strongly religious, even proselytizing, association.[26] Many, even most, of its members were pious and influenced by the Christian obligation to perform charitable works. But they were equally influenced by the spirit of the age, as Catherine Duprat insists: "Far from being pious and conservative, Parisian charities at the end of the Ancien Régime were founded, then directed, by liberals and patriots."[27] She includes the Society for Maternal Charity in this group. However, religiosity varied greatly among later branches of the organization, as well as individual members, and waxed and waned over the course of the nineteenth century. But this carefully balanced tone that Fougeret brought to the bylaws regulating her new organization, emphasizing moral behavior more than religion, would find its way into subsequent redactions.

Although the society was founded in May, the official bylaws were not issued until the organization met in assembly on February 13, 1789.[28] Regular meetings were ordinarily held in a room at the Hôpital des Enfants Trouvés, but the society's first general assembly took place on January 4, 1790 at the Tuileries palace in the presence of the queen, Marie Antoinette, who had accepted the title "founder" and "protector" of the organization.[29] This may reflect a strategic choice on the part of queen. The October Days of 1789 had forced the royal couple to return to Paris under the watchful eyes of their subjects; the queen undoubtedly welcomed the opportunity to publicly display her love for "le peuple." The bylaws lauded "leurs Majestés" and the government more generally for their efforts "to spread the sources of public prosperity, the population, and morality, and thus for encouraging the work of and providing material assistance to the fledgling association."[30]

A close reading of the *règlement* offers insight to both the goals and worldview of the women who helped Madame de Fougeret found the Society for Maternal Charity. Its purpose, the bylaws stated bluntly, was to "prevent the abandonment of legitimate children at the Enfants Trouvés." These legitimate children, they stressed, were abandoned by charity, with neither a hospice dedicated to their needs, nor assistance in their early years (6).[31] They believed that the foundling hospice should be the resort of the single mother. The legitimate infant, who possessed an "état"—a position in life—through his parents, lost more through abandonment than did a bastard.

Poor children in large cities, especially Paris, were at the greatest risk of abandonment, and the *règlement* traced in detail the hard choices facing the impoverished family. The life of an indigent laborer was a harsh one; lacking property, subsisting on a low salary that could easily disappear with a change in fashions, or even a change in the season, he scarcely earned enough to pay for his food. "However, he becomes a father; that which should assure his happiness, serve as his consolation, becomes a subject of tears; the birth of that infant is anticipated with anxiety which presages the misfortune one cannot avoid" (8).[32] The bylaws showed genuine sensitivity to the plight of the poor worker. While the financially pressed father worried about how he could support a child on his paltry salary, the same economic hardship prevented the mother from fulfilling her obligations toward her baby. "The mother shares the work with her husband; her private concerns create more fatigue; if she gives the breast to the child to be born, she will be forced to neglect the rest of the family, she resigns herself to a sad separation" (8). Consequently, the mother reluctantly sent her child, "he who should remain in her arms," to a costly wet nurse, who generally lived far away from any surveillance on the part of the mother and who threatened the poor parents with prison if they could not keep current on her wages.[33] Parish assistance was insufficient for these desperate parents, and as a result the Foundling Hospital, designed for illegitimate children whose mothers could not keep them, became the refuge of legitimate children, as well. There, "The loss of his personal status is certain; that of his life is likely" (11). The bylaws stressed that one could not blame this abandonment on the depraved morals of the parents; rather, poverty led to this unhappy result.

Following this impassioned introduction, the body of the bylaws outlined the society's makeup, its administration, and eligibility for assistance. Anyone willing to contribute in cash or labor could become a member. A subscription system of 96 *livres* per year assured a steady base of revenues. Membership was open to both sexes to encourage a large membership (16). General assemblies of all the subscribers and *bienfaiteurs* (donors) of such a large organization would not be possible—instead, a report (*compte rendu*) would be sent out every six months, providing financial information, as well as the good results of the society's work.

However, the membership of the administration was much more limited. Noting that "the Maternal Charity was established by women, because they are called by Providence to assist abandoned children and indigent mothers," the administrative positions were accordingly restricted to women and "require[d] all the virtues which belong to their sex" (28–29). A *présidente*, elected by all the *dames administrantes* and assisted by two vice presidents, would lead the organization. Members would also elect a secretary to manage correspondence, the registers of admissions, the yearly accounts, and the *procès-verbaux* (minutes of meetings), and a treasurer to maintain the finances of the society (29–30). These two positions were the only in the administration that could be filled by a man, either a *souscripteur* or a *bienfaiteur*. The position of secretary would, by preference, be filled by a woman if one willing to perform the hard work of maintaining the society's minutes and extensive correspondence could be found. However, the *règlement* acknowledged that it would be difficult for a woman to serve as treasurer. The complicated rules of bookkeeping would be too much for most women, in addition to the fact that the position could legally be held only by an "independent individual" (*une personne libre*) (34–36).

A *dame députée*, elected and assisted by the *dames administrantes*, served as the liaison between her district and the Administrative Council (30). The *dames administrantes* were the workhorses of the organization, their "work and cares being of all the good works the most precious" (40).[34] Their financial contributions, presumably less important, were anonymous, discreetly placed in a trunk at assembly meetings. Only a *dame administrante* could propose another for membership. Those presented were expected to possess qualities "specific to the duties of the Maternal Charity" (38). Each week, the *dame députée* was to call together all the *dames administrantes* of her section for an accounting of the week's activities (31). These reports would constitute the chief topic of discussion at the weekly committee meetings that the president, vice presidents, secretary, treasurer, and *dames députées* were to have at the Hôpital des Enfants Trouvés (30).[35]

The *dames députées* and their *administrantes* were the eyes, ears, and public face of the organization. They would maintain correspondence with the *curés* of the parishes located in their section of the city, keep them informed of which mothers the society was assisting, and obtain recommendations for assistance. They would also cultivate ties to the *commissaires* of the Philanthropic Society, who were active at the grassroots level and who "already assisted them whenever asked" (32–33). These women also had permission, at their discretion, to maintain informal contact with and to invite assistance from individuals who were not part of the Administrative Council and might even be ineligible (32–33); they wanted to spread their net as widely as possible. But actual membership was tightly controlled. The bylaws devoted considerable space to the wise selection of their administration. The society would grow and prosper only if the credentials and conduct of its administration were unimpeachable; "it can sustain itself only through public favor [*bienveillance*], and only virtue can hold that favor" (37–38).

The society carried out its primary work through the disbursement of funds. Its funds would be distributed among the fifteen *départements* of Paris, based on the size of the section, the number of poor people living there, and the funds available (26). The founders were determined that the organization would remain on a financially sound footing. No child could be "adopted"—that is, taken under its care—unless the society had enough money on hand to provide the full 192 *livres* to which each mother and child was entitled. That amount was broken down as follows (97):

| | |
|---|---|
| A layette | 20 *livres* |
| Delivery costs | 18 |
| For the first year | 96 (8 per month) |
| For the second year | 48 (4 per month) |
| Petty assistance, for clothing and other needs | 10 |
| | 192 *livres* |

The society provided care only for the first two years of the infant's life, when it was most vulnerable, "trusting in Providence for the continuation of the education of these innocent creatures" (21). From a practical standpoint, the founders assumed that after two years, mother and child would have bonded and the parents would be unlikely to abandon their child, even in the face of continuing hardship. Naturally, financial considerations dictated the two-year limit, as well.

"Economies" would also help maintain the financial viability of the organization. For example, parish or any other charitable assistance would be deducted from the 192 *livres*. Any sums left over if a child died while under the care of the society would revert to the general fund to be redistributed (23–24). Funds not used by one section of the city would be reassigned to another that had been forced to turn away eligible mothers (26–27). If a child died during the month of its birth, the layette would be returned to the society (57).

Of course, the most difficult task for the administration of the Society for Maternal Charity was to determine which mothers and families should receive assistance. According to the bylaws, all legitimate children born into indigence were eligible for assistance; but given scarce resources, the *admin-*

*istrantes* had to choose among many worthy claimants (48). To facilitate these choices, the bylaws divided the poor into four groups and vowed to assist only "the most unfortunate" among them, at least until their resources were more abundant (49).

The categories were as follows (50–51):

1. Women with at least one child living who had lost their husband during their pregnancy; those with at least one child who had a husband completely disabled; and those who had at least two children and were completely infirm themselves.
2. All large families, with at least three children living, if the oldest was still a child. Children of "different beds" under the age of sixteen would be counted.
3. Women with at least two living children who had been abandoned by their husbands. However, the causes of the abandonment would be "carefully investigated."
4. Women with at least two living children whose husband was unemployed or who did not practice a profession or trade that would allow him to support his family during that time. Members of this particular group would also be very carefully investigated.[36]

Indigent mothers applied to the society in their ninth month of pregnancy, presenting a copy of their marriage certificate, certification of poverty, a character reference from their parish priest, and a certificate signed by their principal landlord (*locataire*) and several neighbors. They needed to provide proof that the husband and wife requesting assistance lived together and that the wife was a respectable woman. Widows were also required to provide the death certificate of their husband, and those claiming disability, documentation from a doctor or surgeon (51–52). Any mother discovered falsifying pertinent information would immediately lose assistance.

These stipulations highlight a key goal: "The maternal charity has in mind not only the conservation of infants; its purpose includes the restoration of the morality of the people. To fulfill this worthwhile goal, it must strengthen the bonds of families, make children dearer to their fathers and mothers, and help children to develop the habit of gratitude and respect toward their parents." To begin this "great work," the society required that all mothers breast-feed their infants (48–49). This practice, in the years to come, would remain the touchstone of maternal societies throughout France—that the mothers assisted must breast-feed their children or, if this was not physically possible, "artificially" feed their infants themselves with a spoon, a cup, makeshift bottles, or even rags soaked in cow's or goat's milk.[37] The society wanted to make sure that the mothers they helped did not separate themselves from their children. The only mothers excused from this obligation were those medically incapable of feeding or caring for their children, as well as widowed servants who could not keep their children with them and had no relatives to help them. In these two cases, the society would pay to place the child with a wet nurse.[38] If the mother died during the two-year assistance period, the society would care for the infant for the remainder of the time with funds from its reserve.

While promotion of mother–child bonding was the chief aim of the Society for Maternal Charity, the founders lauded other moral benefits. The bylaws noted triumphantly that their organization had led numerous couples to change their illicit unions to holy ones. "To obtain its donations, mothers and father have mended, at the feet of Altars, the scandal they have created and have raised to the status of legitimate child those who were condemned to never be acknowledged by the authors of their days" (12).

Unlike most future charitable and welfare organizations, the society provided assistance directly to the mother for her benefit and the benefit of her child, bypassing the father. In fact, if a recipient of assistance was obliged to leave Paris for a short time, the stipend would be paid neither to her husband nor to another family member—rather, it would be set aside for the mother until her return, a pointed recognition that the husband's interests might not always coincide with those of the mother of his child (54).[39] The early members of the society showed solidarity with the abandoned mother against the wayward husband: "We will calm the sorrows of an abandoned wife. How often we have encountered these unfortunate victims of the disorder of their husbands, who remain alone after having watched all their personal property disappear, without bed, without clothing, surrounded by children lying in straw, ready to give birth to a new unfortunate wretch."[40] The society thus drew a tight link between the welfare of the mother and the child, and it celebrated, on many levels, a unique bond between women, stressing the benefits of face-to-face contact, sisterly advice, and the shared experience of childbirth and motherhood. Its first seal—"Moses saved from the waters, and confided to the care of his own mother by the daughter of Pharaoh"—underlined this theme.[41]

An illustrious "Table of Individuals Composing the Society for Maternal Charity" was included in the printed règlement, headed by the king, the queen, and the princes and princesses of the blood. The duchesse de Cossé served as president,[42] the duchesse de Crosne and Madame de Flesselles as vice presidents, Madame de Fougeret as secretary, and Monsieur le Président de Ménerville as treasurer.[43] Countesses, viscountesses, and marquises were listed among the *dames députées* and *administrantes*, as well as among the subscribers, who also counted a strong contingent of duchesses among their ranks. Fougeret had drawn on her court and salon connections, as well as her husband's philanthropic friends, to solicit support for her new organization.[44]

With financial and symbolic backing from the highest levels of society, the members of the Society for Maternal Charity set out to do their work. The first report on their efforts appeared on July 3, 1789, in the *Compte rendu des six premiers mois de l'année 1789*.[45] The society reported that it had received a total of 69,619 *livres*, including 2,928 from the royal family, 23,713 in 247 paid subscriptions, and 24,000 from the royal lottery.[46] Two governmental entities, the Caisse d'Escompte (Discount Bank) and the Ferme Générale (Tax Collection), together provided 15,000 *livres* but had requested that it be used to assist a larger number of mothers who might not be able to fulfill the stringent criteria of the Society for Maternal Charity.

The 54,619 *livres* available to provide the complete allotment of 192 *livres* assisted 240 mothers, 205 of whom had given birth to 209 children by the time the account was issued. Of those, 3 were stillborn and 24 had already died. The 15,000 *livres* of the Caisse d'Escompte and the Ferme Générale provided lesser assistance to 228 mothers, of whom 200 had given birth to 202 children. Of these, 4 were stillborn, 31 had died within the first six months, and 14 mothers had placed their child with a wet nurse.

The *compte rendu* noted that mortality was much higher among those infants who had received the smaller sums, and it also drew attention to the fourteen women who had ceased to nurse their children. This lesser assistance was so small that many mothers, even those who had hoped to nurse their children, were forced to put them out to wet nurses so that they could more easily earn a salary (4). This problem highlighted what would prove to be a constant struggle within the maternal societies—was it better to provide assistance to more mothers, but at a lower level, or to provide a higher level of assistance to fewer? The administrators of the society argued that insufficient assistance did not permit a mother to stay home with her child.

The *compte rendu* included a *Tableau général du nombre des Meres & des Enfans assistés par la Charité Maternelle depuis le premier Mai 1788, époque de son établissement* (6), which noted that since its founding, the society had assisted a total of 690 mothers giving birth to 702 children. But the account made no mention of the tumultuous political events that had accompanied the first year of the Society for Maternal Charity's existence, as revolution broke out in the spring of 1789, despite discreet reference to "the disasters that have brought sorrow to France" and that "have prodigiously increased the number of poor this year." Three hundred mothers had already applied

for assistance that the society could only offer to sixty-six with current funds
(6). But it would soon become impossible to ignore the political and social
changes sweeping across France, as the society members were obliged to
come to terms with the changing landscape. The course of the French Revolution would have shattering consequences for the structure, functioning, and
personnel of the Society for Maternal Charity.

By the time the *compte rendu* was prepared for 1790, those changes had
already begun to affect the society on a number of levels.[47] The year had been
a difficult one for the economy and, consequently, for the people of France:
"No task has ever been more distressing and more discouraging than that
which [the society] has to fulfill today." Many of their original supporters had
suffered financial reverses or had fled the country. Madame de Cossé, the
society's beloved *présidente,* known for her personal service to the poor, had
recently died. The rapidly increasing number of poor in the city made these
setbacks all the more disheartening (1–2). The *Almanach national pour l'année
1790,* which offered a generally laudatory account of the society, also stressed
that 1789 had been a particularly difficult year. "Among the children born
since 1789, the loss was more considerable; it can be attributed to two causes:
the severity of the cold this winter & the poor quality of bread & of flour in
the months of July, August & September. During this period, the children
suffered from diarrhea, which led to the deaths of many of them."[48]

The *compte rendu* reflected the continuing problem of intense and widespread poverty in France, aggravated by various factors. The year 1789, despite
euphoria on the part of some for the anticipated political changes, had been a
difficult one—a hard winter had increased the price and led to the scarcity of
foodstuffs. The economic and political crises of that year led to strong popular
support for bold governmental action that would ameliorate the problem of
poverty in the country.[49] This sentiment was reflected in a speech by Jacques
Lambert, *inspecteur des apprentis de l'Hôpital Général,* titled "Address to the
National Assembly for the purpose of forming a committee within [the As-
sembly] to implement in a particular manner the great principles of justice
decreed in the Declaration of the Rights of Man and in the Constitution for
the protection of the nonpropertied class." This discourse, first presented
to the Assembly of the district of Saint-Étienne-du-Mont on November 27,
1789, was approved by the representatives of the Commune of Paris and sent
on to the National Assembly. After much debate, the National Assembly, in
late January 1790, established the core of what would become the Comité de
Mendicité, led by François-Alexandre-Frédéric, duc de la Rochefoucauld-
Liancourt, noted philanthropist and friend of many members of the Society
for Maternal Charity.[50] Its tasks were to rid Paris of vagabonds, to end the

abuses of the hospital system, and to reform the old system of charity. Its task was nothing less than the total reorganization of public assistance in the wake of the liquidation of the resources of the church, the traditional source of charity in France.[51]

The members of the Comité were those men who had been most active in the philanthropic movement. Many were members of the Philanthropic Society, and they believed that the government should play an important role in guaranteeing social and economic protection to its citizens; and in fact, these guarantees constituted a key right of citizenship. According to Alan Forrest, the notion of *le droit à la subsistance*—that all men should be able to support themselves and their families—was central to Revolutionary thinking on poverty. La Rochefoucauld-Liancourt laid out this "right to subsistence" in January 1790 in an attempt to redefine the concept of charity. He argued that since poverty inevitably accompanied political and social change, society as a whole was obliged to provide assistance to the poor; the less fortunate should not be dependent on individual contributions from the rich.[52] The only question was, how best to provide the necessary assistance to the poor without encouraging laziness and crime? These two conflicting views of the poor—victims of society versus slothful vagabonds and potential criminals—continued to shape the debate over public assistance and charity during, and long after, the Revolution.[53]

Despite the much-vaunted "right to subsistence," some members of the Comité believed strongly that private charity could continue to play a role in lessening the plight of the poor: "it relieves the Treasury, it inspires and develops public spirit."[54] In fact, Catherine Duprat argues that the early period of the Revolution—from 1789 through year II—was exceptionally favorable to the growth of philanthropic associations, which had many partisans among the government's new officials.[55] Private charity could be particularly useful in assisting the "deserving poor," those who were poor through no fault of their own. Mothers and children, as well as the old and the infirm, fit into this category. Not surprisingly, the Philanthropic Society and the Society for Maternal Charity were touted as exemplars of private charity.

But despite official approval from the Comité, the Society for Maternal Charity received considerable scrutiny. Since it received substantial financial assistance from the government, the Comité carefully investigated both the goals and the results of the society's work.[56] In a decree issued on July 3, 1790, the National Assembly agreed provisionally to continue to provide the 2,000 *livres* per month drawn on the lottery while awaiting a report on the society's activities.[57] La Rochefoucauld-Liancourt met numerous times with the society's *dames commissaires* Mesdames de Mesgrigny, de Vergennes,

Lavoisier, and Poivre, to learn about its operations and presumably to help them present it in the best possible light, thus strengthening its case before the National Assembly.

The report that the society eventually presented was, according to the Comité, "a clear testimony to the humanity, the charity, to the tender & respectable solicitude, of the severity of principles of this gathering of female Citizens who, bringing into the homes of the unfortunate assistance & consolation, have, as has already been said, diminished to a remarkable extent the number of legitimate children left at the Enfans-Trouvés."[58] The *mémoire* stressed that the Society for Maternal Charity served a particular and important function, caring for poor legitimate infants, for whom neither hospitals nor foundations had been established (4). As did the bylaws, the *mémoire* stressed that maternal breast feeding was "the founding principle of the Maternal Charity." The goals were to strengthen family ties and, by forcing mothers to stay home with their children, to protect them from disorder and, most importantly, from mendicancy. Any mother under the care of the society caught begging would lose her assistance (10–11).

Mendicancy was one of the scourges that the Comité de Mendicité was committed to eliminate, a fact that the authors of this *mémoire* clearly realized. In a variety of ways, this document was carefully calibrated to appeal to the members of the Comité and the National Assembly, reflecting the political savvy of these women—a political savvy future members would share. The authors emphasized their chief goal, preventing the abandonment of legitimate children. This aim gratified a group struggling with the overwhelming burden of foundlings in Paris. The *mémoire* pointed out that the Foundling Hospital had not been created for legitimate infants and yet, according to hospital registers, twelve to fourteen hundred legitimate children were abandoned in Paris each year (14). The "surcharge" of their presence resulted in "the greatest harm for all the children in general," most notably, terrifying mortality. But aware perhaps of the heated debates taking place over paternal rights and obligations in the National Assembly,[59] the *mémoire*'s authors also shrewdly spoke in terms designed to appeal emotionally to the men of the Comité: "This violation of the sacred rights of paternity [child abandonment], committed daily by the poor of Paris, appeared to be a disorder essential to combat through respect for morality" (12–13).

The authors smoothly insisted that they could solve these problems better than the government could. Neither the law nor coercion could stop these disorders, but the gentle consolation of charity could. By demanding that the mothers they assisted nurse their babies, and through exhortations and benefits, they could bring about real societal reform (13). The *mémoire*

celebrated the good effect that the society had already had on the moral behavior of the poor: bringing together families, persuading mothers to fulfill
their duties, urging fathers to show "industry and activity," and encouraging
those involved in "scandalous" unions to marry (16). In short, "*la Charité
Maternelle* brings into the midst of families the love of order, of work, of
obligations & domestic concord" (17).

But the authors also emphasized their society's benefits for the health of
poor families, independent of the moral benefits. The society discouraged
the women it assisted from giving birth at the Hôtel-Dieu, lethal for parturient women, and instead encouraged them to give birth at home, protecting
"precious mothers" from the contagion of the hospital. Among the nearly
one thousand women assisted by the society since its inception, only two had
died in childbirth, and among the babies themselves, only one-fifth had died
in the first year of life. The *mémoire* contrasted these results triumphantly
with the Foundling Hospital's disastrous statistics (17).

The authors of the document asserted that a number of babies equal to
those abandoned each year needed assistance, as well, and that ideally, the
society would assist between two and three thousand legitimate infants—a
goal that they acknowledged was financially impossible to accomplish at this
point (15). At a time when legislators were emphasizing accountability and
results in public spending, surely the government should continue to fund
so worthwhile and effective an organization.[60]

The Comité agreed. Impressed by "its respectable purpose, the natural &
sacred sentiments it engenders," the Comité indicated that the nation should
enthusiastically support the proliferation of such charities (18). The current
political circumstances meant that a number of wealthy people had been
forced to leave Paris, thus reducing the resources of the charity at the same
time that the need for its help had increased. As a result, the Comité agreed
that the society would need at least temporary assistance and recommended
that it be given, for three years, 15,000 *livres* per year drawn on the funds of
the lottery (18–19).

The Society for Maternal Charity lobbied for a continuation of the full sum
of 2,000 *livres* per month that it had enjoyed under the Old Regime.[61] In the
end, when presenting the society's report before the National Assembly on
January 21, 1791, La Rochefoucauld-Liancourt suggested that since the Comité
was still preoccupied with the reorganization of public assistance, it might be
best for the time being to continue to allot the full amount. The National Assembly agreed. The decree passed, and Louis XVI signed it five days later.[62]

As the Comité had recognized in its report, the society depended heavily
upon the annexes of the royal lottery to carry out its work. The account for

1790 listed its revenues for that year at 52,924 *livres,* of which 24,000 were the proceeds of the lottery. In addition, the royal family donated 3,790, which meant that 27,790 *livres,* or more than half of the society's funding, came from the government.[63] This amount represented a sharp drop from the 69,619 *livres* the society had received for the first six months of 1789, as recorded in their first *compte rendu.* This total did allow the admission of 306 mothers for assistance in 1790, some conjointly with the Philanthropic Society.[64] But the accounts indicated that without official support, the charity would scarcely be able to function.

That support had its positive and negative aspects. As Queen Marie Antoinette became increasingly unpopular in France, the society continued to praise her, both as mother and *dame charitable.* The *compte rendu* of 1790 included a celebration of her charitable activities: "In the midst of all these sorrows, one great consolation appears. The Queen, as *Chef* and founder of the Society, is informed of these troubles and shares them. Her compassion extends to all the Poor, they all concern her and appear worthy to her of her care; but this association over which she is pleased to preside, and whose intentions are so touching for a tender Mother, has become her preferred object." Accordingly, the queen had asked that layettes and money to cover childbirth expenses be distributed to three hundred of the neediest mothers, at her expense, with preference given to nursing mothers.[65] This sympathetic portrait of the queen stands in sharp contrast to the harsh portrayals of Marie Antoinette commonplace in the popular press in the early Revolutionary years.[66] No doubt the queen saw her services to poor mothers as a means of counteracting her negative public image, although the more nurturing representation did not take hold in the popular imagination. However, her efforts would not be forgotten by subsequent generations of charitable women, especially when her daughter, the Duchess of Angoulême, became *protectrice* of the society in 1814.

The funds voted by the National Assembly constituted little more than a reprieve. Political winds were changing rapidly in France. While in early 1791 the National Assembly could still offer praise and support for an organization administered by wealthy women with strong royal backing, this was not the case by the end of 1793. The flight to Varennes in June 1791 had destroyed the political viability of the monarchy, as the king and his family flagrantly demonstrated their lack of loyalty to the Revolutionary government. The storming of the Tuileries and arrest of the royal family in August 1792, followed by the declaration of the French republic, removed the society's strongest backers. An ever-increasing number of its supporters were in exile or prison by the end of 1793.

Further complicating its position was the government's increasingly hostile attitude toward private charities. While the Comité de Mendicité had seen poverty relief as a state obligation, it had also supported private charity. In contrast, a decree issued on June 24, 1793, asserted that "public assistance is a sacred debt and . . . society owes subsistence to the unfortunate, whether by procuring work for them . . . or by assuring the means of subsistence to those who are unable to work."[67] Under Jacobin "*étatisme*" (state control), there was little role for private charitable initiative.[68] Those proffering it lacked both faith in the ability of the government to care for its own and Revolutionary zeal. The government of the National Convention was exceptionally ambitious in its plans to care for the nation's poor. The decrees of March 19, June 28, and August 19, 1793, legislated the work of the Comité de Mendicité.[69] The law of June 28, the centerpiece of a Jacobin policy dedicated to the notion of public responsibility for the needy, established assistance for the physically disabled and home medical care.[70] The convention planned to reform both the hospital system and home assistance.[71] Isser Woloch stresses the continued importance of voluntarism in the welfare system of Jacobin Paris, in particular among the hardworking sectional welfare committees, but recognizes that organized private charity had fallen from favor.[72] Care for the poor was now a public, not a private, responsibility. One could make the case that the suppression of charities reflected more than the Jacobin government's antipathy toward private assistance. Paul Nourrisson argues that it represented the triumph of Jacobin doctrine, which had been drawn from the principles of Jean-Jacques Rousseau's influential *Social Contract*. Because the National Convention—the state—represented the general will, which was sovereign, it had to destroy all individual initiatives, such as private charities, that might impede its reach.[73] Accordingly, the Convention abolished all educational, literary, scientific, and charitable societies. The individual owed complete loyalty to the state and was to have confidence in its ability to provide for its citizens' needs. An organization such as the Society for Maternal Charity, which drew its support from elite women, most notably aristocrats and the royal family, now considered enemies of the state, had little hope of surviving the Jacobin reign.

The *Tableau de la Société Maternelle pour l'année de 1793 (vieux stile)* displayed a grim awareness of its declining fortunes. Revenues that year had sunk to 38,431.30 *livres,* which included 22,000 that they had received from the lottery funds before that source was discontinued. Still, the *Tableau,* adopting the language of the Revolutionary government, also expressed some desperate hope that the government would recognize the value of this organization.[74] "The utility of this initiative, the good that has resulted, is the

certain guarantee of public interest. This interest is its sole wealth; in order
to perpetuate it, to give it new life, we offer today an account of our work.
We present it to the People, to their Representatives, and to the authorities
created by them" (3).

The *Tableau* included a recapitulation of the society's activities and results
since 1788. It had provided assistance to 2,103 mothers and 2,136 children
between 1788 and 1793, although 60 of those mothers had not yet given birth
(10–11). Only 8 women had died, either in childbirth or while still nursing
their child. Infant mortality rates had increased since 1788, however. Of the
1808 children born between 1788 and 1792 (including 29 sets of twins and 1
set of triplets), 22 were stillborn, while 51 left the care of the society, leaving
1,735 children. Of those, 403 died before the age of one (11).

The society members were proud of this record. The mortality rate was
relatively low compared to that of children abandoned in hospitals or sent to
wet nurses and would have been even lower if "this experiment" had taken
place among well-to-do families, living in spacious and healthy quarters:

> But where did it take place? In the heart of the most extreme poverty, without
> [fresh] air, in the confined quarters of Paris, where often the father & mother
> have five or six children & sometimes an elderly [relative] living in a single
> room, when they lack the basic necessities of life, where the mother, in addition
> to the demands of a large family, must perform other labor, necessary to the
> subsistence of all these individuals. This is the condition [in life] of the majority
> of mothers chosen by the society, & still the children, remaining attached to
> the maternal breast, thrive [*se sont élevés*] (12–13).

The society had reason for satisfaction. In 1792 the Paris foundling hospice
reported that one-fifth of babies died in their first year of life, and three-fifths
by age three.[75] At the hospital of Rouen, the infant mortality rate stood at
70 percent in 1793.[76]

The *Tableau* adopted the language of the Revolutionary government in its
presentation, noting that "a large number of children whom death would have
harvested have been raised for the *Patrie*," suggesting that these children,
during a time of war, were an important national resource; the society also
highlighted the services that its record could provide to the nation:

> Its observations and its accounts provide precious information for humanity
> and can serve as the basis for more extensive research concerning the lives of
> children raised and nursed by their mothers compared to those sent to a wet
> nurse; on the life and the health of nursing mothers, compared to those who do
> not fulfill Nature's wishes; on the means to preserve humankind, and to stave
> off the dangers that surround the cradle (3–4).

This rhetoric was designed to appeal to a government that sought to encourage mothers, including single mothers, to fulfill their "maternal obligations."[77] The *Tableau* further noted that the female citizens who created, organized, and administered the Society for Maternal Charity would be happy to share their wisdom with the nation; that their methods interfered with no one's liberty, since the mothers assisted were asked only to fulfill the command of nature and breast-feed their children. Significantly, the *Tableau* insisted that since the society operated quietly, without fanfare, it did not "harm equality" but "to the contrary, it secretly joins those who distribute with those who receive and creates perpetual bonds between them of Union and Fraternity" (4). One of the strengths of the society under the Old Regime had been its appeal to the upper reaches of society. Now its members tried to persuade the government of their lack of ostentation and their dedication to the goals of equality and fraternity.

While they expressed the hope that "this account will not be the last that they will have to present to the People" (4), it was their last under the Revolutionary government. The society cooperated with the sectional *comités de bienfaisance* well into 1794, but in the chaos of the Reign of Terror, and the nationalization of all charitable endowments on 23 *messidor* year II of the new Revolutionary calendar (July 11, 1794), the Society for Maternal Charity quietly ceased to function.[78] Its founder, Madame de Fougeret, had been thrown into jail on November 19, 1793, along with three of her children. Her husband was condemned to death by the Revolutionary Tribunal on May 11, 1794, and died on the scaffold. Madame de Fougeret herself was not released until October 1794, following the reaction of *thermidor* and the end to the Terror.[79]

Despite ambitious plans to reform the system of welfare in France, the Jacobin government delivered little that it promised.[80] According to Alan Forrest, "the most grandiose projects of Jacobin welfare legislation fell victim to the ravages of inflation, the cost of the military buildup, and the anti-interventionist policies of the *thermidorian* period."[81] The nationalization of lands of the church, one of France's largest charitable sources under the Old Regime, as well as sustained attacks on the clergy during the Reign of Terror, was disastrous for the poor who had nowhere else to turn.[82] The committed and enlightened—indeed, "Enlightenment"—approach of the individuals who had worked on the Comité de Mendicité and the best efforts of the Convention failed miserably in the end. While rejecting "counterrevolutionary social history" that condemns "the French Revolution as having been one unmitigated disaster for the poor," Forrest argues that by the late 1790s, the poor were no better off, despite rights and privileges gained as a result of Revolution. He cites the financial difficulties, as well as the bureaucratic shortcomings and failure of the highly centralized government to take into account local circumstances in imposing legislative solutions from the center, to explain the failure of the Revolutionary government to achieve its social-welfare goals.[83] If public assistance improved at all, it was because of the committed activities of neighborhood cadres, for example, the *comités de bienfaisance* that emerged as part of Paris's revolutionary civic order in 1793.[84]

Nowhere were the failures of the national social-welfare policy more evident than in the struggling foundling hospices. The Jacobin government had had far-reaching plans for the *enfants trouvés*. Sensitive to the stigma of the word *bastard* (*bâtard*), the National Convention tried to remove its sting with legislation, the law of 26 *brumaire* year II. In general, the government tried to formulate a more humane policy vis-à-vis abandoned children, whom they saw as the Revolutionary government's future, proclaiming them full and "co-equal citizens, even going so far as to change the names of the *hôpitaux des enfants trouvés* to *hospices des enfants de la patrie* (children of the fatherland).[85] As the government promised to care for all of its needy citizens, it promised a better system to care for foundlings. However, resources available for their care dropped precipitously over the course of the Revolutionary decade, making it impossible for the hospital administrators to pay either suppliers or wet nurses. While some individuals continued to provide charitable assistance to institutions that cared for these unfortunate children, the sums were grossly inadequate. In addition, the social and economic upheaval of the Revolutionary years led many parents to abandon their children at the same time that war and hunger were creating more orphans. Mortality rates among foundlings remained shockingly high, and perhaps worsened, despite the more humanitarian rhetoric of the Revolutionary government.[86]

Less ambitious than its predecessor, the government of the Directory scaled back dramatically the assistance promised by the Convention. Some nineteenth-century commentators commended the wisdom of this. Louis Parturier praised the prudence of the Directory, more cautious than the National Convention, which had tried to do too much and in the end failed to accomplish its social-welfare goals.[87] While the Directory's reluctance to fulfill the promises of its predecessor may be understandable, the government's "prudence" was hardly a matter of relief to the poor. With few private charities to fill the gap between personal resources and government assistance, the poor suffered tremendously. Beggars complained that churches, which had lost their revenues through the nationalization of church lands, could no longer offer them assistance and that informal sources of charity had dried up as the French dealt with inflation and dearth.[88] The habit of charity had been undermined during the Revolutionary years, which meant that institutional and governmental assistance was all that was available to the poor—but the sums were derisory.[89]

In this atmosphere, support for private charitable efforts became less politically toxic, and the government took small steps to encourage their redeployment. Under the Directory, the law of 23 *messidor* year II (a law that nationalized all charitable endowments) was suspended by the decree of 2 *brumaire* year IV and finally terminated by the law of 16 *vendémiaire* year V.[90] But private charities, deprived both of funds and of individuals to staff their organizations, were slow to come back into existence. This was particularly true among those charities that had relied upon elite participation, since many of their members remained in exile until the coup of 18th *brumaire*. In addition, the ferocity of laws condemning political associations, passed under both the Convention and the Directory, dampened enthusiasm for associational life more generally, even though no law specifically outlawed the existence of charitable associations.[91]

Upon coming to power in 1799, Napoleon's government took stronger steps to encourage private charitable efforts.[92] The new minister of the interior, Jean-Antoine Chaptal, comte de Chanteloup, took on the task of regenerating both public assistance and private charities. One of his first projects was to establish the Conseil Général des Hospices, instituted by decree on 27 *nivôse* year IX (January 17, 1801). Its purpose was to oversee the hospices and hospitals of France. Subsequent legislation signed into law on 15 *pluviôse* year IX (February 4, 1801) instituted the prefect of the Seine as president of the Conseil, while the *arrêté* (decree) of 29 *germinal* year IX (April 19, 1801) placed direction of the hospices of Paris and the distribution of home assistance under the same administration.[93] The men chosen to serve on the Conseil were nearly all renowned philanthropists and supporters of private charitable initiatives, including, among others, banker and naturalist Benjamin Delessert; future *ministre des cultes* Félix-Julien-Jean Bigot de Préameneu; and Claude-Emmanuel-Joseph-Pierre, marquis de Pastoret, a respected politician whose wife would play a key role in Paris's maternal society.[94] Chaptal strongly urged the Conseil to support the establishment of private charitable initiatives, and indeed, in the months following the establishments of the Conseil there was a blossoming of new charities, along with the reestablishment of old ones.[95]

Even former members of the Jacobin government saw the wisdom of encouraging *bienfaisance*. The former *conventionnel*, A. G. Camus, speaking for the Conseil des Hospices, boasted of its mandate to encourage private charitable associations.[96] There were, of course, practical reasons for this; the government faced a crippling burden in caring for the poor and wished to encourage the well-to-do to assist those less fortunate. The government could not hope to cope with the problem of poverty without making use of its elite citizens.[97]

One group in desperate need of assistance was the *enfants trouvés*. Between 1795 and 1800, foundling hospices throughout France were in a state of crisis, on the verge of total collapse. With wet nurses habitually unpaid, it was nearly impossible to find care for the hundreds of babies abandoned each year in most departments, and some nurses were asked to care for three or four infants simultaneously. Abandoned children faced almost certain death.[98]

Under these circumstances, some former members of the Society for Maternal Charity saw fit to quietly come together and revive their organization. Reorganized on February 19, 1801 (30 *pluviôse* year IX), on the basis of the original bylaws, it presented its first *compte rendu* on December 7, 1801.[99] Perhaps in search of a more broad-based membership than it had enjoyed under the Old Regime (or perhaps in recognition of the continuing economic difficulties the country faced), the new society reduced its subscription fee by half.[100]

The new *présidente* of the society was Madame Châtillon de Béthune, assisted by *vice-présidentes* Mesdames Eugène de Montmorency and Dupont de Nemours, while the secretary was Adélaïde Pastoret, already renowned for her charitable activities. Catherine Duprat notes that the vast majority of the thirty *dames administrantes* came from the families of philanthropic notables. More than two-thirds of the *dames administrantes* were related to administrators of public assistance and of voluntary associations; sixteen were related to members of the Philanthropic Society. Madame Grivel's husband was administrator of the Philanthropic Society and treasurer of the Society for Maternal Charity. Mesdames de Pastoret and Dupont de Nemours were wives of the president and vice president of the Philanthropic Society and were themselves the founders of numerous other charities.[101]

Many members of the reconstituted society had participated in earlier days. However, there was one notable absence from the list of *dames administrantes*: the original *fondatrice*, Madame de Fougeret. While she remained a subscriber, and while her daughters were members (Madame de Maussion became a *dame administrante* in 1807), she did not participate actively in the revived society. Her fortunes and her health had been adversely affected by her time in captivity and the execution of her husband. Still, while observing that the women who reestablished the Maternal Charity always maintained respectful relations with her mother (and they scrupulously maintained her original *règlement*), Madame de Maussion expressed some pique that Fougeret was never named on the membership lists of the Imperial Society for

Maternal Charity as an honorary member. Madame Fougeret herself noted this slight after Napoleon's takeover of the organization in 1811, writing that "only one of [my] daughters made her fortune, but admitted to the court, she repudiated her mother."[102]

The reestablishment of the society, which took place the day after the signing of the Treaty of Lunéville, received positive reviews from Louis-François Jauffret, the secretary of the Société des Observateurs de l'Homme, in the official government newspaper, the *Journal des Débats,* in its edition of April 21, 1801. Fulsomely proclaiming that the reorganization of "respectable societies" offering charitable services was proof of the return of order and humanity to France, Jauffret predicted that it would "create goodwill toward the principles and views of the current government." In particular, he was pleased that the Society for Maternal Charity, "that institution so beautiful from the perspective of morality, so precious from a policy standpoint," had been reestablished. In a politically adept move, Jauffret linked the reconstitution of the society to Napoleon's "pacification" of Europe after Marengo: "In learning this piece of news, so important to so many respectable but unfortunate families, at almost exactly the same time [that I learned] the details of the festivities celebrated all over on the occasion of the pacification of the Continent, I experience a double pleasure: I seemed to see Peace, preceded by the genius of Victory, enter France smiling and establish itself among us, extending its hand to charity.[103]

The new government also responded positively to the reconstitution of the society and, upon the advice of Chaptal, awarded it a subvention of 1,000 FF per month.[104] However, according to a later account, that amount, along with subscription fees, would not have sufficed without various extraordinary gifts augmenting the society's resources.[105] The Conseil des Hospices, living up to its mandate to encourage private charities, provided an additional 6,000 FF, while the Bank of France, the Caisse d'Escompte, the Administration de l'Octroi (Grant Administration), and bankers of the public treasury also made generous donations.[106]

The society's first *compte rendu* made note of the particular hardship the poor face during the months of winter, when bread became more expensive and work more scarce. In fact, the Interior Ministry promised to double the sum of 1,000 FF during the four winter months to augment the meager funds of the society, which had only 4,394 FF on hand by December 1801. Expressing dismay at the paucity of funds available to help poor mothers, the Administrative Committee stressed that other mothers would understand only too well "the kinds of pain a poor woman is subjected to, at that difficult moment, overwhelmed and without help, who has the compassion of her neighbor as her only resource, [a neighbor] as poor as she is, who lends her sheets for her bed, who watches over her and groans over their shared misery, without the power, however, to comfort her sufficiently." Thus the women who staffed the maternal societies would serve as "interpreter[s] of the suffering of these poor mothers" and carry the message to others.[107]

Their impassioned analysis of the pain, loneliness, and despair of poor mothers, destined to give birth in poverty, reveals the sisterly instincts of the new administrative committee members. In accepting their role as "interpreters" of the suffering of poor mothers, these women took upon themselves the obligation to assume a public role to remind others of the needs of poor women. The common bond of childbirth gave them the moral authority to act on behalf of impoverished mothers.

The appeal was successful, although the sums that the charity raised did not match those they had been able to raise before the Revolution. For the year 1802, the society brought in 41,134 FF, of which they spent 37,249 FF assisting 302 women. For 1803, the number of women assisted jumped to 530, leading the society to spend 59,243 FF, nearly 6,000 FF more than their revenues of 53,438 FF. The revenues increased over the next several years, reaching a peak of 65,659 FF in 1806. From 1804 through 1806, the society was able to assist 500 poor mothers each year.[108] Originally, the amount of assistance was fixed at 116 FF, to be distributed over a period of one year. The Administrative Committee soon decided to raise that amount to 140 FF distributed over a period of eighteen months.[109] By 1805, the amount of assistance was set at 128 FF over a period of fifteen months. Still, the society's administration had to reduce assistance for 100 of the 500 mothers to 66 FF, a circumstance that they regretted, but "[with] requests increasing [so rapidly], [the committee] had preferred to divide the assistance rather than send back some of the poor mothers without any consolation; however, the need to take away from some mothers the assistance so necessary while nursing had been so difficult to the women in charge of distributing it that they wanted keenly to make sure that they would never be in a situation where they had to resort to such measures again."[110]

In the meantime, they attracted eminent contributors to their cause. Joséphine Bonaparte contributed 2,000 FF in 1803, while the wives of Louis and Lucien Bonaparte also made generous donations. Members of the Bonaparte family continued to figure prominently on the list of subscribers, although Joséphine, even after she was crowned empress, never took on the honorary position of president that Marie Antoinette had held.[111] Noble families, old charitable scions, and members of the *monde officiel* served as members of the General Administration. While Catherine Duprat argues that the membership of charities like the Society for Maternal Charity democratized and became broader-based in the years of the Consulate, elite families still dominated its direction.[112]

The society relied heavily upon extraordinary donations. A number of individuals remembered the Society for Maternal Charity in their wills.[113] Money from subscribers made up a relatively small proportion of the receipts most years. This need for regular donations became evident when, after revenues peaked in 1806, the society's receipts dropped precipitously to 39,454 FF in 1807. The number of mothers that the members were able to assist dropped from 500 to 450 for that year. Only judicious use of savings from previous years and *économies* from babies who had not survived allowed them to fulfill their obligations. In the previous three years, the society had received a number of generous extraordinary gifts, including 12,000 FF from the Ministry of Justice, which was discontinued after war broke out again, and 24,000 FF in early 1806 to celebrate the coronation of the emperor in 1804. However, no equivalent gift appeared in 1807; "and to have enough for the pressing needs of winter, we had to pull together all of our savings and our reversions, even taken from next year and in advance, because the calculations of the wisest forethought are silent before pressing misfortune."[114]

The lack of extraordinary gifts certainly hurt the society in 1807, and in the next few years its revenues stagnated. Catherine Duprat sees a more general lethargy in the practice of charitable giving in the years between 1804 and 1811. She attributes this decline in donations to both the lack of real crises in those years, which enjoyed relatively good harvests, and the lack of exhorta-

*Table 1.* Revenues and Expenses of the Society for Maternal Charity of Paris, 1801–10

| Year | Mothers assisted | Children assisted | Deaths (boys) | Deaths (girls) | Revenues | Expenses |
|---|---|---|---|---|---|---|
| 1801 | 302 | 309 | 60 | 48 | 42,710 | 36,495 |
| 1802 | 300 | 310 | 46 | 30 | 41,134 | 37,249 |
| 1803 | 530 | 536 | 68 | 58 | 53,438 | 59,243 |
| 1804 | 500 | 511 | 52 | 61 | 56,948 | 56,160 |
| 1805 | 500 | 509 | 46 | 44 | 59,227 | 53,749 |
| 1806 | 500 | 513 | 66 | 75 | 65,659 | 57,630 |
| 1807 | 450 | 461 | 43 | 45 | 39,454 | 53,194 |
| 1808 | 300 | 302 | 26 | 21 | 41,051 | 36,538 |
| 1809 | 300 | 307 | 29 | 31 | 42,098 | 36,342 |
| 1810 | 350 | 355 | 32 | 33 | 39,397 | 40,782 |
| Totals | 4032 | 4113 | 468 | 446 | 481,116 | 467,382 |

Sources: F. Gille, *La Société de Charité Maternelle de Paris* (Paris: Goupy et Jourdan, 1887), 19; Archives de l'Assistance Publique, Fonds Fosseyeux, 133/14, D-263, *Notice historique sur l'objet de la Société de Charité Maternelle et sur les résultats de ses travaux pendant 30 ans* (1831).

tion on the part of the imperial government, especially after the retirement of
Chaptal in 1804. More cynically, she suggests that now that the Napoleonic
regime had stabilized, it no longer needed to seek popular support through
the promotion of charitable assistance.[115]

Still, the Society for Maternal Charity continued to function and to seek
support for its tasks. Between 1801 and 1810, its members assisted 4,032 mothers and their 4,113 children. Their *comptes rendus* touted their success in
preserving the lives of their young charges, as the mortality rates were comparable to those of the well-to-do.[116] These figures were particularly hearten-
ing in light of elevated infant mortality figures among poor and especially
among abandoned children: "It is unfortunately too well established among
the indigent, in large families, and especially in hospitals that close to two-
thirds of children perish before the end of their first year, and we have the
fortune to have preserved close to two-thirds of ours until the end of eighteen
months."[117] And in fact, the mortality rates of assisted children dropped, then
stabilized during the first ten years of the society's reestablishment, from a
high of 35 percent in 1801 to 18 percent in 1810.

Others saw the value of their model, especially in light of the economic
difficulties that continued to beset French cities, even after the (temporary)
restoration of peace under the Consulate. Consequently, Paris was not the
only city that saw the birth, or rather the rebirth, of a Society for Maternal
Charity. However, the forms that these societies took were exceptionally diverse. Lyon had boasted a maternal society before the Revolution and claimed
to be the model for that of Paris.[118] Avignon's maternal society was founded
on 25 *prairial* year X (June 1802), although the circumstances of its origins
are rather vague.[119] One month earlier, by *arrêté* issued on 25 *floréal* year X
(May 15, 1802), the prefect of the Sarthe, Louis-Marie Auvray, established a
Société Maternelle in Le Mans, "in the manner of that which exists in Paris."
Its primary goals were the same as those of its Parisian counterpart. However
Le Man's maternal society was also charged with the task of procuring "em-
ployment and a condition in life for the young at risk, because of indigence
and idleness, to dissoluteness." All "virtuous women" and young ladies who
wished to participate made a minimum contribution of 30 FF per year to
Madame Garnier, the treasurer, and wife of the director of registration. The
society was established in the wake of the prefect's efforts to reorganize the
Bureau de Charité in the city of Le Mans. Along with the maternal society,
Auvray founded a Société Paternelle and a Société des Célibataires. However,
only the Société Paternelle had any success, and by 1803 the Bureau de Charité
was forced to resume operations as these voluntary societies disappeared
owing to a lack of subscriptions.[120]

The Société de Bienfaisance of Marseille also issued a *règlement* for an "Institution of Maternal Charity as has been established in Paris, in Avignon, and in other cities," and it began operations in year XII.[121] The Charité Maternelle was a "Comité spécial de la Société de bienfaisance" and received approximately 7,000 FF each year from the Administration Centrale des Secours Publics, along with a small amount from individual subscribers to the charity.[122] The members of the society's bureau were subject to approval by the Administration Centrale des Secours Publics and the prefect.[123] Thus Marseille's society was as much a branch of the public-assistance bureau as it was a voluntary association in those early years.

One of the most active maternal charities in the early years of the nineteenth century was that of Bordeaux. The economy of Bordeaux, a maritime city, had been hard-hit by the decline in trade that accompanied the wars of the French Revolution and would never regain the commercial success it had enjoyed in the eighteenth century.[124] This downturn led to efforts on the part of the city's elite to ameliorate the condition of the poor and unemployed. Furthermore, Bordeaux was an unhealthy city, constructed in a swampy area, with poorly developed public hygiene, and many babies died because of intestinal problems.[125] In 1805 the city's Société des Soupes Économiques "determined that it could not make better use of its resources . . . than to apply them to aid poor families at the moment of the birth of a child." The prefect of the Gironde issued the *arrêté* that provided the basis for the Society for Maternal Charity of Bordeaux on 24 *ventôse* year XIII.[126]

According to the text of the *arrêté*, the society, "in the manner of that in Paris, would give assistance to mothers unable to nurse their newborn infants." But there were some significant differences between the new Society in Bordeaux and that in Paris. According to the *arrêté*, members of both sexes who subscribed for at least 20 FF would constitute the General Council. Article 6 guaranteed that men would participate on the Administrative Council, which was to include a member of the Bureau d'Administration of the Société des Soupes Économiques and three members of the *bureaux de bienfaisance* along with six women, "two per *arrondissement*, chosen from those who will devote themselves voluntarily to the surveillance of . . . the mothers assisted," and four subscribing members of the General Council. The membership of the Administrative Council determined that it would be dominated by the men who staffed the Société des Soupes Économiques, by the city's three *bureaux de bienfaisance*, and by officials of the municipal and departmental government.[127]

The structure that emerged in Bordeaux was that of an administrative board staffed by men, with men also holding the positions of president and secretary of the General Council. Women controlled the distribution of assistance and surveillance of its use. In short, men directed the enterprise, and women carried out the practical charitable work, although men also assisted the poor women as doctors and surgeons affiliated with the society. The Bordelais society began to function immediately after the *arrêté* was published, issuing printed *comptes rendus* detailing its activities from 1805 onward.[128]

The founding members of Bordeaux's Society for Maternal Charity reflected the city's social structure and established another difference between the society in Bordeaux and that in Paris. For the most part, the founders were members of "la bourgeoisie négociante" (the commercial bourgeoisie), not surprising in the port city of Bordeaux, as well as individuals engaged in the liberal professions. The president and secretary of the society were physicians (Dr. Capelle, the secretary, would serve in that capacity until 1828); the treasurer was a merchant; and Charles-Jacques Fieffé, who represented the Bureau de Bienfaisance du Nord, was also from one of the family's premier merchant families. In 1806 the Administrative Committee included three physicians, a lawyer, and four merchants, along with the *curés* of the parishes of Saint-Pierre and Notre-Dame. Thus, unlike the Paris society, which was dominated by the official world and the nobility, the maternal society of Bordeaux was controlled by the bourgeois elite of the city.[129]

This male dominance of key positions on the Council ensured a very different tone to the Bordelais society as compared to the female-dominated society in Paris. The administrative board sent out missives along with the yearly *comptes rendus* to encourage the women in their worthy work. However, while the Administrative Council of Paris's society stressed its unity with and concern for its poorer sisters, the men of Bordeaux's society took a sterner tone, admonishing its *dames distributrices* not to let sympathy get in the way of making the best use of the charity's resources. For example, if a child died during the period of assistance, or was left with a wet nurse, or if "immoral or improvident parents" made poor use of assistance, the ladies should take immediate action: "A misplaced pity should never lead you to leave the Comité ignorant, even for a short time, of facts whose knowledge will determine the transfer of assistance accorded to another family in which [those funds] will receive better use, more consistent with the goals of the institution."[130] The board also instructed the *dames distributrices* to avoid giving their charges childbirth expenses immediately following delivery, "to avoid their use for so-called baptismal festivities [*baptisailles*]."[131] In general, the male Bordelais Comité tended to stress stern surveillance more than sisterly sympathy.

Bordeaux's administrative board offered practical medical assistance to indigent mothers, systematizing its links with physicians, surgeons, and midwives who would offer free services. The *comptes rendus* listed the names of the medical professionals associated with the society, along with the parish that each served. Not until its takeover by the imperial government did the Paris society acquire the services of physicians and pharmacists in the same way.[132]

Bordeaux's maternal society remained active throughout the first decade of the nineteenth century, publishing its accounts each year. The number of women they helped each year increased steadily, beginning with 69 in 1805 and reaching 173 in 1810. Unlike the Paris society, they did not benefit from generous funding from the government but relied on subscriptions, donations, and collections.[133]

Thus there was a flowering of maternal societies throughout France in the early years of the Consulate and empire. Certainly, the organizers of these charities were aware of, and often inspired by, the society in Paris. However, while all shared certain traits—an emphasis on assistance in the period immediately following the birth of a child, and encouragement of maternal breast feeding—each adapted its requirements to the needs and concerns of the local population and the specific interests of those staffing the society. Sometimes these charitable efforts succeeded, sometimes they failed. In general, these maternal societies were established with strong support (verbal, if not financial) from the prefect and other local authorities.

Not everyone, however, took an entirely positive view of the widespread emergence of maternal societies in provincial cities. Bordeaux's local historian Pierre Bernadau was quite critical as he noted the creation of the Society for Maternal Charity of Bordeaux on 23 *ventôse* year XIII (1805): "It is odd to see [public] authority intervene to create charities. In the past, the philanthropic societies had no official character, and that was only to the good." He went on to comment caustically again on March 5, 1806: "The Society for Maternal Charity of Bordeaux published the account of its alms and those who have contributed. This show of vanity is not too consistent with the principles of Christian charity."[134] However, his was a minority opinion. In general, maternal charities received praise and encouragement, even when their resources, and thus their effectiveness, remained limited. And Emperor Napoleon was well aware of the favorable press that these societies had received for their efforts.

When the Paris society's administrative board met in general assembly on January 18, 1810, to publish its accounts for the year, there was nothing to indicate that its structure and its fortunes were soon to change dramatically.[135] However, the society of Paris, along with its sister maternal charities throughout France, was about to lose its self-sufficiency as Napoleon Bonaparte developed an intense interest in the ministrations of the Society for Maternal Charity and brought these independent organizations into the imperial orbit.

# 2. "A Grand and Official Institution"

## *The Society for Maternal Charity under Napoleon*

As the Napoleonic empire reached its apogee in 1810, Bordeaux's maternal society issued its annual *compte rendu,* boasting of its successes since its founding in 1805 and noting that fewer than one-seventh of the infants cared for that year had died.

The document went on to observe that: "This happy result, and the other advantages procured for the poor by the societies for maternal charity, could not escape the vigilant eye of the genius restorer of the Empire, who has established, on new and better foundations, European civilization. He wanted to aggrandize and generalize the salutary influences of these institutions, and by his decrees of May 5 and December 19 of last year, he called on all French cities to share the blessings that the Imperial Maternal Society should spread."[1] Napoleon took an intense interest in policies regarding abandoned children. The *Code de la maternité de l'an X* (1801) established procedures regulating the abandonment of children, while under the decree of January 19, 1811, the state assumed responsibility for the care and guardianship of these children.[2] However, as Madame Fougeret had determined in the 1780s, it was better to encourage mothers to keep their children than it was to care for them after the fact of abandonment. The benefits of maternal societies, which had emerged in many French cities, most visibly in Paris, caught the attention of the emperor.

It should come as no surprise that the imperial government would take an interest in an organization that purported to preserve the lives of poor infants—who, with a little care, might grow up to become soldiers in Napoleon's army or sailors in his navy.[3] But the possible pregnancy in 1810 of Napoleon's new wife, Marie-Louise, focused the emperor's attention on the society. Until this point, the budgets of maternal societies had remained modest, despite the illustrious list of supporters. On the average, the Society for Maternal Charity of Paris took in 48,111.60 FF each year between 1801 and 1810, and it assisted 403 mothers, spending roughly 120 FF per mother. Bordeaux's society spent 11,533.17 FF each year caring for about 120 mothers, about 96 FF per mother.[4] But now, with fatherhood approaching, Napoleon wished both to spread his largesse and to honor his new wife, emphasizing, perhaps unwisely, her relationship to the former Austrian queen. Lanzac de Laborie questioned Napoleon's wisdom in this: "Forgetful or disdainful of the unpopularity of the previous queen of France, he multiplied, from the time of his Austrian marriage, evocations and reminiscences of the time of Marie-Antoinette."[5]

Consequently, what was once a private association became "a kind of state institution."[6] On May 5, 1810, Napoleon signed a decree at Antwerp announcing the creation of an Imperial Society for Maternal Charity, with branches to be created in each of the empire's forty-four *bonnes villes* and *chef-lieux*. A General Council, composed of one hundred women throughout the empire, would oversee the provincial branches. Marie-Louise, as patroness, would preside over this General Council, as well as the administrative council of the Paris society. Any societies already in existence throughout the empire were to bring themselves into conformity with the bylaws of the new Imperial Society and to become part of the umbrella organization, for which Napoleon provided a yearly endowment of 500,000 FF.[7] He placed it under the supervision of the minister of the interior and the empress.

But while Marie-Louise's pregnancy provided the incentive to transform the Society for Maternal Charity "into a grand and rich official institution,"[8] there was a practical aspect, as well. Napoleon provided the association with generous funding, but he also expected its members to provide substantial capital for poor French families. The decree at Antwerp specified that subscriptions to the society would cost 1,000 FF. If the one thousand women anticipated in the decree actually joined, this would provide an additional 1,000,000 FF per year in assistance.[9] As Napoleon looked to the notables of France to provide administrators for the empire in return for prestige, he looked to the wealthy to finance and staff social services in return for proximity to the empress and enhanced social standing.[10]

While women from some of France's most prestigious families had joined the original Society for Maternal Charity in Paris, and the upper echelons of urban society participated in the provincial societies, as well, Napoleon planned to use the society to honor his new wife and to contribute to the increasing ritualization of court life.[11] He gave careful instructions to the

Countess of Ségur, one of the Paris society's two vice presidents, regarding the impressive ceremony that would structure the twice yearly meetings of the General Council: "The Empress will be seated on an armchair [*fauteuil*] with a desk in front of her covered with a rich cloth [*tapis*]; to her left and right, the Dignitaries of the Society will be seated on folding stools . . . the Ladies and the Councilors of the Comité Central will stand facing Her Majesty. The Ladies will wear a black dress: they will be given a pattern."[12] Good works were only part of the task of the newly configured Society for Maternal Charity. Another purpose was to glorify the empress and, consequently, the emperor.

In exchange, women invited to join the maternal society would bask in the reflected glory of Napoleon and Marie-Louise. But the social benefits went beyond this. Part of the Napoleonic project was the construction of a new elite; *his* notability, blended with aristocrats from the Old Regime willing to support his government. Their wives were part of this process, as well. By taking on the old aristocratic duty of charitable work, the newcomers could gain respectability, smoothing their entrée into elite society.

Jean-Pierre Bachasson, comte de Montalivet, Napoleon's minister of the interior, who was responsible for organizing and financing the new maternal society, explicitly used its exclusiveness as a recruiting tool. In a letter to his prefects, Montalivet suggested that "a society over which Her Majesty (the empress Marie-Louise) has deigned to preside offers the means for the commendably ambitious to distinguish themselves . . . Thus, apply yourself to making the well-to-do classes realize that this is an important and favorable opportunity for them . . . Make sure that each person you recruit recognizes that, beyond the [good] effects of this new institution in assisting the unfortunate, one can also expect other advantages—particular and honorable distinction for the members of the association." Montalivet made it equally clear that not just anyone would be admitted to the society: "It is needless to say that only ladies who have known how to make themselves esteemed will take part in the society."[13]

Social status alone was insufficient for admission to the Imperial Society. In the same letter, Montalivet asked for "a completely confidential note on the conduct of the Ladies who register." The register of the Society for Maternal Charity, compiled from the information submitted by prefects and other officials, includes headings not only for prosaic information, such as name, age, and the amount paid for subscription, but also for the name and status (*qualité*) of the husband, father, and mother of the subscriber; fortune and prospects; regard that the subscriber and her family enjoy; and particular information on their behavior (*moeurs*).[14] Most officials submitted only the name of the subscriber, her husband's position, and the amount of money for which she subscribed, although a number did offer a brief comment on the women's status and behavior. Under the name of Madame Morton of Bordeaux, the register noted that her "family [was] rightly esteemed in commerce." Madame Monicault, wife of the *directeur des postes,* was praised as "esteemed and well regarded." Madame la baronne de Madières, wife of the mayor of Rouen, "enjoy[ed] public Esteem and the merit of a noble family." While most comments were positive, a few were more scathing. Of Madame la baronne Rivert, wife of the prefect of Ain: "She is thought to be a bit loose, but without scandal—the information we have is only flattering." Madame de Chazal, wife of the prefect of the Pyrénées, "may be respectable, but her conduct has been quite loose, or at least, could appear so, due to the circumstances which led to her marriage." However, it appears that only one woman's application was refused: a fifty-nine-year-old widow from Besançon, "born into one of the oldest families of the Franche-Comté," but whose "senses [*esprit*] appear to lack stability; she often has odd ideas that create the impression that she is not quite right in the head." In his observations, the clerk of the Interior Ministry noted that "the prefect observed that it did not seem appropriate to him that this woman be admitted among the members of the society."[15]

Some prefects were more assiduous than others in responding with this "confidential" information. For example, the prefect of Dijon sent a long letter to Montalivet in which he noted precisely the size of the fortune the women enjoyed, in addition to the number of children, their social activities, and their family background.[16] Others provided minimal information. And it was not always the prefect who offered the critique. As Gabriel Vauthier points out, "Desmousseaux de Givré, prefect at Toulouse, and soon after at Gard, did not send this little note concerning his wife: "Very respectable, but bad form [*ton*]; daughter of a rich bourgeois of Dreux"; and, no more than he, the prefect of Indre-et-Loire concerning "la baronne Aglaé-Louise-Étiennette Lambert, his wife, twenty-nine years old, daughter of Constantin Brossard, cavalry captain, member of the General Council of Calvados, questionable conduct, less than honorable birth."[17]

By examining so closely the status and moral qualifications of the applicants, by highlighting the social enhancement that would accompany participation, and by appealing to "*l'amour-propre* as well as the purse,"[18] Montalivet was simply acknowledging an established fact: the members of the society would continue to be drawn from the upper reaches of French society. These elite women were to model appropriate womanly and motherly behavior.

To further underline his interest in the Imperial Society for Maternal Charity, Napoleon assigned some of his most important ministers and advisors the responsibility of managing the charity. Joseph, Cardinal Fesch, Napoleon's uncle and the *Grand Aumônier* (head chaplain and imperial confessor) of France, was the *secrétaire-général* (permanent secretary). Jean-François-Aimé Dejean, one of Napoleon's generals, the *directeur général des subsistances* and formerly the minister of war, was named *trésorier-général.*[19] Members of the Central Committee included the chief chancellor of the empire, Jean-Jacques-Régis de Cambacérès; the chancellor of the Senate; the governor of the Banque de France; and as *conseillers,* Louis-Philippe, comte de Ségur, the marquis de Pastoret, and the duc de la Rochefoucauld-Liancourt, all known for their philanthropic work.[20] Mesdames de Ségur and Pastoret, one the wife of Napoleon's grand master of ceremonies, the other celebrated for her charitable activities (she was previously secretary of the Paris society), served as vice presidents and managed the day-to-day business of the Society.

Throughout the months of June and July 1810, Montalivet sent frequent instructions to the prefects, exhorting them to give recruitment to the society top priority, and provided detailed information for those who would form the administrative councils in provincial cities. First, showing "care to admit among them only Ladies whose conduct and life in society puts them in the position to be able to hope to see their nomination confirmed by Her Majesty the Empress," the women were to request authorization from the prefect, through the intermediary of the mayor. Once the administration was in place, they would inform the treasurer Dejean and the prefect of its composition. The size of the administrative councils would vary depending on the size of the city, from a maximum of twelve *dames administrantes* in cities of more than 80,000 down to a *conseil* of four women in towns of less than 10,000. Any subscribers exceeding that number would be considered "*dames agréés*" rather than "*dames administrantes*" and would not receive the signed *brevets* from the empress. To receive state funds, the women staffing the council were to find out exactly how many mothers and children in their town required assistance each year, and then to distribute charity independently for at least six months to demonstrate their viability. At that point, they would need to prove to the Central Committee of the Imperial Society that the number of deserving poor exceeded the number they were able to assist using only subscription funds.[21]

However, this show of interest from the emperor probably caused more harm than good. Yvonne Knibiehler and Catherine Fouquet argue that the emperor's coarse manner interfered with the spontaneous growth of maternal societies.[22] His interior minister, Montalivet, experienced difficulty not only in establishing provincial branches, but in obtaining support from among the Parisian elite. In fact, the decision to turn the society into an apparatus of the imperial government led to seven resignations, including those of the president, Madame Chatillon de Béthune, and the vice president, Madame de Montmorency, members of the Old Regime nobility who undoubtedly resented the imperial takeover.[23] Lanzac de Laborie refers to Montalivet's recruitment efforts as a "comédie bourgeoise." At the end of July 1810, now certain that Marie-Louise was pregnant, Napoleon asked Montalivet to send him a list of individuals who had subscribed to the society. On July 31, Montalivet sent a panic-stricken letter to Frochot, prefect of the Seine, asking how he was going to tell the emperor that so far he had received only fifty-nine subscriptions, and that the majority of them did not come from the "*monde officiel.*" A postscript read, "His Majesty demands the first list for tomorrow. What is going to become of us? I would give much to be in bed with a fever tomorrow."

Frochot responded with a verbal shrug of his shoulders, so Montalivet took action. That very evening, he sent a *circulaire* to the *grands dignitaires* and the five ministers who had not subscribed, either for themselves or their wives, as well as to a certain number of senators and high functionaries. The intimidation was clear beneath the smooth prose of his reminder:

> In scanning the subscription list for the Maternal Charity, I did not find your name (*or* the name of Mme X). I did not want to present the list to Their Majesties without warning you of this.
>
> You know of the great interest Their Majesties have put into this institution. The Empress presides over it; she delivers the *brevets.* I do not doubt that the Society will have an important presence, that its members will be particularly singled out by our sovereigns. I would have reproached myself had I not specifically called your attention to a matter of such importance.

The responses poured in, some with grateful notes for the warning, others with ill-concealed resentment. By the end of August, Cardinal Fesch, permanent secretary of the society, was able to present a list of 500 members to the emperor.[24]

Montalivet's thinly veiled threats were less successful in the provinces, where it was more difficult to exercise direct pressure on the local elite.[25] This limited success did not indicate a lack of effort on the part of the prefects.[26] Despite frequent communications and widespread publicity, including posters and newspaper announcements, prefects were not always able to persuade a sufficient number of women to form a local administrative council. The correspondence between the Interior Ministry and the prefects demonstrates the difficulties that prefects experienced. For example, in Le Mans, where Paul Delaunay argues that the Society for Maternal Charity had at best a "virtual existence" under Napoleon, the prefect of the Sarthe was able to register only three women, including his wife. During the food shortage of 1812, with enormous demands placed on Le Mans's charitable services, the local maternal society collapsed entirely.[27] And despite the strong support of the bishop of Limoges, as well as the prefect of the Haute-Vienne, only the wife of prefect Texier Olivier subscribed. Limoges, a relatively poor town in the early nineteenth century, had little associational life apart from the church, and the small commercial and industrial elite indicated little interest in staffing the organization.[28] Dejean, the treasurer of the Imperial Society, finally acknowledged in a note to Olivier, "I have concluded from this that it will be difficult to form an administrative council in Limoges."[29]

According to Gabriel Vauthier, by the autumn of 1810, after Montalivet's entreaties, ten departments had no subscribers to the Imperial Society; sixteen had only one (invariably the wife of the prefect); nine departments had two subscribers (the wife of the *receveur général* was the other individual most likely to subscribe);[30] five had only three; and four had only four. In the departments boasting more subscribers, the sums donated averaged considerably less than the specified amount. In general, the non-French departments of the empire, those annexed to France by Napoleon, were considerably more receptive to the call for subscriptions than those of the former French kingdom; perhaps the officials sent to these annexed territories owed their fortunes to Napoleon and wanted to make a particularly good impression.[31] In some instances, a particularly energetic prefect, such as Antoine-Claire Thibaudeau in the Bouches-du-Rhône, was able to gather a larger-than-expected number of subscriptions. He managed to solicit 24,903 FF in subscriptions, one of the largest contributions outside the department of the Seine. This amount did not, however, necessarily indicate sincere enthusiasm, for either the Imperial Society or for Thibaudeau himself.[32]

The reasons underlying the lack of zeal varied from department to department. In Avignon, the royalist sympathies of the local elite may have dampened enthusiasm for this imperial association.[33] Jean-Pierre Chaline notes that "the reception was cool in Lyon, Marseille, [and] Bordeaux."[34] The bourgeoisie in port cities such as Bordeaux, as well as Marseille, were hostile toward the empire—the economies of both cities had been hurt by the Revolutionary wars and further harmed by Napoleon's Continental System.[35] While both cities maintained thriving maternal societies, it was ultimately in spite of, rather than because of, the heavy-handed tactics of Montalivet and the prefects.

Certain issues emerge again and again in the correspondence of prefects with the Interior Ministry, as well as between the prefect and local maternal societies reluctant to subsume their identity into that of the Imperial Society. The original decree of May 5, 1810, specified a subscription fee of 1,000 FF—a breathtaking amount that was quickly lowered to 500 FF, still burdensome. This would have been even more onerous for provincial notable families, given the smaller fortunes and lower revenues in the provinces. The prefect of the Côte-d'Or wrote to the minister of the interior, "I cannot hide from Your Excellency that in general, provincial fortunes are put off by an annual subscription fee of 500 fr."[36] The subprefect of Saint-Yrieix, in a confidential letter to the prefect of the Haute-Vienne, noted that he could not subscribe for his wife because "Relative to my needs & my obligations, my resources are so modest that I am beginning to give way under the burden that overwhelms me."[37] Hard times could contribute to this reluctance; Alexandre-Gaspard Gary, prefect of the Gironde, noted that few of the city's *négociants* could afford to subscribe, given the lack of trade.[38] In letters to the prefect of the Seine-Inférieure refusing to join the local society, the women of Rouen frequently cited their obligation to care for the poor on their estates outside the city, which meant that they could not take on further obligations.[39] In a detailed letter to Montalivet, the prefect of the Seine-Inférieure emphasized some of the problems he faced trying to organize maternal societies in his department. Many notable families had lost resources, including land, seigneurial dues, and *rentes,* during the Revolution and found it difficult to raise the money necessary for subscription. Other women already made significant contributions to other charities or to individuals. Some were nervous to commit to an organization that required a heavy annual subscription fee.[40]

Another bone of contention was the requirement that provincial societies adopt the imperial bylaws, and the ominous suggestion in the Antwerp Decree that receipts collected in provincial cities would be redistributed throughout France on the basis of need rather than remaining in the town where they were collected. Article 16 read, "The Society is one: all the receipts, no matter what kind, no matter what the source, will be collected together to be distributed, by deliberation of the General Council, among the administrative boards of the various *bonnes villes.*"[41] Few provincial notables were willing to see their donations redistributed in other cities.[42] Charitable work was traditionally local, and contributors wanted to see the concrete results of their good works. The prefect of the Seine-Inférieure also noted in a letter that some women were upset that assistance would be distributed only in urban areas, and not in the countryside, where poverty was even more pressing.[43]

Even in towns that had a maternal society prior to the emperor's decrees, those same charitable women might evince reluctance to join the Imperial Society. In a letter to Montalivet, noting that the only subscriptions to the society were the two taken out by his wife, Prefect of the Gironde Gary first noted the difficult economic times but then added, "For a number of years, Bordeaux has had a Maternal Society, composed of the most commendable individuals, who distribute assistance to the indigent; the charitable ladies who are members of this society, find such pleasure in performing these acts of charity themselves that they fear any influence other than the sentiments that govern them, a fear that I have tried in vain to put an end to."[44] The women and men who had established Bordeaux's maternal society in 1805 did not like the idea of outside interference.

The members of the Paris administrative council took these concerns seriously and stressed in meetings with representatives of the imperial government that money was not all that charitable women contributed. The wisdom of their counsel and their willingness to go into the poor areas of their cities made some women invaluable members, even if they could not contribute cash. Both the society and a growing body of didactic literature stressed the importance of face-to-face contact when assisting the poor and the moral influence that charitable women exercised over mothers and children through their frequent visits and surveillance.[45] These types of activities—going into poor areas to locate mothers in need of assistance, and visiting these families—were labor-intensive and required numerous volunteers. If imperial interference pushed out dedicated *dames visiteuses,* the society's mode of operation, with its religious and psychological underpinnings, would be compromised.

The Paris administrative council was more concerned with its charitable work than with meeting the grandiose goals set by Napoleon. They had operated successfully for ten years; they did not want to see their work, nor that of their provincial counterparts, interrupted. These women made it clear to the representatives of Napoleon's government that, to continue its functions, "the Society [must] not be deprived of the Ladies who, since the formation of the former Society, had distributed aid with the most enlightened zeal and the most tireless devotion . . . the Council believed that it should implore Her Majesty to admit these ladies among those of the new Society without asking of them the subscription [fee] required by the Decree and to rely on their work [*moyens*] and their charity for the sums they would like to give."[46] The administrative council also emphasized that the published list of subscribers should not mention the amount of money donated by the volunteers; their labor was as valuable as cash sums. Finally, they reiterated the provincial societies' concerns about the proposed redistribution of funds.[47]

The minister of the interior also took note of the complaints coming from the provinces. When the *règlement* of the Imperial Society was finally issued at Saint-Cloud on July 25, 1811, it made provision to include as members those women who volunteered their labor, rather than their pocketbook, and the most objectionable articles of the decree were modified. Article 22 now specified that "the product of subscription in the other cities of the empire (outside of Paris) will be put into the coffers of their administrative council." According to Article 36, "The contribution of the Ladies of the administrative council having active functions will be voluntary, their cares beings the most precious benefit; they will depose the amount they wish in a trunk, which will have inscribed on it: *Contribution des Dames ayant des fonctions actives* [Contribution of Ladies in active service]." A subscription of 500 FF was no longer required. Reflecting the reality that few towns had attracted a full staff of *dames administrantes,* Article 13 specified that "the number of Ladies who make up the Administrative Councils" outside of Paris "will be decided on later."[48] Montalivet hastened to send out a *circulaire* to the prefects, highlighting these changes.[49]

Even with these modifications, the provincial societies were slow to establish administrative councils. The Society of Dijon held its first meetings in December 1811 but did not formalize its administrative council until May 9, 1812.[50] Likewise, Lyon's maternal society did not begin its operations until the end of 1811, most likely because subscriptions were so slow to come in.[51] Part of this delay was the result of bureaucratic red tape in Paris.[52] The delay in the organization of the Imperial Society was a particular problem in Bordeaux, where the maternal society had been operating since 1805. On December 15, 1810, doctors Lamothe and Capelle, the vice president and secretary of the Society for Maternal Charity of Bordeaux, sent a plaintive letter to the prefect of the Gironde:

> Our annual functions are coming to a close, & we would see this with satisfaction, if the Imperial Society for Maternal Charity were ready to begin the charitable service that we must yield to it. The report that S.A.E., the *grand aumonier* [Cardinal Fesch], made to Her Majesty the Empress made us hope that this wonderful institution would be established during the course of this month; however, we are halfway through without having received word.

Both men expressed concern that poor mothers and their babies would suffer as they waited for instructions from Paris.[53] Although Cardinal Fesch, via the prefect, urged the society to continue operations until the new administration was organized,[54] Bordeaux's administrative committee stressed that they had very little money to continue operations:

> In effect, Monsieur le Préfet, most of the Ladies who make it a habit to [carry out] these tasks [*soins*] that are difficult & often accompanied by inconveniences . . . have informed us of the certain refusal of nearly all our regular benefactors,

> a misfortune confirmed for us by the small quantity of assistance which we have collected since the beginning of this year, although we have come to the period to renew subscriptions & when our harvest is [usually] the most abundant.

The uncertainty about the society's future and the final shape of the bylaws, still unknown in early 1811, meant that many donors were refusing to re-subscribe.[55] Concerned that Bordeaux's society might be forced to disband, the Central Committee of the Imperial Society forwarded 3,000 FF to Bordeaux's administrative board in April 1811.[56] Still, it was not until late 1811 that the old administrative board of Bordeaux's maternal society transferred operations to the administrative council of the Bordeaux branch of the new Imperial Society.[57]

By August of 1811, a month after the imperial decree publicizing the new bylaws was issued, Cardinal Fesch enthusiastically informed the prefects that "the Maternal Society . . . is already fully active in Paris and will soon be established in all major cities; but the intentions of His Majesty the Emperor would only be partially realized if this precious institution did not spread over the entire empire and extend its benefits to all the unfortunates that it is called to help." More realistic now, he noted that "it would be useful if the Ladies who have already subscribed, no matter how small in number, would wish to meet and begin the organization in the town in which they live."[58]

Despite all these concessions, modifications, and encouragements, many prefects failed to establish effective maternal societies in their cities, even those with demonstrable need. The *Compte rendu à S.M. Impératrice-Reine,* issued in 1813, provides a snapshot of the branches of the Imperial Society in 1812. In that year, there were sixty-two maternal societies throughout the empire in addition to that of Paris; this number fell far short of the societies envisaged in each of the 44 *bonnes villes* and departmental *chef-lieux* in the original decree of 1810; there were 130 *départements* in the French empire that year. In other cases, while the prefect had managed to establish a maternal society in one or more of the towns under his authority, the society was essentially a hollow shell that received all or nearly all its funds from the government rather than collecting additional monies from the city's elite.[59]

Still, the Imperial Society did eventually manage to attract more than enough women to fill the ranks of the General Council. The first list of *dames brevetées* (those subscribing for 500 FF), a total of 500, had been approved by the emperor in August 1810; a second group, ready for presentation to the emperor in November 1811, numbered 610, but the total number for the General Council had been fixed at 1,000. Some would have to be left off the list. One member of the Central Committee expressed concern that " if these

Ladies, once they have met all the necessary conditions for registration, do not receive certificates, . . . their zeal may diminish and we will see an end everywhere to the subscriptions and the organization of administrative councils, and finally that the goal of the decree, which calls for establishments in all the departmental *chefs-lieux* will not be met." On the other hand, he wrote, "we know well that in increasing the number of *Dames brevetées,* we diminish their standing; for anything that is too commonplace loses its value." The Comité decided to solicit the emperor to extend the list of *dames brevetées* to 1,500 or 2,000, so that none on the current list would be rejected; however, once those places were filled, women would be admitted only as *dames agréés* until a space opened owing to the retirement of a *dame brevetée.*[60]

Despite its shaky beginnings, and the resistance of many of Napoleon's functionaries, the Paris branch of the Society for Maternal Charity was extremely active during the Napoleonic years. The functions of the Paris society and the Imperial Society necessarily overlapped, a fact evident in the *règlement* issued in July 1811. A General Council, a Central Committee, and the administrative councils of the provincial maternal societies administered the Imperial Society's affairs. The Central Committee included the vice presidents of the Imperial Society, the permanent secretary, the treasurer, their deputies (*substituts*), six women from the administrative council of the Paris society, and six *conseillers* named by the empress. The General Council was composed of various dignitaries, women named to the council by the empress, and the members of the Central Committee. Twice a year, four women from the Paris administrative council attended a meeting with the empress to report on the situation of the society throughout the empire.[61] The careful notes of the meetings and correspondence of the Paris society reveal the overlap in its functions: caring for the poor mothers of Paris and the coordination of the various maternal societies throughout the empire.

The meetings of the administrative council of the Paris society, as well as those of the Comité Central, presided over by Mesdames de Ségur and Pastoret, focused on a few key issues. First, the disbursement of funds; at the first meeting recorded in the minutes, held on December 22, 1810, prior to the issue of the bylaws, "Madame de Ségur informed the Council that the first and principal object of this meeting would be to deliberate on the measures to take to restart as soon as possible the distribution of assistance carried out by the former Society." As in provincial cities, poor mothers had fallen through the cracks between the disbanding of the old Paris society and the formation of the new Imperial Society. Madame de Pastoret noted that the administrative council believed, "While waiting for the moment when the new organization can begin its operations, we must make use of the methods of the former Society," and she suggested allotting 12,500 FF to the *dames administrantes* to carry out their duties.[62]

Second, the council devoted a significant amount of time—probably the majority of its time—to the presentation of reports by the *dames administrantes:* "their operations, the use of their funds, the number of mothers assisted, and the reasons for the admission or the rejection of the children in their respective *arrondissements.*"[63] The number of reports could be as high as 112 (November 14, 1811) but was more often between 30 and 70. In 1812 the Paris society set as its goal assistance to between 80 and 100 women per month, or around 1,000–1,200 per year.

The council and its vice presidents also served as liaisons between the administration of the Imperial Society and the provincial branches. At a meeting of the Comité Central held at the home of Madame Ségur on August 14, 1811, the committee instructed Cardinal Fesch to have the prefects ask the women "best known for their good works" to organize administrative councils in their cities. At the same time, prefects would determine how many mothers and children needed assistance in the main town of each department and find out how many women had actually subscribed in each of these towns; the plan was that governmental funds distributed to each provincial maternal society would be "proportional to the subscriptions taken out." The council reiterated the need for prefects to confidentially send information on the personal behavior and status of women registering "to be sure that they are in a position to meet with the approval of Her Majesty and obtain a certificate." Finally, the council asked Cardinal Fesch and the baron Dejean to print the list of donors and subscribers for the end of the year. It was understood that "men who subscribe and are approved as members will be registered on the List as Honorary Members, since the spirit of the institution is that it will always be directed by Ladies."[64] Before the administrative councils in the provincial cities were even formed, the members of the Central Committee, for the most part members of the administrative council of the Paris society, were taking steps to shape those provincial societies in their own image. Both Marseille and Bordeaux included men as full members of their administration; the rules were about to change.[65]

The Central Committee took great interest and pride in the provincial administrative councils, reporting at their meeting on September 23, 1811, on the progress that had been made in various towns. The committee members also recognized that these newly formed provincial branches needed a rapid infusion of cash. Dejean reported to the Central Committee "that all the towns which have or plan to create Councils need assistance and have solicited it"; consequently, he proposed adopting a basis for the sharing-out of funds and suggested that it would be appropriate to accord an amount equal to one-third more than the sum total of subscriptions in each town requesting aid.[66]

On the other hand, the Central Committee did not approve of all actions taken by provincial maternal societies. It expressed annoyance with the administrative council of Marseille and refused to approve its budget "concerning the costs and expenses that are forbidden by the bylaws, and wrote to [Marseille's council] to comply with its rules. . . . which allow only for differences between Paris and the departments on the price of layettes and other assistance depending on the town, and which prescribe that all administrative activities be voluntary, except for the functions of an agent, who can be paid." Further, they denied "the expense on the part of the administrative council of Marseille to rent a House where they will meet . . . the Council should meet at the home of the *Présidente*."[67] It may be that the comtesse de Ségur and the marquise de Pastoret maintained larger residences than their provincial counterparts. In other cases, the Central Committee experienced difficulty accessing the accounts of the provincial maternal societies at all. At the December 1812 meeting of the Central Committee, Dejean noted the need to inform the provincial maternal societies that they would not receive any funding from Paris until they sent in their accounts for 1812.[68]

The Central Committee intervened in the operations of the provincial societies in other ways, as well. In particular, its members were concerned that some provincial *dames administrantes* were doing as little work as possible rather entering fully into the spirit of the organization. In his report to the Comité in late 1812, Dejean noted that "[since] some administrative councils are content to distribute monetary assistance to poor mothers in one lump sum, it would seem necessary to notify them that this does not capture the spirit of the institution of the Society for Maternal Charity, its principal object being the preservation of children, [which] can be fulfilled only through monthly assistance, assiduous care, and an active and continuous surveillance."[69] Perhaps some women who had been coerced into joining a maternal society were unwilling to devote the time necessary for an "active and continuous surveillance."

Still, with so much visibility, the Imperial Society for Maternal Charity began to attract the attention of those who wished to associate with a well-connected charitable association. Doctors, surgeons, and pharmacists began to offer free services in the various *arrondissements* of Paris.[70] In its *séance* of September 3, 1811, the Paris administrative council decided it would "write to the physicians who have made offers to inform them that the Maternal Society has approved them, and thank them for their proposed contribution regarding their ministrations to relieve poor women giving birth in their *ar-rondissements.*[71] They continued to accept aid from medical professionals who wished to affiliate with the society.[72]

In the fall of 1811, there seemed to be every reason to believe that the financial situation of the Imperial Society for Maternal Charity was excellent. With the emperor's promise of extensive resources, plus expected yearly subscriptions from France's most notable families, the society expanded its operations and expectations rapidly. The Comité Central invited Comte Dejean and Cardinal Fesch to present the society's accounts at its meeting on November 23, 1811; they triumphantly (and perhaps too optimistically) reported that if one added the subscriptions from Paris (270,000 FF) and from the provinces (339,000 FF) to the 500,000 FF endowment, the total was around 1,100,000 FF. They expected this amount to increase soon, since twenty-three departments had not yet responded to the Interior Ministry, and organizational work had just begun in another thirty: "This situation, at a time when all have barely begun to organize themselves, must give us hope for an extension of the establishment and a considerable augmentation in its revenues in the near future."[73] By September 1811, the Paris administrative council had hired a paid agent at a salary of 2,400 FF per year, in addition to 600 FF for his lodgings, to manage its increasingly complicated affairs.[74]

With such a strong financial picture, the Central Committee requested that Dejean ask the emperor for permission to draw on 200,000 of the 500,000 FF assigned the institution based on projected expenses for the year 1812. It would all go to the provincial maternal societies: "This year, we ask for none of it for the city of Paris, for which subscriptions will suffice for its needs." The financial security of the charity allowed them to admit 1,000 poor mothers to assistance in the year 1811. Furthermore, it allowed the society to increase the types of assistance available. The total value of assistance for each mother had been increased from 128 FF (in the case of the Paris society) to 138 FF in the *règlement* of 1811, but this amount struck the members of the Paris administrative council as insufficient. Sick children now had recourse to free doctors, but they also needed medicine; the society decided to make available *cartes de dispensaire.* In addition, babies could now be vaccinated for free at these clinics. The council also requested that the Central Committee authorize the distribution of food supplies to nursing mothers and their families during the cold winter months.[75] The Paris administrative council received 10,000 FF in *secours extraordinaire* to carry out their projects.[76]

This extension of charitable services might have given the emperor the idea to use the maternal society to provide the staffing for various government initiatives. In 1812, during the famine that spread through France, Marie-

Louise ordered the society to use 150,000 FF of its endowment to distribute bread and *soupes économiques* during the three worst months of winter. Approximately 13,000 destitute Parisians profited from these services.[77]

However, this "mission creep" created some tensions for the *dames administrantes,* especially as it became increasingly clear that their financial situation was not as rosy as they had believed in the fall of 1811. When the empress announced that the 150,000 FF she was providing the Imperial Society to distribute to the poor families of Paris should be taken from their 500,000 FF endowment, the Central Committee responded that the society had not received any of that endowment, including the recently requested 200,000 FF for the provincial societies, and "that even after having helped one thousand families this year, the administrative council of Paris had found a way to add to its assistance the distribution of *soupes économiques* for the sum of 10,000 f., a measure which had the approval of Her Majesty." At the time of the baptism of Napoleon's son, the King of Rome, the society had drawn 200,000 FF on the funds of the endowment, but this money had not been earmarked for the poor mothers under the care of the society. Rather, it had been distributed to the poor of Paris without distinction.[78]

Napoleon might have assigned 500,000 FF to the Imperial Society; however, he showed no compunction in drawing on those funds to fulfill charitable needs more broadly defined, and he expected the *dames administrantes* to use the infrastructure of their organization to carry out the services he envisioned. Some of the money for the distribution of bread and *soupes économiques* was eventually provided by the Philanthropic Society.[79] Furthermore, the Central Committee faced additional expenses that they had not anticipated; for example, the secretariat of the Grand Aumônier requested money to cover the cost of the *brevets* that had been sent to the *dames administrantes* of the General Council. When the empress was asked to cover the expense, she refused, saying that she knew nothing about it (*comme étant chose étrangère à la Maison*).[80]

Napoleon's interest in making use of the charitable infrastructure of the Imperial Society reflected the worsening situation of the nation and his regime, both on the domestic front and in the diplomatic realm. The winter of 1812, even before the Russian invasion later that year, was a particularly difficult one throughout France.[81] The administrative council took note of the sad condition of the people of Paris at its meeting of April 12, 1812, and observed that the 50,000 *écus* that the empress had provided to the poor during the three harshest months of winter would soon be exhausted. Consequently, the council decided "that an entreaty would be made to H.M. in hopes that She would wish to provide to the Ladies of the Administrative Council of the Maternal Society for three more months and from here until the harvest with the facility to distribute 25 thousand f. per month in bread and soup to the mothers of large families and to the shamefaced poor [*pauvres honteux*] whose needs are known to the Maternal Society, leaving to the *comités de bienfaisance* the care of other indigents whom they are likely to have known of for a long time."[82] The worsening economy affected the operations of provincial maternal societies, as well. When asked to resubscribe to the Society for Maternal Charity of Rouen in the spring of 1812, the baronne Fouquet noted that although she would like to, "the present circumstances are so troublesome, so pressing, and so urgent that I find myself obliged daily to help individuals who I know are in profound misery, and that their large families and the lack of work put them in a position where they are unable to provide for their most basic needs."[83] In a similar fashion, the *curé* of Auxonne wrote to the prefect of the Côte-d'Or that "the needs of the indigent who are so numerous in my parish are multiplying tremendously, because of the high cost of commodities and especially the most basic foods; I do not believe that I am able to divert the smallest sum from that which I can use to assist them."[84] In 1812, Bordeaux's administrative council noted that "the causes of extreme poverty have neither lessened nor become less severe during the year 1812, and the number of families forced to request the assistance of the Society was greater still than the previous year."[85]

But the end of the hard winter would not bring an end to the difficulties of the French people. Frustrated with what he regarded as lack of Russian support for his economic and diplomatic projects, and hypnotized by his "Star to the East," Napoleon invaded Russia in June of 1812. Despite his Grande Armée of more than 600,000 soldiers from France and its satellite countries, one of the largest ever known, the campaign was a disaster almost from the start. French troops suffered from disease, heat, and the lack of food as Russian troops pursued a "scorched-earth" policy. While Napoleon occupied Moscow in September 1812, the Tsar refused to talk to him. With no one willing to negotiate a diplomatic solution, short of provisions, and facing the rapidly approaching Russian winter, Napoleon called for a retreat, which began in late October. The disastrous consequences are well known.[86]

The summer and fall minutes of the meetings of the Paris maternal society betray no sign that the husbands of many of the women they were assisting were marching off to war with Napoleon and that bad news from the front was starting to trickle in. In December 1812, the *dames administrantes* prepared for what they knew would be another hard winter, asking permission to use funds freed up by infant deaths to purchase wood, clothing, bedclothes, and bread for their nursing mothers. By this time, the Imperial Society was beginning to feel the financial effects of hard economic times and disaffection with the regime; Dejean noted in his report to the Central Committee, "I cannot determine the number of subscriptions for 1812, because the majority of the subscribers have not responded to the letters that I had the honor to write to them."[87]

The Countess of Ségur suggested another possible reason for declining subscriptions to the society. She noted that the Imperial Society had not yet issued a *compte rendu,* which was supposed to be published annually. She argued:

> It is clear that the number of subscriptions, far from increasing, will decrease if the subscribers are not informed every year concerning the situation of the Society and its use of funds. The punctuality with which the former Society published each year an account and this roster [*tableau*] was one of the principal reasons for its prosperity. One could further state that once the printed list of the Councils is set in order, [it] would arouse the activity of those who are late and who, because of that negligence, would not see themselves inscribed on that list.[88]

Perhaps mindful of Madame de Ségur's words, the Paris society finally issued its *compte rendu* for 1811 on July 17, 1813.[89] In addition, the permanent secretary, the treasurer, and the vice presidents issued the previously mentioned report on the Imperial Society and the use of its funds; while the account was rendered to the empress, and printed with her approval, it was intended for a larger audience. This document provides a positive gloss on the charity's situation in 1812 and early 1813, which, according to the report, had achieved "happy results." The report praised in particular the cities of Brussels, Lyon, Bordeaux, Turin, Genoa, Vercelli, Parma, Plaisance, Florence, Livourne, Marseille, Nantes, Liège, Ghent, Bois-le-Duc, Metz, and Montpellier for the generous donations of their female subscribers.[90]

Treasurer Dejean's account to the Central Committee at the end of 1813 outlined the difficulty the country was now facing. In his division of the 137,000 FF among the society's various branches, he noted that he had taken into consideration the "rank and file of the population, and especially the cessation of some branches of industry or the slowdown of regular works which had provided them with a daily means of work and subsistence."[91] And the war was beginning to intrude into the records of the Société Maternelle. On December 17, 1813, Madame Pastoret received a letter from Count Daru, minister and the director of the Administration of War, in which he noted his difficulties in obtaining old and shredded linens: "I thought that it would be possible to provide the military hospitals with old linens that can no longer be used for layettes, and to convert into shreds [*charpies*] the remnants that would be too small to be used as bandages or compresses."[92]

The number of subscribers to the society continued to drop. As it became increasingly clear to the Parisian elite that Napoleon's days as leader of France were numbered, there was no particular reason for those who had been forced to subscribe to continue to do so. Dejean informed Pastoret and Ségur, "I must no longer hide from you either that the number of subscribers . . . has continued to decline."[93] By March 1814, the Paris administrative council cut in half the amount of financial aid that they could offer nursing mothers.[94]

The fall of Napoleon in April 1814 brought chaos to the financial situation of maternal societies throughout France. On April 18, two weeks after Napoleon's abdication, the Central Committee determined that the Paris society's remaining admission slips would be distributed "only to women who have already given birth, that given the almost complete lack of funds, the 49 slips distributed on 18 April would guarantee only 36 f., that is, a layette of 21 f., & delivery costs of 15 f." The immediate future was grim. Looking for all possible ways to save money, the Central Committee fired the agent managing the society's accounts.[95]

Napoleon's abdication caused the Paris society, as well as member branches, considerable financial difficulty, and a reduction in admissions and the amount of assistance seemed to be the only possible response. In his tome *La Société de Charité Maternelle de Paris,* François Gille cites the *compte rendu* of 1814, published on February 20, 1815, which "demonstrates well enough the great perturbation of the functionaries. The situation had become extremely critical; the Maternal Society, subsidized by the State, suffered not only the general effect of the difficulties unavoidable with any change of regime, but still more, in losing its most important subscribers, whose payments would have permitted it to meet its previous promises, it faced a real financial disaster."[96] A letter from the Interior Ministry sent out to prefects in December 1814 notified them that since the October ordinance had reduced funds for the departmental maternal societies to 60,0000 FF in place of the 140,000 originally assigned, their funds for that year would be about half of what they had expected.[97]

With the fall of Napoleon, the allied governments opposing France, as well as the French elite, turned to the brother of Louis XVI, the former comte de Provence, to head the new government, structured by a new constitution called "The Charter." Many French men and women, exhausted by war, economic hardship, and the pretensions of Napoleon and his family, welcomed the return of the Bourbon monarch, who took the name of Louis XVIII, to Paris on May 3, 1814, although with varying degrees of enthusiasm. Because he was a widower, his niece Marie-Thérèse, Duchess of Angoulême, daughter of Marie Antoinette and Louis XVI, would play a key role in his court. Not only was she the daughter of his deceased brother; she was married to the son of Louis's other brother, the comte d'Artois (the future Charles X). Louis XVIII, settled in the Tuileries palace, worked to reestablish the court life of the Old Regime.[98]

The members of the administrative council, few of whom were particularly loyal to Napoleon, took rapid steps to adjust to the new order of things and to preserve their institution. On May 21, 1814, shortly after the return of the Bourbons, the Paris society addressed a letter to the duchesse d'Angoulême, requesting her patronage:

> We beg you to allow your name to protect once more this institution previously honored by a majestic *suffrage* whose memory supported us for many long years. This new blessing would assure the Maternal Society a true prosperity, assistance to poor families, and the most touching compensation to the zeal of the ladies. Your Royal Highness is perhaps unaware that her name can exert power over virtuous souls.[99]

The Duchess of Angoulême, moved by the connection between her mother, Marie Antoinette, and the Society for Maternal Charity, accepted the invitation to preside over the institution.[100] To strengthen that sympathetic bond, the administrative council searched for the society's register of deliberations from the early 1790s, which bore the queen's signature in several places.[101] The duchess received equally flattering supplications from other maternal societies to step in as protector. Dijon's maternal society, controlled by avowed royalists, including Madame Ranfer de Bretenières, composed a letter to the duchess in which they offered their "congratulations on your return to our homeland so long unhappy because of your absence" and asked her to "deign to place herself at the head of the Society for Maternal Charity!"[102] Bordeaux, the city which first welcomed the return of the Duke of Angoulême in 1814, included in its *compte rendu* for 1815 a flattering account of the visit of the duke and duchess, "our beloved princes," to their city, praising in particular "*la Princesse,* object of so many good wishes and blessings."[103]

Louis XVIII took the views of the Paris administrative council, as well as other maternal societies, into account when he issued the October 31, 1814, ordinance reorganizing the maternal societies. The Imperial Society, established by the decrees of May 5, 1810, and July 25, 1811, was dissolved, and the Society for Maternal Charity of Paris immediately resumed the regime it had followed prior to May 5, 1810. The administrative councils in the departments outside of Paris were ordered to continue their functions until all of their funds were gone—at that point, "there can be established, with the approval of our Minister of the Interior, maternal societies following the example of

Paris, in towns whose population size may necessitate this type of institution, and where a sufficient number of subscribers will come forward." The king agreed to place 100,000 FF at the disposal of the minister of the interior to distribute to maternal societies; of that, 40,000 FF would go to Paris. Heeding the wishes of the women who had requested it, the maternal societies were "placed under the protection of our much-loved niece, the Duchess of Angoulême, who will preside, in that quality, when she finds it appropriate, over the Society for Maternal Charity of Paris.[104]

While the Bourbon government had decided that the organization was a useful adjunct to state services, it was not willing to maintain every maternal society that had existed under the empire. In contrast to Napoleon, who sought to multiply the societies' number as a sign of his own importance and in tribute to the empress, the new government instead wished to determine whether a city or town actually required the services of a maternal society before allowing it to continue. Although a "Note sur la Société de Charité Maternelle," inserted into *Le Moniteur* on November 23, 1814, stated that the Duchess of Angoulême would preserve maternal societies in the cities of Lyon, Marseille, Bordeaux, Rouen, Nantes, Strasbourg, Toulouse, and Orléans, even they were asked to justify their town's need for this particular charity.[105] To this end, in December 1814 the Interior Ministry sent a letter to the prefects noting that "H.M. determined that an institution such as the Society for Maternal Charity is advisable only in large towns where the resources of the hospices and the *bureaux de bienfaisance* do not come close to extending the assistance to indigent mothers necessary to raise their children. Thus, Monsieur, the intention of H.M. is that a Society for Maternal Charity will be established only in the towns where these institutions can truly be *useful and necessary* and where the voluntary subscriptions could be sufficiently numerous to sustain these institutions along with moderate assistance granted by the government." The ministry posed a number of questions designed to determine whether a maternal society was appropriate for that particular city, including the number of poor and the number of births taking place each year among the indigent class; the sufficiency of hospice revenues and the resources of the *bureaux de bienfaisance;* whether the establishment of a maternal society would be useful and necessary in that particular city; the estimated number of indigent mothers who would need assistance from the society each year, and the cost of that assistance; and the estimated total of subscriptions and how much the government would need to supplement that funding each year.[106]

Not surprisingly, no city responded that it could easily care for its poor, and in particular, for poor women giving birth. In fact, all pleaded for generous governmental assistance. Bordeaux's administrative council reported that the society had assisted 273 mothers in 1813 and 285 in 1814—probably about half of those actually needing assistance—and that "the utility of & the necessity for a maternal society in Bordeaux is underlined by the efforts and voluntary sacrifices that the Bordelais made, ten years ago, to establish that institution, which they have supported since that time, through new efforts & donations renewed every year." Given the poor state of the economy in Bordeaux, with the decline in commerce, the society could continue to hope for about 12,000 FF per year in subscriptions but would probably need a total of 30,000–32,000 FF per year from the royal government to care for its poor mothers.[107] The Bureau Central de Charité of Bordeaux, which the prefect queried, as well, reported 3,421 indigent families and 10,938 indigent individuals listed for their city, along with 405 families, and 1,096 individuals "honteuses." Their revenues of 78,243 FF fell well below their expenses in caring for these individuals.[108]

Marseille's administrative council was equally emphatic that its city needed a maternal society. The *dames administrantes* assisted about 530 women per year but, with sufficient funding, could admit up to 1000. The society received about 4,000 FF in donations and subscriptions each year, and 6,000 FF from the Conseil Municipal; however, they required about 31,000 FF per year to assist 530 poor mothers, meaning they would need about 24,000 FF from the government.[109] Marseille's Administration Centrale des Secours Publics agreed that a maternal society was extremely beneficial in a city such as theirs—in 1812 the bureau had assisted 10,058 families, or 40,405 individuals.[110]

Lyon, the second-largest city in France, did not find it difficult to persuade the Interior Ministry that it should maintain its maternal society, even though the mayor of the city was slow to respond with the necessary information.[111] While Dijon was a much smaller town than the others, and its maternal society assisted only about 90 women per year at a cost of 105 FF per mother, it received strong support from the town's mayor, as well as the prefect, and received permission to continue. More modest than the other cities, it requested only 3,000 FF per year from the royal administration.[112] Rouen's maternal society, which received a sum of 6,000 FF from the government in January 1815, continued to operate without interruption, as well.[113] In all, the royal government decided to allow existing maternal societies to continue their operations in twenty-one cities and authorized their creation in ten other locations.[114]

The brief period of the Hundred Days only increased confusion for both the Paris Society for Maternal Charity and provincial branches.[115] However, the relationship between the central government, royal or Napoleonic, and maternal societies showed surprising continuity. During the Hundred Days, the Interior Ministry maintained the decentralization of maternal societies established by the ordinance of October 1814, disbursing funds to the provincial societies and asking that they submit their new bylaws to replace the imperial *règlement*.[116] But with Waterloo, a new and less generous royal regime had clearly asserted control. The new prefect of the Gironde, Camille de Tournon, put it bluntly in a letter to Dr. Capelle, secretary of Bordeaux's maternal society:

> During the unjust and ephemeral government of the usurpation, a sum of ten thousand francs was accorded to the Society for Maternal Charity of Bordeaux . . . His Majesty having accorded . . . only a sum of 60,000 francs in place of 140,000 for the maternal societies in the *départements*. . . . [W]ith the difficult situation of the public treasury not permitting the augmentation of the first of these sums, His Excellency the Minister of the Interior has no choice but to decree a new distribution of assistance for the year 1815. . . . [T]he five thousand that you have already received should be considered as the total assistance you are awarded for 1815.[117]

But even with reduced funding, the royal government continued to supplement the resources of the many branches quite generously. For example, in 1817 the Society of Rouen received 5,125 FF of its 10,049.84 FF receipt total from the Interior Ministry; in 1816, Dijon received 4,500 FF of its 9,423.38 FF in revenues from the government. On March 4, 1819, the prefect of the Rhône noted in a letter to the minister of the interior that Lyon's Society for Maternal Charity had raised only 1,500 FF the previous year, the same amount they had received from the government—a surprisingly small amount, considering the city's size.[118] While some branches that had been propped up by Napoleonic pressure disappeared, in other cases, prefects were able to promote the formation of local societies that had failed to coalesce under the strong-arm tactics of Napoleon and his ministers—for example, in the cities of Le Mans and Limoges. Limoges, perhaps to its own astonishment, was included among "towns whose population size may necessitate this type of institution, and where a sufficient number of subscribers will come forward." This was particularly surprising in light of the fact that, as the minister of the interior noted in the same letter, "The city of Limoges [did not] yet have a maternal society," but nonetheless, he asked the prefect to "make known to the inhabitants of Limoges the stipulations which I have just provided to you, and ask the ladies who intend to contribute to the presence of this institution to send you their names."[119] The first meeting of Limoges's Society for Maternal Charity took place on February 6, 1817, and it issued its *règlement* that same year.[120]

While unhappy about declining subsidies, maternal societies were not necessarily displeased to regain their independence. The Paris society had expressed its frustration and discontent with the imperial bylaws in a "Précis sur la Société de Charité Maternelle de Paris," addressed to the Interior Ministry on June 2, 1814. "The *dames administrantes* who make up the Paris Committee would like at this time to resume the simple administration that the society had until the end of 1810, and no longer take part in the general administration of other Societies established in many departments."[121] The Paris *dames administrantes* had not expected or wanted to oversee a vast administrative apparatus; they wanted to perform charitable works among the poor women of their respective *arrondissements*. In short, they wanted to return to the original intent of their organization. The provincial maternal societies seemed equally content to shake off the tether of the Imperial Society. In its new bylaws, issued on December 13, 1815, Bordeaux's society stated that it "has taken back the existence that it had lost for several years; its benefactors have recovered the ownership of an institution that they founded in the year 1805; they will no longer be strangers to its operations and its successes; they will choose among themselves the administrators, who will exercise the rights of all."[122] However, maternal societies did not, in fact, reclaim their formerly independent status. While a letter sent to prefects in early 1816 indicated that the Interior Ministry was ready to dispense with close control of the annual accounts and regulations of the provincial societies,[123] the new patroness of the organization, the Duchess of Angoulême, quickly took an active role in directing the societies. Her interests included the distribution and use of funds, as well as approval of members.[124] The Interior Ministry carefully perused the accounts in subsequent years and offered frequent advice to the administrative councils in the provinces.[125]

It is not surprising that the Duchess of Angoulême and the Interior Ministry declined to cede control over the maternal societies now scattered throughout France. These charities were still handsomely subsidized; according to Catherine Duprat, at 40,000 FF per year, the Paris Society for Maternal Charity was the most generously subsidized charity in France.[126] Moreover, despite a rhetorical rejection of Napoleonic innovations, the royal government was more than happy to make use of the centralized bureaucratic apparatus that the imperial government had put into effect, which included extensive surveillance of charitable institutions.

The Napoleonic era had pushed the maternal societies of France in a direction that shaped them as semiofficial organs of the state. This hybrid status would continue to be a defining characteristic of maternal societies and shaped their modes of activity, as well as their relationship with the state. As private charitable institutions, they sought local autonomy; as adjuncts of state services, they expected state funding (but never believed that they had received sufficient funds) and carried out many duties assigned by the state, in addition to their core tasks. This tension frequently revealed itself in the relations of maternal societies with the state, and it often had implications for their relations with the women they assisted.

# 3. Modeling Maternal Behavior

*Relations between the* Dames Visiteuses
*and the* Pauvres Mères Indigentes

In 1811, Madame Chastan, wife of a Parisian *charbonnier* (collier), gave birth to triplets. Still caring for a little girl of twenty-eight months, the mother was determined to breast-feed all three babies herself. Her patrons at the Society for Maternal Charity suggested that Madame Chastan place at least one of the three babies with a wet nurse. "'Eh, which would I give up?' she responded. 'No, no, I can nurse all three of them.'"[1] With this story, the Paris society demonstrated in a compelling fashion the success of its organization and approach. Through timely assistance to a struggling mother and the encouragement of maternal breast feeding, they had strengthened the natural bonds that exist between mother and child—so much so that Madame Chastan refused to send any of her babies to a wet nurse. The goal was to duplicate this success through practical and moral assistance to other mothers in need.

Since their inception, maternal societies had promoted two goals: the preservation of children, and the encouragement of women's maternal role. Madame Fougeret, founder of the Society for Maternal Charity, and the charitable women who subsequently staffed the administrative councils saw these two goals as closely intertwined. Napoleon's appreciation for their approach had precipitated his decision to place the society under the authority of the empress and to essentially turn it into an arm of the state. After Napoleon's fall, the decision of the king and his ministers to continue to subsidize maternal societies demonstrated that the values promoted by the organizations crossed political boundaries and enjoyed near-universal support.[2] The 1820s and 1830s were years of political, and even violent, conflict in France, but politicians and policy makers agreed on one point: mothers were the key to orderly family and social life—the moral linchpins of the family.[3] This conception of woman primarily as mother and confined to the domestic sphere, although debated vigorously during the eighteenth century in the salons and the literature of the Enlightenment, was enshrined by Napoleon in the *Code civil* in 1804 and widely accepted as an ideal (although far from reality) throughout the nineteenth century, as well.[4] The fundamental importance of mothers to families, and thus to society at large, justified assistance targeted to help poor women become caring mothers. This perspective helped to firmly establish the Society for Maternal Charity as the doyenne of women's charitable associations.

Historians have focused on the early nineteenth century as a crucial period in the articulation of women's maternal and domestic responsibilities. Jennifer Popiel's recent book demonstrates that while Rousseau's popular prescriptions on education, motherhood, and family life were not implemented in the political and legislative sphere in the eighteenth century, his ideas came to shape modern ideas about family life; by the early nineteenth century, the nurturing mother had replaced the patriarchal father as the key parent in training children and in unifying the family.[5] Denise Z. Davidson's work indicates that class and gender norms were in a process of transformation in the late eighteenth and early nineteenth century across social classes. While working-class women were unable to devote their time to purely domestic pursuits as middle-class and elite women could, Davidson asserts that the ideology of domesticity shaped workers' gender norms, as well.[6] In general, she finds that prescribed gender roles, especially with regard to access to public spaces, were more settled by the 1820s after a period of some ambiguity under Napoleon and the early years of the Restoration government. These norms would come under challenge in the 1830s as utopian socialists and others more politically radical began to contest "traditional" gender constraints; but, as Davidson notes, "the first body of texts arguing for women's 'domestic' existence needed to be created and internalized before subversive discourses could come into existence in opposition to it."[7]

A variety of individuals and institutions framed a gendered social vision that emphasized the nurturing role of the mother at various levels. Bonnie G. Smith identifies elite women as key in both shaping notions of feminine and maternal duties and communicating these ideas not only to their own daughters, but to women of other social classes, a process that we can see at work in the functioning of maternal societies.[8] Rachel G. Fuchs's work highlights the efforts of the state, through its welfare policies aimed primarily at single mothers, to foster maternal responsibility and to discourage child abandonment.[9] Maternal societies first helped to shape, then fought to maintain, a vision of family life in which the loving nursing mother was central, among the working poor as well as the well-to-do. Part of their task was educating poor women to be affectionate mothers who could inculcate appropriate values in their children.[10] Their records emphasize these complex interactions among elite women, poor women, and the local and central governments, illuminating one aspect of the nexus of elite women's culture with that of poor women. This relationship between the *dames visiteuses* and the recipients of their help was key to maternal societies' operations and anticipated outcomes.

It is easy to understand why poor women sought assistance from the Society for Maternal Charity; these women were in desperate straits and turned to an organization that offered practical assistance and, in many cases, a kind word and emotional sustenance. From the time of the society's origins, Madame Fougeret and her fellow *dames administrantes* showed sympathy for the travails of poor mothers and emphasized their sisterly concern as well as their willingness to offer pecuniary help. The reasons that elite women joined the society and that the state lent such strong support are more complex. It is not surprising that both elite women and the state turned to charitable assistance to accomplish personal and social goals. Women sought friendship, satisfying activity, and to "do good" as *dames visiteuses*. Both the central government, represented by the Interior Ministry and the prefects, and local administrators saw value in the charitable donations and free labor of maternal societies' elite members. This cachet made it easier to attract both members and subsidies from the government.

Furthermore, poor mothers—especially those married, virtuous, and untainted by single motherhood—along with their innocent children, were particularly sympathetic charitable objects. Consequently, this charity's goals—to preserve children through the alleviation of poverty and to assist poor mothers in their duties—were appealing in a century when the nurturing and educational role of mothers was increasingly celebrated.[11] And who could better teach poor women to become good mothers than other women? The Society for Maternal Charity was predicated upon this ideal of female solidarity, based on women's shared experience of motherhood. In 1790 the Paris society had argued that its organization "merits the consideration of all sensitive and humane individuals; in particular, it merits the consideration of Mothers; they alone can appreciate the real horror of the situation of these unfortunate women, who dread that inevitable moment when they must know and lose forever [the child] to whom they have just given birth: it merits the consideration of friends of morality and [social] order, and [the society] awaits with confidence the assistance that Providence has not ceased to provide since it came into existence."[12] This emotional language is prevalent in the documents, and especially in the public appeals, of maternal societies. The founders had hoped they could save poor families by inspiring positive emotions—love, respect, gratitude—in place of the disorder and despair that undermined family life among the impoverished. It was this despair and disorder that led to the abandonment of babies, and the subsequent steep augmentation in infant mortality rates. The most important of these positive emotions, capable of bringing an end to this hopelessness, was the love of the mother for her child.

The efforts of Madame de Fougeret to persuade poor women to breast-feed their children reflected this belief in the efficacy of maternal care. Since the time of Rousseau, philosophers, writers, and philanthropists had pinpointed the importance of maternal nursing, not just for its health benefits, but for strengthening the mother–child bond; indeed it was a "sacred duty" that could cement the relationship.[13] They touted a mother's love, not just a re-ligious duty, but a powerful human emotion that could lay the foundations for a healthy society. The founders of the Society for Maternal Charity were convinced that if they provided poor mothers with funds sufficient to allow them to nurse their babies themselves rather than sending them off to a wet nurse, they would tap the wellspring of maternal devotion that lay beneath the surface, crushed by the immense weight of poverty and squalor.

While it is true that both the royal government and moral philosophers recognized that mother love, properly cultivated, could serve the public good, the reality of its deployment was nuanced and complex. Eighteenth- and nineteenth-century individuals were well aware of this complexity, and the language of maternal love—and especially, its cultivation and practice among the poor—reflects some ambiguity. In their seminal work on the history of motherhood, Yvonne Knibiehler and Catherine Fouquet have stressed that while "maternal love has always existed," "from about 1750 onwards, the duties of mothers become the object of an increasingly rich discourse on the part of philosophers, doctors, and statesmen."[14] As we have seen, Jean-Jacques Rousseau in particular idealized the image of the loving mother as vital to the well-being of the infant.[15] But as the founders of the Society for Maternal Charity recognized, intense poverty could dull maternal affection, rupturing the emotional bond between mother and child and leading hope-less mothers to abandon their infants at overburdened foundling hospices. Encouraging poor women to express their love was insufficient; rather, these women needed the resources that would allow that love to blossom.

The records of maternal societies reveal the development of several strands of discourse on emotion, and this particular emphasis gained force in the

1820s and 1830s. The society's mode of operation makes no sense without an understanding of the theme of motherhood and mother love that was elaborated over the course of the eighteenth century and increasingly rooted in "nature." By demanding that the poor mothers they "adopted" breast-feed their infants and keep them at home, the charitable ladies hoped to intensify the "natural" bond that exists between mother and child. In his report to the Lyon maternal society in 1826, Secretary Mottet-Degérando stressed that "one cannot fail to notice that it is humane and moral that mothers nurse their children. It is incontestable that they are better cared for; the father, who sees them raised under his eyes, becomes more devoted to his family, a particular charm holds him there, and in that way, many disorders are prevented."[16] The founders of the society assumed that after two years of breast feeding and caring for her child, the mother—no matter how poor—would find it unthinkable to abandon her baby, and that in fact, this act of caring would draw the entire family together more tightly. They assumed that emotions intensified over time if a woman practiced loving maternal behavior.

But mother love was not the only discourse of emotion at work in the appeals of the society. Eighteenth-century literature celebrated pity and empathy, sentiments considered as natural as mother love.[17] The "natural" sympathy that individuals feel for fellow human beings in distress—especially women and children, *exempla* of the deserving poor—would help to convince the wealthy to provide the resources they needed. Well-to-do mothers and fathers would be especially susceptible to these pleas. The supporters of maternal societies continued to employ this language of empathy throughout the nineteenth century. In his charge to Marseille's *dames distributrices* in 1816, the honorary treasurer L. Dudemaine advised them to draw on this empathy: "Examine the residence of the well-to-do gentleman. This man, who would be tempted to refuse you, also has a wife, he has children who are his joy and his consolation, these auxiliaries will plead victoriously for the unfortunates that you represent."[18] All that was needed was the appropriate spark. Sarah Maza has analyzed the efforts of lawyers to incite public sympathy through melodramatic narratives of virtue assaulted and innocence betrayed.[19] In a similar way, the maternal society hoped to arouse the sympathy of the wealthy in its graphic descriptions of poor but respectable families. By exciting the pity of potential donors, these women hoped to recruit members and raise funds to finance good works. Dudemaine stressed this point, asserting that "One need only approach a Marseillais and his heart will open itself to good works."[20]

The Paris society's original bylaws boldly claimed the right to the public's sympathy: "The plan traced by the Maternal Charity was of a nature to inspire the most tender interest. Save the life and *état* of a multitude of citizens sacrificed to poverty, reestablish morality in indigent families, save them from [committing] a crime, attach a prize to the observation of their duties, such is the enterprise of the Maternal Charity."[21] The bylaws carefully traced the difficult situation of the working family, scarcely able to attend to its own needs: "The birth of a new child becomes the last straw for this desperate family; all is exhausted; the memory of the difficulties caused by [the child] who preceded this one extinguishes the sentiments of nature; his judgment is pronounced; he will be abandoned."[22] No one could help but be moved by this image of the destitute family, unable to care for a beloved child.

The supporters of the Society for Maternal Charity used the same kind of emotional language to incite the sympathy that might lead to action. While William Reddy argues that the emotional regime of the nineteenth century was less overtly sentimental than that of the eighteenth,[23] as late as 1858 the Reverend Monsabré gave a floridly moving sermon in support of Lyon's maternal society in which he traced the travails of the poor mother: "Nature utters terrible cries, but the pressing voice of necessity stifles them. It is in vain that the mother strives to reconcile these two things, especially if the distressing possibility of illness or unemployment come to complicate her dilemma, [her choices are] destitution or abandonment."[24]

The key role of sentiment explains in part why maternal charities emphasized the importance of face-to-face contact. This personal contact would create emotional ties between poor and rich, and it would heighten the natural sympathy that charitable women felt for their charges, as well as respect and affection on the part of poor indigent mothers for their *dames patronnesses*.[25] These relations between women were considered crucial to the organization's success; there could be no progress without kindness on the part of the *dames visiteuses* and without gratitude and submissive behavior on the part of poor mothers.

Sentiment was essential to the appeal of the Society for Maternal Charity. The language of sentiment and nature dovetailed nicely, and the charitable women who staffed maternal societies shared the belief that the maternal bond was a natural one. All women wanted to keep their infants unless poverty and stress ruptured the maternal bond. Consequently, maternal societies dedicated themselves to helping poor women maintain or revive that natural bond with their child so that they could act as responsible and loving mothers. In the words of a Bordelais notable and philanthropist, the vicomte de Pelleport-Burète, the members of the society hoped that "through their generous efforts, all the sentiments of maternity [would be] revived in the woman's heart, even when those sentiments [had] been weakened or extinguished."[26]

Thus, while affection for one's child was "natural," according to moral philosophers, the founders of the society recognized that deprivation could lead to its diminution. This diminished affection was not necessarily because of any moral failing on the part of these poor mothers; rather, it resulted from concrete material conditions. That love could never be entirely extinguished, the Paris society's 1789 bylaws eloquently argued:

> Thus, the abandonment of legitimate children can no longer be attributed to moral depravity, but rather to a lack of assistance . . . [P]aternal and maternal sentiment are not extinguished among the common people; the tears that they shed when imploring the assistance of the Maternal Charity attest to that. Many mothers taken in by [the society] who had never nursed [their children] submitted to that law, and fulfilled their duties with a touching sensibility; among them, several have done more: pressed by remorse, by the desire to once again see the children they have abandoned, they have asked for their return. Some bitterly mourned their deaths; others, happier, were able to take them in their arms, and the caresses they lavished on [their children] would have been enough to gain forgiveness for their faults if repentance alone were insufficient.[27]

It was the concrete act of nurturing that would revive maternal affection: "These mothers nurse their children, fill all the obligations that have been imposed on them; and these same creatures, destined to be rejected, became dear to their families."[28] The baron Dupin wrote warmly of the effectiveness of the society's methods in reviving maternal feelings, noting that "once a child reaches the age of a year, [during which] his mother has nursed him, that she has enjoyed his caresses, his first smile, there is little worry that she will pull away from him and abandon him."[29] If provided with assistance that would render the task of caring for a new baby less overwhelming, the wellspring of maternal love would begin to flow once again, and with it, other benefits crucial to families and to society. A. Cornereau, in his celebration of the Society for Maternal Charity of Dijon, asserted that "in this way, the *Charité maternelle* brings, into the midst of families, love of order, of work, the duties and the unity of households; it restores to the State mothers, precious as mothers of families, and a prodigious number of children."[30] This statement explains the state's interest in maternal societies: the state directly benefitted from stable families, and only good mothers could make families strong.

But a mother needed to do more than nurse her infant to create an affectionate and viable home life—she needed to develop other skills that the *dames visiteuses* could teach her. Part of the equation was *prévoyance,* prudence and thrift in managing resources. In its charge to the *dames distribu-*

*trices,* the administrative board of Bordeaux's maternal society warned that "improvident parents will consume in useless expenses, and all in the same day, that which, well-managed, would have sufficed for all their needs for quite some time."[31] It was the responsibility of the visiting ladies to show these poor mothers a better way, even against their will. While the bylaws and exhortations of individual maternal societies differed in particulars, the tone and emphasis were the same. The *dames visiteuses* should exercise foresight, economy, and prudence, which their charges practiced all too rarely. They might buy a cradle for families who lacked one.[32] The women who staffed the society of Bordeaux were warned to resist any requests for advances, since a lack of foresight too often plunged the poor into "irremediable distress."[33] The *dames visiteuses* were to urge single mothers living with the father of their children to marry, and thus make themselves eligible for assistance; according to the *présidente* of Lyon's society, one of the most important contributions of the Society for Maternal Charity was to "enlighten and to make legitimate before God certain unions which, previously, were the object of scandal."[34]

Good housekeeping and management skills were crucial for the poor mother. But mothering skills were equally essential. In some cases, poor women simply did not know how to be good mothers, despite their own best efforts; "others, obeying the voice of deception or prejudice, will indulge in practices sometimes absurd, sometimes dangerous to their health or the health of their children."[35] Poverty led families to become apathetic and indolent: "From this arises their distrust, their predispositions, and a profound ignorance; from this, bizarre prejudices that must be overcome."[36] In these cases, the *dames visiteuses* should step in with advice. Breast feeding, the linchpin of the society's requirements, not only helped mothers bond with their children, but also improved the baby's odds of survival considerably.[37] The *dames visiteuses* also counseled (or required) vaccination against smallpox, provided infants with their own cradle, and sometimes supplied medical assistance. There is reason to believe that the poor women seeking assistance might have resisted some of the advice proffered; in her study of the infant welfare movement in pre–World War I London, Ellen Ross found that poor mothers defined good and bad mothering very differently from the infant welfare workers and that their views on the appropriate care and feeding of infants and young children diverged significantly.[38]

These different cultures of motherhood undoubtedly led to tensions, if not conflicts. In some cases, the extreme poverty of these families made it impossible for them to behave as the *dames visiteuses* might have liked. Still, with a sympathy that was not always obvious among nineteenth-century moral and social philosophers, who denounced the "moral decadence of the laboring classes" and "the poor and vicious classes,"[39] the women who staffed maternal societies recognized that the behavior of the poor was not the only cause of poverty: "Often, one must agree, poverty appears hideous in the midst of large cities, where one is sometimes tempted to believe it is the result of disorder; but if that cause exists for some families, for how many more is it not illness, feebleness, and inevitable circumstances that have reduced them to distress, to that extremity where the unfortunate no longer tries to help himself, where discouragement immobilizes him with sorrow!"[40] On the other hand, the methods of maternal societies were predicated on the belief that appropriate behavior could at least ameliorate the situation of the poor. The *dames visiteuses* encouraged "moral" behavior to bring out "natural" maternal instincts.[41] Thus mothers who received assistance from the society were to adhere to strict standards of behavior. Continued assistance was contingent on the good use of money provided and on constant attention to the cleanliness, health, and well-being of the child. Maternal societies demanded proof of legal (and in some cases, religious) marriage and good morals, as well as the promise to breast-feed as a partial guarantee of good behavior. The woman had to be poor through no fault of her own, because of a dead, unwillingly absent, or injured husband, or because of her own illness. While the original *règlement* of the Paris society promised assistance to virtuous women deserted by loutish husbands, in practice, the *dames administrantes* evinced some reluctance to give preference to these women. At a meeting of the Paris society's administrative council in 1811, "The Council refused to admit for assistance the child of a woman who had been abandoned by her husband in accordance with the dispositions of the bylaws, which prescribe preferred admission for households whose behavior is proper [*regulière*]."[42]

It was no easy task for maternal societies to locate the neediest and most deserving women. Women carried out most of the work of the organization, visiting poor mothers eligible for adoption by the charity and assessing their needs.[43] The process of identifying these mothers could be a Herculean task; the *dames visiteuses* would call on them in their abodes to assess eligibility, but first they needed to determine who might need help.[44] In 1865 the *présidente* of Lyon's maternal society described the process:

> It must still be recognized that in this search for poverty, which is imposed on us and which obliges us to search even in its final resting places, the poor help us to discover other poor. Our *dames administrantes,* even because of the abundance of the aid they had to distribute, had to enter farther into those remote areas which are the usual refuge of poverty; and there, the ladies found the poor who would have remained unknown to them; they heard the groans which perhaps would never have reached them. It really is good and useful to look for the poor

in his home. He is grateful that you sought him out, for your assiduousness and weariness, which are the most genuine evidence of a profound sympathy. Advice is more welcome; surveillance becomes more energetic.

Equally valuable were the networks that charitable women built up over time. "Moreover, our *dames administrantes* try to bring to this task the wisdom they have gained through long experience in charitable work. They look still for other sources of information, whether in building relations with other charities that visit poor families, or by ensuring the support of the Sisters of Charity responsible for visiting the parish poor."[45]

The *dames administrantes* had always tried to cast a broad net in their search for the neediest and most deserving families. In the early 1790s, under the Revolutionary government, Paris's maternal society had cooperated effectively with the sectional *comités de bienfaisance* that had been put into place to identify and assist the poor in the capital.[46] In many cities, close relations between maternal societies and charitable organizations such as the Philanthropic Society provided another source of information on needy mothers.[47] In others, maternal societies posted handbills and larger signs informing the neighborhood of their presence. In 1812 the Prefecture of the Rhône printed a poster publicizing the existence of the Imperial Society for Maternal Charity, specifying the parameters of each *arrondissement* of Lyon and listing the *dames administrantes* in charge of each district.[48] Part of Dijon's administrative costs included the outlay for informative *circulaires* to be posted throughout the town; the posters listed the conditions for admission, the types of assistance available, and the names of the *dames visitantes* responsible for each parish of Dijon. The *affiche* also listed midwives and surgeons affiliated with Dijon's maternal society.[49]

Under Napoleon, as well, the vice presidents of the Paris society were proactive in seeking out those eligible for assistance. On February 9, 1812, Mesdames Ségur and Pastoret sent a form letter to the twelve mayors of Paris asking for help:

> The Administrative Council of the Maternal Society, to fulfill the desires of H.M. the Empress, has recourse to the cares and the experience of Monsieur the Mayor of the. . . . *arrondissement* in order to know in a precise manner the name of the families registered for the assistance that MM. the members of the *comités de bienfaisance* distribute, the daily needs of each of these families, and the causes of disability that must give them the right to extraordinary assistance which H.M. the Empress allows them, with the understanding that they are not exempted from Labor, but to spare them the difficulty caused by the temporary increase in the price of bread.[50]

Throughout the nineteenth century, maternal societies continued to work closely with their local *comités* and *bureaux de bienfaisance* to identify eligible families. Often, the *bureaux* would refer eligible women to the local maternal society, as this helped them to keep their own costs lower.[51] Maternal societies also entertained individual solicitations for assistance. These could come from a variety of sources; for example, in 1812 M. le Curé de Clichy la Garenne sent a note to Madame Pastoret asking for assistance on behalf of the wife of a day laborer.[52] Generally, requests for assistance were funneled through the prefect. Bordeaux's archives record a number of these cases. Françoise Lacouture, wife of an unemployed worker, sent her request for assistance via the mayor of Bordeaux, who passed it on to the prefect, who in turn gave it to the administrative council.[53] The prefect of the Gironde tried to persuade Madame Guestier, *présidente* of Bordeaux's maternal society, to take charge of a child born under mysterious circumstances to *la femme* Gallet, a married woman, whom the foundling hospice refused to admit.[54] In 1858 the prefect notified Madame Guestier that the commandant of the Municipal Guard had requested assistance "in favor of the wife of a corporal in that Guard who just gave birth, and is unable to nurse her child."[55] In Lyon, the prefect of the Rhône passed on a request for the shoemaker Bertrand, who asked for assistance on behalf of his wife.[56] In October 1870, the prefect of the Seine-Inférieure forwarded a number of requests for assistance to the baronne Le Mire, *présidente* of Rouen's maternal society; the crisis brought about by the Franco-Prussian War undoubtedly strained the city's resources.[57] In a few cases, the requests came from higher authorities; in 1864 la dame Blanchère solicited the intervention of the empress herself to gain an increase in her monthly assistance from Lyon's maternal society; the minister of the interior passed her request along.[58]

Once needy families were identified, the process of selection began. Identifying, vetting, and assisting these poor mothers was laborious and often emotionally grueling, as the women had to turn down many desperately poor mothers while choosing those they could assist. Our best evidence for the process comes from the records maintained by the Society for Maternal Charity of Paris for 1790–93 and 1810–14, but other maternal societies appear to have followed similar procedures. At their regular meetings, the *dames administrantes* presented information on mothers and children in need of assistance in their parish or *arrondissement;* the women in attendance voted on whether to admit each particular woman, then determined the degree of help she would receive.[59] In general, each parish or *arrondissement* received a prearranged proportion of admission cards. In its early years, the Paris society decided on a regular basis how many admission slots to accord each parish, based on total resources; the larger and poorer parishes were allowed to admit more families.[60] Lyon explicitly laid out its process of apportionment in its bylaws: "In the month of October, each year, the Administrative Council decides provisionally the number of mothers it believes it will be able to admit in each *arrondissement* during the following year, in view of resources anticipated and realized over the course of the exercise. A number of admissions proportional to the population and the number of poor it contains is attributed to each *arrondissement*."[61] Each *dame distribuante* would receive a certain number of admission cards to give to eligible mothers in her district. Determining the type and amount of assistance was an important part of the process; in all cities, the *dames administrantes* carefully sifted through evidence to determine who would receive the full complement of *secours,* which usually included childbirth expenses, a layette, and pecuniary assistance for up to eighteen months.

Once worthy recipients of assistance were located and accepted, it was the task of the *dames visiteuses* to monitor mothers under the care of the society in their *arrondissement* or parish to make sure that they behaved as proper mothers at all times. According to instructions, the women in charge of distributing aid were to visit families under their surveillance frequently. This would allow them to examine whether the infant and its swaddling clothes were kept clean and whether it was suitably cared for and nourished. They were also to give the mother instructions and words of comfort "dictated by their experience and their wisdom." Most important, the visits were to take place frequently, ideally on random days and at random times. Unannounced visits were essential to guarantee the good conduct of the mothers. If a *dame distributrice* had reason to believe that pecuniary gifts might be used unwisely [*mal employé*], she was usually authorized to convert them into assistance in kind.[62] Through careful surveillance, by setting a good example, and through a bit of blackmail, the maternal societies would help shape poor women into the kind of mothers they ought to be.

But the demand for appropriate behavior did not only reflect the belief that a moral mother would be a better mother. While some philanthropists objected to the demand for a marriage certificate, and in particular, proof of religious marriage, on the grounds that all poor mothers deserved assistance (and these voices would come to dominate by the end of the century, under the secular Third Republic), others fiercely justified the choice to help only poor women of impeccable moral behavior. In 1821 the baron Dupin defended maternal societies against their detractors, noting that "they would forget that the attentions of the ladies of the Society are, of all their benefits, the most precious; that the mothers of families would not agree to put themselves in contact with fallen women [*filles déshonorées*]; that consequently, to demand more would be to destroy the institution. One cannot lose sight of certain moral distinctions. Without a doubt, every suffering being has a right to public assistance, but a wife deserves more consideration than a concubine."[63] This defense of "*distinctions morales*" reflects the class elements embedded in the mode of operation of maternal societies. Class and gender norms were potent ideologies that structured the society's workings. The decision to recruit a female membership was deliberate. The Society for Maternal Charity directed its appeals primarily toward women, touted as more tender, more sympathetic, more willing to come to the aid of their suffering sisters. These appeals also reveal the class- and gender-specific nature of perceived emotional response. The founders of the society assumed that women's natural pity for the less fortunate, and especially for children, would allow them to overcome their understandable disgust at the repellent living conditions of those they helped. Their sympathetic natures would lead poor women to trust in their advice.[64] And while maternal love was an emotion that transcended class boundaries, the selfless motherly insights of the elite *dames visiteuses* would serve as model and inspiration for the poor women they assisted. The original bylaws of the Paris society underlined these perceptions: "The Maternal Charity was founded by women, because they are the ones called by Providence to the assistance of abandoned children and indigent mothers; and the Administration of this establishment demanded all the virtues specific to their sex . . . a tender sensibility, a particular fondness for children capable of surmounting repugnance for the details of poverty, a zeal always kept alive by sentiment, a religious respect for duties imposed and laws adopted, finally that modesty which brings them to beseech advice from enlightened persons and to receive it with gratitude."[65] While all women were called to take part in the work of the Society for Maternal Charity, mothers in particular could be expected to have sympathy with its goals.

Thus the activities of the society were predicated on the ideal of sisterly solidarity: women helping women. The president of Lyon's maternal society went so far as to say, "they become the mothers of poor mothers!"[66] The society's elite supporters also believed that the generosity and kindness of the *dames visiteuses* could bring about true reconciliation between social classes and inspire genuine gratitude on the part of the poor for the rich.[67] Fears of class unrest and socialist upheaval grew stronger over the course of the 1830s and 1840s. These fears were particularly acute in traditionally revolutionary cities like Paris, and in cities with class-conscious workers, such as Lyon. Lyon experienced upheaval more than once over the course of the 1830s. The uprising of 1834[68] was the largest urban disturbance in France between the

revolutions of 1830 and 1848, and the 1848 event prompted a desire for class
reconciliation (as well as repressive measures) on the part of Lyon's elite. Lyon's
*compte rendu* for 1849 reveals an intense desire to use the resources of the
society as a means of conciliation after the frightening upheavals of 1848; the
*présidente,* Madame Delahante, addressed the members along these lines:

> I ask all for whom the period of financial difficulty and anxiety was only tempo-
> rary to please realize that charity ruins no one, and that the gifts one distributes
> among the poor procure the only durable and desirable riches; it also seems to
> me that, more than ever, it is so necessary to see extended *[voir s'augmenter]*
> relations of the rich with the poor, and more than ever, they must be shown
> the warmest and most active sympathy, in seeking the salvation of souls at the
> same time as the relief of poverty, and in joining the consolation of religion
> to temporal aid.[69]

Loving assistance to poor mothers, coupled with religious exhortations,
could prevent future revolutionary activity and diminish the hatred of the
poor for the rich. Thus maternal societies and their supporters promoted
the hopeful view that they could reconcile social classes and perhaps nip
the dangers of socialism and other "false doctrines" in the bud—a particular
concern in working-class cities. Madame Delahante's speech emphasized
this possibility:

> Perhaps the rich, more disenchanted with the things of this world, and more
> struck by their instability, will be more disposed to come to the assistance of
> the poor; and they, in turn, finally understanding the untruth of all the false
> doctrines that [others] have dared to preach, will understand that [those doc-
> trines] can lead them only to a more profound misery, and will be more grateful
> toward those who extend a hand and seek to alleviate their ills.[70]

This was also the message delivered by the Reverend Montsabré in a sermon
touting the benefits of the Society for Maternal Charity of Lyon in 1858. He
presented a compelling narrative:

> A worker, led astray by false doctrines, walked the pavement of a crowded street,
> carrying a young child in his arms. He saw at a distance a group of women
> sumptuously dressed. What could he do, seeing them? Grumble and complain.
> But one of them, noble by birth but more noble still because of her character
> *[esprit]* and virtue, drew away and approached him.
>     What a beautiful child you have there, she said to him, let me embrace him.
> *Et voilà,* that poor man who just a moment ago was disagreeable, vanquished
> by such kindness. Trembling, he brought his dear little one forward, two large
> tears rolling down his cheeks. It was a mysterious baptism which purged all
> hatreds. He left, blessing those whom he had cursed and, returning to his home,

said, "Wife, the things I have been told are not true; a rich lady, young and beautiful like an angel, embraced our child." You see, then, a maternal caress, just like that, had reconciled him with society.[71]

This evocative vignette highlights the secondary concerns and goals of maternal societies and, for listeners, stressed that charity could be a crucial social act.

The possibility that maternal societies might promote better relations among social classes led both local governments and the French state, represented by the Interior Ministry and prefect, to lend them often enthusiastic support. Alisa Klaus suggests that the French government saw private charities not only as a way to aid in the protection of maternal and infant health, but also as a means of quelling class conflict.[72] In his hagiographic account of the Society for Maternal Charity of Rouen, another industrial city that feared that effects of worker unrest, Charles Des Alleurs explicitly recognized that this was one of the goals of the charity: "In this way, create between the rich and the poor these moral bonds, which prevent the latter from giving way to discouragement, to despair, and especially from being led astray by evils which can give rise to envy, and consequently, to consider the prosperity of those favored by fortune a blessing for him, since he directly reaps the fruit! Now, then, these same bonds become for the rich an occasion to do good in an enlightened manner, and with double profit, for the hand which receives and the hand that gives."[73] From an early date, policy makers were aware that the society could possibly help calm class conflict and political strife. Already in 1815, a letter from the prefect of the Rhône to the minister of the interior noted that the Society for Maternal Charity was particularly useful in "a manufacturing city where destitution is always triggered by a *cause générale* that strikes the entire working class at the same time" as was the case in Lyon.[74]

Of course, the efforts of maternal societies did not prevent class conflict in 1830, the year of the July Revolution, nor did it prevent revolution in 1848. Still, this interest in the moderating influence of maternal societies continued over the course of the century, especially as the elite became more conscious of offending the pride of working-class families. A *compte rendu* published by the Society for Maternal Charity of Lyon in 1867 outlined the tensions among working-class families of that city who suffered from unemployment and suggested that "it is, perhaps, possible for the Charité Maternelle to be able to enter into these abodes without offending the sensibilities of these poor families."[75] A similar argument can be found in several of the *comptes moraux* of the Limoges society: "The Maternal Charity is one of the most edifying among all the charitable organizations that take care of poor families in Limoges; it is best liked by the working class, and most easily accepted. By directly addressing the needs of children, it appears to better assuage the sensitivity of the worker."[76] This may not have been entirely wishful thinking; Annie Flacassier suggests that the home assistance offered by the *dames visiteuses* gave the bourgeoisie of Bordeaux a more profound understanding of lower-class misery in their town and led to more sustained charitable efforts that, despite their limitations, created a more peaceful social climate in Bordeaux than in many other nineteenth-century French cities.[77]

To most effectively improve class relations, the women who staffed maternal societies focused on those who would appreciate their services and be more receptive to their advice. Despite genuine sympathy on the part of the *dames visiteuses* for the women they assisted, they also wanted to target the poor mothers and families most susceptible to their message. These were the "deserving poor," those mothers who appeared most selfless and dedicated to their families—in short, "good mothers." To a certain extent, this focus on married mothers may explain the successes they frequently touted: reduced mortality rates, prevention of child abandonment, healthier children, and happier families. Maternal societies were already serving a population of the poor better off than the truly destitute; these were married women rather than the single mothers who were the poorest and most vulnerable.[78] Even if widowed, or married to disabled spouses, these families were "respectable," more likely to be embedded in the community, with access to social networks and resources. If married in a religious ceremony, they were likely members of a church, another source of support. Those less receptive—and in the eyes of the *dames administrantes,* less moral and less deserving—did not merit equally sympathetic attention. While its supporters favored the ideal of class reconciliation, the underlying message of the society was sometimes harsh, undergirded by an uncompromising adherence to class hierarchies:

> You will follow, MESDAMES, in all these types of situations, the impulse of your zeal and your prudence, that of the generous interest you take in the condition of the poor; you will give them advice, instructions, or console them, depending on the circumstances; you will remind them sometimes that the able-bodied poor must earn his living by working, and that he has no right to the assistance of charity, public or private; finally, in a case where their misconduct would require it on your part, a severe tone, you threaten them, if necessary, with the loss of the benevolence and the assistance of the Society.[79]

The *dames administrantes* rigorously upheld the rules governing morality. Admission to assistance was not pro forma. In 1815, despite a personal request by the mayor of Bordeaux, that city's Society for Maternal Charity did not accord assistance to the Chagneau family, as the unhappy parents could not provide proof of a religious marriage and had only two instead of the required three children.[80] The Fourcade family was likewise turned away for not fitting the "class of poor admissible according to our bylaws."[81] A Madame Gallet was refused assistance when inquiries turned up "information . . . extremely unfavorable"; in addition, she was unable to produce certification of religious marriage.[82] One can only assume that a similar response awaited Marie Fauré when it was discovered that the husband on her marriage certificate was Joseph Cassadon, rather than Pierre Blanc, the man she claimed as her spouse.[83]

On the other hand, if the *dames administrantes* truly believed that a woman deserved assistance, they could on occasion find a way to work around the rules. In 1811 the baronne de Baulny of the Paris society had

> proposed assistance for a woman, mother of five children, three of whom had been born in a legitimate marriage & two others [born] outside of marriage, their father having died before he was able to carry out the union he had promised to enter into. The Council decided that, according to its statutes, she was not admissible, but that Mme de Baulny could allow her some assistance provided that it was not given in the name of the Society, and that it would be drawn from funds remaining in Mme de Baulny's possession following the death of some children to whom the Society had awarded assistance.[84]

The *dames visiteuses* kept the nursing mothers under careful surveillance once they were admitted. The minutes and *comptes rendus* occasionally make note of women who had been dropped from the rolls for improper conduct, beginning with the earliest records. At a meeting of the Paris society on February 20, 1790, Madame Lavoisier denounced *la femme* d'Orléans, "who made a false declaration to her concerning the number of her children." *La femme* Fosse had also lied about the number of her children, and as a result, both suffered the same penalty: "to lose now and in the future the Assistance of the Society."[85] In 1817, nine women previously assisted by Bordeaux's society "deserved to have their assistance revoked."[86] The reasons that women lost their assistance varied; in 1819, three women were dropped from Bordeaux's rolls for refusing to have their children vaccinated; in 1821, two women placed their children with a wet nurse, in contravention of the rules.[87] Rouen's president provided fewer details, simply noting in the *compte moral* for 1857 that "in general, the assisted families show gratitude for the help that is given to them, and those whom the ladies have to complain about or find fault with the conduct are very small in number; only three women have incurred the sorrow of losing a portion of the sums that they had been granted."[88]

Those who questioned the motives or methods of the *dames administrantes* found themselves cut off from any prospect of assistance. At a meeting held on November 9, 1812, Madame de Ségur shared a letter she had received from the minister of the interior, Montalivet, that noted, "I learned that one of the Ladies of the Maternal Society to whom *la femme* Cordier, a pregnant mother of a family, had been recommended by the Bureau de bienfaisance of the Porte St. Denis, refused her assistance solely because the marriage the woman had entered into before the mayor of her *arrondissement* did not receive the blessing of the church." Montalivet politely scolded the administrative council for suggesting that a nonreligious marriage was unacceptable. Madame de Ségur responded on December 12 that the report was false; that in fact, Madame Cordier had not been refused assistance, but that she had requested admission too early. She was not due to give birth until January 1813 and had been asked to resubmit her request in December. The vice president noted defensively that "one can cite more than one hundred examples of women assisted who had been united with their Spouses only through a civil marriage." However, she went on to say, "I must observe to Your Excellency that being free to make these choices according to our conscience, we need give no explanation to the poor in case of admission or refusal; and it is reasonable to think that those who have not been chosen complain of that misfortune as an injustice." Not surprisingly, when Madame Cordier came back seeking assistance in March of 1813, "The Ladies unanimously refused admission to that woman."[89]

Even those guilty of insufficient gratitude were deemed unworthy of assistance. In a letter from 1816, Bordeaux's administrative council informed the *dames distributrices* that if they ever assisted a woman who ignored the consideration she owed them, her assistance should cease immediately, because she was clearly unworthy of it. The administrative council wished to see its "estimable collaborators respected."[90] However, most poor mothers at least outwardly demonstrated appropriate gratitude; Elie Lefébure, president of Rouen's Society for Maternal Charity, reported that the women they assisted usually "receive their advice and even their admonishments submissively, and act disposed to comply."[91]

This bifurcated attitude toward the poor families they assisted highlights contradictions in class and gender solidarities on the part of the *dames visiteuses*. Certainly, they were sympathetic to the trials of poor mothers. Their tone was far more compassionate than that of the male social and moral economists described by Rachel Fuchs.[92] In fact, the male members of Bordeaux's administrative council issued the harshest pronouncements concerning the behavior of poor mothers, urging stern surveillance on the part of the *dames visiteuses.* Ultimately, however, like most of the educated French middle classes and elite, members of the society believed that "the cause of poverty rests primarily with the poor."[93] The exception to this were the *pauvres honteux,* the "shamefaced poor," who had enjoyed greater fortune at one point in life. The Society for Maternal Charity of Marseille noted that "one Lady is in charge of keeping a secret register of mothers who had held a distinguished rank in society and whom the reverses of fortunes plunged into poverty."[94] But even the entrenched poor could become good mothers. The bylaws, *comptes rendus,* and other communications promoted the idealized potential of the poor nursing mothers. The sketches that adorned the covers of some *compte rendu* painted a tender picture of these poor mothers surrounded by their children, while the philosophical bases of the society celebrated the ability of poor mothers to love their children deeply and maintain their families under difficult circumstances.

But even more than the romanticized vision of the poor nursing mother, maternal societies and their supporters promoted an idealized view of their female members, as this exhortation from Bordeaux's bylaws of 1810 suggests:

> The Society builds its fondest hopes also on the charitable zeal and active cooperation of its benevolent ladies. Essentially compassionate and consoling, they will remember to good purpose their days of sorrow and solicitude; they will recognize that it is principally up to wives and mothers like themselves to bring comfort and life to mothers and children languishing in a garret of misery. In fulfilling this respectable ministry, a sole sentiment animates them—the love of humanity.[95]

A later set of bylaws, issued in the wake of Napoleon's fall from power, developed even more fulsomely this view of women performing charitable works:

> The blessings that we collect could not produce the relief desired without the help of our virtuous ladies, chaste wives and tender mothers, who feel in their hearts an overabundance of that maternal love which the Author of nature created for the conservation of the human race during the first years of life . . . These ladies will continue to employ their charitable activity in favor of the unfortunate objects of our solicitude; they will let shine a few moments of happiness in the refuge of pain and misery by bringing consolation, effective assistance, and the counsel of their wisdom.[96]

Still, despite their compassion for poor mothers, the *dames administrantes* never lost sight of the fact that it was their role to select, to judge, and to supervise. As the president of Lyon's society told the general assembly of *dames administrantes:* "and if we speak here of surveillance, it is because, as you are aware, the exercise of charity requires not only that pity so easy and sometimes so sweet; one must combine it with firmness and prudence, in order to manage to separate the poor who merit assistance from those who solicit it, taking advantage of [their] destitution."[97] Pity was laced with a strong dose of moral superiority. The women who staffed maternal societies could be harshly judgmental, and that judgment played itself out in various attempts at the social control of the lower-class families that they assisted. Any mother who placed her child with a wet nurse, kept any pertinent information from her sponsor, or was accused of "bad conduct" (*inconduite*) was immediately cut off from assistance "for now and in the future."[98] Never did the society's members express sympathy for acute poverty if it drove women to lie or to bend the rules. And in some cases, they viewed the poor recipients of their assistance with more distaste than sisterly concern, as was revealed in the Paris society's charge to Queen Marie Antoinette when she met them in assembly on January 4, 1790: "May her courage render her superior to the disgust which the details of poverty cause . . . May her indulgent goodness lead her to pity rather than to reject these people degraded by vices and excesses which are the fruit of despair and poverty."[99]

Despite sometimes harsh attitudes about the poor, and confidence that the *dames visiteuses* could serve as role models, not all charitable ladies lived up to their own high ideals. In 1860 the prefect of the Gironde received an angry letter from Jean-Louis-Similien de Bièvre, *colleur de papiers peints* (wallpaper hanger), whose wife had given birth to twin girls in May 1859. Madame Olivier, *dame distributrice* of the St. Seurin quarter of Bordeaux, was in charge of delivering layettes and cash assistance to the de Bièvre family. Instead, she had kept the money for herself and told de Bièvre that "the coffers of the Society are empty." De Bièvre complained to both the secretary of Bordeaux's society and to the prefect, thus exposing the duplicity of Madame Olivier, who was forced to repay the society the two hundred francs she had stolen and to resign in disgrace. It took all of Secretary Guiraut's diplomatic skills to persuade Monsieur de Bièvre not to drag Madame Olivier into court and bring scandal to the society.[100]

This incident hints at the tensions between the society's members and the poor families they were supposed to assist. While social mores taught that the poor had no claim on the largesse of the elite, individuals like de Bièvre clearly felt a moral right to the aid of the Society for Maternal Charity, at least once they had received a promise of assistance. Others went further, believing that they had a right to aid if their families met the conditions for assistance. Madame Cordier had been convinced that she was entitled to assistance and angrily made sure that her complaints were heard by the appropriate authorities when she believed she had been unjustly denied help.

Undoubtedly, many poor mothers resented the moralizing that accompanied their assistance. Bordeaux's administrative council explicitly recognized this resentment, noting that the society retained authority over nursing mothers less through gratitude than through fear. For this reason, the council suggested that it was important to provide monthly monetary supplements. Since mothers received the gift of delivery expenses and the layette soon after giving birth, there was nothing left to fear except potential loss of that cash payment. Without it, the mother would become deaf or disobedient to the advice and remonstrances of her patron, "who no longer [would have] coercive means to bring her around when the voice of reason and wisdom was insufficient." Without the carrot of monthly payments, poor mothers might send their children to wet nurses or become wet nurses themselves; they would no longer consider it in their best interest to be "clean, careful, and regular."[101] The Central Committee of the Imperial Society made a similar point when it criticized some provincial maternal societies for handing over cash to the nursing mothers in one lump sum rather than distributing it in small amounts during their regular visits.[102] At times, coercive techniques were necessary to exert social control.

The work of Ellen Ross on charitable assistance and the British working class suggests some truth to this belief; these poor women carefully weighed the demands of infant welfare workers against the potential material benefits they could obtain."[103] The *dames administrantes* considered their advice to be as important as the material inducements that they offered; the president of Rouen's maternal society noted that the society "makes it an unceasing obligation not only to distribute assistance, but also comfort, and kindly advice in the midst of poor families at the very moment they experience greatest need of them."[104] Perhaps some poor mothers appreciated the kind words, but others undoubtedly tolerated unsolicited advice to obtain more tangible assistance.

Still, many poor mothers did internalize the lessons the Society for Maternal Charity sought to impart, or at least they learned to create an image of themselves that met with the approval of their social betters. In 1830, Madame Guillaume, mother of three children and recipient of assistance from the maternal society of Bordeaux, volunteered to care for the child of a woman sent to prison for three months, a child "whom she nursed like the most tender of mothers," a story that met with warm approval.[105] Another

exemplar of the poor and dutiful mother was Madame Gosselin, who asked
Bordeaux's society for assistance when her husband was called away on military reserve duty in 1838: "That young mother shed many tears, clasping her
newborn to her breast . . . As she prayed fervently, as she made her other
two children pray, God inspired her. 'The Society for Maternal Charity,' she
said, 'cared for my child; it is only through [the society] that I can hope to
find alleviation of my sorrows'; immediately, with her youngest child in her
arms, she went to see several members of the Society."[106] Madame Gosselin
was the very image of the pious and devoted wife and mother, as well as a
grateful recipient of assistance.

Lyon's society also recounted its successes for its members and donors;
for the year 1846 the president, Madame Delahante, reported, "Not only did
we grant material assistance to the same number of nursing mothers as the
previous year, but several religious and moral outcomes have given us great
consolation." She noted that *dames administrantes* had helped to arrange the
marriage of two couples living in sin so that they could receive assistance from
the society and that others had prevented several mothers from abandoning
their children at the foundling hospice.[107]

Given their firsthand experience with these poor families, struggling under the burden of too many children, the *dames administrantes* must have
been keenly aware of the problem of fecundity among the poor. While the
French state encouraged a high birthrate,[108] the members of the society
could not help but be aware of the cost of high fertility among the poor as
they read the roster of women requiring assistance and listed the number
of children to whom they had already given birth: "Marie Ailboue, wife of
Gabriel Duchesse, companion *salpêtrière* [worker with saltpeter], rue de
Charonne, 5 children living, pregnant with 8th . . . Catherine Barthélemy,
wife of Honoré Boulaire, companion joiner, rue du Faubourg St. Martin, 5
children living, pregnant with 12th . . ."[109] The report of the Imperial Society issued in 1813 made reference to children who "perish in the middle of
families where fecundity aggravates indigence."[110] In fact, it may be that the
society's insistence that poor women breast-feed their children was partly in
recognition of its contraceptive benefits. Certainly, the contraceptive benefits
of breast feeding were known.[111] While never explicitly mentioned in the accounts and correspondence of the societies, it is plausible that Malthusian
sentiments undergirded this particular bylaw, although the health benefits—
widely recognized—were undoubtedly key. So the evidence here is mixed; as
Stuart Woolf notes, the historian is left with only "tantalizing questions" on
this particular issue.[112] The Society for Maternal Charity of Bordeaux revealed
ambiguous sentiments vis-à-vis family planning among the poor:

The maternal societies' statutory exclusion of women who do not have at least three children is not only because of the modest resources of the societies. If new households with only one or two children were admitted to our assistance, individuals reduced to the most frightful destitution would no longer be halted in their marriage schemes, foreseeing the misery that the resulting children would soon bring. Now, then, it is advisable neither for morality nor for the public interest, to facilitate unions entered into under such unfavorable circumstances; for any augmentation of the population is nowhere a desirable thing, but only that of a healthy, active and virtuous population, and one that can support its needs through its work or through honest industry.

This statement in Bordeaux's *compte rendu* would seem to suggest that the society's members opposed the high fertility among the poor. However the account goes on to say:

> Moreover, if the [gift of] life we received from our parents would seem to be a blessing that we are bound to restore to the *patrie,* it is no less true that a charitable institution is less obliged to favor the discharge of that debt than to recompense and to soothe the large families which make up for the sterility of certain marriages, and that of the celibate.[113]

The ambivalence we see here reflects the debate ongoing in France since the eighteenth century over populationist policies versus the demographic anxiety extreme poverty engendered.[114] But while the fecundity of these poor families served to underline the distance between rich and poor, the accounts of maternal societies over time came to emphasize the important role they played in helping these families. By the 1870s, in the wake of the Franco-Prussian War, support for large families would be a patriotic duty.[115]

Clear class boundaries structured relations between the *dames adminis-trantes* and the mothers they assisted. Christine Stansell argued in her work on women of the city of New York that evangelical moral reform groups helped to strengthen class and social identity on the part of their members, as the middle classes sought to differentiate themselves from those above and below them in the social hierarchy.[116] For the members of the Society for Maternal Charity, poor women remained the "Other." Kathleen McCarthy has highlighted widely divergent attitudes about hygiene, privacy, and child-rearing practices among those of different class status, as well as the revulsion many charitable women and social activists felt at the living conditions of the poor.[117] It was their shock at the unsanitary living conditions of the poor that led Bordeaux's maternal society to purchase beds for some of these families: "The father, the mother, and the children were gathered in the same bed, or in two at most; a grandfather, a grandmother, were sleeping with their grandchildren of both sexes, brothers with sisters, the healthy with the sick, even with the dying; and to excuse this disorder as dangerous for health as for morals, the most respectable mother responded that she could not do otherwise."[118]

Things had not changed much since the eighteenth century, when Louis-Sébastien Mercier described the plight of the urban poor: "An entire family occupies a single room with four bare walls, where straw mattresses have no sheets and kitchen utensils are kept with the chamber pots. All together the furniture is not worth twenty crowns, and every three months the inhabitants, thrown out for owing back rent, must find another hole to live in. So they wander, taking their miserable possessions from refuge to refuge . . . Their naked children sleep helter-skelter."[119] The bylaws of some maternal societies had provision for members to hand off certain duties to the sisters of working religious orders, in recognition that "ladies" would experience greater shock at the condition of the poor than nuns, accustomed to this type of work.

However, embedded in the most obvious and carefully maintained markers of rank and difference—the privilege of class and money—was a dialectic that in some ways undercut the boundaries that separated charitable women from those they served. Those women most celebrated for their good works were those who ventured fearlessly into the poorest abodes and maintained affectionate ties to the women they helped. In his eulogy of Madame de Pastoret, the comte de Falloux recounted that a poor woman hospitalized at the Hôtel-Dieu with a broken femur, who could nurse her infant only with difficulty, relied on Madame de Pastoret, who came faithfully each day to place the baby at the mother's breast and to help it sleep afterward.[120] This kindly support was the ideal.

Further, the structure and membership of the Society for Maternal Charity were predicated on the ideal of solidarity between women. Celebrating the reestablishment of the society in 1801, the *Journal des Débats* stressed that the women staffing the organization were particularly well suited to this kind of work:

> It is ladies who have established this Society; its members are women. Who can better bring consolation into these hovels of poverty and sorrow? Who can more successfully go before these fathers and mothers, more unfortunate still than guilty, ready to push away the child who will be born of them, and to thus lose their right to all the charms of parenthood? Who better than mothers to assist mothers and protect children? Finally, who can, better than they, vanquish the selfishness and insensibility of men, soften their hearts to the condition in life of virtuous poverty and persuade the rich to contribute to charity?[121]

Their special status as women and mothers conferred upon them the qualities necessary to perform this kind of charitable work, creating "natural"
links between them and the poor mothers they assisted, as well as links to
potential donors.

The nature of their charitable work intensified these links. The bylaws of
every maternal society stressed the importance of personal service to the poor,
and sustained, personal contact. The visiting ladies performed a function
similar to latter-day social welfare workers, going into poor neighborhoods,
seeking out those most in need of assistance, counseling poor women, and
helping to keep families together.[122] The correspondence and accounts reveal
no fear on the part of these women that their efforts exposed them to contagion, even in a city like Marseille where the *dames administrantes* were well
aware that frequent outbreaks of cholera created large numbers of orphans.[123]
Poor mothers came to know their *dames administrantes* and approached them
personally with their tales of hardship. In a discourse presented at the general assembly of Lyon's maternal society in 1832, *présidente* Madame Prunelle
noted that, owing to the city's economic hardships, "This year, mobs [of poor
mothers] rush up to your *Dames administrantes,* and these ladies, who are not
authorized to admit a larger number of mothers to assistance, groan over so
much misery that they do not know how to relieve."[124] Surely this intimate,
face-to-face contact served both to create sympathetic relations and to undercut distance between classes, if not hierarchy, especially as the members
of the society visited the neighborhoods and homes of the poor.[125]

Supporters of maternal societies celebrated these links between rich and
poor women. The baron Dupin applauded that "between the indigent mothers and the charitable ladies who assisted them, reciprocal bonds of attach-
ment are created that will continue into the future. The former will always
find with the latter an advisor, a [source of] support. One will tell them, one
will help them find the means to exercise honest industry and to support their
family; they will be guided in their domestic conduct; order and foresight
will keep misery at bay."[126] L. Dudemaine, honorary treasurer of Marseille's
maternal society, wrote in 1816, "Virtue, sentiment, all generous attachments
are linked by a chain to the hearts of the charitable."[127]

More generally, the administrators of maternal societies encouraged physical service to the poor on the part of all of their members, believing that it
would solidify the links between elite and poor. The Paris society bylaws
specified that "in no case should any lady ask someone to replace her in carrying out her functions unless it is one of the ladies of the *comité* who will
sign her reports, or one of the sisters of charity in her *arrondissement*,"[128] thus

underlining the obligation of each woman to carry out her work personally.[129] Bordeaux's *présidente,* protesting the desire of the Duchess of Angoulême to personally approve each *dame administrante,* argued that such a requirement would discourage charitable women who were not known at court and who feared that they might face rejection, while at the same time women who were less meritorious "*would be able to* [underlined in original] remain in these functions, while abandoning to the Sisters of Charity everything they find unpleasant; which would destroy the moral relations which the institution ought to establish between the rich & the poor, for the good of all."[130]

The precise relationship between local religious orders and maternal societies is unclear. The society of Rouen welcomed assistance from local *religieuses.* However, the president of the Rouen society specified that "those whose absences or exceptional circumstances prevent from fulfilling the duty that they accepted are replaced by the worthy sisters of Miséricorde or St. Vincent de Paul, who carry out this mission with the devotion and pious abnegation which distinguishes them."[131] The phrasing suggests *présidente* Le Mire's recognition that ideally the women would carry out these tasks themselves. The members of the Society for Maternal Charity of Limoges appear rather less assiduous; in their case, "Assistance is distributed through the care of the Sisters of Charity in cooperation with the *dames administrantes.*"[132] The Sisters of Charity/St. Vincent de Paul also "deliver each month to Madame *la Présidente* a memo with the requests [for assistance] that were made, and those which deserve to be honored."[133] This arrangement would seem to reduce the direct involvement of maternal-society members in the distribution of assistance.

Religion played a somewhat muted role in many of the maternal societies, but its influences were present in all. Most had close ties to local churches. Often, the local bishop or archbishop, as well as the local Protestant pastor, was an honorary member of the society's administration.[134] *Compte rendus* often make note of church collections; frequently the local priest or bishop preached a sermon and donated the proceeds. These *quêtes* and sermons could be an important source of revenue. While we lack the sources that would clarify the reasons that women chose to join maternal societies, we can assume that religious devotion drew many to charitable work. Charity, both material and spiritual, had traditionally been considered an obligation of the Christian woman of the upper classes.[135] It was a virtue that brought equal, though different, benefits to rich and poor, since "charity, in working to destroy the vices and the sorrows of humanity, easily brings together all ranks and conditions, maintains that fraternity established by the Gospel and by Nature, and ennobles the powerful and the rich, in making them use the advantages they have received from Providence to relieve those deprived of them."[136]

This religious emphasis found its way into the *comptes rendus* of many of the provincial societies. The maternal society of Rouen stressed its commitment to "neglect nothing to maintain religious sentiments, the spirit of conciliation, and good conduct among the families that it protected."[137] The women of Dijon's maternal society described themselves as "dedicated to the exercise of Christian charity toward poor women giving birth and their children."[138] The Lyon society touted the religious benefits of its works in 1836: "Say you, Mesdames, that in addition to the children saved for the care and the tenderness of their parents, many other religious effects are obtained by the pious ladies who administer this charity. How many children owe them the fortune of receiving baptism! how many households have received the nuptial blessing as a result of their efforts at the time when the request for assistance was made!"[139] Still, many of the societies were ecumenical, welcoming the contributions of Catholic, Protestant, and Jewish supporters alike. Bordeaux's society was one of the most consistently religiously pluralistic. This strong ecumenical flavor was not the case in every city; Annie Flacassier points out that the three religious faiths coexisted peacefully in Bordeaux and that many of the city's merchants were Protestant or Jewish.[140] But Paris also counted a number of Protestant and Jewish women among their *dames administrantes,*[141] and Lyon placed Catholic and Protestant women in charge of different *arrondissements* of the city.[142]

Politicians under the Third Republic who objected to the religious and moralizing requirements of maternal societies complained bitterly about the requirement for proof of a religious marriage. This proof was not, however, usually part of maternal society bylaws, at least in the first half of the century.[143] An exception is the society of Rouen; part 3, article 3 of their bylaws, which had been in effect since 1823, specified that for admission to assistance, the poor mothers had to furnish "a certificate verifying that they have received a nuptial blessing."[144] However, in a number of cases, even if religious marriage was not required in the bylaws, it was enforced in practice. Bordeaux, which did not require such marriage on the part of its recipients in its 1810 and 1815 bylaws, noted the obligation for a religious ceremony several times in the *comptes rendus.* However, that religious ceremony did not have to be a Catholic one; indigent Protestant and Jewish mothers, according to Bordeaux's bylaws, had the same claim to assistance as Catholic ones. Under the Second Empire and the patronage of the very Catholic empress Eugénie, however, the requirement for a religious marriage was formalized.[145]

A number of maternal societies revised their bylaws in the late 1840s and 1850s as part of the process of obtaining the status of *utilité publique* and used this opportunity to make a religious marriage, "before the minister of their religion [*culte*]," part of the bylaws.[146]

For most of the century, even under the more secular government of Louis-Philippe, few government officials or politicians objected to the moral and religious requirements of the Society for Maternal Charity. And, in fact, its rhetoric attracted support from successive royal and imperial governments and from the upper reaches of French society. Clearly, the society's appeal had resonance, in large part because it was perceived as efficacious. If the government, through agents like the Society for Maternal Charity, could persuade poor mothers to manage their emotions in such a way that the performance of maternal love was assigned a higher priority than the fear of poverty, the state could succeed in its goal of reducing the number of abandoned infants. If sympathy on the part of elite women was strong enough, they would willingly scour poor neighborhoods to find the indigent mothers requiring their services, and they would provide the necessary advice, practical assistance, and infrastructure. Hence, the sentimental culture pioneered by writers like Rousseau was channeled in a socially useful way to achieve practical goals.

The tone the society employed in its appeals reveals an important shift in attitude about emotion in the eighteenth century that continued into the nineteenth. It reveals a new conviction that sentiment should and does structure one's behavior. In previous centuries, churchmen had encouraged charitable donations as part of one's "Christian duty." Rousseau in particular, but other *philosophes,* as well, had convinced many to regard their fellow human beings, especially mothers and children, with sentiment and to offer help if possible. The state traditionally regarded child abandonment as evidence of poverty and moral failing, a problem with few solutions other than building more foundling hospices, at the same time making it more difficult for mothers to legally abandon their children.[147] In contrast, Madame de Fougeret and those who followed her drew on new philosophical currents about human sentiment and focused on the mother–child bond as the solution to the problem of child abandonment—a bond that, while "natural," required encouragement and nurture. The women of the Society for Maternal Charity consciously used and manipulated sentiment for the purpose of fulfilling specific policy goals. They believed that mother love could be nurtured, then exploited, to prevent child abandonment. Pity and affection for fellow human beings could be encouraged to foster charitable giving and work among the poor.

William Reddy's work traces this overt employment of sentimentalism in the eighteenth century, as well as a shift to a new "emotional regime" in the nineteenth, one that emphasized reason and self-interest among men. Sentimentalism lived on, especially among women;[148] certainly, maternal societies and their supporters continued to make emotional appeals in support of their work. Over the course of the century, however, these appeals for assistance became less floridly emotional and more matter-of-fact, focusing on the benefits of maternal societies to the state and society rather than the social obligation to help mothers and children living in misery. Even as the cult of motherhood continued to flourish, maternal societies began to stress their own usefulness to the state, a shift we see clearly by the 1850s in their *comptes rendus.* In 1870 the Society for Maternal Charity of Bordeaux eschewed graphic descriptions of desolate mothers and abandoned children in its yearly account, instead warning of the dangerous effects of declining French birthrates. Drawing on historical comparisons with the decaying Roman Empire, when Polybius argued, "Mothers no longer love their children, they spend as little time with them as possible, and fathers say nothing, as long as the family fortune does not diminish," the report warned that "From the day that the number of children decreases, the family suffers . . . With an only child, egoism takes hold; the father and mother keep him entirely to themselves and forget that he is part of society; military service becomes a terrible misfortune; ideas of nationality disappear; the family isolates itself, thinks only of itself, and becomes indifferent and passive."[149] By supporting large families and reducing mortality rates, the maternal society performed an essential social duty, which also served the state.

The message of maternal societies would have had less resonance had the state not so strongly supported it. French regimes—royal, imperial, and even republican—took such an active role in establishing, funding, and controlling maternal societies because they shared the goal of encouraging suitable maternal and familial behavior on the part of the poor women receiving assistance. The state's goals were more far-reaching, however; it also wished to encourage appropriate behavior on the part of the elite women proffering that assistance.[150] If these women were to serve as appropriate role models for poor women, their behavior was a legitimate subject of official interest. This consideration accounts for the careful inquiry into the background and behavior of the women invited to join the Imperial Society in 1810 and 1811. It also accounts for the demand on the part of the Duchess of Angoulême, and later, Empress Eugénie, that they be allowed to personally approve any woman admitted to administrative councils throughout the country.[151] Thus we see a multiplicity of influences operating throughout society crystallized in the workings of the Society for Maternal Charity. Through organizations like these, the French elite and the state promoted their conception of motherhood on the national and the provincial levels and helped to shape the nineteenth-century celebration of domesticity and civic motherhood.[152] Certainly, the state sought another benefit, as well: a reduction in child abandonment and in mortality rates. But the clear consensus was that loving mothers and strong families would lead to these other social goods.

It is unlikely that the women who received assistance from maternal societies adopted wholesale their values concerning motherhood and appropriate gender roles for women, but they did not entirely reject them, either. Unlike their elite counterparts, poor mothers recognized that they must contribute to the family economy, whether at home doing piecework, or working outside the home. This need to earn money shaped their relations with their own children and their ideas about what constituted "good" maternal practices. However, as we have seen, they were careful to emphasize their maternal virtues in contacts with their elite patronesses. And, as Catherine Hall points out in the context of the British working classes, certain aspects of middle-class discourse on femininity, masculinity, and domesticity had resonance with these men and women.[153] Through the targeted used of charity, the French elite transmitted a message about the meaning of motherhood and family to the poor. As Bonnie G. Smith discovered, the charitable ladies of Lille tried to reshape the behavior of the recipients of their assistance "in their own image," hoping to promote their own model of feminine behavior until it became a social norm.[154] The state supported these efforts and attempted to promote its own policies through these organizations. These efforts on the part of the state to maintain this surveillance over maternal societies eventually led to tensions between the Interior Ministry and some provincial branches; because the state so clearly saw them almost as a branch of the government, it frequently asserted its right to intervene in their mode of operation.

# 4. In the Public Interest

*Charitable Associations*
*and Public-utility Status*

By the 1840s, the Society for Maternal Charity was a mature organization, boasting decades of successful outreach and consistent governmental support. All branches claimed to serve the public interest and attracted support from those most committed to the common good. The society devoted itself to goals—the preservation of children and appropriate maternal behavior—that met with the approval of state and municipal authorities. But even associations devoted to a good cause could incite consternation on the part of a French government that wanted them to serve as obedient tools to carry out its policies.

So far this study has mainly considered the charitable efforts of maternal societies and the government's desire to use them to achieve particular policy goals: to prevent the abandonment of children, to lower infant mortality, to funnel resources to poor nursing mothers, and to strengthen families by teaching women to become "better" mothers. The surveillance that these elite women provided was an important tool in the state's efforts to create more stable families. However, the Society for Maternal Charity was also an association, and the French state's relationship with associations was historically a troubled and ambivalent one.[1] Paul Nourrisson notes that the French state traditionally looked askance at associations and sought to control their activities and status.[2] At the same time that the *dames visiteuses* monitored the behavior of mothers under their care, national authorities monitored the activities of maternal charities.

The state had always taken an intense interest in the activities and the financial health of maternal societies, demanding accountability and the right to approve the membership and regulations. But in the 1840s these demands grew more onerous. In 1850 the administrative council of the Society for Maternal Charity of Bordeaux requested an opinion on its legal status from three local consultants. This *mémoire* was part of a process that had begun eight years earlier, when the society had requested what it thought would be pro forma authorization to accept two modest bequests. However, "to its great surprise, Monsieur the Minister of the Interior refused to accord or to cause that authorization, *given that the Society would not have a legal existence, that it had not been lawfully recognized as an establishment of public utility.*"[3] The stubborn insistence on the part of the charity's administrative council that the society did indeed possess this legal status, and the equally resolute insistence on the part of the government that the society had not followed the prescribed forms to acquire the official status of *utilité publique,* had led to a twelve-year standoff between the two—a standoff that illuminates not only the government's heightened interest in controlling associations, even women's charities, but also the centralizing tendencies of the French government, as well as local resistance to those efforts.

While we may understand the desire for control over political organizations that might pose a threat to public order, especially given the French proclivity for revolutionary activity, why did the state seek to control benevolent organizations such as charities? Especially those controlled by women? Most historians agree that French administrators generally ignored the associational activities of women, and indeed, most female groups appear to have garnered little notice from authorities.[4] While Annie Grange suggests that this lack of interest may be because there were so few female associations,[5] Catherine Duprat argues that their official "silence"—the absence of general assemblies and frequent publications, as well as their careful cultivation of the traditional, nonthreatening image of *dames de charité*—kept these associations largely out of public view, even though female *sociétés de bienfaisance* often received more generous treatment from municipal and national officials than did their male counterparts. However, most female associations lacked visible political and financial clout.[6]

But this was not true of maternal societies. Their political and financial importance invited governmental surveillance, especially by the 1840s. As part of its process of centralization, and in an effort to exert greater control over potentially subversive political, and other, associations, the July Monarchy took a series of steps to bring them all under closer scrutiny. Despite impeccable credentials as a model charity and despite its "unthreatening" female leadership, maternal societies, after decades of relatively smooth sailing, faced the same demands for accountability and conformity as male associations.

Why did this scrutiny increase in the 1840s? While most historians, follow-ing Alexis de Tocqueville's lead, emphasize the intensification of central plan-ning and control under the Revolutionary and Napoleonic governments, Da-vid H. Pinkney focuses instead on the period of the July Monarchy (1830–48), when the government's procedures and institutions changed considerably to facilitate its expanding functions. He argues that the 1840s were the decisive years in the centralization of France, citing improvements in transportation and communication, the greatest barriers to the consolidation of state power in earlier years.[7] Stéphane Gerson suggests that it was the July Monarchy that "set into motion the divergent forces of liberalization and governmental intrusion."[8] These two forces may appear inherently contradictory, but as Patrick Joyce argues, freedom—liberalism—is not just absence of restraint, it is also a mode of governance, a technique of rule.[9] As the government's ability to extend its administration improved, previously autonomous organizations found themselves subject to greater interest and regulation, in part because governmental ministers sought to use these putative private associations to achieve particular goals through strategies of positive governance.[10] But since associations did not always believe that the strategies suggested by state au-thorities would achieve the desired outcome, it is not surprising that this greater push for control led to local resistance, at least in some instances.[11] This was the case for a number of maternal societies.

The perceived religiosity of some associations was also potentially prob-lematic. The ministries of neither Louis-Philippe nor Napoleon III regarded religious organizations as purely benevolent and nonpolitical, and many charities were tainted by their identification with Legitimist groups that op-posed both the Orléanist and Bonapartist regimes.[12] In fact, the anticlerical stance of many July Monarchy officials and of the later government of the Third Republic led to suspicion about the activities of overtly religious chari-table groups, especially if families hostile to the current regime dominated the membership.[13] Not surprisingly, a number of the *dames administrantes* were, in fact, allied with Legitimists; for example, the Dijonnais family Ranfer de Bretenières, very prominent in the Society for Maternal Charity of Dijon, became notoriously affiliated with ultraroyalists.[14] And in a well-known ex-ample of political protest, Madame de Pastoret, whose spouse was linked with the Bourbons and who was personally close to the Duchess of Angoulême, stepped down from the vice presidency of the Paris society in 1830 following the July Revolution, although she continued to serve on the administrative council.[15] It was not only the French government that worried about the political activities of religious women working in association; in her study of nineteenth-century Oneida County, New York, Mary P. Ryan found that whereas in 1827 the *Evangelical Magazine and Gospel Advocate* had dismissed women's reform activities lightly, by 1835 the editor considered female associations dangerous weapons of religious conservatives.[16]

But there was another reason for state interest in charitable organizations, especially popular and influential ones like the Society for Maternal Charity. They were the frequent recipients of donations and legacies, and they used these funds to provide services that the state could not afford to supply. Larger maternal societies relied heavily on donations and gifts from wills to build up their resources. In his account of the Paris society, François Gille noted substantial bequests from "charitable individuals" nearly every year. These legacies were usually invested in bonds [*rentes*] at 3 to 5 percent.[17] After 1855, the minister of the interior, in concert with the minister of finances, decided that the excess funds of all maternal societies should be placed in the Treasury Department's current account to earn interest.[18]

These contributions could play an important role in the finances of maternal societies. Bordeaux's society received thousands of francs in donations and legacies over the course of the nineteenth century, as did Lyon's.[19] Marseille's archives record a number of legacies ranging in size from 100 to 2,000 FF between 1825 and 1850.[20] Even a small maternal society, such as that of Dijon, occasionally received bequests.[21] However, to accept donations and legacies, charitable organizations required approval from the government and an enhanced legal status, that of *utilité publique*. This status of "public utility" gave a charity recognized legal rights, although it still officially remained a private establishment.[22] Jean-Luc Marais notes that from early in the nineteenth century through the Second Empire, the state exercised increased surveillance over donations and bequests to all associations, even those whose public utility was legally recognized. Furthermore, from 1830 until the 1860s, the stricter rules applied in particular to religious or ecclesiastic establishments, although they were also extended to other types of beneficiaries.[23] In the 1840s, as the French government became increasingly suspicious both of associations and their financial sources, even charities such as maternal societies were forced to prove their legitimacy and their public utility if they wished to establish perpetual sources of funding. In fact, authorities may have been more suspicious of bequests to female-controlled charitable organizations, fearing that the religious fervor of women would lead them to act against the interests of their family when determining the disposition of their property and potentially dissipate the family fortune.

And while in general the state worried more about male associational activity, with its overt political implications, those female-led organizations that achieved local or national—and thus political—importance also invited governmental scrutiny of their bylaws, fiscal activities, and charitable practices. Even women's charitable activities could have a political component. And in some cases, the activities of women such as the *dames administrantes* could seem more problematic than similar activities on the part of men. With their primary focus on social issues, especially those related to maternity and children, and an approach that did not always dovetail with official policies, women's groups could present unexpected challenges to municipal and national authorities, even as their female membership frequently allowed them to escape official notice.[24]

The state exercised control over associations in a variety of ways, but most notably through legislation, through surveillance (or *police*) and, as we have seen, through subventions to favored organizations.[25] French governments demanded that charities, like all associations, obtain legal recognition, a requirement rooted in the Ancien Régime.[26] The Revolutionary and Napoleonic regimes that followed were perhaps even more suspicious of associational life. The Le Chapelier Law and the debate that accompanied its passage in 1791 set the parameters for future generations. "The State alone is the site of the *formulation and the control of the public interest* [*intérêt général*]. Between this public interest and private interests, nothing must exist in the midst of society."[27] Napoleon was even more overtly hostile toward associations. His government evinced intense distrust of any individuals or groups acting outside the tutelage of the state, and the Napoleonic Code (1804) regulated associational activities.[28]

The penal code also regulated associations. Any group of more than twenty people meeting regularly required government authorization and municipal permission prior to all meetings. This unpopular law was the subject of much debate over the course of the century. Still, until the Law on Associations passed in 1901, the strictures of the penal code changed little, although its application was more or less severe, depending upon the regime.[29] Despite changes from republic to empire to monarchy to republic to empire again, continuity best defines the French state's philosophical and legal approach to associational activity.

While explicitly political, rather than charitable, associations were the primary concern of the legislators who fashioned articles 291–94 of the penal code,[30] charities also fell under the requirements of the law. While charities dedicated to the young, the old, poor women, prisoners, and others in need flourished in the nineteenth century, few had the visibility and resources of maternal charities in cities such as Paris, Bordeaux, Lyon, and Rouen. Consequently, few sought official recognition, and most possessed no assets beyond the voluntary contributions of members and occasional collections or fund-raisers.[31] The administration tolerated these associations, as long as they kept reasonably accurate accounts and conformed to the relevant laws.

However, officially tolerated charitable associations were subject to the goodwill of the state and donor willingness to contribute to their operating costs.[32] Therefore, their existence was likely to be ephemeral. To guarantee its long-term existence, especially in the face of competing state interests, a charitable organization needed recognition as *utilité publique*.[33] Associations *reconnues d'utilité publique* (recognized as having public utility) enjoyed a civil personality and were recognized as *gens de mainmorte*—institutions, such as corporations (in this case, a charity), that could possess property or other gifts in perpetuity—since they served the state and commune in the exercise of their functions.[34] Mortmain, the perpetual ownership of goods by a collectivity, had long been a concern for the French government and people, who resented the untaxable wealth of ecclesiastical institutions in particular.[35] It fell within the purview of the state, as part of its policing function, to carefully control which organizations were accorded public-utility status and the benefits that accompanied it.[36]

The governments of Charles X (1824–30) and, in particular, Louis-Philippe (1830–48) developed and elaborated the theory undergirding the status of *utilité publique*. Because these associations performed a service of "general interest," the state was willing to cede some power over their operations and property. These establishments with public-utility status enjoyed some autonomy—including the right to freely administer their resources in most cases.[37] But only associations whose public utility was recognized and that possessed resources sufficient to guarantee their existence could obtain this status and subsequently accept donations and legacies.[38] And even if an association were recognized as useful, national and municipal authorities might have concerns about its potential political role.

For maternal societies, this recognition and legal status were crucial. By the 1840s these societies, with their long and respectable history, were proud of both their independence and their public utility. In its report to the Comité de Mendicité in 1790, the Paris society had asserted that "the Maternal Charity is a free & independent association."[39] In 1836 the Interior Ministry had agreed to augment the budget of maternal societies by 20,000 FF, because "the utility of the Societies for Maternal Charity is generally recognized."[40] But the precise legal status of provincial branches was less clear-cut than many of their members believed. When Napoleon's government collapsed in April 1814, and the Imperial Society dissolved, the official status of provincial branches became murky. On October 31, 1814, when the royal government issued the ordinance reorganizing maternal societies, the Paris society was instructed to "immediately resume the administration that directed it prior to the decree of 5 May 1810." The administrative councils of provincial branches were ordered to continue their operations until they had exhausted the funds on hand; then, according to article 5 of the decree, the Interior Ministry would approve maternal societies in cities large enough to need and support them.[41] As we have seen, Bordeaux, Marseille, Lyon, Rouen, and Dijon received permission to continue operations, and Limoges was encouraged to found a maternal society.

But did this ordinance, coupled with the decree of 1811, confer, or at least implicitly recognize, the public-utility status of these newly independent maternal societies? Apparently it did so for the Paris society. Its annual accounts state proudly that it was "recognized as *utilité publique* by the decree of 25 July 1811."[42] However, for societies outside of Paris, the meaning of this ordinance became a subject of intense debate.

Not immediately—throughout the 1820s and 1830s, numerous maternal societies were allowed to accept donations, and to invest in *rentes* and property on behalf of their organization.[43] In 1818, Bordeaux's society made the solicitation of legacies a financial strategy:

> We will renew here our invitation to affluent and charitable individuals who know how to read into the future. They will see that any helpful institution must be protected against the cooling off of zeal which led to its founding, against the insufficiency of precarious collections, against the possible increase in the needs of the poor, and that security can only be founded on a stable annual revenue. That these individuals, then, profit from the time that God [*Providence*] has granted them to enjoy, the fullness of their intellectual faculties, and all the activity of a good and loving heart; that they will then make their final arrangements in favor of the unfortunate who so often provoked their compassion, and for whom they gave such abundant charity. It is [when one is in] a state of good health that these resolutions must be carried out.[44]

The account revealed no uncertainty about the right of the Society for Maternal Charity of Bordeaux to accept legacies. However, the official status of the provincial branches of maternal societies would be aggressively challenged in the 1840s, to their great surprise and consternation.

In early 1842, the prefect of the Gironde made a routine request on behalf of the Society for Maternal Charity for authorization to accept a bequest of 1,000 FF.[45] On February 9, the minister of the interior inquired whether the Bordeaux society "had been recognized as an establishment of public utility by royal ordinance, and consequently if it is qualified to incur [obligations] and to receive [donations]."⁴⁶ The prefect responded that "a decree of 5 May 1810 authorized, with the approval of the Minister of the Interior, the establishment of Societies for Maternal Charity following the example of Paris in all towns whose population [is large enough] to necessitate an institution of this genre. By a letter of 16 May 1816, Monsieur the Minister of the Interior announced to Monsieur the Prefect that the city of Bordeaux was included among those where the Society for Maternal Charity would be retained. The bylaws were approved by one of my predecessors on 13 December 1815." The prefect went on to remind the minister that the Bordeaux society had been established according to the rules of that era and had subsequently received regular assistance from the state, as well as authorization to accept bequests on numerous occasions. Consequently, there was no reason to refuse authorization to accept this particular bequest.

In his response, written on May 25, 1842, the minister of the interior outlined his disagreement with the prefect's logic. While acknowledging that the Imperial Society, established by the decrees of May 5, 1810, and July 25, 1811, had indeed been eligible to receive gifts and bequests with the authorization of the government, he went on to remind the prefect "that a royal ordinance dated 31 October 1814 abrogated (first article) that organization and declared (second article) that the Society for Maternal Charity of Paris would immediately resume the administration that directed it prior to the decree of 5 May 1810, in (third article) that the administrative councils established in the departments would continue their functions only until their funds on hand were exhausted . . . By article four, the same ordinance determined the organization of the Societies for Maternal Charity which could take shape in the future in the departments." As a result, according to the minister, the larger umbrella that had organized the Imperial Society for Maternal Charity no longer existed, and the only legal existence that the Bordeaux society now enjoyed was that conferred with the approval of its bylaws on December 13, 1815. However, while that ministerial authorization provided legal recognition, it did not confer the status of *établissement d'utilité publique*. Public-utility status alone would qualify a maternal society to receive bequests and donations and to conduct other acts of civil life. Only a royal ordinance could provide an association with the coveted title of *utilité publique*, according to an *avis du Conseil d'État* issued on January 17, 1806. Thus the minister suggested that Bordeaux's society prepare a formal application for public-utility status.⁴⁷

The minister's assertions seemed to allow no room for argument or compromise. However, Bordeaux's administrative council had no interest in complying with the minister's demands that it seek legal recognition; the bureaucratic requirements were substantial and could interfere with the smooth functioning of the charity. Their arguments were twofold; first, the members believed that they already enjoyed the status of *utilité publique,* much as the society of Paris did; and second, they did not wish to submit their bylaws and statutes once again to the minister of the interior, who might demand that they make numerous changes. The bylaws had been carefully tailored to the particular circumstances of Bordeaux, and they saw no reason to change them in accordance with national standards.[48]

The Society for Maternal Charity of Bordeaux was not alone. In fact, numerous maternal societies throughout France found themselves in the same position in the mid-1840s. After enjoying years of what they believed was formal recognition by the central government dating to the creation of the Imperial Society, the provincial branches were suddenly required to seek public-utility status if they wished to accept donations and legacies and thus assure a stable long-term existence. Between 1846 and 1850, nine maternal societies requested and received public-utility status, presumably at the demand of the Interior Ministry.[49] And it was not only the branches of the Society for Maternal Charity that came to the government's attention in those years; other charitable institutions were also asked to provide proof of their legal status following routine requests for prefectoral approval of legacies.[50]

Although the Interior Ministry recognized and accepted its public-utility status, even the Paris society faced increased scrutiny. In 1843 the minister of the interior wrote a letter to the prefect of the Seine in which he noted that the Society for Maternal Charity of Paris had invested in five bonds on the Canal of Burgundy for the sum of 5,407.25 FF. He pointed out testily that "the Society of which we are in charge, having been authorized as an establishment of public utility, can make no acquisition, no loan and no investment of funds, except for governmental bonds, unless specially authorized by a royal ordinance" and that "the purchase of the five bonds on the Canal of Burgundy consequently took place illegally." However, he did not, at this late date, wish to forbid the society's investment: "Not wishing to go back over a fait accompli, I believed that I should approve the account in question. But I would ask you, M. le Préfet, to take the necessary steps to make sure that this irregular purchase is regularized as soon as possible."[51] Because of its well-connected members and prominent position in the capital, the Interior Ministry declined to pursue the matter, beyond a strongly worded rebuke and a request that the treasurer "regularize" the purchase. Provincial maternal societies would not be so fortunate.

The Society for Maternal Charity of Marseille received its first warning in 1844. A letter from the Interior Ministry in January of that year notified the prefect of the Bouches-du-Rhône that the approved bylaws of the society were not on file.[52] The Marseille society quickly printed up a copy of its bylaws, which, according to its records, had been submitted to the prefect on January 5, 1816.[53] The *présidente*, Madame de Pontevès, pointed out to the prefect that her society had submitted its bylaws to the minister of the interior Vaublanc back in 1816, only to be told that his approval was unnecessary.[54]

Subsequent ministers had not shared M. Vaublanc's laissez-faire attitude. In fact, only a few months after Vaublanc sent his missive, the undersecretary of state for the Interior Ministry sent a letter to the prefects countermanding Vaublanc's order and instructing them that all charitable institutions must submit yearly reports on their activities.[55] A response to the prefect's letter of May 10, 1844—not sent until August 28, 1847—made it clear that, as far as Louis-Philippe's Interior Ministry was concerned, Vaublanc's orders had long since been superseded. Simple approval might be acceptable for smaller organizations; however, the Society for Maternal Charity of Marseille, "because of its sizeable resources, and also because it requires the civil capacity to be able to accept the Millot bequest, or other bequests and donations that it may receive, should be recognized as an establishment of public utility." He enclosed a copy of the model statues and bylaws that he had prepared for maternal societies seeking official recognition to follow.[56] Madame de Pontevès was as unhappy with this demand as Madame Guestier had been.[57] But the minister was no more accommodating than he had been with Bordeaux's maternal society and demanded that the society of Marseille adopt the national standards.[58]

The documentation is less complete for other cities, but the Interior Ministry began to demand that additional maternal societies fulfill the same requirements. At its meeting of April 29, 1842, the secretary-treasurer of the Society for Maternal Charity of Lyon, Perret-Lagrive, read to the gathering a letter from the interior minister that had been sent to the prefect of the Rhône concerning a legacy of 1,200 FF bequeathed to Lyon's maternal society by Madame Jourdan in 1839. In the letter, the minister explained to the prefect that as a result of the royal ordinance of October 31, 1814, Lyon's society was "no longer qualified to receive Legacies & donations, [and] as a result, M. the Minister of the Interior cannot authorize the Maternal Society of Lyon to receive the liberality of Mad. Jourdan unless the Administrative Council of that Society makes its request & obtains approval of its bylaws by a new royal ordinance."

This demand caused considerable flurry: "The Administrative Council, which had never been aware of the existence of that ordinance of 31 October 1814 & which could find no trace in its archives despite all of its searching, recognizes the legality of the Minister of the Interior's refusal to authorize acceptance of the legacy of Mad. Jourdan." As a result, "the Administrative Council voted unanimously so that the request of approval of its statutes & bylaws, as well as the reconstitution of the Society's civil status would be addressed to the prefect of the Rhône to be sent on to M. the Minister of the Interior, & assigned M. Perret-Lagrive . . . to furnish for that purpose all the evidence and documents necessary, and to take all [necessary] steps."[59]

A few years later, Rouen faced the same situation. Charles des Alleurs, the secretary and biographer of Rouen's society, recorded his difficulties in accessing a bequest left to the society by M. Bouctot. "At the beginning of the year 1845, I became more active in my efforts to obtain legal recognition." However, he also faced complications: "Despite the support I sought from some of our Representatives, and from one of my closest relatives, a deputy for many years, who arranged a meeting with the Minister himself for me, the obstacles seemed to multiply."[60] Dijon's maternal society ran into difficulty, as well, when it tried to accept a legacy from M. Bounder, a former doctor.[61] There is no evidence that the Limoges society received any legacies in the 1840s; however, in 1844 an undersecretary at the Interior Ministry informed the prefect of the Haute-Vienne that the royal ordinance of October 31, 1814, required that all maternal charities in France submit their bylaws for approval. He noted that he had no copy of Limoges's bylaws in his offices and requested either a certified copy or, if none existed, that a copy be submitted for his approval.[62]

This heightened interest in charitable associations raises the question: Why did the central government suddenly become so concerned over the legal status of these well-respected charities in the 1840s, charities that the minister of the interior clearly recognized as useful and worth preserving? Even the issue of donations and legacies had not been important in earlier years. The government had authorized the societies of Marseille, Bordeaux, Lyon, and Rouen to accept a number of bequests in the 1820s and 1830s. These bequests were duly approved by the prefects and by royal ordinance. And why was the Interior Ministry so interested in regulating seemingly minor points in the bylaws and statutes of these local charitable associations?

It seems that a number of factors converged to bring the uncertain legal status of maternal societies to the attention of the government in the 1830s and 1840s. The Interior Ministry's heightened interest in charitable associations reflected the July Monarchy's more general concern with the regulation of associational life. Louis-Philippe's government had replaced the more conservative—and more fully legitimate—Restoration monarchy in 1830 but faced a dilemma. Legitimists—stalwart supporters of the Bourbon monarchists—opposed the July Monarchy, and some openly plotted against

Louis-Philippe, whom they saw as a usurper.[63] But because of its revolutionary origins, the government also found it difficult to rein in various groups that wanted to "continue the revolution" and forge a more democratic polity. Even celebrating the origins of the July Monarchy could be a tricky proposition, since those festivities revived memories of the barricades and the promise of a more inclusive government. Each year, the ceremony's approach created a certain amount of revolutionary unrest.[64]

Following the July Revolution of 1830 and the establishment of the new Orléanist monarchy rather than a more democratic form of government, a strong republican movement emerged in France, supported by networks of opposition societies. Socialist aspirations also played a role and increasingly came to dominate the manifestos of associations. Organizations such as the Société des Droits de l'Homme channeled discontent with the regime and created "disorder," especially after the radical Amis du Peuple was forced to disband following the June insurrection of 1832.[65] These societies circumvented penal-code restrictions by subdividing into groups of fewer than twenty individuals, thus placing themselves outside the jurisdiction of article 291.[66] As unrest increased in 1833, the government tried to quell disorder by prosecuting not only revolutionary societies, but also newspapers; however, juries showed little enthusiasm for returning guilty verdicts.[67]

This political and social unrest that followed the July Revolution provided the backdrop to the law of 1834, which tightened enforcement of article 291 of the penal code.[68] During debate over the passage of the law of 1834, deputies tried to exempt charitable associations, among others, but met with little success. The government feared that subversive societies would use any loopholes to their advantage. The pro-government *Journal des Débats* argued, "If one leaves associations, whether religious, or scientific, or literary, a pretext, the battle becomes pointless; for they will all fling themselves into the exception established by the law, and, to make use of the energetic expression of M. Dupin, they will all rush out the door that remains open [*elles se précipiteront toutes par la porte qui restera ouverte*]."[69] More to the point, supporters of the law recognized that seemingly benign institutions were often far from neutral from the state's perspective. Consequently, the law passed with few amendments in April 1834 and granted the government great latitude to control all associations.[70] Both the July Monarchy and future regimes would make use of this power. For example, under Napoleon III, the law would be used to target the Society of Saint Vincent de Paul, a well-respected religious charity that was, however, perceived as hostile to the Second Empire.[71]

The new strictures of the law of 1834 led numerous charitable associations to reassess their legal standing vis-à-vis the state, a development that, accord-

ing to Catherine Duprat, would have logically led to an increase both in requests for legal authorization and the dissolution of more marginal charities.
But the new law also inspired associations to seek public-utility recognition to
solidify their legal status. A spate of charities that had not worried about their
legal status in earlier years went through the cumbersome approval process
after 1834. The Caisse d'Épargne was awarded public-utility status in 1835, the
Orphelines de la Providence in 1836, the Société pour le Placement en Apprentissage des Jeunes Orphelins and the Philanthropic Society in 1839, and
the Asile-ouvroir de Gérando in 1843. The case of the Philanthropic Society
is particularly interesting. It had been in existence since 1780 but until 1839
had not felt the need to seek public-utility status.[72]

While the law of 1834 was intended to regulate political and popular organizations, the government also had reason to be concerned specifically with
charitable associations. As the problem of indigence absorbed the attention
of philanthropists and policy makers, the government sponsored numerous
inquiries into poverty in France. In 1840 the minister of the interior, Charles,
comte de Rémusat, opened an *enquête* (investigation) on pauperism and
public and private charity. The replies of prefects highlighted the reality of
suffering throughout the country.[73] The Interior Ministry also increased its
efforts to reduce the numbers of abandoned children, although these efforts
often had unintended collateral consequences.[74] It was in response to these
far-reaching problems that the number of voluntary associations devoted to
the needs of France's poor continued to multiply.[75] The uncontrolled proliferation of new charities, as well as the overlapping functions of public and
private charitable groups and the competition for scarce francs, undoubtedly
heightened the state's desire to tighten surveillance of charities that might be
the beneficiaries of large donations.[76]

Donations to charitable associations raised governmental concern on
several levels. The public was ambivalent about, and in some cases hostile
to, mortmain, which had allowed ecclesiastical authorities to exempt their
property from taxation. French legislators used this public distrust to justify, at least in part, the seizure of church property during the Revolution
of 1789. That same hostility led to the spoliation of corporate societies and
charitable institutions.[77] Why the apprehension about donations and mortmain? Barthélemy Terrat outlined a number of reasons for official concern
in a pamphlet defending the benefits of mortmain.[78] First of all, the state had
the responsibility to defend the interests of family members who might lose
their inheritance as a result of too-generous donations to charities, especially by individuals under the sway of vanity or excessive religious fervor.[79]
The language Terrat employed suggested concern that women in particular

might be susceptible to these dangerous impulses.[80] Legal reforms during the Revolution of 1789, codified in the Napoleonic Code of 1804, had mandated the equal division of family property, enhancing women's inheritance rights considerably.[81] Accordingly, the law limited the amount that an individual with legitimate heirs could funnel elsewhere.[82] Bequests to charitable organizations could sometimes prompt legal action and bitter recriminations on the part of heirs. In 1866, François Nicolas Guiraut, longtime secretary of the Society for Maternal Charity of Bordeaux, died; three testaments that he had written all named the society his universal heir. M. Guiraut, a lifelong bachelor, also left a life annuity to his unmarried sister, who contested the will and began to sell off M. Guiraut's most valuable property. The society brought legal action and managed to order the liquidation of the estate to its benefit, preserving about 10,000 FF for its coffers. In this case, the prefect took the side of the Society for Maternal Charity—Demoiselle Guiraut had been quite well provided for by her parents—but in other cases, family members might have been able to show genuine harm.[83]

However, the state's concerns went beyond solicitude for disinherited family members. Large donations to charitable institutions had potential economic repercussions, as well. From an economic standpoint, the government was concerned that mortmain would interfere with the free circulation of goods. This fear was not new to the nineteenth century; Anne-Robert-Jacques Turgot, controller general under Louis XVI, had similar suspicions concerning the generous benefactor. Celebrated jurist and a member of the commission that drafted the Napoleonic Code, Félix-Julien-Jean Bigot de Préameneu argued that the government "should know the nature and the quantity of the property that is thus placed outside of the market; [the government] must even prevent a blameworthy excess in these transfers [*dispositions*]."[84] The laissez-faire economic approach of the July Monarchy may have made its ministers suspicious about the economic consequences of large donations to charitable organizations. But there were fiscal implications, as well. The state receives tax payments when property changes hands; because mortmain property does not change hands, the government no longer benefits from these taxes.[85] Consequently, government ministers could perceive these donations as capital "squandered" on the poor, diverted from private investment that could enrich both individuals and state coffers.

Furthermore, private charities like the Society for Maternal Charity were in direct competition for bequests and legacies with institutions of public assistance. Prior to World War I, local initiatives, but especially private donations, bequests, and investments, financed the majority—about 60 percent—of national hospital costs.[86] Consequently, the system of public assistance could not exist without a continuous influx of private resources, which gave the government additional incentive to regulate the status of charitable organizations.

The July Monarchy considered the religious nature of many charities problematic, as well. Despite the fact that the queen, Marie-Amélie, was quite pious, the king and his advisors were not.[87] The particular philosophical and anticlerical bent of the Orléanist regime also contributed to its suspicious attitude toward *associations de bienfaisance,* especially those of religious, and often Legitimist, inclination.[88] Orléanist officials were supportive of both property rights and the rights of the state, and very distrustful of the church. Consequently, they worried about the accumulation of riches in the hands of establishments with the right of mortmain, especially ecclesiastical institutions.[89] This distrust accounts for the fact that the state reserved to itself the right to approve any bequest to a charitable association, and the wariness was only partially attenuated by the good works that many religious associations performed.[90] While the Society for Maternal Charity was ecumenical and assisted women of all religious denominations, state officials perceived it as a fundamentally religious institution, directed by pious and politically conservative women. This was, in fact, often the case. However, the society attracted women from families of various political inclinations, and the religiosity of the organization varied over time and from branch to branch.[91] Still, the official perception that the society was an intensely religious organization would lead the government of the Third Republic to sharply reduce its subsidies by the 1880s.[92]

Furthermore, Catherine Duprat suggests that under the Restoration and the early phases of the July Monarchy, active and well-connected philanthropists had played a key role in governmental agencies such as the Interior Ministry— including individuals such as Adrien-Étienne de Gasparin and the comte de Rémusat, both of whom served as ministers of the interior. However, by the early 1840s this close association between governmental ministers and philanthropic societies had come to an end—both Gasparin and Rémusat had gone into opposition at this point—as the Interior Ministry ceased to consult volunteers associated with either private charitable associations or public assistance for advice. As a result, the influence of philanthropists over the administration of assistance declined.[93] This split undoubtedly rendered the administration less sensitive to both the contributions and the concerns of charitable organizations and more likely to be suspicious of their motives.[94]

Taken together, these factors created an inhospitable atmosphere for associational activity and led to increased scrutiny on the part of the July Monarchy vis-à-vis all associations, including maternal societies. The new stability of the ministerial regime after 1840 under François Guizot, whose ministry would govern France until 1848, along with Charles-Marie-Tanneguy, comte Duchâtel, as minister of the interior, created the conditions for bureaucratic intrusiveness.[95] Still, the Society for Maternal Charity was a highly favored organization, and the Interior Ministry was willing to facilitate the status of *utilité publique* for maternal societies in larger French cities. By reducing the number of abandoned children that the state and municipalities would have to support, as well as funneling assistance to poor families, these societies performed an important function that the government appreciated. While the government was parsimonious in granting legal recognition to charities in general, its eagerness to bring the branches of maternal societies into compliance so that they could receive legal recognition highlights the society's privileged—and respected—position.[96] Since both the Interior Ministry and the maternal societies themselves had an interest in gaining legal recognition for the societies and assuring their continued existence, it should have been an easy matter to resolve.

However, resolution was not a speedy process. The legal situation of the societies of Marseille, Rouen, and Bordeaux was not resolved under the July Monarchy. The new republican government, installed in February 1848, was equally determined to make sure that large maternal societies fulfilled the necessary legal requirements, even as other, more urgent matters occupied their time. While the relative stability of the Soult–Guizot–Duchâtel ministry may have provided the breathing space for the Interior Ministry to set into motion its examination of the legal status of maternal societies, the unrest of 1848 did not deflect its determination to bring about conformity. In June of 1848, in the midst of the Second Republic's most troubled period—street fighting would break out in Paris before the end of the month, culminating in the notorious June Days—the wheels of the bureaucracy continued to roll. Perhaps the inertia of the bureaucratic machine is the most telling explanation for the ministry's continued insistence that the maternal societies revise their bylaws. As Balzac wrote of the costly bureaucracy that Napoleon put into place and that subsequent regimes maintained scrupulously, "There are forty thousand government clerks in France . . . for this price France possesses the most inquisitorial, fussy, ferreting, scribbling, paper-blotting, fault-finding old housekeeper of a civil service on God's earth. Not a copper farthing of the nation's money is spent or hoarded that is not ordered by a note, proved by vouchers, produced and reproduced on balance sheets, and receipted for when paid; orders and receipts are registered on the rolls, and checked and verified by an army of men in spectacles."[97] The minute attention of various Interior Ministry clerks to the particulars of the maternal societies' bylaws suggests the truth of Balzac's scathing critique. It is also possible that the tumult of the period led to an increased rigidity on the part of officials following up on the initiatives of previous administrations. In June 1848 the Interior Ministry sent letters to the prefects of both the Bouches-du-Rhône and the Gironde demanding to know why they had not yet submitted applications for public-utility status.[98] Madame Guestier's response to the prefect's query indicated her continued belief that the minister's demands were intrusive and redundant.[99]

The back-and-forth between the Interior Ministry and the Society for Maternal Charity branches of Bordeaux, Marseille, and Rouen took place against the backdrop of both continued political unrest and heated debate in the Constituent Assembly (and later the Chamber of Deputies) over the appropriate role of public assistance and private charities.[100] As administrations rapidly changed over the course of 1848 and 1849, Madame Guestier continued her dialogue with the Interior Ministry via the prefect, hoping that at some point a minister would accept her contention that the Bordeaux society's legal existence had been securely established since 1815, or would at least agree to recognize the statutes and bylaws approved in 1815 without the need for modification. However, despite what one would assume were more pressing concerns during this chaotic period in French political history, the minister of the interior continued to insist that the Society of Bordeaux follow the models provided in revising its statutes and bylaws.[101] In the meantime, bequests continued to pile up.[102] Perhaps the endless discussions concerning liberty of association kept the issue on the front burner for the *fonctionnaires* at the Interior Ministry. This rigidity belied the fact that the government of the Second Republic was much more sympathetic to associational activity than the July Monarchy had been. While prohibiting secret societies, new legislation debated and passed in July of 1848 gave political clubs liberty (although subject to governmental approval), while nonpolitical private associations were simply required to declare their existence to municipal authorities. Charitable and industrial associations were exempted from even this formality.[103] Effectively, the new legislation abrogated article 291 of the penal code, as well as the law of 1834, permitting almost complete freedom of association.[104] But these changes in the law had no effect on the situation of provincial associations seeking public-utility status.

For Madame Guestier and the rest of Bordeaux's administrative council, the bylaws proposed by the minister contained two problematic points: the obligation to establish and send to the Interior Ministry an annual budget each year (in addition to the annual *compte rendu* already provided), and the obligation to hire a paid *receveur*.[105] The permanent secretary (*secrétaire-*

*général*) of the interior dismissed the society's complaints, but four months later, Bordeaux's administrative council was still contesting the Interior Ministry's demands.[106] It made one more effort to resist compliance. On June 4, 1850, Messieurs Lacoste, Saint-Marc, and Vaucher rendered the legal opinion already cited on the official status of the Society for Maternal Charity. The consultation rapidly traced the institutional history of Bordeaux's society and its assets, many of which had come from donations.[107] However, despite the fact that the government had previously authorized the society to accept these donations, in 1842 the ministry had suddenly challenged its legal existence and denied it the right to "conduct any act of civil life." The *mémoire* expressed the administrative council's deep outrage at the demand that it abandon the bylaws that had governed the society for thirty years to adopt the statutes and bylaws proposed by the central government. The legal opinion supported the administrative council's contention that the ordinance of October 31, 1814, conferred legal status upon the Bordeaux society, in the same way that it had upon the Paris society, whose legal existence had never been challenged.

But the *mémoire* went on to make another point about the Bordeaux maternal society's right to receive legacies and make sales of property. An *avis du Conseil d'État* of January 17, 1806, did seem to suggest that the Bordeaux society required special approval from the Conseil d'État for public-utility status.[108] However, the consultants noted that the *avis du Conseil* applied only to "establishments of charity and *bienfaisance* directed by independent societies [*sociétés libres*] *which gather in a maternity hospice, [or] building for the ill and orphans, [or] the old,* and that the Society for Maternal Charity, which offers home assistance, is not an establishment of that genre." For this type of charity, all that was necessary was an ordinance authorizing its establishment, since its public utility was well recognized without specific mention. Under the terms of the *avis du Conseil,* the society did not require special approval as a public utility in order to receive donations, because it effectively had that capacity—a capacity that the government had previously recognized. Not only had it received funds from the government, but it had always been authorized to accept donations and legacies until the contretemps of 1842.[109]

The consultation, like other representations in the past, fell on deaf ears, despite the support that it received from Bordeaux's municipal council.[110] However, in March of 1851 the Interior Ministry's secretary did add a conciliatory note concerning the model statutes and expressed his willingness to accept even substantial variation to accommodate local customs and needs.[111] The prefect forwarded the letter to Madame Guestier with the curt suggestion that she give up the fight.[112] After all, as the secretary stressed to the prefect in a later letter, dated September of 1853, formal recognition as a *utilité publique* would mean that the society's legal status could never again be contested. The tone of this particular letter suggests some concern on the part of the secretary that Bordeaux's society might disband if pushed too far. He urged the prefect to move carefully while persuading the administrative council to comply with the letter of the law. "The steps that I have indicated that must be followed in this affair demand great restraint, and you must show great tact in your communications on this subject with the Board. You will offer advice on the means to reconcile the exigencies of the law which must be executed with the legitimate sensitivity of charitable persons so useful to the poor and so worthy of consideration. In a word, try to eliminate this error, but avoid compromising the existence of the charity."[113]

This attitude suggests a more flexible approach on the part of the Second Empire than had been the case with earlier administrations. This flexibility may seem surprising in light of the authoritarianism of the early Second Empire, which some have labeled a "police state." In 1852 the government had abrogated the legislation of 1848 that guaranteed liberty of association; this decree of March 25, 1852, replaced the law of 1848 with stricter regulation of public association and assembly.[114] This change would suggest a harsher attitude toward private associations. However, while Napoleon III's government showed a continued interest in regulating charitable organizations, it also wished to encourage charitable action and by many measures showed a favorable attitude toward the charities on which they depended to solve many of France's social problems.[115] While his government did not want to see independent networks flourish throughout France, Napoleon III was aware that associations controlled by the state, carrying out state-sanctioned activities (especially to assist the working class and the poor), were extremely useful.[116] Empress Eugénie was well known for her charitable activities, including the *présidence* of the Society for Maternal Charity, which enhanced its already favored position.[117]

However, it was not until 1854 that the prefect of the Gironde finally forwarded to the minister of the interior the required 150 copies of the statutes adopted by Bordeaux's society; six months later, in October 1854, the prefect sent an urgent note to the minister, reminding him that the statutes still had not been approved.[118] The numerous changes that took place in the governance of maternal societies may have slowed the bureaucratic machinery and the approval process of *utilité publique* applications. The decree issued on March 25, 1852, set into motion a process of putative administrative decentralization. Supervision of maternal societies shifted from the Interior Ministry to the prefect, who could now approve their annual accounts (although he was still required to forward the information to the minister, along with the *compte moral* and the list of the members and subscribers). The decree of February 2, 1853, transferred ultimate control to the newly crowned Empress Eugénie. Finally, on April 15, 1853, the emperor promulgated a new *règlement* for maternal societies, one that confirmed their regional autonomy and their particular statutes but that reinforced the earlier decrees of 1852 and 1853.[119]

Against this backdrop, Bordeaux's administrative council had adopted its (slightly) revised bylaws on February 15, 1853,[120] and formally approved its new statutes on December 13, 1853. They were not ratified by imperial decree until February 24, 1855, as the administrative council made adjustments to comply with changing requirements.[121] Despite their eventual submission to the government's demands, the administrators of Bordeaux's society remained convinced that they had been in the right all along. The cover of the *Statuts et règlement de la Société de Charité Maternelle,* reissued in 1909, states that the Bordeaux society had been "recognized as *utilité publique* by the decree of 25 July 1811." They never conceded the point.

The resistance on the part of the Society for Maternal Charity of Marseille was not as fierce as that of Bordeaux; however, Madame de Pontevès was equally unhappy at the prospect of adopting the model statutes and bylaws and made her discomfort clear in a strongly worded letter to the prefect. Like Madame Guestier in 1848, she had hoped that the changing administration would look more sympathetically at her request. This was not the case. Still, she noted that her administrative council "thought that it could not submit to the desires of Monsieur the Minister without having presented to him its observations concerning two articles which contain stipulations [that are] in essence contrary to the customs and ways of our region." The first article that Madame de Pontevès objected to was article 9, which required the election of a *secrétaire-trésorier* as a joint and unpaid position. Currently, an honorable and solvent individual was willing to serve as treasurer for free; however, the position of secretary involved a good deal of day-to-day written work, and with so few men of leisure in the commercial port city of Marseille, it was impossible to find someone who could fill that position gratis. Thus it was necessary to separate the two functions.

However, article 12 of the statutes caused the greatest concern. It seemed to suggest that materials—such as layettes, food, bottles, and other items—used to assist the poor mothers of Marseille would be deposited at the home of the *présidente,* who would also hold council meetings at her home. Every three months, each *dame administrante* would receive the materials and cash necessary to assist the women under her patronage. Each mother would then present herself at the home of the *dame administrante* in her *quartier* to receive this assistance.

The implications of this system were more than disturbing: it was clear to Madame de Pontevès that "our lodgings are too narrow; that our President could not receive the materials [at her home]; and that the *dames administrantes* could not agree to receive at their homes a crowd of women who are strangers, coarse and most often carrying their nurslings with them. This inconvenience is such that the Prefecture . . . despite a room and a large courtyard earmarked for that purpose, no longer wished to continue because of the noise and the congestion caused by these women." This was why "from the time of its creation, a place has been set aside specifically for this charity in order to hold the material goods [for the poor women] and for the meetings of the council of the *dames administrantes*. The ladies meet at a set time each week to receive the poor women who request assistance and deliberate to decide who has a right [to assistance] and who should be rejected according to the report of the ladies who visited them." This system of administration required a concierge, who provided a number of services; Madame de Pontevès asserted that to pay separately for the services rendered by the concierge would double the costs to the society, undoubtedly to deflect criticism that a concierge was an unnecessary luxury for a charity.[122] Her defensive tone harkened back to the early days of the Society for Maternal Charity of Marseille, when both the prefect and the Interior Ministry criticized its expenses.[123]

In forwarding her comments to the Interior Ministry, the prefect dismissed Madame de Pontevès's desire to keep the functions of secretary and treasurer separate. Since most of the society's funding came from the state, the department of the Bouches-du-Rhône, and the city of Marseille, and since it earned only 118.50 FF in *rentes* per year and owned no property, he did not believe that the functions of either were particularly onerous; the two positions could easily be combined, and performed for free. On the other hand, he expressed sympathy with their objections to article 12, agreeing that it would be difficult to make distributions from their homes and that their observations on this point should be taken into consideration.[124] The Interior Ministry's secretary concurred but nonetheless agreed to "provisionally accept the request of the Maternal Society, and . . . submit it along with the collection of statutes and bylaws for the ruling of the Conseil d'état" if Madame de Pontevès would just send along the documents.[125]

Some trifling squabbling over the particulars of the statutes and bylaws continued throughout 1849 and into 1850.[126] But finally, on January 2, 1851, the president of the republic (the future emperor, Napoleon III) granted the

Society for Maternal Charity of Marseille formal recognition "as an establish-ment of public utility."[127] The functions of secretary and treasurer remained separate, according to the statutes approved. The bylaws specified that all functions would be performed free of charge, except that of secretary. The meeting place of the administrative council was left deliberately vague.[128]

While not quite as combative as the experiences of Bordeaux and Mar-seille, the process for obtaining public-utility status could be a lengthy and contentious one for other societies, as well. Dijon seemed to experience the least difficulty, perhaps because it was willing to accept the recommended modifications to its statutes and bylaws with little dispute; the society had put into motion the process to obtain public-utility status in 1847 and was *reconnue d'utilité publique* on May 31, 1850.[129] Lyon, having started the process in 1842, received its approval as an *établissement d'utilité publique* on February 3, 1846.[130] Unlike Bordeaux or Marseille, Lyon's society had accepted from the start the legitimacy of the ministry's complaints and did not attempt to assert its legal standing; this acquiescence undoubtedly speeded the process along, although it still took four years.[131]

The Rouen society had begun the process for obtaining public-utility status in late 1844 or early 1845, with some urgency; a note sent out by the prefect to discuss its legal status read, "Several legacies having been made to the Society for Maternal Charity, it is essential that the poor be able to enjoy the generosity of donors. To obtain authorization to accept them, it is necessary that its organization be legally established by a royal ordinance; to cut short as much as possible the delays that have arisen in the formal procedures, I wanted to bring together Madame *la présidente* and *messieurs les officiels* in a meeting."[132] Beginning in 1846, "The Society made new and lively solicitations to be recognized and in this way to manage to draw on several of the legacies that it had been willed, and that the heirs did not want to discharge without the production of legal authorization."[133] Charles Des Alleurs continued his efforts in 1847, distressed that "without legal recognition for the Society, all the legacies which represent a considerable amount, remain necessar-ily in limbo, to its great detriment." His rather elliptical account suggests that Rouen's society experienced difficulties similar to those of Bordeaux and Marseille. After consulting with the prefect, Des Alleurs determined that "the Government, apart from its aversion to these kinds of recognition, also wanted, in the statutes and bylaws that it recommended we accept, to reserve for itself certain rights which seemed contrary to the privileges that the Society had enjoyed for a long time; especially relative to the election of the ladies, the members of the Board, etc., and many meetings that year were devoted to discussions concerning the statutes and bylaws, which the

Minister himself presented as condition, sine qua non, for recognition of the Maternal Society of Rouen." The society protested these demands: "we were obliged, so to speak, to fight every foot of the way; but finally, when it seemed that the Society would receive almost complete satisfaction, it was plunged into uncertainty by the Revolution of February 1848." Despite the turmoil of this revolutionary year, the Rouen society continued its negotiations, obtaining legal recognition in 1849.[134] Des Alleurs immediately sent a letter to the prefect, asking for his approval to accept 22,000 FF in legacies and donations that had accumulated in the previous five years.[135]

Limoges's administrative council did not seek public-utility status in the 1840s while the other cities were going through the process. However, it took them several years just to obtain legal approval of their bylaws. They, too, were ordered to bring their *règlement* into conformity with the model bylaws sent out by the Interior Ministry in 1847; after a protracted correspondence via the prefect, the bylaws were finally approved on July 20, 1849.[136]

Even after the contentious discussions and carefully negotiated modifications of statutes and bylaws, maternal societies were still subject to unilateral changes in their operating procedures. In May 1855, the president of Rouen's society, Elie Lefébure, sent a message to the prefect of the Seine-Inférieure, noting that the administrative council had changed article 4 of its bylaws in response to Empress Eugénie's desire to personally name the presidents and vice presidents of maternal societies.[137] When the prefect submitted these changes for approval by the Conseil d'État, the permanent secretary of the Interior Ministry responded huffily that this would be unnecessary. "As I informed you in my message of last 18 April, Article 4 of the statutes was for all intents and purposes modified by a decision of H.M. the Empress."[138] Any desire for control on the part of the empress, or indeed, the Interior Ministry, superseded the internal regulations of the individual maternal societies. Perhaps Rouen's decision to vote officially on these requested changes was a mild assertion of their autonomy.

The obsessive interest of the Interior Ministry and the empress in the smallest details of the operations of provincial maternal societies suggests that while statesman like Guizot may have championed a laissez-faire approach to the economy, the state's attitude toward associations most decidedly was not hands-off. The impulse of the French state since the Ancien Régime, intensified during the Revolution and Napoleonic era, was toward greater regulation, bureaucratization, and centralization. This process continued under the July Monarchy and the Second Empire. By placing his wife at the head of the Society for Maternal Charity, Napoleon III assured continued official interest and interference.[139] Part of that process was to effectively wield, and in some cases to tighten, the laws regulating associations that had been part of the *Code civil* under Napoleon. The view was that a well-run state, even a "liberal" state, should make sure that voluntary associations serve the public good—or at least, that they do not run counter to it.[140]

Charitable associations, like maternal societies, fell under the scope of administrative law, which was increasingly intrusive as relations between the French citizenry and executive authority became more highly regulated and formalized, first under Louis-Philippe, then under Napoleon III. In this context, it is easier to understand the resistance on the part of Bordeaux, Marseille, and Rouen's maternal societies to the central government's effort to make uniform their bylaws and statutes with little regard for or understanding of local needs. Stéphane Gerson found a similar subversiveness on the part of provincial elites who sought to preserve and celebrate local histories outside the uniform blueprint provided by the Ministry of Public Instruction.[141] Timothy Smith, in his study of efforts to introduce welfare programs into Lyon in the nineteenth and twentieth centuries, also finds resistance to state interference in the delivery of charity and the development of public-assistance policies. He quotes the president of Lyon's Civil Hospices, who observed in 1909 that his predecessors had fought a battle "against a sort of legislative centralization" that had "sought to impose uniform laws on the country without regard for local circumstances."[142] Maternal charities were not alone in their desire to maintain local autonomy in the face of increasing encroachment by national authorities. This is not to say that they were hostile to the Interior Ministry, nor were they unwilling to collaborate with the government. They did so on numerous occasions and usually allied themselves with a government that offered them financial and verbal support. Dijon and Lyon demonstrated no particular resistance to fulfilling the requirements for public-utility status; perhaps their *dames administrantes* were less invested in the particular practices of their societies and did not believe that the demands of the Interior Ministry threatened their effectiveness. But the predominant spirit of cooperation did not prevent maternal societies from resisting direction they considered contrary to their interests, or contrary to the interests of the mothers they served.

In contrast, French administrations saw these charities as an extension of the government, providing useful social services that it could not, or chose not to, provide, a topic that will be more fully explored in the next chapter.[143] As Jean-Luc Marais notes, an *établissement d'utilité publique* "exists only because the state gives birth to it." And "the State only gives [a charity] life to fulfill a function which it delegates to it."[144] This utilitarian and state-centered view of charitable associations under its patronage strengthened the government's determination to provide careful regulation of and surveillance over them. But it also led to struggles between the government and the charities themselves. As Paul Nourrisson points out, the French government tended to regard private charities as an auxiliary of state action, while their members viewed themselves as independent individuals coming together to serve the public good.[145] Charities saw themselves as representing local needs and interests, and their members sometimes resented the efforts of the state to control their activities. This tension could potentially undercut the cooperative relationship that both the state and the charities themselves desired. And despite its desire to regulate and control, even the government recognized at times that it could not push its agenda too far; recall the secretary's advice to the prefect that he show "great tact" in his communications with Bordeaux's maternal society and to "eliminate the error, but avoid compromising the existence of the charity."

While in most cases the French state may have regarded women's associations as "domestic" while those of men were "civic,"[146] those of women could also have civic, even political, implications. Catherine Duprat, highlighting the "silence" of women's associations in the first half of the nineteenth century, suggests that their stereotypical feminine image and the lack of a strong public voice could in fact be an important asset for these groups, masking their true goals—which, she acknowledges, were far from apolitical.[147] When women's groups sought to promote a particular moral, sometimes religious, vision for society, and to influence government policy toward women and children, the political implications became evident even to men who might resist acknowledging the influence of women in the public sphere.[148] This was especially true of a large, generously subsidized, and powerful association like the Society for Maternal Charity. The political potential was clear as Napoleon I took control of and expanded the reach of the maternal societies and as subsequent ministries subsidized, worked through, and maintained control over them. It would become clearer under the secular Third Republic, which objected to the policy of many maternal societies to assist only mothers married in a religious ceremony. The efforts of maternal societies to accept bequests, as well as governmental subsidies, invited official scrutiny of their statutes, bylaws, and finances. The ministry was willing to allow some flexibility in those bylaws, as long as they did not come into overt conflict with governmental goals and as long as maternal societies publicly submitted to governmental tutelage. But from the inception of the Society for Maternal Charity, the state was well aware of its political potential and was determined to exercise control and surveillance, while the societies themselves sought autonomy and local control.

The female membership may even have introduced certain complications as the state sought to regulate these organizations under laws that were conceived to control male associations. Maternal societies never promoted an overtly feminist political vision and, in fact, supported the most traditional domestic view of family life and the maternal role, but this did not always alleviate official concern. The perceived religious identity of these women aroused suspicion under more secular French regimes, perhaps already under the July Monarchy, but certainly by the time of the openly anticlerical Third Republic. And the nature of their charitable activities—assistance to poor mothers and their families—at a time when the state was increasingly concerned about fertility, infant mortality, and population growth meant that prefects and the Interior Ministry would take a particular interest in the activities of the various branches of the Society for Maternal Charity and would intervene frequently in their operations, a corollary to their generous subventions.

# 5. "Seconding the Views of the Government"

## *Maternal Societies and the State*

When the Society for Maternal Charity issued the organization's first bylaws in February 1789, the language reflected Enlightenment optimism, with its faith in the potential benefits of combined philanthropic and governmental action:

> The government, eager to extend the sources of public prosperity, the popula-
> tion, and [good] morals, has encouraged [our] work and doubled [our] strength
> by a considerable donation; businesses have seconded the views of the Govern-
> ment by enriching us; the number of subscribers has increased; and this Society,
> having only zeal as its guide; for hope, only the concern it should inspire; for
> arms against all the obstacles opposed to its establishment, only the need to
> attack a disastrous evil . . . [1]

While giving credit to the *compagnies* that had provided money to their fledgling organization for "seconding the views of the Government," the maternal society believed that it was seconding the views of the government, as well. From the time of its origins, the links between the Society for Maternal Charity and the French government were strong, as the state relied on maternal societies to provide social services that it would not, or could not, provide.

The operations of the various branches of the society and their relation-ship with the government provide insight to the provision of social services in France in the years before the welfare state and suggest why the variation in services to the poor in different regions of the country was so great, even in a state so centralized. The Society for Maternal Charity would serve as a model for the provision of social services to poor mothers and their children under the Third Republic and beyond. The visibility of the *dames visiteuses* in providing assistance, advice, and surveillance to poor families undoubtedly made it easier for administrators under the Third Republic—and even earlier—to accept women as inspectors in situations where their maternal and domestic skills would be useful.[2]

Although charitable ladies have sometimes been mocked as elitist and overly moralistic,[3] Jean-Pierre Chaline argues that many took their work very seriously and they could, in fact, be quite effective. He suggests that "the common view today of the *dame patronnesse* probably leads us to underestimate the influence which . . . these women could have, exercising power, utilizing funds that were sometimes considerable."[4] While we have seen that the Society for Maternal Charity attracted support, and its most illustrious members, from the highest reaches of French society—Queen Marie Antoinette, Empress Marie-Louise, the Duchesse of Angoulême, Queen Marie-Amélie, and the Empress Eugénie all served as *présidentes*—the workhorses were the *dames distribuantes, dames visiteuses* or *dames administrantes,* and, for some societies, the *dames associées.*[5] Madame Pastoret, the society's first secretary after its reconstitution in 1801, and later its vice president, serves as exemplar of the *dame administrante.* Celebrated for her willingness to seek out and personally provide help to those in the poorest areas of Paris, she had already founded at her own expense a *salle d'asile,* the first crèche in Paris, in the year 1800. She was also known for her zealous participation in other charities, such as the Visite des Hôpitaux. Her contemporaries praised both her "esprit" and her charitable works; her husband famously said of her that she "loved to do well the good she did" (*aimait à faire bien le bien qu'elle faisait*).[6]

The marquise de Pastoret was one of the most visible faces of the Society for Maternal Charity in its early years. Wife of a prominent statesman and philanthropist, she was in her own right one of the best-known and respected *dames de charité* in the capital. One of the most prestigious and powerful charities in France, the society attracted women who were influential and well connected in the provinces as well as in Paris. Madame Guestier, longtime *présidente* of Bordeaux's maternal society, was a member of that city's most famous wine family, owners of the commercial house Barton and Guestier.[7] From the time of its founding, Bordeaux's society was dominated by its commercial bourgeoisie, traditionally the most influential group in this port city located in France's premier wine country.[8] Madame Delahante, who served nearly twenty years as president of Lyon's society, was a member of a well-connected family involved in finance;[9] she was succeeded by the comtesse de Soultrait. The chief positions in Rouen's maternal society were held by members of the aristocracy, along with the wives of some of the city's most powerful *négociants* (including the baronne Elie Lefébure, wife of one of Rouen's mayors, who served as *présidente* for over twenty-five years). Admission to Rouen's society was perhaps even more exclusive than in some other cities. It was not until the 1840s that the wives of Rouen's influential textile bourgeoisie began to supplant the aristocrats and wives of high officials who dominated during the Restoration.[10] The aristocratic bent of Dijon's maternal society was also clear; the comtesse de Melfort served as its head for twenty-five years, from 1820 through 1845, followed by the baronne d'Aisy, then the comtesse de Macheco.[11] The positions passed frequently from mother to daughters, who were undoubtedly trained to take a leadership position in this charitable organization.[12]

Although they worked cooperatively with governmental officials for the most part, at least through the early 1870s and the advent of the Third Republic, these women were sufficiently self-confident to oppose what they sometimes saw as unwelcome infringements on their activities.[13] All branches demanded the right to adapt the "official" national bylaws of their organization to fit specific local conditions.[14] And while the prefect or other local officials sometimes sent women to the maternal society for assistance to ease the burden on local public assistance, the ladies firmly refused to assist anyone not meeting the requirements set out in the bylaws.[15] They were seldom intimidated by local, or even national, authorities.

In fact, their participation in such a prestigious organization may have heightened the sense of efficacy and influence on the part of these women and provided them with a sense of political effectiveness and social utility in collaboration with like-minded individuals.[16] Katherine Lynch notes that "women's participation in voluntary associations helped to create the kind of social networks and social experiences that built women's sense of citizenship."[17] Clearly, the *dames administrantes* received some benefit, some pleasure in return for their concerted efforts on behalf of poor mothers. Catherine Duprat notes the enormous number of feminine charitable organizations that had developed in France by the time of the July Monarchy, outstripping their male counterparts and demonstrating that many women enjoyed participating in these associations.[18] The [male] vice president and secretary of the Society of Bordeaux explicitly recognized what these women might gain through membership. "You are assured equally pleasing successes, Mesdames, if you unite your efforts, in each *arrondissement*, to reach the same goal; thus, we invite you to form relationships among yourselves that will certainly be agreeable as well as useful, because they will be based upon the esteem that you merit equally, and the numerous services that you have rendered for the public welfare. Called to deputize for each other in

your functions when it is necessary or convenient, it will be easy to create
that happy union of views and means leading to the comfort of the poor."[19]
As Dr. Capelle, the secretary of Bordeaux's maternal society, recognized,
participation in charitable organizations created networks, social and professional, among these women. And as Duprat argues, these good relations
among colleagues were essential; they facilitated the smooth functioning of
these groups and ensured the performance of what were often demanding
and thankless tasks.[20] Many of these women served together in multiple
charities, and while these interactions leave little trace in the archives, aside
from heartfelt eulogies when a longtime member died or was forced to step
down,[21] we can assume that friendships based on common interests and a
sense of mission were powerful and enduring.

Furthermore, the democratic sociability of charitable organizations could
heighten women's sense of political efficacy and prepare them for civil life,
although their claims to participation differed from those of men. For women,
charitable work could be the critical link between their familial and more
public roles, a form of civic engagement. Their dedicated work allowed them
entry into national debates concerning the social claims of poor mothers and
their children, as well as other issues.[22]

Certainly, women participated in the Society for Maternal Charity for the
status it conferred. Napoleon and his interior minister Montalivet explicitly
underlined the "particular and honorable distinction for the members of the
association" when trying to persuade the elite women of the empire to join
the Imperial Society in 1810.[23] But while the desire for status may explain
the membership of some women who contributed little to the functioning
of their society, it does not make clear the devotion and long-term membership of the "workhorses."[24] Jean-Pierre Chaline underlines the seriousness
and sense of responsibility with which the members of maternal societies
carried out their duties.[25] These women performed hard and often unpleasant work, going into the poorest sections of their cities and dealing with the
intense misery from which their class status usually protected them. In fact,
the *réglement* issued by Bordeaux's Society for Maternal Charity in 1815 suggested that some ladies might be "too sensitive and too delicate to regularly
fix their gaze on the misfortunes of the poor" and that they should instead
focus on soliciting wealthy individuals for monetary assistance.[26]

But many women were willing to carry out this work themselves. Perhaps
not all—we have seen how Limoges's *dames administrantes* relied on the
Sisters of Charity to help with their work, and this was undoubtedly the case
for other women, as well. In Paris, toward the end of the Second Empire, "a
particularly high-class category of fifty '*Dames protectrices*' with the special

mission of collecting offerings counted no less than four marquises and five duchesses, not to mention a dozen countesses or baronesses; another significant presence next to them were the wives of the great Jewish bankers." These women were not performing the laborious work of personal assistance and surveillance. But even women of high rank served as *dames visiteuses*. According to Chaline, most of the eighty *dames administrantes,* each in charge of distributing assistance in one sector of each of Paris's twenty *arrondissements,* were of less elevated social status than the duchesses, countesses, and marquises among the *dames protectrices.* Still, included among them were the comtesse Walewska, the duchesse Decazes, and, from a prominent Protestant banking family, Madame Hottinguer.[27] In the provinces, a division between the noble *quêteuse* and hardworking woman of bourgeois status seems not to have existed. While it is true that in Lyon, *présidente* Madame Prunelle noted that she was "called to the honor of presiding over their gatherings, but does not share their work," this distinction seems to have been related more to her age and health than to her rank. While Madame Prunelle identified her chief tasks as recruiting members and raising money, she fulsomely praised the hard work of Lyon's *dames visiteuses,* "going themselves to visit [the poor mothers] in their sad abodes, and very often, not content to simply hand over the gifts of the Society, but helping them over and above with all their means."[28]

Certainly, the *dames distributrices* made it clear that they wanted contact with the families they assisted to be on their own terms. Madame de Pontevès, *présidente* of Marseille's society, did not want poor women coming to her home in search of assistance. Still, all maternal societies emphasized the need for personal contact between charitable ladies and the recipients of assistance, frequent visits to the homes of the poor, and constant surveillance. The documents provide much more evidence of sustained contact between the visiting ladies and the mothers they adopted than they do of efforts to avoid that duty.

Participation in an important and influential charitable organization like the Society for Maternal Charity could convey status of a kind different from that stressed by Napoleon, his interior minister, and the prefects who sought to encourage women to join the Imperial Society in 1810. While these men focused on the benefits of association with the empress and other *dames du monde,* the women who participated most fully in the activities of this charitable association showed less pride in their connection to the social elite than they did in the good works they performed. The Revolutionary period had brought attention to the multiple ways in which individuals—citizens—could attain higher status through service to the public good. Through associational activities, concerned citizens could promote a variety of political and social goals. Catherine Duprat traced the rise of philanthropic associations in the eighteenth century and the key role that the individuals linked with these groups played in formulating a new image of citizenship and enlightened concern for fellow human beings.[29] As Suzanne Desan points out in a review of Duprat's work, the philanthropic agenda shaped a wide range of educational, judicial, and economic reforms, and the humanitarian ideals of the philanthropists undergirded a number of other political discourses of the late eighteenth century and into the nineteenth.[30] Women had far fewer opportunities than men for explicitly political engagement; however, these charitable organizations offered women opportunities for civic activity that could heighten their sense of political efficacy.

It seems likely that the "democratic sociability" of the women who staffed the maternal societies also created a sense of political efficacy on their part. A number of historians have argued that civic associations under the Old Regime provided a space in which individuals could learn the practice of citizenship.[31] Because women did not emerge from the Revolutionary process with participatory rights in the political process, historians have ignored that they, too, underwent a political learning process through active membership in voluntary associations such as the Society for Maternal Charity.

The nature of associational activity taught its members modes of organizational and political behavior. Beginning in 1790, the Paris society kept careful minutes of its meetings. Members in attendance voted on matters including acceptance of new members, the election of officers, and which families to admit to the society's care.[32] This tradition of keeping minutes was renewed under Napoleon; the council of the Paris society maintained a careful register of all official correspondence, as well as *procès-verbaux* (minutes) of their meetings.[33] Provincial maternal societies also kept registers of at least important *séances,* as these records were often attached to legal documents and records of votes. These democratic exercises that undergirded associational activities instilled the practices of citizenship.

The public act of issuing a *compte rendu* each year mandated accountability on the part of the administrative boards. After 1810, all maternal societies that received state funds were required to submit yearly accounts. Larger and wealthier maternal societies often printed theirs for distribution. In addition to receipts and expenses, these *comptes rendus* also frequently incorporated commentary on a variety of issues, including the benefits of breast feeding, the difficult lives of poor mothers and their children, and the government's responsibility to subsidize their work. But these records also ensured public accountability. In them, the members would recount their works for the year,

*Table 2.* Average Revenues of the Branches of the Society for Maternal Charity

| | Average yearly revenues (in French francs) | | | | Not including revenues from the central government | |
|---|---|---|---|---|---|---|
| | 1815–30 | 1831–45 | 1846–60 | 1861–70 | 1815–45 | 1846–70 |
| Paris | 70,340 | 85,112 | 82,931 | * | 16,684 | * |
| Bordeaux | 19,848 | 26,708 | 34,530 | 42,897 | 16,124 | 29,535 |
| Lyon | 11,050 | 17,165 | 26,467 | 53,265 | 6,300 | 16,768 |
| Rouen | 14,299 | 22,347 | 23,918 | 24,048 | 14,885 | 25,376 |
| Marseille | 19,125 | 20,651 | * | * | 10,052 | * |
| Limoges | 3,366 | * | 4,741 | 6,006 | 1,866 | 1,811 |
| Dijon | * | * | 3,198 | 2,588 | * | 1,678 |

*Insufficient data from these years.

Source: The data are drawn from a wide variety of *comptes rendus* and correspondence, and from Charles Des Alleurs, *Histoire de la Société de Charité Maternelle de Rouen* (Rouen: Imprimerie de Alfred Péron, 1854). For the archival material on which the table is based, see citation in text.

including how many families they had assisted, the mortality of infants under their care, how many children had been vaccinated, and other achievements. For example, in the *compte rendu* for 1831, the *présidente* of the Society for Maternal Charity of Lyon applauded its members for all they had accomplished that year and announced, "You are going to hear the report that we had to prepare to justify in your eyes the use of the funds with which you entrusted us."[34] This praise was not just for ears of the members present; it was also a reminder to municipal and national authorities that their organization deserved financial support. These women became skilled politicians, promoting and defending their record and methods to political authorities, as well as lobbying government agents for more funds.

We see political skills on display among the women in the society's leadership roles. Those who served in the chief administrative positions, such as president or vice president,[35] maintained extensive correspondence with influential members of the government whom they lobbied for additional funds; they kept records and sometimes managed substantial budgets, particularly in the large cities. Paris, as the largest society, had receipts of 93,088.60 FF in 1849, while Bordeaux in 1850 took in 41,381.84 FF. Lyon, in 1868, enjoyed revenues of 101,194.40 FF.

The long tenure of and public esteem for many of the *présidentes* of provincial organizations both brought them local standing and underlined it, and their success indicated their ability to work with local and national authorities.[36] They were undoubtedly empowered by their positions of influence and sense of efficacy. Charles Des Alleurs, secretary and historian of Rouen's society, made this case emphatically:

These [maternal] societies, increasing in numbers, present in the essential and constitutive elements of their personnel the elite of the population, whether by their fortune or by their status. They have also shown great animation, when the occasion arises, in defense of the privileges they have successively acquired, whether for the election of their members, their presidents, vice presidents, and other officers. They have always maintained, in these relations with superior authorities, that outspokenness and that noble independence which . . . proves that the individuals who are affiliated with these institutions in an intimate way are proud of them and honored.[37]

Consequently, these women were not timid in making their case to government officials concerning organizational needs, nor did they hesitate to call on potentially useful contacts. They often showed keen political instincts, even to the extent of proffering negative comparisons with previous regimes. In 1817 the administrative council of the society of Lyon wrote a particularly pointed letter to the maréchal Marmont, duc de Raguse, *lieutenant du roi*, bemoaning the lack of financial support that the Restoration government had provided: "We were not afraid to address ourselves to [Your Excellency] to implore you to support our just complaints before the Government, and even to insist that it may not be politically wise for the assistance that was abundantly provided by the previous government to be withdrawn by the King." The women undoubtedly hoped that the unfavorable comparison between the generous Napoleonic regime and the more frugal Restoration government would spur the king to more munificent behavior.[38]

This spirited activity on behalf of their organization and the poor women they served could sometimes lead to conflict with governmental representatives. For example, costs were often a matter of disagreement among the local societies, the prefect, and the central government. In 1815 the prefect of the Bouches-du-Rhône demanded to know why the expenses of Marseille's maternal society had doubled since 1807. The administrative council responded defensively, pointing out that the amount of aid they provided to poor mothers had increased considerably, thus augmenting their costs.[39] Bordeaux's society responded coldly to the suggestion by the Interior Ministry that they should cut expenses by firing their paid male secretary and persuading a member to perform those functions for free.[40] Autonomy could be an issue with even more salience for the administrative councils of local societies. Certainly, the desire for independence and the right to act as they saw fit in the interests of poor women inspired *dames administrantes* in both Bordeaux and Marseille to resist efforts to modify their bylaws and statutes; Lyon's society strongly defended its decision to award most poor women the full 100 FF complement of assistance when challenged, as we will see.

It is not surprising that the women staffing the administrative councils of provincial towns fought hard to maintain autonomy for their organizations in the face of an ever-encroaching state that employed a variety of weapons to exert control over this important charity. The Society for Maternal Charity, whose administration was composed almost exclusively of women,[41] provided a unique opportunity for elite women themselves to shape not only the nature of their charitable activities, but also the nature of their organization. Maria Luddy points out that women's involvement in philanthropy provided them with personal and group authority and power.[42] This power could create tensions with male authorities, who sometimes argued that any public role on the part of women was unseemly. Certainly, women's charitable activities could come into conflict at times with "the dictates of domesticity."[43] Kathleen D. McCarthy argues that American women also extended their maternal responsibilities beyond the home to assist dependents and the dispossessed. They justified their activities through religion, the ideology of republican motherhood, and the cult of domesticity; politicians and others questioned their moral authority when their causes became more secular and less firmly embedded in "womanly" concerns.[44] However, these women could legitimately counter that their assistance of poor women and children was an extension of the domestic sphere writ large, "charity recast as a domestic function."[45] Their positions gave them a voice in debates taking place, over the course of the nineteenth century, concerning motherhood, child welfare, and social policies.[46]

Their voices could be progressive and sympathetic at times. These charitable women expressed real concern for poor mothers and their families. The original *règlement* of 1789 outlined the plight of the poor working family and illustrated why the birth of a child could occasion distress rather than joy. While the financially pressed father worried about how he could support his child on his paltry salary, the same economic hardship prevented the mother from fulfilling her obligations toward her baby. This was the dilemma that maternal societies hoped to prevent.[47]

While perhaps not always sharing the humanitarian priorities of maternal societies, the state certainly shared the practical goal of preventing child abandonment and strengthening poor families. The government's consistent, although modest, support underlines this. The investment that the Bourbon, Napoleonic, and subsequent governments made in maternal societies provided a substantial return. Napoleon had set aside a 500,000 FF endowment for them, with 100,000 FF reserved for the Paris society, although only a small portion of this was regularly provided. Under the Bourbon Restoration, maternal societies were guaranteed 100,000 FF per year, with 40,000 FF going to Paris and the additional 60,000 divided among the provincial societies.[48] By the 1840s and 1850s, the Interior Ministry generally allotted 120,000 FF to the maternal societies, with 45,000 FF reserved for the Paris society. By the 1860s, that sum had been increased to 140,000 FF.[49] This amount does not include the contribution of departmental and municipal governments, which varied considerably from city to city. While under Napoleon some maternal societies had subsisted entirely on funds from the central government, under the Restoration, July Monarchy, and Second Empire, Interior Ministry funding was welcome but constituted a relatively small portion of their revenue. This was particularly true of the well-established maternal societies in large cities; these societies received larger subventions from the central government than did the smaller ones (such as Dijon), but they were able to raise more funds from other sources. Although Limoges was a large city, its maternal society was never as independent and active as those of Bordeaux, Lyon, or Rouen; one-third to nearly half its revenues came from the Interior Ministry. (See also Table 2.)

Each year, the central government allotted funds to maternal societies throughout France, and this funding, although less generous than under Napoleon, provided assistance to the "deserving poor" and allowed for the reassignment of public funds to other concerns. Prefects, acting both as agents of the central government and as local administrators trying to fund successful social-welfare enterprises, forcefully, but not always successfully, encouraged municipal and departmental councils to provide subsidies to local maternal societies.[50]

*Table 3.* Percentage of Revenues from the Central Government

|           | 1815–45 | 1846–70 |
|-----------|---------|---------|
| Paris     | 20%     | *       |
| Bordeaux  | 16%     | 10%     |
| Lyon      | 12%     | 16%     |
| Rouen     | 14%     | 14%     |
| Marseille | 15%     | *       |
| Limoges   | 45%     | 33%     |
| Dijon     | 31%     | 29%     |

*Insufficient data from these years.

Source: The data are drawn from a wide variety of *comptes rendus* and correspondence, and from Charles Des Alleurs, *Histoire de la Société de Charité Maternelle de Rouen* (Rouen: Imprimerie de Alfred Péron, 1854). For the archival material on which the table is based, see citation in text.

Although subsidies from the Interior Ministry provided the lion's share of funding for many of these societies (especially in small, poor towns), local subscriptions and donations could bring in substantial sums. Society members sponsored balls, lotteries, and fund-raisers door-to-door (*quêtes à domicile*) and at their churches to bring in additional funds. In her study of *la vie élégante* in Paris in the first half of the nineteenth century, Anne Martin-Fugier notes the growing importance of charitable activities such as collections in churches and neighborhoods, concerts, balls, sales, and sermons. According to Martin-Fugier, "Philanthropy is an aristocratic tradition, part of the ostentatious expenditure that the bourgeoisie sought to appropriate for itself: to practice philanthropy was to legitimize oneself as a member of the ruling class."[51] An important function of these events, she argues, was to demonstrate the social utility of the elite.[52] Maternal societies could raise significant sums through various fund-raisers.[53] The example of Bordeaux is particularly instructive. By 1834, Bordeaux's maternal society no longer recorded money collected through individual subscriptions. Rather, the chief local fund-raisers included collections conducted in the various parishes of the city, directed by the *dames administrantes* from that particular district, as well as yearly balls and the annual raffle and sale (*loterie et vente*). In 1834 these fund-raisers brought in 17,611 FF; by the 1840s the society was regularly raising 20,000–30,000 FF per year through its various efforts, an amount that constituted about 60 percent of its revenues.[54] Lyon, with a larger population than Bordeaux, raised far less money through collections and balls (about 16 percent of its total revenues) but continued to collect subscriptions. Still, Lyon, like most major cities, relied on these events to raise funds; the smaller amount they raised may be due to the proliferation of charities in Lyon under the Restoration and beyond, resulting in a lesser return for any one charity.[55] Rouen's society also worked actively to raise money; in a letter to the prefect of the Seine-Inférieure, written in 1838, Elie Lefébure explained that her organization's resources would be far below its needs "if we had not found the means to supplement [our revenues], sometimes with door-to-door-collections, concerts, plays, balls, etc."[56] It brought in about 28 percent of its revenues through these extraordinary means.[57]

Sometimes the queen or other members of the royal family would contribute an item for a local auction.[58] Martin-Fugier's account suggests the popularity of these kinds of events for charitable purposes; their expansion throughout the century may have made it more difficult for maternal societies to raise money, as they found themselves competing with an ever-growing number of charitable causes. Perhaps this difficulty accounts for the Paris society's apparent decision to avoid the balls and collections that other societies regularly employed; François Gille's account does not note any fund-raisers of this nature until 1874, when the duchesse de Mouchy organized a *fête villageoise* in the Besselièvre Garden, complete with fourteen boutiques with goods for sale. The diminution of the society's resources had forced this expedient.[59]

Paris was less dependent on these efforts to raise money, because the society there received donations and legacies from numerous benefactors. The wealthier and better-established societies all invested donations and legacies in *rentes* that provided a yearly return. Consequently, while the Paris society reported a royal subvention of 40,000 FF in 1823, along with a 3,000 FF contribution from the Duchess of Angoulême, other donations, investments, and subscription fees added 21,763 FF to the total receipts for the year.[60] In 1841, contributions and investments added nearly 37,000 FF to the royal treasury's contribution of 45,000 FF.[61] Bordeaux's society raised 15,663 FF in addition to the 2,500 FF provided by the government in 1828.[62] In 1868 the Society for Maternal Charity of Lyon augmented the 6,200 FF provided by the Interior Ministry with another 64,017 FF.[63] While 40,000 FF of this sum came from the *département* of the Rhône and the city of Lyon, it still represented a significant contribution to the welfare of France's poor that the central government did not have to provide from its coffers. (See Table 2.)

But while the money raised was essential, *dames administrantes* believed that their personal ministrations were as valuable as the pecuniary assistance they provided.[64] These women performed a function similar to latter-day social-welfare workers, going into poor neighborhoods, seeking out those families most in need of assistance, counseling poor women, and helping to keep families together.[65] This was not easy work. Catherine Duprat underscores just how demanding the charitable obligations of a *dame distribuante* could be. In the last years of the July Monarchy, the *administrante* of a rich *quartier* of Paris never had fewer than ten families to care for, while that of a poor area might be responsible for twenty to twenty-five women and their nurslings.[66] In addition, members of the administrative council had to judge the qualifications of each poor mother concerning her eligibility for admission to the society. They spent many hours in meetings, listening to the reports of the *dames administrantes* on various sections of their city.[67]

Best of all, from the point of view of the government, these women performed their tasks for free, serving as an unpaid quasi-branch of the French public-assistance services. In Paris alone, the society assisted between 600 and 900 families a year.[68] In a large city like Lyon, the society assisted nearly as many women—for example, 654 in the year 1866.[69] Between 1816 and 1853, the Rouen society provided aid to between 230 and 460 women and

*Table 4.* Average Number of Mothers Assisted per Year

|            | 1815–30 | 1831–45 | 1846–60 | 1861–70 |
|------------|---------|---------|---------|---------|
| Paris      | 636     | 808     | 891     | 1353    |
| Bordeaux   | 269     | 441     | 641     | 808     |
| Lyon       | 123     | 184     | 263     | 581     |
| Rouen      | 256     | 324     | 394     | 419     |
| Marseille  | 415     | 414     | *       | *       |
| Limoges    | 107     | *       | 308     | 352     |
| Dijon      | *       | *       | 71      | 59      |

\* Insufficient data from these years.

Source: The data are drawn from a wide variety of *comptes rendus* and correspondence, and from Charles Des Alleurs, *Histoire de la Société de Charité Maternelle de Rouen* (Rouen: Imprimerie de Alfred Péron, 1854). For the archival material on which the table is based, see citation in text.

their families each year.[70] Bordeaux's Society for Maternal Charity gave cash, in-kind, medical, and moral assistance to 10,168 mothers between 1805 and 1840, an average of 282 families per year.[71] By 1866 they were caring for over 1,000 mothers per year.[72] These figures indicate why the government increased its financial support for maternal societies over the course of the nineteenth century.

While in general, maternal societies in larger cities cared for more poor mothers, the correlation is not perfect. Bordeaux, a smaller city than Lyon, cared for nearly twice as many mothers per year on average throughout most of the nineteenth century (the numbers in Lyon increased significantly in the 1860s when they entered into affiliation with the Service des Enfants Assistés). However, because of the demands of the local economy and the desire to make sure that workers would be available when necessary, Lyon's silk magnates created a relatively generous system of social protection beginning in the 1830s. This system, along with the wide range of charities available, made the society's care less essential in Lyon than in many cities.[73] So in addition to the size of the city, the number of mothers assisted also reflected the zeal of the women who staffed the maternal societies, and perhaps the availability of other types of assistance.

Certainly, we should not exaggerate the impact of charities like the Society for Maternal Charity. The problem of poverty was crushing in nineteenth-century France, and maternal societies could not care even for all those who met their exacting requirements. And the sums they provided were not enormous. Still, their assistance was more generous than the temporary aid that officials were empowered to offer mothers who attempted to abandon their children at the Hospice des Enfants Trouvés in Paris in an effort to persuade these desperate mothers to keep their babies. This assistance, which could last up to four months, included a *demi-layette* and 5 FF per month for four months if the mother was willing to nurse her own child. If she wished to send it to a wet nurse, the hospice provided a *demi-layette* and 26 FF to transport the child and to pay for the first month of wet nursing. Married women were not even offered this aid, since they could apply to their local *bureau de bienfaisance*.[74]

In contrast, the imperial regulation for the Society for Maternal Charity, issued in 1811, had fixed assistance for each mother at 138 FF, which included a layette, the costs associated with childbirth, an allowance of 6 FF per month for fourteen months, and a sum of 13 FF "in small assistance at the discretion of the [administering] lady."[75] But the amount and type of assistance varied significantly from city to city. In Marseille, the 1844 bylaws fixed the maximum aid for each mother at 119 FF—18 FF for the layette, 3 FF for the childbirth costs, 90 FF for sixteen *mois de lait* ("milk months") at 6 FF per month, and 8 FF "in assistance chosen by the Ladies." However, the bylaws explicated that

> experience has shown us that there are many occasions when assistance can be divided among several individuals since needs are not the same nor equally urgent for each of them; it is based on the report of the *Dame administrante* or of the *Dame associée* that the Committee decides the amount of assistance; so it is in such circumstances that a layette and childbirth costs suffice as assistance, there are others where the poor health of the mother requires a wet nurse for her child; thus there would be only nourishment to pay for; often, however, the Council could only allow three francs per month, assistance known in Marseille since time immemorial by the name of "demi-lait"; sometimes the demi-layette suffices.[76]

Bordeaux's bylaws from 1815 capped the amount per mother at 103 FF (a layette for 25 FF, 18 FF for the costs of childbirth, and 5 FF per month for twelve months).[77] Lyon's *Règlement du détail* specified assistance amounting to 100 FF for each mother—10 FF for birth expenses, 20 FF for the layette, a second *trousseau* for 10 FF, and twelve months of *nourrissage* for 60 FF.[78] Limoges's bylaws also suggested a maximum of 100 FF, divided up slightly differently than Lyon's (15 FF for the layette, 15 FF for birth costs, 60 FF in twelve monthly payments, and 10 FF in *petit secours*).[79] Dijon's 1852 bylaws specified a "first class" of women receiving 5 FF for childbirth expenses, 5 FF at the discretion of the *dame visitante*, 4 FF per month for ten months, and a layette valued at 14 FF; this fixed the maximum amount at 64 FF. However, a second class of less needy women would not receive the 40 FF in monthly

*Table 5.* Assistance Amounts

| Year of publication of bylaws | Maximum assistance |
|---|---|
| Paris (1816) | variable, depending on receipts |
| Lyon (1847) | 100 FF |
| Bordeaux (1815) | 103 FF |
| Rouen (1849) | layette + 50 FF |
| Marseille (1844) | 119 FF |
| Limoges (1817) | 100 FF |
| Dijon (1874) | 64 FF |

Source: The data are drawn from a wide variety of *comptes rendus* and correspondence, and from Charles Des Alleurs, *Histoire de la Société de Charité Maternelle de Rouen* (Rouen: Imprimerie de Alfred Péron, 1854). For the archival material on which the table is based, see citation in text.

payments.[80] Mothers assisted by Rouen's maternal society were eligible for a layette and up to 50 FF in cash (which had to cover delivery costs); the society would also lend sheets to the new mother for up to a month, at which point she was to return them to the society, freshly bleached. In general, Rouen's society assisted only women giving birth to their fourth child and whose other children were all under the age of nine.[81]

In practice, the actual degree of assistance depended upon the funds raised by that particular branch and the perceived needs of the mother. Bordeaux's society provided an average of 75 FF in assistance to its mothers between 1815 and 1840, considerably below the official maximum of 103 FF.[82] The society of Rouen fixed its assistance at 50 FF per mother, although less needy women constituting a "second class" were accorded only 25 FF in assistance.[83] In Dijon, according to the bylaws of its society, the mothers received 64 FF in assistance (including childbirth costs and a layette), plus a cradle. A second class of mothers received only delivery fees, the layette, and 15 FF in cash.[84] Along with Dijon, Rouen's assistance was the least generous of the major maternal societies, at least on paper—although in reality, Limoges, offering its mothers less than 20 FF on average, was the least generous.[85] But in many cases—perhaps most—the straitened finances of maternal societies meant that few mothers actually received the maximum assistance.

Lyon was the most generous of the maternal societies; by midcentury it was spending an average of approximately 95 FF per family assisted. This munificence, however, led the Interior Ministry to reprimand the society. In a sharply worded letter castigating the administrative council for failing to raise as much money as one would expect in such a large city, the permanent secretary of the Interior Ministry suggested that "while waiting for an increase in revenues to permit leaving no needy family without the benefits of the charity, there would perhaps be grounds to divide the resources of the association among a greater number of women, reducing the actual amount of assistance. The Society of Lyon is the only one that allows 100 francs per family; in Paris, the rate of assistance is 80 fr., and still less in other large cities. Thus, the Society of Bordeaux was able to assist, in 1845, twice the number of women that Lyon [could] with resources that were not significantly greater."[86] In response to such criticism, Lyon did revise its allocation per family downward slightly. However, in 1861 the society continued to defend its decision to provide more generous assistance, arguing that "the assistance provided by the charity must be of real value if the Society wants to attain the goal it has in view."[87]

In an age when wages were low and irregular for the working classes, and the provision of social welfare scattered piecemeal among numerous, though inadequate, public assistance and private charitable institutions, the Society for Maternal Charity was an important piece of the puzzle and touched the lives of some of France's poorest citizens.[88] Huge disparities in public and private assistance existed between municipalities, and the state provided little money for this purpose.[89] In general, the amounts provided to the needy were extremely small. Frances Gouda notes that during the crisis years of the late 1840s, the French *bureaux de bienfaisance* provided assistance amounting to a national average of 10.42 FF annually (or 12.70 FF when administrative costs were added for each recipient). According to the 1841 census, the *bureaux de bienfaisance* managed to donate an average of 10.60 FF per individual

*Table 6.* Average Amount of Assistance per Mother per Year (in French Francs)*

|           | 1815–30 | 1831–45 | 1846–60 | 1861–70 |
|-----------|---------|---------|---------|---------|
| Paris     | 92      | 84      | 85      | 94      |
| Bordeaux  | 75      | 63      | 52      | 53      |
| Lyon      | 105     | 90      | 95      | 90      |
| Rouen     | 57      | 70      | 65      | 69      |
| Marseille | 47      | 50      | **      | **      |
| Limoges   | **      | **      | 14      | 17      |
| Dijon     | **      | **      | 49      | 44      |

*Figures were calculated by dividing total yearly expenditures by the number of mothers assisted, which includes overhead costs. Consequently, assisted mothers did not receive the full amount suggested in these numbers.

**Insufficient data from these years.

Source: The data are drawn from a wide variety of *comptes rendus* and correspondence, and from Charles Des Alleurs, *Histoire de la Société de Charité Maternelle de Rouen* (Rouen: Imprimerie de Alfred Péron, 1854). For the archival material on which the table is based, see citation in text.

(as a national average). Most generous was the department of the Seine, which allowed 26.26 FF annually, while in the department of the Nord (an industrial region), needy individuals received as little as 6.76 FF.[90] No wonder Catherine Duprat stresses, "It remains that at a time when the sums allowed by Public Assistance to registered indigents were far from reaching 100f per year and per family, the 100f from the Maternal Charity could seem to be a very substantial allocation."[91]

Of course, some branches of the society had a greater impact than others. We have already seen that there was a wide disparity in the resources that different maternal charities were able to marshal. Smaller organizations, such as the Society for Maternal Charity of Arles, were unable to attract much support, either from the families of the town (few of whom were wealthy) or the government, which believed that townspeople should contribute the majority of funds.[92] This situation limited the assistance they could offer. Furthermore, charitable women were simply less assiduous in some towns. The *comptes moraux* of Limoges's maternal society make reference to their reliance on the "Sisters of Charity affiliated with the *bureau de bienfaisance* who like to lend their help to the Society for Maternal Charity, coming to its assistance for the distribution of aid and surveillance which the Society must exercise over the little children."[93] Hazel Mills notes a long tradition in France of nuns carrying out charitable work refused as too unpleasant by lay *dames de charité*.[94] The documents of Limoges suggest that the women of that city spent little of their own time in personal charitable activities and relied heavily on the Sisters of Charity to carry out the society's work. The small sums they were able to offer each mother (around 15 FF per family) suggest that their fund-raising efforts were not particularly successful, either. In general, the members of Limoges's maternal society, many of them wives of leaders in the porcelain industry, took a more utilitarian than charitable approach to their work. Their efforts to finance a day-care center in 1862 were based more on a desire to get working mothers back to the factories than to help the overburdened women who sought the charity's assistance:

> A desire for crèches has often been expressed in Limoges. They would have the greatest utility in a manufacturing city where the porcelain factories employ a large number of women. When they do not have sufficient funds to procure wet nurses, and what wet nurses! they renounce the workshop to care for their children; they then lose the habit [*habitude*] for work, which is replaced by that of mendicancy. The majority of ladies who are members of the Société Maternelle would willingly subscribe to the establishment of a crèche if M. the Minister would kindly lend his generous assistance and furnished, through the intermediary of M. the Prefect, the instructions and bylaws necessary for the creation and maintenance of an *oeuvre* so worthy of interest.[95]

Still, many maternal societies maintained a high profile, and the Interior Ministry was fulsome in its praise for their good works, as were local officials. Their appreciation for these good works led local and national governments to subsidize maternal societies; but with these subsidies came restrictions. Under Napoleon, the maternal societies ceased to experience some of the independence they had enjoyed in their leaner years. This continued to be the case under subsequent governments.[96] All maternal societies receiving subsidies were expected to keep the Interior Ministry (via the prefect) updated on their activities and personnel.[97] They were expected to promote the goals of the royal or imperial government. And if a maternal society wished to obtain the appellation *utilité publique,* the government demanded exacting compliance with its requirements.

Starting under Napoleon, the Society for Maternal Charity began to provide staffing for other initiatives of the central government, a trend that would continue under subsequent regimes. For example, vaccination against smallpox became a national health imperative in the first decades of the nineteenth century, and all branches of the society adopted vaccination as a goal. The Society of Bordeaux pioneered this requirement; in 1808 the society awarded a "gratification pécuniaire" to all nursing mothers under its care who agreed to have their child vaccinated.[98] Article 45 of the 1811 *règlement* for the Imperial society directed that "All children adopted by the Society will be vaccinated through the care and at the expense of the Administrative Council." The statements of expenditures that provincial branches submitted to the Interior Ministry included an entry for the number of children vaccinated. Provincial branches instituted various incentives to make sure that the vaccinations were, in fact, carried out. For example, the *état* for the Society for Maternal Charity of Dijon specified that mothers must submit a certificate from a surgeon specifying that their child had been vaccinated before receiving the stipend for their final months under the society's care;[99] in 1861 Lyon's society reported that "the second *trousseau* would no longer be delivered until the nursing mother produced a vaccination certificate."[100] By making the provision of assistance contingent upon vaccination of the infant, the various branches of the society furthered the government's goal of vaccinating all children, especially the poor.[101] However, some maternal societies were more assiduous than others about recording these efforts. Lyon did not begin to track vaccinations until 1859, but as late as 1864 the Interior Ministry complained that the information was still not recorded in Lyon's *comptes rendus.*[102]

The government used the infrastructure of maternal societies to provide other charitable services, as well, especially during times of crisis. As we saw earlier, during the famine of 1812, Marie-Louise ordered the society to use

150,000 FF of its endowment to distribute bread and *soupes économiques* to the poor of Paris during the three worst months of winter, to the benefit of approximately 13,000 destitute Parisians.[103] Other societies regularly provided social services not explicitly mentioned in their bylaws. For example, in 1824, Bordeaux's society distributed beds to poor families to prevent unsanitary sleeping conditions.[104] The Paris society used its funds to apprentice twenty-eight little girls who had lost their parents while under its patronage.[105] In 1837, Marseille's maternal society set up a system to distribute bread and meat to needy mothers through local bakers and butchers.[106]

Many societies provided to families free medical services beyond those offered at the time of childbirth. Most listed, in their *comptes rendus,* affiliated doctors, midwives, and pharmacists willing to provide free medical services, and individual maternal societies sometimes provided nursing mothers with *cartes dispensaires* that allowed them access to medical centers and medications. The Imperial Society first made note of this practice in the minutes of a meeting held on November 23, 1811:

> When the children of nursing mothers are sick, the ladies of the Council must provide care for them. Several physicians have generously offered their services; they were welcomed. But these services are not sufficient; it would be necessary to provide free of charge the necessary drugs and place at the disposal of the Ladies, for their respective *arrondissements,* 40 clinic admission cards which would cost 1,200 francs. For several years, the former Society had recognized the advantages of these measures. It is combined now with another advantage; the clinics vaccinate free of charge, and the certificates are accorded only when the children have been vaccinated.[107]

Perhaps because of Napoleon's personal interest in the operations of the Imperial Society, doctors and pharmacists offered their services eagerly; in 1812 the administrative council celebrated the good works of M. LeMaire, pharmacist of the society, for "the care with which [he] . . . furnishes medication free of charge to poor women giving birth in his *arrondissement.*"[108] Because so many doctors and surgeons requested affiliation with the society, the administrative council in Paris was forced to establish rules for admission to these positions. The number of doctors was limited to twenty-four (two per *arrondissement*), while that of surgeons was set at twelve. Two society-affiliated doctors had to attest to the skills of any new physician, who was also required to prove that he was a doctor in medicine. The *arrêté* composed by the council noted that doctors and surgeons known for their charitable assistance to the poor would receive preference.[109] The society also appointed pharmacists to each *arrondissement.*[110] It is not clear whether medical personnel continued to

associate officially with the Paris society after the termination of the Imperial Society. The Paris *comptes rendus* extant after 1815 no longer list doctors,
surgeons, and pharmacists as affiliates of the society.

The relationship of medical personnel with the society formally continued in other locales. In its first *compte rendu,* issued in 1805, the Bordeaux
society listed not only affiliated doctors and surgeons, but also midwives
willing to deliver the babies of poor mothers.[111] From the start, Bordeaux's
maternal society was uniquely embedded in the city's medical community.
Doctors Lamothe and Capelle were its cofounders, and Dr. Capelle its long-
serving secretary. Victor Lamothe had served as physician at the Hospice
des Enfants-Trouvés, as well as the Maternity Hospice, and participated as
an examiner for Madame Coutanceau's midwifery students at Bordeaux's
*école d'accouchement* (childbirth school). He was also the chief vaccinator
in Bordeaux. These professional and personal ties created links among the
maternal society, the foundling hospice, the *dépôt de vaccin,* and the doctors,
midwives, and other medical personnel of the city.[112] Unlike many maternal
societies, Bordeaux's always listed a full complement of doctors (one to three
per parish), pharmacists, and *accoucheuses* associated with the charity in its
yearly accounts.[113]

Rouen's maternal society was less integrated with that city's medical community. Its 1823 bylaws required that a doctor and a surgeon affiliate with
the charity; Charles Des Alleurs, the eventual secretary-archivist, began his
association with the society as its physician.[114] Rouen's society was unique in
its formal association with a dentist, M. Weille; in his history of the society,
Charles Des Alleurs remarked, "This nomination was made outside the bylaws; both the old and the new [bylaws] make mention only of a physician
and a surgeon."[115] It seems unlikely that one doctor and one surgeon associated with the society of Rouen could provide the same level of care as the
twenty-plus doctors and surgeons, and nearly twenty midwives, who served
in Bordeaux.

Lyon's society, beginning in 1830, listed one or two doctors responsible
for each *arrondissement.* In general, the *arrondissements* were fully staffed
throughout the 1840s, although most districts had only one physician once
the number of *arrondissements* increased in the mid-1840s. By 1850, only
nine of the city's sixteen *arrondissements* enjoyed the services of an associated
doctor; the account of 1852 noted that "in the *arrondissements* which lack
free doctors/obstetricians, the Administrative Council will supply [aid] by
paying midwives to go assist mothers giving birth in their homes."[116] Perhaps
Lyon's maternal society lacked the close ties to the medical community that
Bordeaux's enjoyed.[117]

Additional services beyond those specified in the bylaws were geared to the circumstances of the region that the society served and to the interests of its members. The terrible tragedy of the six shipwrecked fishing boats near La Teste in March of 1836, which killed 68 fishing men, leaving 160 orphans, spurred Bordeaux's maternal society to extend its assistance beyond its city limits. The twelve pregnant widows of La Teste inspired the sympathy of the *dames administrantes,* who were sure that their generosity in this exceptional case would meet with the approval of donors.[118] As we have seen, Limoges's administrative council tried to sponsor a crèche that would provide child care for the poor mothers of Limoges, many of whom worked for the porcelain industry there and were undoubtedly employed by the husbands of the maternal society members.[119] During the crisis years of the early 1860s in Rouen, triggered by the "cotton famine" caused by the American Civil War, Rouen's maternal society extended its assistance to women with only one child and began to distribute bread to all mothers eligible for assistance; in recognition of this extraordinary assistance, the Municipal Council voted a subsidy of 600 FF in 1863 and 1864.[120] After the frightening revolutions of 1848, Lyon's maternal society, whose *dames administrantes* were particularly concerned about the effects of socialist teachings on silk workers, distributed mass and prayer books to the poor families of their city "to counterbalance . . . the evil that has been done to them by so many perverse and foolish doctrines which seek to deceive them about their true interests."[121]

Throughout the century, prefects showed interest in sponsoring maternal societies in their departments.[122] While some branches that had been propped up by Napoleonic pressure disappeared after 1814, in other cases prefects were able to promote the formation of local societies that had failed to coalesce under the strong-arm tactics of Napoleon and his ministers—for example, in the cities of Le Mans and Limoges.[123] As the Bourbon and subsequent governments continued to funnel money through maternal societies, they presented an attractive option for local administrators.[124] Local governments would have appreciated that the formation of a Society for Maternal Charity brought in additional monies from the central government, always welcome to the prefect as well as municipal officials, especially since state authorities refused to bear the entire cost of foundlings and delegated most of that expense to departmental governments.[125]

For overburdened prefects, dealing with problems of poverty, abandoned children, and high infant mortality, a maternal society could fill a number of functions. Its assistance could help to reduce the number of abandoned children. This was a particularly pressing issue, since the number of abandoned infants increased dramatically after the Revolution of 1789 and remained a serious issue until the advent of the Third Republic. According to baron Dupin, the nineteenth-century historian of French public assistance, the number of *enfants trouvés* under state care prior to the Revolution of 1789 was about 45,000, while by 1821 the number was closer to 60,000. The number of abandoned children left in the care of departmental governments fluctuated over the course of the nineteenth century and was often related to state policies that could make it more or less difficult for a poor mother to abandon a baby.[126] For example, in Lyon between 1835 and 1840, the average number of children abandoned was 1,918 per year for a population of approximately 200,000.[127] The costs could be enormous, especially for departments such as the Rhône with a large city. In a meeting held on September 15, 1842, the members of the General Council of the Rhône deplored "the ease with which the newborn from neighboring departments, and even from abroad, arrive by land and sea conveyances which depose them at the Hospice de la Charité, which results in an increase in expenses somewhere around 200,000 f."[128]

The first major effort to use harsher policies to reduce child abandonment came in the 1830s. Rachel Fuchs and Janet Potash argue that the push was related to efforts to cut state aid for foundlings (especially after the recession of 1826–29) but was also part of the larger "social question"—the fear of poverty, and the immoral and potentially criminal behavior that resulted from social ills. Social economists and others perceived child abandonment as a symptom more of depravity than of *misère* and argued that strict policies to discourage abandonment could be effective. Maternal societies, which shored up the family structure, could be part of the puzzle,[129] but so were government policies that would make it difficult, indeed shameful, to abandon a child. These policies included *déplacement* (moving foundlings from the department in which they were abandoned to other jurisdictions so that it would be more difficult for the mother to locate the child if her circumstances changed); aid to poor (especially single) mothers; and closing the *tours,* or "foundling wheels," which allowed for the anonymous abandonment of infants.[130] Some departments were quicker than others to adopt these draconian policies; the municipal council of Croix-Rousse, a working-class suburb of Lyon, complained bitterly that not only had the Department of the Rhône failed to institute policies that would discourage child abandonment, but that indeed, single mothers were treated too generously: "there is a kind of bonus incentive for unmarried women with child."[131] Communications between the prefects of the various departments and the Interior Ministry suggest that harsh measures such as *déplacement* and the closing of *tours* could be effective; however, the correspondence also suggests that the social and emotional costs of these measures was high.[132]

The Interior Ministry, as well as the prefects who carried out national policies, worried primarily about the cost of caring for abandoned children. But mortality rates for these abandoned children were also extraordinarily elevated. Early in the nineteenth century, as many as 750 per 1,000 of all abandoned children died within twelve months; by the third quarter of the century, about 667 per 1,000 died as infants (a spike in infant mortality occurred during the Franco-Prussian War, 1870–71). Despite minor fluctuations, these mortality rates remained relatively constant until the 1880s, when they decreased slightly.[133] Earlier in the century, baron Dupin had considered child mortality over the first twelve years of life. Writing in 1821, he observed that for every twenty-five children abandoned, only about three or four were still alive after twelve years, a mortality rate of 840 per 1,000 live births. In contrast, he noted, the results for children assisted by a Society for Maternal Charity were much better. In general, thirteen or fourteen would still be alive after twelve years, a mortality rate of 440 per 1,000.[134] The *compte rendu* from 1810 for Bordeaux's society confirmed these good results: "Among the babies who have participated in the assistance of the Society, only one-seventh have fallen victim to the dangers that afflict man in the first year of his life. This mortality is less than that observed by most authors who have written on the life expectancy of humans."[135] Yet Catherine Duprat suggests that infant mortality rates were still high among those assisted by the Paris Society for Maternal Charity; the number of deaths at twelve months established the annual average rate at 153 per 1,000 live births for the period 1815–19 and at 133 per 1,000 for the decade 1831–40.[136]

Still, those rates compare favorably with the mortality rates for children left in the care of the Enfants-Trouvés, and even compared with the results for state-assisted children cared for at home. A later *enquête* carried out in 1860 under the Second Empire found a significantly lower mortality rate for children raised by their mothers with some assistance from the state (a model similar to that pioneered by the Society for Maternal Charity, although without the surveillance of the *dames visiteuses*) than for that of children raised in foundling hospices—about 300 deaths per 1,000 live births, in place of 570 per 1,000 for infants (*du premier âge*).[137] For the babies born in 1857 and adopted by the society of Lyon, the mortality rate was around 300 per 1,000, the average suggested by the *enquête* for assisted children.[138] However, the secretary-treasurer of Lyon's society remarked that this figure was, in fact, unusually high: "it must be attributed to extreme poverty and [food] scarcity."[139] For Bordeaux, the rate was 100 per 1,000 for infants assisted by its maternal society, as compared to a national average of 160–200 per 1,000 for all infants.[140] In general, mortality rates for the children assisted by maternal societies fluctuated dramatically from year to year, for reasons related more to economic circumstances than to the ministrations of these charities. Still, the Interior Ministry carefully tracked and commented on the infant mortality rates recorded by maternal charities each year, raising questions whenever rates appeared to spike.

Perhaps more important than the promise of comparatively lower mortality rates, maternal societies removed some of the financial and labor burden from the *bureaux de bienfaisance* and public sources of welfare. In 1821, Dupin argued that while it cost 762 FF to care for an *enfant trouvé* through age twelve, it cost the Society for Maternal Charity only about 100 FF to prevent the abandonment of a child altogether.[141] The *enquête* of 1860 indicated that it was six times cheaper to provide assistance to a nursing mother than it was to care for a foundling or abandoned child, that is, an average of 1,403.30 FF from birth to age twelve, compared with an average of 232.92 FF in temporary assistance to an indigent mother who wanted to keep her child.[142] As we have seen, maternal societies usually provided even smaller amounts of cash. These potential savings had resonance for an administration paying millions of francs each year to support abandoned children.[143] However, this support for temporary assistance did not address the fact that the mother and child were left to their own resources after the first two years of assistance.[144]

The close association with the state and shifting national concerns is reflected in the perceptibly changing public voice of the Society for Maternal Charity over the course of the nineteenth century. While the organization retained its focus on assisting the poor mothers of large families at the time of childbirth, and on the encouragement of breast feeding, and moral surveillance, the tone and meaning of that focus shifted in ways that reflected century-long trends. In some cases, this shift led to changes in bylaws. When Bordeaux's maternal society revised its statutes and bylaws in 1853 and 1854, it changed the nature of assistance available to poor mothers. In place of the 103 FF limit, encompassing a layette, birth expenses, and a monthly allowance, the society was now authorized to accord to each mother a layette, a cradle, 5 francs for childbirth costs, a quarterly allowance of 15 FF, and either 21 FF to pay for four months of bottles, or 30 FF to pay a wet nurse for the same length of time. These last two costs were authorized only in cases when the mother could not nurse the child herself; but this possibility reflects a move away from the exclusive insistence on breast feeding, and a greater emphasis on encouraging the mother to keep her child with her, if at all possible. The society was willing to pay for a wet nurse if the mother absolutely could not breast-feed.[145] Still, the consequences of paying for a wet nurse were not always happy. In 1852, M. Guiraut, the secretary of Bordeaux's society, sent a letter to the prefect of the Gironde, noting:

> On 29 April 1851, at the request of Pascal Pradeau and his wife Marguerite Jaubert, living at rue Belleville 129, Parish St. Eulalie, the Maternal Society placed their newborn child with a wet nurse . . . not long afterward, Pascal Pradeau and his wife Marguerite Jaubert left Bordeaux, abandoning their child, and since that time, they have not reappeared.

The society had paid 180 FF to keep the baby with its wet nurse; but now the administrative council had determined that "in consequence of the abandonment of that child whose period of breast feeding has reached an end, there is reason to place it with the Foundling Hospice."[146]

While the primary intent at the time of the society's founding was to prevent the abandonment of legitimate infants, that concern, over time, took a backseat to encouraging marriage, reducing infant mortality rates, and improving the health of children. The *comptes rendus* of several maternal societies made frequent reference to their success in encouraging marriage among the poor who wished to receive the benefits of the Society for Maternal Charity.[147] Maternal societies probably worked with other charitable organizations, such as the Société de Saint-François Régis, which was committed to helping poor couples with the extensive paperwork and fees necessary to legally marry in France. Like maternal societies, Saint-François Régis emphasized religious marriage and the reinforcement of familial bonds.[148] Barrie Ratcliffe's study of cohabitation among the Paris popular classes suggests that many clients of Saint-François Régis sought the organization's help because they wanted access to charitable resources.[149] In 1838 the Society for Maternal Charity of Bordeaux celebrated the numerous marriages it encouraged, "admirably seconded by those whose mission is to bring back to the path of morality those individuals who have strayed," suggesting their links to these other organizations and their interest in facilitating marriage among the poor.[150]

The state's growing concerns about depopulation and the welfare of the nation's children were reflected in the shifting emphasis of maternal societies. By the late 1860s, Bordeaux's maternal society listed, in its yearly accounts, mortality rates for the infants that members assisted and began to express concern over depopulation. While these anxieties would intensify after 1871, as Joshua Cole points out, fears about infant mortality and depopulation cannot be attributed solely to the Franco-Prussian War, as they date back to earlier years.[151] By the late nineteenth and early twentieth centuries, the Paris society focused primarily on the health needs of infants, sponsoring prenatal and lactation consultations, as well as a *maison maternelle* (house for mothers) and an *oeuvre de berceaux* (a charity that provided cradles to poor women).[152] Other provincial societies began to provide similar services.[153] This emphasis on the well-being of children reflects national trends dating from the 1850s and 1860s.[154] In 1856, prefects received a *circulaire* from the Interior Ministry instructing them to replace the expression "assistance to single mothers" with "assistance to newborn children," emphasizing children rather than mothers, especially single mothers.[155] Still, maternal societies stressed the health benefits they offered mothers, as well. François Gille, in his hagiographical account of the Paris society, drew attention to its emphasis on home birthing. At a meeting that took place on December 5, 1853, the administrative council reminded its members of article 21 of the society's bylaws, which denied birth costs to mothers who delivered their babies in the hospitals of Paris. Gille underlined the benefits of this regulation:

> To really understand the advantages of this preventive measure, it must be known that, for a long time already, the administration of Public Assistance, along with doctors, struck by the number of [cases of] puerperal fever which raged, in the form of an epidemic, in the maternity wards, rightly gave their attention to averting the harm by trying out a new system. The Society, by requiring the women it helps to give birth at home, had found the most efficacious means of prevention against disease: we speak of the dissemination of those giving birth, and their isolation from source of contamination, for it must be recognized, and we must not be afraid to affirm that without any prejudice, the mortality in the hospitals of Paris is and always will be higher than that experienced at home.[156]

Until the regular use of antisepsis in hospitals beginning in the late nineteenth century, home delivery was certainly preferable to the lethality of maternity wards.[157]

Over time, many maternal societies modified their rhetoric, and sometimes their services, to reflect national priorities and maintain their funding. By the time of the Third Republic, the Paris society was careful to stress that it assisted all poor mothers in childbirth "**without distinction of nationality or religion**" [bold in original text], clearly conscious of the government's antipathy to exclusive religious charities.[158] However, while these assorted accounts reflected growing national issues, the focus of the various branches of the Society for Maternal Charity also remained intensely local. Lyon's society continued to worry about the effects of the employment cycle on its silk workers, and the charitable women of Rouen carefully pegged the degree of their assistance to the price of bread, concerned about the effect of that expense on the city's poor.[159]

But the same women who looked with such sympathy upon the "deserv-ing poor" could be quite harsh toward those they deemed less moral and less deserving. Furthermore, they would go only so far to accommodate the changing views of the national government. The declining fortunes of the Society for Maternal Charity after 1871 were directly related to its refusal to assist certain mothers. As the secular government and reformers of the Third Republic became increasingly concerned with the problem of depopulation, the society's resistance to assisting any but the legally (and in some cases religiously) married put them at odds with the government.[160]

Lyon provides an interesting case study, both of how the government used maternal societies to deliver social services and of how the secular regimes that came to power under the Third Republic grew disenchanted with the philosophical bases of these proudly moralistic charities. The Service des Enfants Assistés, part of the Civil Hospices of Lyon, was responsible for the care of abandoned children and for temporary assistance to both single and married indigent mothers and their infants. Lyon's public-assistance services were, in fact, in advance of many cities; the local administration consciously tried to prevent the abandonment of children by distributing assistance to both single and married poor mothers at the time of the infant's birth.[161] The service had offered temporary assistance to 373 legitimate children in 1862, and 275 in 1863; the decreasing number reflected both an improved economy in 1863 and "the strictness brought to the estimation of the parents' resources." However, "in order to more confidently join the spirit of charity to the thorough investigation necessary to really know the position of the legitimate parents applying [for assistance], the administration of the hos-pices and that of the department contacted the Society for Maternal Charity, which consented to undertake, beginning in 1864, the allocation of assistance for legitimate children." This new arrangement would offer advantages: "to [avoid] placing legitimate mothers in the same category as single mothers, to soften the harshness of home visits through the intervention of charitable ladies, and also to assure a double maternal surveillance over the children nursed by their mothers."[162]

Lyon's society determined that it would have to increase the number of its *dames distributrices* to care for more poor women. In addition, the ad-ministrative council debated changing its bylaws in order to perform its new functions. The bylaws specified that the society could offer assistance only to women who nursed their babies. However, like most other maternal societies, Lyon over the years had introduced numerous exceptions to that "absolute rule," expending considerable resources on bottles and wet nurses for mothers unable to breast-feed their infants—"experience had shown that one could not follow it without refusing assistance to families deserving keen interest [owing to their] extreme poverty." However the new situation of the Lyon society, effectively serving as a branch of the Service des Enfants Assistés, would require that they increase the number of exceptions, "for we must not forget that our new mission is to prevent, more than ever, the abandonment of newborn babies, and that our Charity must try to be anywhere that danger is to be feared." However, the administrative council ultimately decided not to revise this particular rule, "the first of our institution." Rather, it would always be "by means of exception that mothers will be authorized not to breast-feed their children; and yet any time the *Dames administrantes* are unable to impose this absolute obligation, they will substitute exhortations and advice." The women would apply the rules at their discretion.[163]

This change in policy led to a significant increase in both the revenues and the workload of Lyon's maternal society. The city of Lyon and the Department of the Rhône had each regularly provided 3,000 FF per year to the charity. In 1864 that amount increased to 13,000 FF from each source. By 1866 the society was receiving 20,000 FF annually from both the city and the department; in 1871 the department's contribution jumped to 30,000 FF. The number of mothers admitted to assistance increased from 406 in 1863, to 567 in 1864, to 686 in 1867, and to 713 in 1869.[164] The value of the labor provided by the society was considerable and eased the workload of the Service des Enfants Assistés.

However, the fall of the Second Empire in late 1870, and the increasingly secular bent of the Third Republic in the following years, brought about for Lyon's maternal society dramatic changes that foreshadowed future adjustments in the relationship between the government and all maternal societies. In 1871 the Municipal Council of Lyon discontinued the Society's 30,000 FF subsidy. In 1872 they restored 10,000 FF, but this was a temporary measure. On July 11, 1873, the prefect of the Rhône called for an extraordinary session of Lyon's Municipal Council to discuss the matter of the maternal society's subsidy. The prefect supported a continued allocation of 10,000 FF; however, discussion over the matter was heated and reflected new political realities. The Rapport de la Commission des finances noted that "the association of maternal charity is a *lay* Society [emphasis mine] directed by ladies, spreading around them assistance designed to relieve the suffering very often undeserved, and who consequently put into practice solidarity resulting from the observation of duties dictated by the inequality of the conditions of fortune among the citizens of the same country." The reporter, M. Causse, recounted the benefits provided by the *dames administrantes,* noting the free help of society members who visited the assisted families and concluded that "if its statutes did not exclude from the benefits of the Society the mothers of families who are in every way respectable, but have requested only a civil celebration of their marriage, one could only applaud and encourage the devotion that the ladies in charge of the direction of the Society for Maternal Charity have shown." However, "in a country as divided as ours, lay charitable societies distance themselves from their goal when their benefits are subordinated to religious practices, the observation or abandonment of which establish the right for admission or rejection to the assistance of the Society." In short, the paragraph of the statutes requiring proof of religious marriage was no longer acceptable for a charity receiving municipal subsidies. The council viewed it as "a breach of liberty of conscience, an absolute liberty . . . which our laws have sanctioned for a long time."[165] Consequently, the Municipal Council made approval of the 10,000 FF subsidy to the Society for Maternal Charity contingent upon removal of paragraph 3, article 4 from the third section of its statutes.[166]

The maternal society of Lyon faced resistance not only from the city government. The General Council of the Rhône, representing the department, had accorded the society a subvention of 30,000 FF in 1872; however, in doing so, the council had ordered that "a Commission, composed, in Lyon, of the general Councilor of the canton, the Councilor of the *arrondissement* and the officer of the registry office; in the rural communes, of the general Councilor of the canton, the Councilor of the *arrondissement* and the mayor of the canton, or in his absence, of a mayor of the cantonal district, named by administrative authority, will designate the mothers of families who will receive the subvention." The General Council, like the Municipal Council, disliked the society's religious qualifications. At its meeting of September 10, 1873, M. Durand, the *rapporteur*, noted that the society had ignored its deliberations and "continued to distribute the subvention which you accorded them in conformity with its statutes," specifically the requirement for a religious marriage. As a result, M. Durand moved that the subvention of 30,000 FF should be revoked for 1874. M. Dalin objected, noting the many services of the society and pointing out that with winter approaching, the refusal of this credit would "reduce to the point of death a host of mothers of families and doom to certain death a considerable number of their children." Surely the General Council did not wish to assume such a grave responsibility? M. Grinand responded coldly that this impasse was entirely the fault of the society for refusing to modify its statutes. M. Ballue added, in a tone of outrage, that "in the account of the Society, a certain sum had been spent to distribute catechisms . . . What relief could a catechism bring to a woman in labor? One must say, in all truth . . . It is a question here of an exclusive sect,

I will not say religious, but ultramontane. Now, we fight ultramontanism, which we consider an enemy of modern society. The General Council cannot, in voting for the requested subvention, provide arms to an implacable enemy." On a vote of 15 to 9, the *conseil* rejected the maternal society's request for a subvention.[167]

In a meeting that took place on November 21, 1873, the prefect was able to convince the Municipal Council that, given the General Council's decision to withhold funding, a subvention of at least 10,000 FF was essential so that the maternal society could continue to function. Stressing the society's respect for all religions, regardless of sect, the council awarded 10,000 FF for 1873 but decided to delay a decision concerning funding for 1874.[168] The die had been cast. The municipal and departmental government's long support for the Society for Maternal Charity had come to an end.[169] It is true that the society's administrative council had been unwilling to compromise on its statutes; when faced with the Municipal Council's ultimatum in August 1873, the administrative council protested, declaring that it could "under no circumstances modify its statutes along the lines demanded by the Municipal Council."[170] Twenty years later, despite their diminishing resources, the women would not budge. In a letter to the prefect of the Rhône, the departmental inspector for the Service des Enfants Assistés reported that the *présidente* of the society of Lyon "told me quite categorically that the admission of children was strictly contingent upon their status as a legitimate child, and that the statutes subordinating the right to assistance to the religious marriage of the parents were rigorously carried out" (while noting in the margin of the letter "whatever the [religious] cult might be").[171]

The religiosity of maternal societies was a complicated and controversial issue and was the subject of frequent debate among supporters and detractors after 1870. While their *comptes rendus* and the *comptes moraux* frequently employed the more secular language of "love of humanity," there was a strong spiritual component to their work, which varied in intensity from place to place. For example, the Society for Maternal Charity of Besançon, like many maternal societies, cooperated closely with the city's *dames de charité,* a lay religious group. After 1846 it was known as the "Société Maternelle de Sainte Anne de Besançon" and followed an explicitly religious program, although assisting women of all faiths.[172] Most societies were ecumenical. In more religiously pluralistic cities like Bordeaux, the local Society for Maternal Charity counted among its benefactors the Jewish consistory, the archbishop of Bordeaux, and M. Martin, *ministre du culte protestant.*[173] In a similar fashion, Paris and Lyon welcomed both members and poor mothers of various religious backgrounds, although many of the individual women were without a doubt highly religious.[174] Susan Grogan suggests that politicians like Paul Strauss, who relied on the original constitution of the Society for Maternal Charity in his critiques of the organization, exaggerated the religious bent of the institution and refused to acknowledge that many branches of the society had evolved in a more secular direction over the years, while still maintaining moral requirements.[175]

This concern about the religious requirements of maternal societies would become more salient with the fall of the Second Empire and the increasingly anticlerical stance of the Third Republic. In fact, it may be that some maternal societies stiffened their resistance to secularism in reaction against the sometimes bullying tactics of state and municipal authorities. Religion emerged as an issue in different locales at different times, depending upon the political composition of the municipal and departmental councils, and the local political culture. By the 1880s, it would emerge as an issue on the national level; this would signal a significant shift in the relationship between the French state and the Society for Maternal Charity.

# Epilogue

## Toward a Welfare State

Over the course of its nearly one-hundred-year existence, the Society for Maternal Charity had drawn strong support from every regime. But France's defeat in the Franco-Prussian War of 1870–71, and the changes that followed, presaged significant shifts in the maternal society's political fortunes, although the specific nature of those changes was, for a long time, unclear. The complicated political landscape in France following the fall of the Second Empire in September 1870 made it difficult to know what type of government would eventually emerge. Until the crisis of May 16, 1877, which eventually led to the resignation of the monarchist president, Marshal Patrice de Mac-Mahon, it was even unclear that the ultimate form of government would be republican. Monarchist candidates drew strong support in the elections of February 1871—the first held after the French defeat at the hands of the Germans—and maintained power until 1876, when Republicans won control of the Chamber of Deputies.[1]

But it was less the form of government than political strife between fervent Catholics and equally zealous anticlericals that signaled the decline of the Society for Maternal Charity's political and social influence. The secular bent of the Department of the Rhône's General Council, as well as Lyon's Municipal Council, brought an early end to local subsidies for Lyon's maternal society, and other maternal charities faced similar challenges vis-à-vis local authorities. But as anticlerical sentiments intensified at the national level, it became increasingly difficult for the French state to support provincial maternal societies, especially those that refused to compromise on religious and moral requirements for their recipients.

For a time, the republican government continued to subsidize maternal societies throughout the country at a national level. The Society for Maternal Charity had stepped up during the nation's time of need in 1870–71; the Paris society changed the residency requirements in its bylaws so that it could assist poor mothers fleeing Alsace and Lorraine in the wake of annexation by Germany.[2] Maternal societies throughout the country struggled to provide additional assistance at a time of extreme hardship for the poor, and when the government sought, more than ever, class reconciliation and to combat depopulation. In 1874 the minister of the interior appointed a representative from Paris's Society for Maternal Charity to serve on a Comité Supérieur de Protection des Enfants du Premier Âge, suggesting its continued political significance.[3] Madame Mac-Mahon, wife of the French president, did not serve as president of the Paris society as previous queens and empresses had, but she offered visible support, attending the *fête villageoise* fund-raiser in 1876.[4] In 1883 the minister of the interior sent a *circulaire* to prefects concerning subsidies for maternal societies and crèches throughout the country. Reiterating its support for the Society for Maternal Charity, and praising the good results of these organizations—the minister noted that, as proof of its interest, the Interior Ministry had obtained a grant of 146,000 FF for maternal societies and crèches in 1881—he stressed that prefects should encourage municipal and departmental governments to support these societies enthusiastically, with generous subsidies if they were already in place, and to take the initiative to encourage their creation where they did not exist.[5]

But at the same time, the Conseil Supérieur de l'Assistance sent prefects a model of statutes and bylaws for maternal societies. While still noting that the society provided assistance to "enfants légitimes," article 18 of the model bylaws specified among the required documents that mothers seeking assistance must present only a civil marriage certificate, not proof of religious marriage. This change in requirement indicated the future line of conflict between maternal societies and the government.[6]

The Interior Ministry made explicit its new position regarding the bylaws of maternal societies in March of 1888. In another *circulaire* to prefects, the minister noted that it had been called to his attention that numerous maternal societies required that mothers seeking assistance provide proof that their marriage took place "before the minister of their *culte,*" suggesting that women married in a civil ceremony were ineligible. He went on to write,

> I do not know if the restrictive provisions in question are rigorously followed, and
> I beg of you to inform me about that in a very precise manner. But in any case,
> I would prefer to see disappear a rule manifestly in opposition to the principle

of liberty of conscience; and if that rule is inscribed in the statutes of the Society cited above, I would be obliged if you could consult the administrators in order to see that the statutes are revised and that there is no longer any distinction between indigent individuals who had their unions consecrated before the minister of an acknowledged religion, and those whose marriages are purely civil.[7]

The prefects obediently researched the information, and by 1894, the ministry was able to report that sixteen branches still enforced the marriage requirement, while another twenty-two still had the rule in their bylaws but did not enforce it. This finding suggests that fewer than half of the maternal societies throughout France had any kind of religious marriage requirement on the books by the mid-1890s.[8] Still, the reporter for the Conseil Supérieur argued that this requirement was one reason that many maternal societies had lost significant local popularity and financial support.[9] This is a case in which the perception might have been as important as the reality; clearly lawmakers and officials perceived maternal societies as intolerant, sectarian organizations, and even a shift away from religion-based requirements might not have changed that view.

And not all maternal societies were willing to make that shift. Despite disapproval from all levels of government, a number of maternal societies continued to refuse the new, more secular approach that the central government dictated for those that still wished to receive a subsidy.[10] Limoges's maternal society responded to the prefect of the Haute-Vienne on April 9, 1888, that "the Society for Maternal Charity of Limoges, up to this time, has assisted all indigent mothers without regard for politics or religion; but it is impossible for it to annul any of its bylaws . . . The Society hopes that M. the Minister will render justice to the manner in which it has always tried to distribute the assistance with which it has been entrusted."[11] Dijon's response to its prefect's query, via the mayor of Dijon, was even more forceful: "The Society for Maternal Charity of Dijon executes very faithfully the bylaws that were adopted by the Conseil d'État in its meeting of 7 January 1875." The mayor noted drily that "one cannot say in a more explicit and more correct manner that the Maternal Society does not see fit to accept the observations of the Minister concerning Part 3 of Article 26 [of its bylaws] and that indigent mothers whose marriage is purely civil are now and will continue in the future to be deprived of the assistance of the Society."[12]

Dijon's maternal society had never received any funding from its departmental government, and seldom from the municipal government, although in the 1880s and early 1890s, the municipal government occasionally provided 1,000 FF per year as part of an effort to improve child welfare. It could, however, generally count on a small subsidy from the central government. For example, in 1890 the society received 1,500 FF. However, by 1895 it had lost all subventions from any governmental entities.[13] The last subsidy from the municipal government was granted in 1891. In 1893 and 1894, the mayor of Dijon informed the prefect that he could not support a subvention to the society because of "partiality" in its decisions on aid; in particular that "the Society accords no assistance to single mothers and it accords it to married women only after taking account of their religious and political opinions."[14] This was a new and potentially more damaging accusation; maternal societies had not previously been accused of political bias in their decisions on assistance. The Interior Ministry followed suit soon afterward. In a letter to the prefect in 1896, the minister inquired whether it was true that Dijon's society refused assistance to those not religiously married. The prefect, in a draft response dated February 22, 1897, acknowledged that this was the case but suggested that a subvention was still justifiable, based on the organization's good works. However, a sentence affirming, "I believe that I must add that all the ladies who belong to the Society for Maternal Charity of Dijon are most honorable, and several belong to sincerely Republican families," was crossed out.[15] Perhaps the prefect thought that this was stretching the truth a bit—Dijon's society was long known for the conservative, indeed royalist, bent of its members. A letter from the Interior Ministry dated June 20, 1901, inquired about the nature of maternal-assistance charities in the Côte-d'Or; the prefect's response stressed the confessional, and indeed, the proselytizing function of Dijon's Society for Maternal Charity.[16]

Lyon's society, of course, lost its departmental and municipal funding in the 1870s when it also lost its position as an adjunct of that city's Service des Enfants Assistés. It received its last subvention from the Interior Ministry in 1894. In a letter dated December 21, 1894, the prefect of the Rhône reported, in response to a query from the minister of the interior, that "article 28 of the interior bylaws of the Society imposes on mothers the obligation to give proof of their marriage before a minister of their faith in order to obtain the benefit of the Society's assistance; I believe that I must add that this clause is rigorously enforced."[17] Predictably, the minister responded in April 1895 that "I have not accorded a subvention to this Society, because assistance is dependent upon proof of a religious marriage."[18]

As the government withdrew funding, some societies expressed anger at what they perceived as the unfair treatment of married mothers by the government. Bordeaux's society had chosen "unanimously" to renounce both its municipal and its departmental subsidy in 1881 rather than to revise its religious requirements.[19] Perhaps this reluctance to change the bylaws was related to what these bourgeois members of maternal societies saw as a fundamental injustice in public assistance. In 1875, Bordeaux's maternal society had deplored the fact that public assistance awarded significantly more financial help to single mothers than the society was now able to provide to "legitimate wives"; it noted that it was difficult for the charitable individuals associated with Saint-François-Régis to convince poor couples that married life was a better choice when it meant a diminution in the resources available to care for their child.[20]

Frequently, *dames administrantes* seemed to conflate single mothers and those married only in a civil ceremony, as did government officials in their discussion of maternal societies. And as Rachel Fuchs demonstrates, legislators were now less willing to brand women in long-term consensual relationships as immoral, regarding *concubinage* as the functional equivalent of marriage.[21] Perhaps this explains why so many maternal societies refused to admit a group of women whom they considered not only immoral, but already excessively favored by the government.

The Paris society, more attuned to national politics, was ahead of its provincial counterparts in complying with the government's wishes. By the 1870s, its *comptes rendus* contained no mention of a religious marriage requirement.[22] Still, in 1876 the city of Paris discontinued its 10,000 FF subvention. François Gille, secretary-treasurer and defender of the society, professed ignorance as to why the municipal government would withdraw its support from a charity that had enjoyed the support of diverse regimes over the years; however, he noted that "the charitable institutions from which the municipal council withdrew its subsidies all had, they say, a religious character, and that was the deciding factor in their elimination from the city budget."[23]

An even crueler blow followed in 1882 when the minister of the interior proposed the repeal of article 6 of the decree of October 31, 1814, which had guaranteed a subvention of 100,000 FF to maternal societies throughout France, with 40,000 FF reserved for the Paris society.[24] While this sum had increased over the years, the minimum was guaranteed by law. The minister of the interior justified abrogation of the law by noting that the number of maternal charities throughout France had increased dramatically, and it was unfair to reserve such a large proportion of the subsidy for the Paris society. Now Paris was dependent upon the grace of the government for any subvention at all. While the society managed, through intense lobbying, to extract 13,000 FF from the ministry in 1883, this marked the end of reliably generous support by the central government.[25]

By the 1890s, it was clear that the Society for Maternal Charity had lost the preeminence it had claimed as the doyenne of charitable associations for women and children. The Interior Ministry and prefects now grouped it with crèches and similar associations when making inquiries about local charities. In fact, the inspector of the Services des Enfants Assistés des Établissements de Bienfaisance et de la Protection du Premier Âge in the Department of the Rhône noted in a letter to the prefect in 1892 that a state subvention to local crèches would be a better investment than a subsidy for the Society for Maternal Charity.[26] This does not mean that it lost all support. Donations to the Paris society continued to increase after 1871; while it spent 85,295 FF in assistance to mothers in 1871, by 1880 the society was able to spend 138,605 FF.[27] However, maternal societies could no longer assume that the elevated social position of their members, and their long record of service was sufficient. There was much about their traditional goals and values, their emphasis on moral behavior, the advancing age of many members, and even the aristocratic titles that still dominated membership lists that suggested these societies were simply becoming outmoded.[28] If they wished to remain relevant, they needed to provide services that mothers demanded and that the government would support.

Consequently, the Paris Society for Maternal Charity continued to expand the nature of its services into the twentieth century in an effort to keep up-to-date. The *compte rendu* of 1925 provided a Tableau des Consultations de Nourrissons (baby clinics) and made note of a Commission des Berceaux (cradles) and a Commission d'Hygiène Maternelle, both offshoots (*filiales*) of the Society for Maternal Charity. The account also noted their sponsorship of a Maison Maternelle, a Maison de l'Enfance and a Maison de Petit. By the early 1930s they had added prenatal consultations, consultations on anti-venereal prophylaxis, and an x-ray center.[29] As they had once worked with religious orders to provide assistance, the members of the Paris society now worked closely with the nurses at the Caisses de Compensation; one nurse, in a letter read to the general meeting of the Society in 1925, applauded the "aide morale" of the *dames visiteuses* and noted how much more responsible mothers were about attending consultations in areas with a maternal society.[30]

These new services reflect that the goals of the society had shifted, at least in emphasis, the result of long-term social, economic, cultural, and demographic changes in France. The Society for Maternal Charity had always sought "the preservation of children," but by the late nineteenth and early twentieth centuries, this meant something different than it had in 1788. Child abandonment, the raison d'être for the society's creation, had become much less of a concern since the late 1860s; however, child health and welfare, as well as encouraging large families, drew increasing attention under the Third Republic and beyond.[31] Reducing infant mortality had always been a goal of the society; children raised by their mothers had a much better chance of survival than those abandoned to a foundling hospice. But Dominique Banquey, in a study of Bordeaux's society from 1865 through 1895, notes that "in the period under study, the Society for Maternal Charity focused more than it ever had on reducing infant mortality," in ways beyond simply the prevention of abandonment.[32] François Gille's account bears this out; over time, he increasingly emphasized the success of the Paris society in lowering infant mortality.[33] Maternal societies and the government still focused on mothers as the moral center of the orderly family; good mothers would ensure healthy babies. But now more tools—and tutelage—were available to assist mothers in their efforts to raise their children successfully.[34] And while mothers with at least three children had always received preference, the society's explicit goal was now "to assist large families," and furthermore, to encourage parents to have large families—this was, in fact, the purpose of all the additional services that the society offered.[35]

This emphasis only increased after World War I. Ideally, *présidente* de Beauverger stated in a *rapport moral*, every family should have at least four children: "Large families are indispensable if France wants to maintain her position as a great nation."[36] This espousal of governmental policies ensured that the society would continue to enjoy official support—a representative of the Ministre du Travail, de l'Hygiène et de l'Assistance, et de la Prévoyance Sociale presided over their meetings in the 1920s and offered fulsome praise for their efforts. In 1923 the Paris Municipal Council began to provide them with a subvention of 18,000 FF, which they used to distribute milk. However, the government's financial support was significantly smaller proportionally than it had been in earlier years. Out of more than 1,000,000 FF in revenues, the national government provided 50,000 FF in 1925, a sum that was raised to 82,500 FF in 1926.[37] The national government now touted the society's traditional support for large families, maternal breast feeding, and strengthening the bond between mother and child as official policy. Good mothers and strong families meant a strong nation.[38] The methods of maternal societies supported the goals of the central government, and as a result, they continued to receive support for their mission, as long as they adhered to government rules on religion. But they were no longer the leading providers of services to mothers; their methods were now largely duplicated by others charities and by public assistance.[39]

The Society for Maternal Charity was one of the most important charities in nineteenth-century France, both in the number of poor it touched and in the path it provided to the future provision of family assistance. It paved the way for the social-welfare state in France, specifically social welfare for families, and both charitable associations and public assistance programs would use its methods. Catherine Rollet-Echalier, in her study of the evolution of assistance for children, explicitly makes that connection; under the Third Republic, the *bureaux de bienfaisance* as well as public assistance functioned in the same manner as maternal societies had for nearly one hundred years: "home visit and interview, report, decision on the amount, the nature, the duration of aid, etc."[40] Susan Grogan sees these "visiting ladies" as the precursors of the state-employed *inspectrice* of the twentieth century, while Linda L. Clark's work suggests that women's volunteer work in positions of "maternal authority" eventually paved the way for paid careers in social welfare.[41] Certainly, the "lady patrons" or "lady visitors," called upon to help watch over assisted children under the Third Republic, sound like the maternal societies' *dames visiteuses*—even bearing the same name.[42]

But the maternal society's founders and members also led the way in searching for the best means to keep families together and to preserve the life and health of children. Dominique Banquey makes this case: "In practical terms, it certainly functioned effectively, however, in a limited sense, because of its nature as a private charity: short-term assistance, restricted to the category of disadvantaged children, kept in their homes, firm surveillance by unqualified personnel." However, he goes on to say, "In theoretical terms, one can in contrast recognize that it had enormous importance. It had understood that the diminution of infant morbidity and mortality begins with simple preventive measures, such as maternal breast feeding, hygiene, vaccination, measures to apply in the first instant to children at high risk."[43] Mothers—domesticated mothers who cared properly for their children, and who created stables homes—were the key to ensuring that children received these essential services. Maternal charities sought to teach mothers these skills and about the needs of their children, and to provide the assistance that made these benefits possible. But, as Banquey underlines, eventually the state recognized that the protection of children was too important a task to be left in the hands of charitable organizations, especially ones espousing rigid moral requirements. Child protection had to come under the care of the state and a wide panoply of secular associations.[44]

But how best to handle the complicated issue of assistance to needy mothers and their children remained, and remains, a fraught issue. It may seem surprising that as the Third Republic became increasing secular, indeed anticlerical, it continued to provide any support to the Society for Maternal Charity, whose philosophy and moral stance now stood in opposition to its own. In fact, the government did not completely cut off subsidies to maternal societies maintaining religious requirements until the 1890s. Perhaps it was because these charities had performed an important role throughout the century in allowing the French government to sidestep a question that had never been resolved since the heady days of the French Revolution: did the poor, even the deserving poor, have a *right* to assistance? Did the state have an obligation to care for those who could not care for themselves?[45] Moralists had heatedly debated this question ever since the Directory quietly abandoned the promise of the Comité de Mendicité and the Convention to provide subsistence to those who could not support themselves. The state was reluctant to assume the obligation of universal care, especially while grappling with the intense problems of poverty, which were complicated by the onset of industrialization. Here, associations—especially those whose public utility was recognized, and who, for the most part, shared the state's vision of family life—could play a crucial role. By funneling money to organizations like the Society for Maternal Charity—a charity whose goals garnered almost universal sympathy throughout most of the century—the government could alleviate some poverty, and especially its concomitant problems of child abandonment and high infant mortality, without significantly increasing its own responsibilities and obligations.[46] The centralizing tendencies of the government led the ministers of the interior to exert pressure on these purportedly independent charities to control their goals and activities, pressure that the *dames administrantes* sometimes resisted. However, the influences worked in two directions. Alisa Klaus argues that in France, as in other Western countries, women's voluntary associations were a key force in the transition from private charity to a public welfare system, while Catherine Rollet-Echalier sees a direct link between maternal charities and future laws on assistance to large families.[47] However one might feel about the religious and moralizing tendencies of many of these charitable ladies, it is hard not to be impressed by the herculean task they took on, intervening to help mothers and save children through their personal assistance, as well their efforts to cajole and shame state and local authorities into more generous subsidies. Their genuine sympathy for these families speaks to us from the pages of their accounts and correspondence; their moral judgments on single mothers and disorderly poor families sometimes seem less harsh than those of today's politicians. And their emphasis on the benefits of breast feeding and maternal bonding sound more compelling to us today than it might have to their critics in the late nineteenth century.

Jane Jenson has argued that the depopulation crisis and the social doctrines of solidarism in France created a context in which state policies to accommodate women's work and maternity could emerge, even while French women gained comparatively few citizenship rights, not receiving the right to vote until 1944.[48] However, the tradition of the very specific social agenda of the Society for Maternal Charity, with an emphasis on motherhood and children, also helped to set the tone for both protective legislation and the development of welfare services under the Third Republic, as well as more feminist demands for greater rights and protections for women as mothers.[49] The legislation passed under the Third Republic tended to be narrow in scope. It focused on the welfare of the child, and consequently on the needs of the mother.[50] As Rachel Fuchs notes, "The relatively uncontroversial idea of saving babies' lives became the linchpin of the social welfare programs developed in late nineteenth-century France."[51] Welfare programs supported by legislators like Paul Strauss and eventually adopted were often quite similar in method and philosophy to those pioneered by maternal-society members.[52] While most historians of nineteenth-century charitable organizations mention the Society for Maternal Charity as one of the most important French women's philanthropic groups, they have not given due weight to its influence and to the continuity in the ideology and methods of assistance to poor women and children from the Old Regime through the Third Republic. The political significance of these charitable associations is clear.

The methods and ideology of maternal societies were not, of course, adopted wholesale by the French government. Debates over legislation both before and during the Third Republic reflected the same tensions that the *dames administrantes* were forced to consider: the emotional and physical needs of the child versus the economic needs of the family; the dependence of both the family and society at large on the labor-force contribution of women; and the domestic image of women and mothers versus the reality of most women's lives. These questions emerged in all industrial nations over the course of the past two centuries as states and voluntary associations grappled with how best to manage the problem of poverty among mothers and children. Different states have experimented with different solutions based on the specific cultural context, the nature of voluntary associations within the country, and the willingness of the state to provide direct assistance. However, no country has achieved a completely satisfactory solution to the problem of familial poverty. The debates linger today, reflecting the intractable nature of these problems; the structural problems are too intense, and the conflicts over values and choices too strong. The history of the Society for Maternal Charity outlines one effort to alleviate poverty by strengthening families; while its direct influence eventually waned, its methods and goals helped to shape twentieth-century policies on family assistance.

# Notes

## Introduction: Maternal Societies in the Nineteenth Century

1. Archives Départementales du Rhône (ADR) 3X 1849, *Compte rendu présenté aux dames composant la Société de Charité Maternelle de Lyon, année 1846* (Lyon: Imprimerie d'H. Brunet, Fonvielle et Cie, 1847), 4. Unless otherwise indicated, all translations in this volume are my own.

2. The titles and functions of the various female members of the society would change over time and differed depending on the location. In most cities the *dames administrantes* were those on the conseil d'administration; the *dames visiteuses* or the *dames associées* visited and delivered resources to the families. Under the Second Empire, a category of *dames protectrices,* charged with fund-raising, would emerge in Paris. These terms translate clumsily into English and have been left in the original French.

3. By the 1840s, Lyon's Hospice de la Charité was relatively lenient about letting parents reclaim abandoned children, often asking for only a token sum to compensate for the cost of caring for the child. See Janet Ruth Potash, "The Foundling Problem in France: 1800–1869: Child Abandonment in Lille and Lyon," PhD diss., Yale University, 1979, 201–2.

4. According to a report by the Congrès National d'Assistance Publique et de Bienfaisance Privée, held in Bordeaux in 1903. See *IIIe Congrès national d'assistance publique et de bienfaisance privée. Bordeaux: 1er au 7 juin 1903.* 3 vols. (Bordeaux: Imprimerie G. Gounouilhou, 1904), 1:14.

5. Linda K. Kerber's "Separate Spheres, Female Worlds, Woman's Place: The Rhetoric of Women's History," *Journal of American History* 75:1 (June 1988): 9–39, was one of the first to do so. In a more recent article, Leonore Davidoff discusses the slipperiness of public/private when placed in opposition to each other, while still arguing that the concept is a useful one. "Gender and the 'Great Divide': Public and Private in British Gender History," *Journal of Women's History* 15:1 (Spring 2003): 11–27.

6. See Katherine A. Lynch, "The Family and the History of Public Life," *Journal of Interdisciplinary History* 24: 4 (Spring 1994): 665–84.

7. The total *recettes* for 1846 were 25,849.48 FF, but that included a balance of 5,440.48 FF from the previous year. ADR 3X 1849, *Compte rendu*, 1846, 5.

8. I have chosen to translate the charity's name as "Society for Maternal Charity" rather than "Society of Maternal Charity" to avoid awkward repetitiveness, since it is frequently followed by "of Bordeaux," "of Paris," or "of Lyon."

9. Archives Nationales (hereafter AN) F[15] 2565, *Compte rendu à S.M. l'Impératrice-Reine et Régente, Protectrice et Présidente de la Société de la charité maternelle, par S.A. Em. le Secrétaire général et S.Ex. le Trésorier général de la situation de la Société dans tout l'empire, et de l'Emploi de ses fonds; et par les Dames du Conseil d'Administration de Paris, des opérations de ce conseil* (Paris: Imprimerie Impériale, 1813). See also the *Almanach royal et national pour l'an M DCCC XXXI* (Paris: Chez Guyot et Scribe, 1831), 886; *Almanach impérial pour M DCCC LIII* (Paris: Chez Guyot et Scribe, 1853), 1081; *Almanach impérial pour M DCCC LXII* (Paris: Chez Guyot et Scribe, 1862); Evelyne Lejeune-Resnick, *Femmes et associations (1830/1880): vraies démocrates ou dames patronnesses?* (Paris: Publisud, 1991), 175; and Alisa Klaus, "Women's Organizations and the Infant Health Movement in France and the United States, 1890–1920," in *Lady Bountiful Revisited: Women, Philanthropy, and Power,* ed. Kathleen D. McCarthy (New Brunswick, N.J.: Rutgers University Press, 1990), 167. Catherine Rollet-Echalier notes that these societies multiplied especially under the Second Empire. *La politique à l'égard de la petite enfance sous la IIIe République* (Paris: Presses Universitaires de France, 1990), 9–10.

10. "Womanly Duties: Maternalist Politics and the Origins of the Welfare States in France, Germany, Great Britain, and the United States, 1880–1920," *American Historical Review* 95:4 (October 1990): 1079.

11. "Women's Voluntary Associations: From Charity to Reform," in *Lady Bountiful Revisited,* 45.

12. Catherine Duprat indicates that in the first half of the nineteenth century, subsidies never constituted less than 65 percent of the total revenues of the Paris branch of the Society for Maternal Charity. *Usage et pratiques de la philanthropie: pauvreté, action sociale et lien social, à Paris, au cours du premier XIXe siècle,* 2 vols. (Paris: Association pour l'Étude de l'Histoire de la Sécurité Sociale, 1996–97), 2:622.

13. Quoted in Duprat, *Usage et pratiques,* 2:615.

14. Joseph-Marie de Gérando, *De la bienfaisance publique,* 4 vols. (Paris: Jule Renouard et Cie, 1839), 2:7.

15. Already under the Ancien Régime, charities like the Société Philanthropique had preceded the Society for Maternal Charity. Under the Restoration government, the July Monarchy, and the Second Empire, voluntary associations similar in organization to the Society for Maternal Charity continued to appear. See Catherine Duprat, *"Pour l'amour de l'humanité": le temps des philanthropes: la philanthropie parisienne des Lumières à la monarchie de Juillet* (Paris: Éditions du C.T.H.S., 1993), and *Usages et pratiques.* Duprat points out that female voluntary associations in particular tended to follow the model of the Society for Maternal Charity, in "Le silence des femmes: associations féminines du premier XIXe siècle," in *Femmes dans la cité, 1815–1871,* ed. Alain Corbin, Jacqueline Lalouette, and Michèle Riot-Sarcey (Grâne: Créaphis, 1997), 85.

16. Alisa Klaus, among others, testifies to the expansion of welfare provided in this manner under the Third Republic in *Every Child a Lion: The Origins of Maternal and Infant Health Policy in the United States and France* (Ithaca, N.Y.: Cornell University Press, 1993), 129–35, and "Depopulation and Race Suicide: Maternalism and Pronatalist Ideologies in France and the United States," in *Mothers of a New World: Maternalist Politics and the Origins of Welfare States,* ed. Seth Koven and Sonya Michel (New York: Routledge, 1993), 196–98. See also Rollet-Echalier, *La politique à l'égard de la petite enfance,* 247.

17. See Rachel G. Fuchs, "The Right to Life: Paul Strauss and the Politics of Motherhood," in *Gender and the Politics of Social Reform in France, 1870–1914,* ed. Elinor Accampo, Rachel G. Fuchs, and Mary Lynn Stewart (Baltimore: Johns Hopkins University Press, 1995), 82–105; and Rollet-Echalier, *La politique à l'égard de la petite enfance,* part 2.

18. Well into the twentieth century, a representative of the Ministre du Travail, de l'Hygiène, de l'Assistance, et de la Prévoyance Sociale presided at the annual meetings of the Society for Maternal Charity of Paris, offering both kind words and limited financial support. See Archives de l'Assistance Publique (AAP 4771) for examples of the society's *comptes rendus* for the years 1925, 1926, and 1933.

19. Janet Ruth Potash, in her study of the foundling problem in nineteenth-century France, concurs: "The obvious motive for limiting the number of foundlings was financial." "The Foundling Problem in France," 182.

20. Ibid., 294. For an excellent study of French policy concerning child abandonment, see Rachel G. Fuchs, *Abandoned Children: Foundlings and Child Welfare in Nineteenth-Century France* (Albany: State University of New York Press, 1984).

21. For more on this, see George D. Sussman, *Selling Mother's Milk: The Wetnursing Business in France, 1715–1914* (Chicago: University of Illinois Press, 1982), chap. 7; and Joshua Cole, *The Power of Large Numbers: Population, Politics and Gender in Nineteenth-Century France* (Ithaca, N.Y.: Cornell University Press, 2000), esp. chap. 5. Both discuss the Roussel Law of 1874; see also Émile Chevalier, *L'assistance dans le campagne: indigence, prévoyance, assistance* (Paris: Librairie Nouvelle de Droit et de Jurisprudence, 1889), 259–63.

22. Paul Strauss argues that it was under the direct influence of Rousseau that Madame de Fougeret founded the Society for Maternal Charity in 1788. *L'enfance malheureuse* (Paris: Bibliothèque-Charpentier, 1896), 167–68.

23. William M. Reddy, *The Navigation of Feeling: A Framework for the History of Emotions* (New York: Cambridge University Press, 2001), 146.

24. See, for example, Anne Vincent-Buffault, *The History of Tears: Sensibility and Sentimentality in France,* trans. Teresa Bridgeman (New York: St. Martin's Press, 1991); Sarah Maza, *Private Lives and Public Affairs: The Causes Célèbres of Prerevolutionary France* (Berkeley: University of California Press, 1993), especially 84–85; David Denby, *Sentimental Narrative and the Social Order in France, 1760–1820* (Cambridge: Cambridge University Press, 1994); G. J. Barker-Benfield, *The Culture of Sensibility: Sex and Society in Eighteenth-Century Britain* (Chicago: University of Chicago Press, 1992).

25. Nicole Fermon, *Domesticating Passions: Rousseau, Woman and Nation* (Hanover, N. H.: Wesleyan University Press, 1997); Carol Blum, *Rousseau and the Republic of Virtue: The Language of Politics in the French Revolution* (Ithaca, N.Y.: Cornell University Press, 1986).

26. The term "the civilizing process" comes from Norbert Elias's seminal work *Über*

*den Prozess der Zivilisation* (Basel: Haus zum Falken, 1939). It appeared in English as *The Civilizing Process,* trans. Edmund Jephcott (New York: Urizen Books, 1978). Barbara H. Rosenwein has outlined the influence of Elias's model on the study of emotions in history in several important pieces; see especially pages 237–40 in the conclusion of her edited volume *Anger's Past: The Social Uses of an Emotion in the Middle Ages* (Ithaca, N.Y.: Cornell University Press, 1998) and "Worrying about Emotions in History," *American Historical Review* 107:3 (June 2002): 821–45. For an example of this influence, see the introduction to *The Soft Underbelly of Reason: The Passions in the Seventeenth Century,* ed. Stephen Gaukroger (London: Routledge, 1998), 1–14. Peter N. Stearns has been one of the most important historians of the history of emotions and coined the term *emotionology* in a article written with Carol Z. Stearns, "Emotionology: Clarifying the History of Emotions and Emotional Standards," *American Historical Review* 90:4 (October 1985): 813–36. According to Stearns and Stearns, *emotionology* defines "the attitudes or standards that a society, or a definable group within a society, maintains toward basic emotions and their appropriate expression; ways that institutions reflect and encourage these attitudes in human conduct, e.g., courtship practices as expressing the valuation affect in marriage, or personnel workshops as reflecting the valuation of anger in job relationships."

27. Reddy defines *emotive* as "A type of speech act different from both performative and constative utterances, which both describes (like constative utterances) and changes (like performatives) the world, because emotional expression has an exploratory and self-altering effect on the activated material of emotion." *The Navigation of Feeling,* 128. For Reddy's analysis of emotives, and their power to build, change, and intensify feelings, see *The Navigation of Feeling,* 103–11, and "Against Constructionism: The Historical Ethnography of Emotions," *Current Anthropology* 38:3 (June 1997): 327–40.

28. There is an extensive literature on the "origins" of maternal love; see Élisabeth Badinter, *Mother Love, Myth and Reality: Motherhood in Modern History* (New York: Macmillan, 1981); Yvonne Knibiehler and Catherine Fouquet, *Histoire des mères du moyen âge à nos jours* (Paris: Montalba, 1977); Lawrence Stone, *The Family, Sex and Marriage in England, 1500–1800* (New York: Harper and Row, 1979), 267–99; and Bonnie G. Smith, *Ladies of the Leisure Class: The Bourgeoises of Northern France in the Nineteenth Century* (Princeton, N.J.: Princeton University Press, 1981), just to name a few.

29. Philippe Ariès, in his influential *Centuries of Childhood: A Social History of Family Life,* trans. Robert Baldick (New York: Vintage Books, 1962), suggested as much and fostered much subsequent debate.

30. Badinter, *Mother Love,* 117–19.

31. Mary Lynn Stewart discusses the high participation of French women in the labor force, especially as compared to married British women. *Women, Work, and the French State: Labour Protection and Social Patriarchy, 1879–1919* (Kingston: McGill–Queen's University Press, 1989), 20–25. See also Joan W. Scott and Louise A. Tilly, "Women's Work and the Family in Nineteenth-Century Europe," *Comparative Studies in Society and History* 17:1 (January 1975): 36–64; Marilyn J. Boxer, "Women in Industrial Homework: The Flowermakers of Paris in the Belle Epoque," *French Historical Studies* 12:3 (Spring 1982): 403. In her study of Oneida County, New York, Mary P. Ryan found that in 1855, 4.3 percent of native-born and 1.4 percent of foreign-born wives worked for pay, while in 1865, 6.0 percent and 3.8 percent did so, respectively. *Cradle of the Middle Class: The Family*

in *Oneida County, New York, 1790–1865* (Cambridge: Cambridge University Press, 1981), 172, 271.

32. See Philip Nord, "The Welfare State in France, 1870–1914," *French Historical Studies* 18:3 (Spring 1994): 830–32; Stewart, *Women, Work, and the French State*, 43–44, 57, 67–68. In many cases, the women themselves preferred to work at home, which made it easier to balance competing obligations; see Boxer, "Women in Industrial Homework," 416. Rachel G. Fuchs discusses how difficult it was for mothers to care for a baby at home and work for wages in *Poor and Pregnant in Paris: Strategies for Survival in the Nineteenth Century* (New Brunswick, N.J.: Rutgers University Press, 1992), 164–65. On the efforts of Limoges's maternal society to sponsor a crèche, see chap. 5 of this volume.

33. See, for example, Strauss, *L'enfance malheureuse*, 201–2, as well as chap. 5 and Epilogue of this volume.

34. June K. Burton speculates about this issue in *Napoleon and the Woman Question: Discourses of the Other Sex in French Education, Medicine, and Medical Law, 1799–1815* (Lubbock: Texas Tech University Press, 2007), 202–3.

35. For background information on and the documents resulting from the work of the Comité de Mendicité, see *Procès-verbaux et rapports du Comité de Mendicité de la Constituante, 1790–1791*, ed. Camille Bloch and Alexandre Tuetey (Paris: Imprimerie Nationale, 1911).

36. Contemporary works include, among many others, Ferdinand Béchard, *De l'état du paupérisme en France et des moyens d'y remédier* (Paris: Librairie de Charles Douniol, 1853); Joseph-Marie de Gérando, *De la bienfaisance publique*; Honoré-Antoine Frégier, *Des classes dangereuses de la population dans les grandes villes et des moyens de les rendre meilleures*, 2 vols. (Paris: J.-B. Baillière, 1840); Jules Siegfried, *Quelques mots sur la misère; son histoire, ses causes, ses remèdes* (Havre: Librairie de J. Poinsignon, 1877); and a slightly later work, Paul Strauss, *Assistance sociale: pauvres et mendiants* (Paris: Félix Alcan, 1901). Rachel Fuchs examines the arguments of many of these individuals, as well as others, in chap. 2 of *Poor and Pregnant in Paris*.

37. For example, Baron A. De Watteville, *Statistique des établissements de bienfaisance: rapport à son excellence le Ministre de l'Intérieur sur l'administration des bureaux de bienfaisance et sur la situation du paupérisme en France* (Paris: Imprimerie Impériale, 1854); Commission d'Enquête sur le Service des Enfants Assistés, *Enfants assistés: enquête générale ouverte en 1860, dans les 86 départements de l'empire* (Paris: Imprimerie Impériale, 1862); Ministère de l'Intérieur, rapport au Ministre sur la situation des bureaux de bienfaisance en 1871 par M. Paul Bucquet, *Enquête sur les bureaux de bienfaisance* (Paris: Imprimerie Nationale, 1874). Louis Chevalier considers many of these reports, as well as those of Villeneuve-Bargemont, Villermé, and Buret, in his *Classes laborieuses et classes dangereuses à Paris pendant la première moitié du XIXe siècle* (Paris: Plon, 1958), trans. Frank Jellinek as *Laboring Classes and Dangerous Classes in Paris During the First Half of the Nineteenth Century* (New York: H. Fertig, 1973); see also Cole, *The Power of Large Numbers*, esp. chap. 5.

38. See *Exposition universelle de 1889: Congrès international d'assistance*, tenu du 28 juillet au 4 août 1889, 2 vols. Bibliothèque des *Annales économiques* (Paris: G. Rongier et Cie, 1889); and Congrès National d'Assistance Publique et de Bienfaisance Privée, Bordeaux, 1903, *IIIe Congrès national d'assistance publique et de bienfaisance privée*. Bordeaux: 1er au

7 juin 1903 (Bordeaux: G. Gounouilhou, 1905). *La Revue Philanthropique,* no. 39, July 10, 1900, covers the display on "Assistance publique et bienfaisance privée" at the Exposition of 1900. See also *La Revue Philanthropique,* no. 61, May 10, 1902; no. 68, December 10, 1902; no. 75, July 10, 1903.

39. Introduction to *Women, Philanthropy and Civil Society,* ed. Kathleen D. McCarthy (Bloomington: Indiana University Press, 2001), 2; Koven and Michel, "Womanly Duties," 1,079–80, 1,093.

40. Klaus, "Women's Organizations and the Infant Health Movement," 167. Stuart Woolf argues that, from the time the society was appropriated by the Napoleonic court, it became an appendage of the imperial administration. See "The Société de Charité Maternelle, 1788–1815," in *Medicine and Charity before the Welfare State,* ed. Jonathan Barry and Colin Jones (London: Routledge, 1991), 109. Susan Grogan underlines the fact that the state's "reliance on women's voluntary work cannot be overlooked." "Philanthropic Women and the State: The Société de Charité Maternelle in Avignon, 1802–1917," *French History* 14:3 (2000): 307n79. I discuss this issue in "Maternal Societies in France: Private Charity before the Welfare State," *Journal of Women's History* 17:1 (2005): 87–111.

41. "The French Revolution and the 'New' Elite, 1800–1850," in *The American and European Revolutions, 1776–1848,* ed. J. Perlenski (Iowa City: University of Iowa Press, 1980), 189.

42. Frances Gouda, *Poverty and Political Culture: The Rhetoric of Social Welfare in the Netherlands and France, 1815–1854* (Lanham, Md.: Rowman and Littlefield, 1995), 5.

43. Susan Grogan makes a similar point in "Philanthropic Women and the State," 319, as do Jean-Pierre Chaline, "Sociabilité féminine et 'maternalisme': les sociétés de charité maternelle au XIXe siècle," in *Femmes dans la cité,* 17; and Sarah A. Curtis, "Charitable Ladies: Gender, Class and Religion in Nineteenth-Century Paris," *Past and Present* 177 (November 2002): 121–56. See also Adams, "Maternal Societies in France."

44. Archives Municipales de Lyon (AML) 111 WP 051, letter from the Interior Ministry, Division du Secrétariat, to the prefect of the Rhône, March 11, 1867.

45. On the development of civil society, see Philip Nord's introduction to *The Republican Moment: Struggles for Democracy in Nineteenth-Century France* (Cambridge, Mass.: Harvard University Press, 1995), 1–14; as well as his introduction to *Civil Society before Democracy: Lessons from Nineteenth-Century Europe,* ed. Nancy Bermeo and Philip Nord (Lanham, Md.: Rowman and Littlefield, 2000), xiii–xxxiii.

46. William J. Novak, "The American Law of Association: The Legal-Political Construction of Civil Society," *Studies in American Political Development* 15 (Fall 2001): 163.

47. Karen M. Offen notes that "'Civil society' was, historically speaking, an area fundamentally marked by gender struggles; indeed campaigns to include—or exclude—women are central to understanding its history and should be central to its definition." "Feminists Campaign in 'Public Space': Civil Society, Gender Justice, and the History of European Feminisms," in *Civil Society and Gender Justice: Historical and Comparative Perspectives,* ed. Karen Hagemann, Sonya Michel, and Gunilla Budde (New York: Berghahn, 2008), 98.

48. Lynch, "The Family and the History of Public Life," 676–78.

49. On women's efforts to claim rights as women, see Karen M. Offen, "Depopulation, Nationalism, and Feminism in Fin-de-Siècle France," *American Historical Review* 89:3 (June 1984): 648–76.

50. *Creating the Welfare State in France, 1880–1940* (Montreal: McGill–Queen's University Press, 2003), 27.

51. Steven M. Beaudouin, "'A Neutral Terrain': Public Assistance, Private Charity, and the State in Third Republic Bordeaux, 1870–1914," PhD diss., Carnegie Mellon University, May 1996.

52. Smith, *Creating the Welfare State,* 33.

53. Françoise Bayard and Pierre Cayez, *Histoire de Lyon: du XVIe siècle à nos jours* (Le Coteau: Horvath, n.d.), 245. The population sank to 88,662 by year 8, before beginning its recovery under Napoleon.

54. Robert J. Bezucha, *The Lyon Uprising of 1834: Social and Political Conflict in the Early July Monarchy* (Cambridge, Mass.: Harvard University Press, 1974), 11–13.

55. On Lyonnais prosperity, see Bayard and Cayez, *Histoire de Lyon,* 245–47.

56. For a particularly useful examination of class conflict and revolt in Lyon, see Bezucha, *The Lyon Uprising.*

57. Ibid., 25.

58. On the evolution of Lyon's system of poor relief, see Timothy B. Smith, "Public Assistance and Labor Supply in Nineteenth-Century Lyon," *Journal of Modern History* 68:1 (March 1996): 1–30.

59. Potash, "The Foundling Problem in France," 140.

60. Ibid., 7; Denise Z. Davidson, *France after Revolution: Urban Life, Gender, and the New Social Order* (Cambridge, Mass.: Harvard University Press, 2007), 144–50.

61. A table prepared in 1863 listed nearly 60 charitable institutions in the Department of the Rhône, most of them in Lyon. At this time, the Society for Maternal Charity of Lyon (which appeared first on the list) counted 344 *dames sociétaires* among its members; some of the other charitable organizations, for example, the Société pour le Patronage des Jeunes Filles, listed 2,500 *dames sociétaires.* AML 744 WP 074, "Tableau des oeuvres particulières de bienfaisance du département du Rhône, certifié par Monsieur le Sénateur chargé de lad. du département du Rhône: Lyon, 14 January 1863."

62. ADR 3X 1848, "Société de Charité Maternelle de Lyon: allocations et subventions, 1812–1895," undated printed document.

63. Bibliothèque municipale de Lyon (BML), Fonds Coste 113277, "Institut de Bienfaisance Maternelle"; José Rivert, *Les oeuvres de charité et les établissements d'enseignement libre de 1789 à 1945. Histoire, régime juridique actuel, réalisations Lyonnaises* (Lyon: Librairie Catholique Emmanuel Vitte, 1945), 47–50.

64. Potash, "The Foundling Problem in France," 5.

65. Mary Lynn Stewart-McDougall, *The Artisan Republic: Revolution, Reaction and Resistance in Lyon, 1848–1851* (Kingston: McGill–Queen's University Press, 1984), 4–5.

66. ADR 3X 1850, Société de la Charité Maternelle de Lyon, *Rapport présenté aux dames composant la Société de la Charité Maternelle, année 1826,* 7; 3X 1848, letter from the conseil d'administration of the Société de la Charité Maternelle de Lyon to the mayor of the Croix-Rousse, February 6, 1817; 3X 1849, letter from the *présidente* of the Société de la Charité Maternelle de Lyon to the mayor of the Croix-Rousse, December 18, 1848; list of mothers assisted by Lyon's maternal society in Croix-Rousse, 1848. On December 9, 1848, the treasurer of the Société de Charité Maternelle of Lyon sent out letters to the mayors of both the Croix-Rousse and Vaise, asking them to send the *mandats* for the

allocations they had promised to the maternal society for 1848. In 1852 the three suburbs were absorbed into the city of Lyon. Bayard and Cayez, *Histoire de Lyon,* 255.

67. Louis M. Greenberg, *Sisters of Liberty: Marseille, Lyon, Paris, and the Reaction to a Centralized State, 1868–1871* (Cambridge, Mass.: Harvard University Press, 1971), 215; Potash, "The Foundling Problem in France," 7.

68. Christine Adams, entry on "Bordeaux" in Jonathan Dewald, gen. ed., *Europe 1450– 1789: Encyclopedia of the Early Modern World,* 6 vols. (New York: Charles Scribner's Sons, 2003), 1:281–83; Beaudouin, "A Neutral Terrain," 35–36.

69. Steven M. Peterson, "The Social Origins of Royalist Political Violence in Directorial Bordeaux," *French History* 10:1 (1996): 56–85.

70. Camille Jullian, *Histoire de Bordeaux depuis les origines jusqu'en 1895* (Bordeaux: Feret et Fils, 1895), 715–22.

71. Ibid., 715–16.

72. Municipalité Bordelaise, ed., *Bordeaux, aperçu historique: sol, population, industrie, commerce administration,* vol. 3: *Administration* (Paris: Librairie Hachette et Cie/Bordeaux: Librairie Feret et Fils, 1892), 466.

73. Édouard Feret, *Statistique générale topographique, scientifique, administrative, in- dustrielle, commerciale, agricole, historique, archéologique, et biographique du département de la Gironde,* 3 vols. (Bordeaux: Feret et Fils and G. Masson/Emile Lechevalier, 1878–89), 1:320; Archives Municipales de Bordeaux 312 Q, 1881, "Conseil d'administration, assemblé générale des bienfaiteurs de la Société de Charité Maternelle de Bordeaux, rapport sur l'exercice 1880." On the Gradis family, see Charles Higounet, gen. ed., *Histoire de Bor- deaux,* 8 vols. Vol. 5, *Bordeaux au XVIIIe siècle,* ed. François-Georges Pariset (Bordeaux: Fédération Historique du Sud-Ouest, 1968), 348.

74. Much of the preceding information is from Steven Beaudouin's "A Neutral Terrain," 42–62.

75. Annie Flacassier, "La Société de Charité Maternelle de Bordeaux de 1805 à 1815," *105e Congrès, Comité d'Histoire de la Sécurité Sociale* (Caen: Comité d'Histoire de la Sécurité Sociale, 1980), 44–45.

76. Dominique Banquey, *La Société de Charité Maternelle de Bordeaux: un organisme de protection maternelle et infantile aux XIX siècle?* Thèse pour le doctorat en médecine, Thèse no. 282 (Bordeaux: A.C.E.M.B., 1976), 16. The other largest maternal societies were Paris, Lille, Lyon, and Rouen, depending on the factors considered. See Archives Dé- partementales de la Côte-d'Or (ADCO) 22 X G, article 3, *Circulaire* from the Interior Ministry, Secrétariat-général, 3e bureau, "Sociétés de Charité Maternelle, Rapportement annuel 1856."

77. André Jardin and André-Jean Tudesq, *Restoration and Reaction, 1815–1848,* trans. Elborg Forster (Cambridge: Cambridge University Press/Paris: Éditions de la Maison des Sciences de l'Homme, 1983), 255.

78. Raoul Busquet, *Histoire de Marseille* (Paris: Éditions Robert Laffont, 1945), 327.

79. Ibid., 354.

80. Greenberg, *Sisters of Liberty,* 9 and 27.

81. Raoul Busquet and Joseph Fournier, *La vie politique et administrative,* volume 5 of *Les Bouches-du-Rhône, encyclopédie départementale,* gen. ed. Paul Masson, part 2: *Le bilan*

*du XIXe siècle* (Paris: Librairie Honoré Champion/Marseille: Archives Départementales des Bouches-du-Rhône, 1929), 90.

82. Busquet, *Histoire de Marseille*, 328.

83. Ibid., 334. Augustin Fabre also stresses the disastrous effects of war and the interruption of trade on Marseille's economy, along with an epidemic that ravaged the city during the winter of 1812–13. Fabre, *Histoire des hôpitaux et des institutions de bienfaisance de Marseille*, 2 vols. (Marseille: Imprimerie et Lithographie de Jules Barile, 1854–55), 2:383.

84. Busquet, *Histoire de Marseille*, 341–42. On epidemics in Marseille, see Lt. de Crouzet, *Précis historique sur la Société de Bienfaisance et de Charité de la ville de Marseille* (Aix: A. Makaire, 1864), 46, 53; Fabre, *Histoire des hôpitaux*, 383; Busquet, 343. On more than one occasion the correspondence of Marseille's maternal society with the prefect of the Bouches-du-Rhône makes reference to the problems caused by recurrent outbreaks of cholera in the city. See, for example, Archives Départementales des Bouches-du-Rhône (ADBR) $X^2$ 26, letter of December 27, 1854.

85. William H. Sewell, *Structure and Mobility: The Men and Women of Marseille, 1820–1870* (Cambridge: Cambridge University Press/Paris: Éditions de la Maison des Sciences de l'Homme, 1985), 268–69.

86. Émile Camau, *Les institutions de bienfaisance, de charité, et de prévoyance à Marseille: guide de l'assistance* (Marseille: Agence de l'Assistance par le Travail, n.d.), 11. A "Supplément et modifications au règlement de la Société de Charité Maternelle de Marseille" specifies in article 10 that "Genovese women and other foreigners will not be admitted to different types of assistance except after ten years of residency in Marseille." ADBR $X^2$ 26, *Règlement pour la Société de Charité Maternelle de Marseille* (Marseille, 1844), 12. In contrast, the Paris Society for Maternal Charity, by the late 1860s, explicitly assisted women "without distinction of nationality or religion."

87. On the poverty of and discrimination against Italian immigrants, see Sewell, *Structure and Mobility*, 267–68.

88. In fact, one of the *dames administrantes* was given the specific task of caring discreetly for the *dames honteuses*. ADBR $X^2$ 26, *Règlement pour la Société de Charité Maternelle de Marseille*, 8. Comte Alban de Villeneuve-Bargemont, *Statistique du Département des Bouches-du-Rhône*, 4 vols. (Marseille: Chez Antoine Richard, 1826), 3:481. This had long been a tradition for Marseille's maternal society; the *compte rendu* for 1819 noted that the 403 families assisted "included 27 shamefaced families for whom assistance was larger." AN $F^{15}$ 2565, État des recettes et dépenses pour la Société de Charité Maternelle de Marseille pendant l'exercice 1819.

89. Jean-Pierre Bardet, *Rouen au XVIIe et XVIIIe siècles* (Paris: Société d'Édition d'Enseignement Supérieur, 1983), 375. These rural domestic-industry workers suffered enormously during periods of economic crisis; many elite women of Rouen declined the minister of the interior's invitation to subscribe to the Society for Maternal Charity in 1810–12 because they needed to help the poor living on their properties in the countryside surrounding Rouen. See Archives Départementales de la Seine-Maritime (ADSM) 3XP 217, letters to the prefect written in 1810 and 1812.

90. Jean-Pierre Chaline, *Les bourgeois de Rouen: une élite urbaine au XIXe siècle* (Paris:

Presses de la Fondation Nationale des Sciences Politiques, 1982), 307. See also his essay "Sociabilité féminine et 'maternalisme,'" 74.

91. ADSM 3XP 213, *Comptes de la Société Maternelle de Rouen pour l'exercice 1853, vérifiés et approuvés dans l'assemblée générale de la Société du janvier 1854.*

92. Yannick Marec, *Pauvres et philanthropes à Rouen au XIXe siècle* (Rouen: Recueils Pédagogiques d'Histoire Régionale, 1981), 9–11. Much of the following information on Rouen comes from Marec's essay.

93. Ibid., 43–47.

94. Ibid., 15.

95. Ibid., 17.

96. Ibid., 28.

97. Chaline, *Les bourgeois de Rouen,* 309.

98. The terminology is that of Robert Joseph Aldrich, "Modernization without Industrialization: The Case of Dijon and the Côte-d'Or," PhD diss., Brandeis University, Department of Comparative History, October 1979. Much of the following description of Dijon in the nineteenth century comes from his thesis, as well as from Pierre Lévêque, *La Bourgogne de Lamartine à nos jours* (Dijon: Éditions Universitaires de Dijon, 2006), esp. 119–50 and 279–83.

99. Between 1851 and 1911, Dijon grew from 32,253 inhabitants to 76,847. In contrast, the rest of the department, notably the rural areas, lost 94,847 during the same period. Jean Guichard, "Notes de démographie," *Dijon et la Côte-d'Or,* tome 3: 40e Congrès de l'Association Française pour l'Avancement des Sciences (Dijon, 1911): 279–88.

100. This continued to be the case into the twentieth century. In a confidential note, the commissaire central de Police, Dreyfus, reported to the prefect of the Côte-d'Or that the directing members of the Society for Maternal Charity of Dijon "can be assumed to belong to the reactionary element," although he did go on to note that "there are, among the *dames administrantes,* assigned to distribute assistance, and the lady patrons, [members of] all religious faiths." ADCO 22 X G, article 5, note from the commissaire central de police, Dreyfus, April 11, 1908.

101. ADCO 22 X G, articles 2–4. The Interior Ministry frequently chided the prefect for his inability to secure a departmental or municipal subsidy for the Society for Maternal Charity. See ADCO 22 X G article 3, correspondence from the minister of the interior to the prefect of the Côte-d'Or, especially 1862–75.

102. Lévêque, *La Bourgogne,* 149.

103. Ville de Dijon–Archives municipales, *Pauvreté, hygiène et santé à Dijon avant 1914* (Dijon, 1990), 13.

104. John Merriman, *The Red City: Limoges and the French Nineteenth Century* (New York: Oxford University Press, 1985), xiii–xiv. Much of the following information on Limoges is drawn from Merriman's account.

105. Henri Demany, *40 Maires pour Limoges: du rouge au point à la rose au coeur* (Limoges: Éditions de la Veytizou, 1989), 66–67.

106. See Archives Départementales de la Haute-Vienne (ADHV) 3X 15, *Comptes moraux.*

107. Paul Ducourtieux, *Histoire de Limoges* (Marseille: Laffitte Reprints, 1975; Réimpression de l'édition de Limoges, 1925), 253.

108. ADHV 3X 15, *Compte moral,* March 30, 1864.

109. Pascale Gourinal, "L'assistance aux enfants trouvés et abandonné à l'Hospice de Limoges, 1789–1850, " T.E.R. d'Histoire moderne présenté à l'U.F.R. des lettres et sciences humaines de Limoges, 1988, 24.

110. *Histoire du Limousin et de la Marche,* publié sous la direction de René Morichon, 3 vols. (Limoges: Éditions René Dessagne, 1972–76), 2:84n6.

111. Monique Lachtygier, "Tableau de la vie ouvrière à Limoges de 1804 à 1848," mémoire pour le Diplôme d'Études supérieures, Université de Poitiers, November 1958.

112. Merriman, *The Red City,* 21.

113. Olivier Faure, "Health Care Provision and Poor Relief in 19th Century Provincial France," in *Health Care and Poor Relief in 18th and 19th Century Northern Europe,* ed. Ole Peter Grell, Andrew Cunningham, and Robert Jütte (Aldershot, England: Ashgate, 2002), 313. Frances Gouda indicates that between 1833 and 1853, the number of people receiving *secours à domicile* in any given year ranged from about 700,000 to 1.2 million. If combined with those receiving institutional assistance in hospices and hôpitaux, 1.2–1.8 million received assistance yearly, between 3.5 and 5 percent of the national population, peaking sharply in the crisis years of 1846–47. *Poverty and Political Culture,* 76.

114. Davidson, *France after Revolution,* 187.

115. See Chapter 5. This does not suggest that government assistance supplanted private charity; until World War I, France's charitable institutions provided far more assistance than did public-assistance institutions. Smith, *Creating the Welfare State,* 18.

116. Smith, *Ladies of the Leisure Class.*

117. Fuchs, *Poor and Pregnant in Paris.*

118. See Michel Foucault, *An Introduction,* vol. 1 of *A History of Sexuality,* trans. Robert Hurley (New York: Vintage Books, 1990); and Jacques Donzelot, *The Policing of Families,* trans. Robert Hurley (New York: Random House/Pantheon Books, 1979).

119. For a particularly negative view of the elite charitable woman, see Lejeune-Resnick, *Femmes et associations.*

120. Davidson, *France after Revolution,* 146.

121. Klaus argues that French women were excluded from policy making because of centralized state structures and a tradition of social intervention; she notes that "The specific political conditions under which women organized for 'maternalist' goals in France prevented them from becoming a distinctive female political force," while Lejeune-Resnick sees *dames patronnesses* as simply reinforcing the political goals of men, and upholding the bourgeois social structure. Klaus, *Every Child a Lion,* 92; Lejeune-Resnick, *Femmes et associations,* 15, 19.

122. *Rousseau's Daughters: Domesticity, Education, and Autonomy in Modern France* (Durham: University of New Hampshire Press, 2008).

123. Jean L. Cohen and Andrew Arato, *Civil Society and Political Theory* (Cambridge, Mass.: MIT Press, 1992), ix., quoted in Lynch, "The Family and the History of Public Life," 674. Evelyne Diebolt also asserts that "participation in philanthropic organizations offered numerous women the possibility of participating in various civil and public activities. This made it possible for them to exercise a certain authority in social, economic, and political life in France." See "Women and Philanthropy in France from the Sixteenth to the Twentieth Centuries," in *Women, Philanthropy and Civil Society,* 29.

124. Lynch, "The Family and the History of Public Life," 675; Kathleen D. McCarthy, "Women and Political Culture," in *Charity, Philanthropy, and Civility in American History,* ed. Lawrence J. Friedman and Mark D. McGarvie (Cambridge: Cambridge University Press, 2003), 179–97.

125. Smith, *Ladies of the Leisure Class,*134, and chap. 6 for her analysis of the political implications of women's domestic and social charitable activities.

126. See Suzanne Desan's review article, "What's after Political Culture? Recent French Revolutionary Historiography," *French Historical Studies* 23:1 (2000): 170.

127. See Adams, "Maternal Societies in France."

128. Duprat's work, based on her *thèse* at Paris I, completed in 1991, was published in three volumes by the Association pour l'Étude de l'Histoire de la Sécurité Sociale: *Le temps des philanthropes,* and the two volumes of *Usage et pratiques.* While her study is impressively broad and detailed, she focuses exclusively on philanthropic activity in Paris.

129. The vast and very rich literature includes, among others, *Maternity and Gender Policies: Women and the Rise of the European Welfare States, 1880s–1950s,* ed. Gisela Bock and Pat Thane (London: Routledge, 1991); *Women, the State, and Welfare,* ed. Linda Gordon (Madison: University of Wisconsin Press, 1990), and her *Pitied but Not Entitled: Single Mothers and the History of Welfare, 1890–1935* (New York: Free Press, 1994); Koven and Michel, *Mothers of a New World,* as well as their article "Womanly Duties," and Kathryn Kish Sklar's "A Call for Comparisons" in the same issue of the *American Historical Review;* S. J. Kleinberg, *Widows and Orphans First: The Family Economy and Social Welfare Policy, 1880–1939* (Urbana: University of Illinois Press, 2005); Molly Ladd-Taylor, *Mother-Work: Women, Child Welfare, and the State, 1890–1930* (Urbana: University of Illinois Press, 1994); McCarthy, *Lady Bountiful Revisited* and *Women, Philanthropy, and Civil Society;* and Susan Pedersen, *Family, Dependence, and the Origins of the Welfare State: Britain and France, 1914–1915* (Cambridge: Cambridge University Press, 1993). The essays in Birgitta Jordansson and Tinne Vammen's edited anthology *Charitable Women: Philanthropic Welfare, 1780–1930* (Odense: Odense University Press, 1998) focus primarily on the late nineteenth and twentieth centuries, as well.

130. Accampo, Fuchs, and Stewart, eds., *Gender and the Politics of Social Reform;* Allan Mitchell, *The Divided Path: The German Influence on Social Reform in France after 1870* (Chapel Hill: University of North Carolina Press, 1991); Rollet-Echalier, *La politique à l'égard de la petite enfance;* Stewart, *Women, Work, and the French State.* Many of the essay collections cited in the previous note also treat the French case. Fuchs, *Poor and Pregnant in Paris* does cover most of the nineteenth century but focuses on the legislative agenda for single mothers post-1871.

131. Koven and Michel, "Womanly Duties," 1,099.

132. Lynch, "The Family and the History of Public Life," 676.

133. In *The Rise of Caring Power: Elizabeth Fry and Josephine Butler in Britain and the Netherlands* (Amsterdam: Amsterdam University Press, 1999), 12, Annemieke van Drenth and Francisca de Haan contend that "the rise of caring power provided the context in which women began to feel responsible for 'those of their own sex' and developed a new sense of collective gender identity."

134. Jane Jenson, "Representations of Gender: Policies to 'Protect' Women Workers and Infants in France and the United States before 1914." In Gordon, *Women, the State,*

*and Welfare,* 152–77. The other essays in the book also focus on the gendered ideology that contributed to the nature of welfare provision in various historical contexts. For a discussion of the nature of, and the feminist underpinning of, maternalism, see Koven and Michel, "Womanly Duties," and their introduction to *Mothers of a New World;* Gisela Bock, "Poverty and Mothers' Rights in the Emerging Welfare States," in François Thébaud, ed., *A History of Women in the West,* vol. 5: *Toward a Cultural Identity in the Twentieth Century* (Cambridge, Mass.: Belknap Press of Harvard University Press, 1994), 402–32; and van Drenth and de Haan, *The Rise of Caring Power,* 169–70. Maternalist arguments, which focused on women's rights as child bearers and child rearers, were similar those of the "familial feminists" that Karen Offen discusses in her "Depopulation, Nationalism, and Feminism," and to those of the "relational feminists" that she outlines in "Defining Feminism: A Comparative History," *Signs* 14 (Autumn 1988): 119–57, and *European Feminisms, 1700–1950: A Political History* (Stanford, Calif.: Stanford University Press, 2000), 21–22.

## Chapter 1. *The Origins of the Society for Maternal Charity*

1. Archives de l'Assistance Publique (hereafter AAP) B-832[17], *Réglemens de la Société de la Charité Maternelle,* arrêté à l'Assemblée du 13 Février 1789 (Paris: De l'Imprimerie de Seguy-Thiboust, 1789).

2. On the treatment of abandoned children under the Ancien Régime, see Rachel G. Fuchs, *Abandoned Children: Foundlings and Child Welfare in Nineteenth-Century France* (Albany: State University of New York Press, 1984), 1–16.

3. Fuchs, *Abandoned Children,* 10. Claude Delasselle analyzes the number of children admitted to the Foundlings Hospital over the course of the late seventeenth and early eighteenth centuries in "Abandoned Children in Eighteenth-Century Paris," in *Deviants and the Abandoned in French Society: Selections from the Annales, E.S.C.,* vol. 4, ed. Robert Forster and Orest Ranum, trans. Elborg Forster and Patricia Ranum (Baltimore: Johns Hopkins University Press, 1978), 47–82. See also George D. Sussman, *Selling Mother's Milk: The Wetnursing Business in France, 1715–1914* (Chicago: University of Illinois Press, 1982), 22.

4. A child admitted to the Foundling Hospital had approximately one chance in ten of surviving to the age of ten. However, the excellent reputation of the Foundling Hospital of Paris blinded many to this grim fact, including Rousseau, who abandoned five of his children there. Delasselle, "Abandoned Children," 76. Janet Ruth Potash suggests that some parents might not have realized how slim their abandoned child's chance of survival was. "The Foundling Problem in France, 1800–1869: Child Abandonment in Lille and Lyon," PhD diss., Yale University, 1979, 13. The expense of caring for abandoned babies led to a number of failed efforts to find a more economical method than wet nursing to provide nourishment for abandoned children. See Marie-France Morel, "À quoi servent les enfants trouvés?: les médecins et le problème de l'abandon dans la France du XVIIIe siècle," in *Enfance abandonnée et société en Europe, XIVe–XXe siècle: actes du colloque international organisé par la Sociéta Italiana di Demografia Storica, la Société de Démograhie Historique, l'École des Hautes Études en Sciences Sociales, l' École Française de Rome, le Dipartimento di Scienze Demografiche (Università di Roma–La Sapienza), le Dipartimento Statistico*

*(Università di Firenze), Rome, 30–31 janvier 1987* (École Française de Rome: Palais Farnèse, 1991), 837–58; Christine Adams, *A Taste for Comfort and Status: a Bourgeois Family in Eighteenth-Century France* (University Park: Pennsylvania State University Press, 2000), 205–7.

5. Sussman, *Selling Mother's Milk,* 66–67. Sussman suggests that mortality rates would have been even higher in a city like Lyon, where the wet-nursing business was completely unregulated and unsupervised.

6. Quoted by la baronne de Beauverger, "Madame de Fougeret, première présidente de la Société de Charité Maternelle, et deux des présidentes qui lui ont succédé," *Revue Médico-sociale de l'Enfance* 1er année, no. 4 (1933): 250.

7. Michael W. Flinn, *The European Demographic System, 1500–1820* (Baltimore: Johns Hopkins University Press, 1981), 41; Delasselle, "Abandoned Children," 62.

8. Suzanne Desan, *The Family on Trial in Revolutionary France* (Berkeley: University of California Press, 2004), 197; Katherine A. Lynch, *Family, Class, and Ideology in Early Industrial France: Social Policy and the Working-Class Family, 1825–1828* (Madison: University of Wisconsin Press, 1988), 115–18.

9. *Histoire des mères du Moyen Age à nos jours* (Paris: Montalba, 1977), 135.

10. Ibid., 135–43.

11. Stuart Woolf, "The Société de Charité Maternelle, 1788–1815," in *Medicine and Charity before the Welfare State,* ed. Jonathan Barry and Colin Jones (London: Routledge, 1991), 99.

12. Ibid., 101; Delasselle, "Abandoned Children," 71–78; Fuchs, *Abandoned Children,* 11.

13. Olwen H. Hufton, *The Poor of Eighteenth-Century France, 1750–1789* (Oxford: Clarendon Press, 1974); Cissie Fairchilds, *Poverty and Charity in Aix-en-Provence, 1640–1789* (Baltimore: Johns Hopkins University Press, 1976).

14. Quoted in Delasselle, "Abandoned Children," 70.

15. The following information on the life of Madame de Fougeret is drawn from three biographical notes: la baronne de Beauverger, "Madame de Fougeret, première présidente"; Anonymous, "Une femme de bien: Mme de Fougeret, fondatrice de la Société de Charité Maternelle: 1746–1813," *La Presse Médicale* (August 30, 1905, annexe, no. 69): 553–54; and a biography written by Madame de Maussion, née Fougeret, published in *Portrait et histoire des hommes utiles, hommes et femmes de tous pays et de toutes conditions qui ont acquis des droits à la reconnaissance, par des travaux, des tentatives, des perfectionnements, des découvertes utiles à l'humanité, etc.* (Paris: Bureau de la Société Montyon et Franklin, n.d.),

16. Monsieur d'Outremont was also a member of the commission formed by Necker in 1777 for the reform of the hospitals of Paris. Catherine Duprat, *"Pour l'amour de l'humanité": le temps des philanthropes: la philanthropie parisienne des Lumières à la monarchie de Juillet* (Paris: Éditions du C.T.H.S., 1993), 75.

17. Rachel Fuchs outlines the dangerous and uncomfortable voyage of babies to their rural wet nurses in *Abandoned Children,* 12.

18. Victor Lamothe, a Bordelais physician and member of the Academy of Bordeaux, conducted an unsuccessful experiment in the 1780s to try to find the "best and most economical method to provide a substitute to breast milk" for abandoned infants. Adams, *A Taste for Comfort and Status,* 204–7.

19. Biographical note, Madame de Maussion, n.p.

20. Duprat, *Le temps des philanthropes.*

21. Ibid., 75. These attitudes on the part of the Philanthropic Society in 1784 may account for the confusion about the date of the maternal society's founding.

22. *Compte rendu par le comité philantropique à l'assemblée générale de la Société,* le 14 décembre 1787. Extrait du procès-verbal dudit Comité, du 11 décembre (Paris: Chez Clousier, 1787[?]); see also Bibliothèque Historique de la Ville de Paris (BHVP) 4369[8] *Calendrier Philanthropique, Année 1789* (Paris: Clousier, 1790). I thank Harvey Chisick for the reference.

23. Woolf, "The Société de Charité Maternelle," 102.

24. For example, in 1790 the Society for Maternal Charity reported in its *compte rendu* that it had admitted twenty-four mothers conjointly with the Société Philanthropique, and these women were to be assisted for one year by the maternal society, then pensioned for two more years by the Philanthropic Society. See Archives Nationales (AN) AD XIV 12, *Compte rendu par l'administration de la Société de la Charité Maternelle pour l'année 1790,* 5. See also BHVP Mss. 996, rès. 34, *2ème registre des délibérations de la Société de Charité Maternelle* for more examples of their cooperation.

25. Duprat, *Le temps des philanthropes,* 75.

26. Paul Strauss, *L'enfance malheureuse* (Paris: Bibliothèque Charpentier, 1896), 200–202; Rachel G. Fuchs, *Poor and Pregnant in Paris: Strategies for Survival in the Nineteenth Century* (New Brunswick, N.J.: Rutgers University Press, 1992), 127–28.

27. Duprat, *Le temps des philanthropes,* 376.

28. Camille Bloch, *L'assistance et l'état en France à la veille de la Révolution (généralités de Paris, Rouen, Alençon, Orléans, Châlons, Soisson, Amiens)* (Paris: Librairie Alphonse Picard et Fils, 1908), 357.

29. Ibid. For the minutes of the meeting of January 4, 1790, at which society members were presented to the queen, see BHVP Mss. 996, rès. 34, 1–6. Gabriel Vauthier offers a detailed account in "Marie-Antoinette et la Charité Maternelle," *Revue du Dix-huitième Siècle* 5 (1918): 145–49.

30. AAP B-832[17], *Réglemens de la Société de la Charité Maternelle,* 5.

31. These parenthetical page numbers are from the bylaws text, AAP B-832[17], *Réglemens de la Société de la Charité Maternelle,* as I have quoted the documents extensively.

32. The period of the French Revolution was one of intense debate over the rights of fathers. See Rachel G. Fuchs, *Contested Paternity: Constructing Families in Modern France* (Baltimore.: Johns Hopkins University Press, 2008), 30–41.

33. Sussman, *Selling Mother's Milk,* 58–61.

34. When the Paris Society for Maternal Charity was reconstituted under Napoleon, the *dames députées* disappeared. As explained in note 2 of the Introduction, the titles and functions of the various female members of the society changed over time and differed depending on the location.

35. For the minutes of the society's meetings, 1790–93, see BHVP, Mss. 996, rès. 34.

36. As maternal societies were created in different cities, their bylaws would sometimes give preference to different categories of mothers.

37. Until the development of abundant fresh cow's milk, and sanitary, easy-to-clean bottles and rubber nipples late in the nineteenth century, artificially feeding babies was

neither desirable nor safe. Sussman, *Selling Mother's Milk,* 11, 164–66; Fuchs, *Abandoned Children,* 3, 138–39.

38. While most future maternal societies also paid for a wet nurse or bottles and milk for mothers physically incapable of feeding their child, rarely was an exemption provided for "veuves domestiques." In the case of the 1789 bylaws, the widowed servant mothers were required to contribute some money to pay for their child's *nourrice.*

39. This differed from much public assistance, in which relief to married women generally depended on how "deserving" their husbands were. As Rachel G. Fuchs notes, "Married women belonged to the domicile of their husbands, which denied them a right to poor relief as individuals, privileging their husbands and male kin. *Gender and Poverty in Nineteenth-Century Europe* (Cambridge: Cambridge University Press, 2005), 202–3. Susan Pedersen found that the idea of giving welfare benefits directly to mothers was highly controversial in prewar England and perceived by some as an attack on working men, while in post-1871 France, family policy would be linked to a nationalist and patriarchal social vision in support of high birthrates. *Family, Dependence and the Origins of the Welfare State: Britain and France, 1914–1945* (Cambridge: Cambridge University Press, 1993), chap. 1.

40. BHVP Mss. 996, rès. 34, 3.

41. Biographical notice, Madame de Maussion, n.p.

42. The first appeals to join the Society for Maternal Charity were sent out under the name of the duchess of Cossé, who already held the title of "Supérieur des Enfans-Trouvés." Biographical notice, Madame de Maussion, n.p.

43. The président de Ménerville of the Cour des aides was the son-in-law of Madame de Fougeret. Woolf, "The Société de Charité Maternelle," 102.

44. Stuart Woolf gives heavy weight to these family and social ties, arguing that "like their successors, the ladies of our society could operate in a male world only through their network of relatives," and he credits these networks with the organization's financial success in its early years. Woolf, "The Société de Charité Maternelle,"102. See also Duprat, *Le temps des philanthropes,* 79–80.

45. See AN AD XIV 12, *Compte rendu des six premiers mois de l'année 1789,* rendu par l'administration de la Charité Maternelle, le 3 Juillet 1789. Page numbers to specific references in *comptes rendus* provided in parentheses in text.

46. Catherine Duprat notes that 177,000 *livres* of the revenues from the royal lottery was used for assistance each year, and of that, 120,000 *livres* was given to the Hôpital des Enfants Trouvés. *Le temps des philanthropes,* 76n72.

47. See AN AD XIV 12, *Compte rendu, 1790.*

48. *Almanach national pour l'année 1790* (Paris: Chez Cuchet, 1790), 84.

49. On efforts by the royal and municipal governments, as well as the church and philanthropists to ameliorate the subsistence crisis of the winter of 1788–89, see Lisa DiCaprio, *The Origins of the Welfare State: Women, Work, and the French Revolution* (Urbana: University of Illinois Press, 2007), 19–20.

50. *Procès-verbaux et rapports du Comité de Mendicité de la Constituante, 1790–1791,* ed. Camille Bloch and Alexandre Tuetey (Paris: Imprimerie Nationale, 1911), i–x ; Duprat, *Le temps des philanthropes,* 294–98. On le duc de la Rochefoucauld-Liancourt, see Ferdinand-Dreyfus, *Un philanthrope d'autrefois: la Rochefoucauld-Liancourt, 1747–1827* (Paris: Plon-Nourrit, 1903).

51. Ferdinand-Dreyfus, *Un philanthrope autrefois*, 152; Isser Woloch, *The New Regime: Transformations of the French Civic Order, 1789–1820s* (New York: Norton, 1994), 243; DiCaprio, *The Origins of the Welfare State*, ix–x and 30–34.

52. Alan Forrest, *The French Revolution and the Poor* (New York: St. Martin's Press, 1981), 27.

53. Fuchs, *Gender and Poverty*, esp. 12–13, 38–41.

54. Ferdinand-Dreyfus, *Un philanthrope autrefois*, 162.

55. Duprat, *Le temps des philanthropes*, 381–82.

56. This was part of the Comité's comprehensive investigation into the various institutions of French social welfare in the early years of the Revolution. For a detailed look at their work, see DiCaprio, *The Origins of the Welfare State*, 35–40.

57. Bloch and Tuetey, *Procès Verbaux*, 94–96.

58. AN AD XIV 12, *Rapport sur l'établissement de la Charité-Maternelle de Paris,* par le Comité de Mendicité (Paris: Imprimé par l'Ordre de l'Assemblé Nationale, 1790). This is also reprinted in Bloch and Tuetey, *Procès verbaux*, 693–703. The following information is taken from the *Rapport;* the page numbers for specific citations are in parentheses in the text.

59. Fuchs, *Contesting Paternity,* 30–34.

60. DiCaprio notes that "the Revolution introduced a new sense of government accountability for all forms of public spending . . . revolutionary welfare placed a new emphasis on the actual *results* of providing assistance rather than the efficacy of charity (good works) in ensuring the salvation of the charitable contributor." *The Origins of the Welfare State,* 45.

61. Bloch and Tuetey, *Procès verbaux,* 149 and 228.

62. Ibid., 720–21; AN AD XIV 12, Loi relative à l'établissement connu sous le nom de la Charité Maternelle de Paris, January 26, 1791.

63. AN AD XIV 12, *Compte rendu, 1790,* 4.

64. Ibid., 5.

65. Ibid., 2.

66. The essays in *Marie-Antoinette: Writings on the Body of a Queen,* ed. Dena Goodman (New York: Routledge, 2003), attest to the unpopularity of the queen, which intensified during the early years of the Revolution.

67. Charles Beaumont, *Extension de la capacité civile des associations privée de bienfaisance* (Avesnes-sur-Helpe: Éditions de l'Observateur, 1936), 11.

68. Bloch, *L'assistance et l'état,* 448–49; Duprat, *Le temps des philanthropes,* 342–57; Isser Woloch, "From Charity to Welfare in Revolutionary Paris," *Journal of Modern History* 58:4 (December 1986): 801; Léonie Chaptal, "Le centenaire de 1814: le mouvement social en 1814," *La Revue Hebdomadaire,* no. 9 (February 28, 1914): 513.

69. Louis Parturier, *L'assistance à Paris sous l'Ancien Régime et pendant la Révolution* (Geneva: Mégariotis Reprints, 1978; Réimpression de l'édition de Paris, 1897), 200.

70. Duprat, *Le temps des philanthropes,* 336; Woloch, "From Charity to Welfare," 801.

71. Alan Forrest's *The French Revolution and the Poor* is the most complete account of the Revolutionary government's efforts to reform the system of poor relief throughout France.

72. Woloch, "From Charity to Welfare," 801.

73. Paul Nourrisson, *Histoire de la liberté d'association en France depuis 1789,* 2 vols. (Paris: Librairie de la Société du Recueil Sirey, 1920), 1:106–7.

74. The society achieved its highest revenues of 77,192 livres in 1789. AN AD XIV 12, *Tableau de la Société Maternelle pour l'année de 1793 (vieux stile)* (Paris: De L'Imprimerie de Mayer et Compagnie, year II), 13. The following information is taken from this *tableau.*

75. Forrest, *The French Revolution and the Poor,* 125.

76. Between 1793 and year V, the death rate rose from 70 percent to 95 percent. Olwen H. Hufton, *Women and the Limits of Citizenship in the French Revolution* (Toronto: University of Toronto Press, 1992), 82.

77. Desan, *The Family on Trial,* 210–16.

78. Woloch, *The New Regime,* 279, and "From Charity to Welfare in Revolutionary Paris," 794n30; Hufton, *Women and the Limits of Citizenship,* 86. Catherine Duprat notes that the society's funds had dried up by year III. *Le temps des philanthropes,* 414.

79. Biographical notice by Madame de Maussion; "Une femme de bien," 554.

80. See DiCaprio, *The Origins of the Welfare State,* 106–9.

81. Forrest, *The French Revolution and the Poor,* 83.

82. William Doyle outlines the disastrous consequences of the nationalization of church land for the poor, as it could no longer provide charitable assistance it had distributed before the Revolution. *The Oxford History of the French Revolution* (Oxford: Oxford University Press, 1989), 400.

83. The conclusion to Forrest's book *The French Revolution and the Poor* covers these defects in the Revolutionary government's efforts at public assistance.

84. Woloch, "From Charity to Welfare," 811.

85. Lynch, *Family, Class, and Ideology,* 119; Adams, *A Taste for Comfort and Status,* 172; Forrest, *The French Revolution and the Poor,* chap. 7.

86. Alan Forrest details the problems of the foundling hospices under the Revolutionary government in *The French Revolution and the Poor,* chap. 7. See also Lynch, *Family, Class and Ideology,* 119.

87. Parturier, *L'assistance à Paris,* 224.

88. Forrest, *The French Revolution and the Poor,* 75.

89. Isser Woloch and Alan Forrest underline the meager funds for poor relief under the Directory both in Paris and nationwide. "From Charity to Welfare," 807–8, and *The French Revolution and the Poor,* 84–85.

90. Chaptal, "Le centenaire de 1814," 514. However, these laws were far from a panacea, since there was no compensation for the losses that institutions of charity, especially the hospitals, had suffered from years II–IV, and since only lands and buildings, not *rentes,* were restored. Forrest, *The French Revolution and the Poor,* 56–58.

91. Duprat, *Le temps des philanthropes,* 413–17.

92. Léon de Lanzac de Laborie, *Paris sous Napoléon,* 8 vols. *Assistance et bienfaisance approvisionnement* (Paris, 1908), 5:134.

93. Parturier, *L'Assistance à Paris,* 245.

94. La Rochefoucauld-Liancourt and Mathieu de Montmorency were asked to serve but declined.

95. Duprat covers Chaptal's efforts in some detail in *Le temps des philanthropes,* 422–25. See also Chaptal's own discussion of his efforts on behalf of poor assistance in Paris in

Jean-Antoine Chaptal, comte de Chanteloup, *Mes souvenirs sur Napoléon* (Paris: Plon, 1893), 59–63.

96. See Lanzac de Laborie, *Paris sous Napoléon*, 5:134.

97. Duprat, *Le temps des philanthropes*, 422.

98. Claude-François-Etienne Dupin, *Histoire de l'administration des secours publics* (Paris: Chez Alexis Eymery, 1821), 311–12; Forrest, *The French Revolution and the Poor*, 131–33; Lynch, *Family, Class, and Ideology*, 119.

99. F. Gille, *La Société de Charité Maternelle de Paris* (Paris: V. Goupy et Jourdan, 1887), 9.

100. Duprat, *Le temps des philanthropes*, 462.

101. Ibid., 467.

102. Biographical note, by Madame de Maussion.

103. *Journal des Débats*, 1 *floréal* year IX (April 21, 1801), quoted in Duprat, *Le temps des philanthropes*, 430.

104. Chaptal provided encouragement along with the assurance of 12,000 francs per year. Bibliothèque Nationale (hereafter BN) Fonds Français Mss. 11368, *Procès-verbaux de la Société de Charité Maternelle*, séance of May 11, 1812.

105. AN F$^{15}$ 1939, "Précis sur la Société de Charité Maternelle de Paris," June 2, 1814.

106. Gille, *La Société de Charité Maternelle de Paris*, 10; Duprat, *Le temps des philanthropes*, 452.

107. This information from the *compte rendu* of December 7, 1801, is taken from Gille, *La Société de Charité Maternelle de Paris*, 10–11. A passage very similar to this, questioning whether the society ought to increase its public appeals, appears in the *compte rendu* of December 1807, following an extremely poor year for revenues.

108. The numbers are from Gille, *La Société de Charité Maternelle de Paris*, 19, and AAP Fonds Fosseyeux, 133/14, D-263, *Notice historique sur l'objet de la Société de Charité Maternelle et sur les résultats de ses travaux pendant 30 ans* (1831).

109. AAP, Fonds Fosseyeux, 791 FOSS 14 n. 2, *Compte rendu de la Société de Charité Maternelle dans l'assemblée générale du 25 Frimaire An XII*, 1–2.

110. AAP, Fonds Fosseyeux, 791 FOSS 14 n. 2, *Compte rendu de la Société de Charité Maternelle dans l'assemblée générale du 29 décembre 1806*, 3.

111. The *compte rendu* issued on December 20, 1804 (29 *frimaire* year XIII), noted that "some ladies of the board, having been admitted, since the general assembly, into the presence of her majesty the empress, received evidence of her interest in and her benevolence for this institution. She wished to promise them that each month she will give a sum to augment the assistance that the maternal society distributes." AAP, Fonds Fosseyeux, 791 FOSS 14n2, *Compte rendu*, 5 (fn).

112. Duprat, *Le temps des philanthropes*, 461–62.

113. Gille records the various legacies bequeathed to the society between 1801 and 1810. *La Société de Charité Maternelle de Paris*, 12–13.

114. AAP Fonds Fosseyeux, 791 FOSS 14 n. 2, *Compte rendu par l'administration de la Société de Charité Maternelle dans l'assemblée générale du 28 décembre 1807*.

115. Duprat, *Le temps des philanthropes*, 468–69.

116. AAP, Fonds Fosseyeux, 791 FOSS 14 n. 2, *Compte rendu*, 1804, 5.

117. AAP, Fonds Fosseyeux, 791 FOSS 14 n. 2, *Compte rendu*, year XII (1803), 1.

118. Stuart Woolf, "The Société de Charité Maternelle," 100; AN F¹⁵ 2565, Letter from the conseil d'administration of the Société de Charité Maternelle of Lyon to Monseigneur, le Maréchal, duc de Raguse, lieutenant du Roi, October 11, 1817.

119. Susan Grogan, "Philanthropic Women and the State: The Société de Charité Maternelle in Avignon, 1802–1917," _French History_ 14:3 (2000): 299.

120. Paul Delaunay, _La Société de Charité Maternelle du Mans et ses origines_ (Le Mans: Imprimerie Monnoyer, 1911), 7–8.

121. Bibliothèque Municipale de Marseille, 50.079, Société de Bienfaisance de Marseille, _Charité maternelle: arrêté du comité administratif de la Société de Bienfaisance de Marseille, pour l'institution de la Charité Maternelle,_ arrêté au Bureau de Direction, le 28 floréal et 15 messidor an 12, et adopté par le comité administratif de la Société de Bienfaisance,

122. Archives Départementales des Bouches-du-Rhône (ADBR) X² 26, "Extrait, parte in qua, des registres des delibérations du Conseil Municipal de la ville de Marseille," July 10, 1810.

123. ADBR X² 26, extracts from the registers of the Administration Centrale des Secours Publics, March 30, 1808, March 29, 1809, and May 19, 1810; letters from the administration Centrale des Secours Publics to the prefect, May 9, 1808, April 30, 1809, and May 21, 1810.

124. See Steven M. Beaudoin, "'A Neutral Terrain': Public Assistance, Private Charity, and the State in Third Republic Bordeaux, 1870–1914," PhD diss., Carnegie Mellon University, 1996, chap. 1.

125. Annie Flacassier, "La Société de Charité Maternelle de Bordeaux de 1805 à 1815," in _105e Congrès, Comité d'Histoire de la Sécurité Sociale_ (Caen: Comité d'Histoire de la Sécurité Sociale, 1980), 36.

126. Christine Adams, "Constructing Mothers and Families: The Society for Maternal Charity of Bordeaux, 1805–1860," _French Historical Studies_ 22:1 (Winter 1999): 70–71.

127. For the text of the _arrêté,_ see Archives Départementales de la Gironde 4J 727, handwritten extract from _L'écho du commerce de Bordeaux,_ n. 2623, n.d.

128. The _comptes rendus_ for these years can be found at the Bibliothèque Municipale de Bordeaux (BMB) D 11096.

129. See Flacassier, "La Société de Charité Maternelle de Bordeaux," 42–43, for a discussion of the social demographics of the society's founding members.

130. BMB D 11096, letter from le comité d'administration aux dames distributrices des secours de la Société, et surveillantes de leur emploi, 20 _thermidor_ year XIII, 2.

131. BMB D 11096, letter from le comité d'administration aux dames distributrices des secours de la Société, et surveillantes de leur emploi, 20 _thermidor_ year XIII, 2.

132. In the _procès-verbal_ from a meeting held on March 22, 1813, the conseil d'administration considered the requests of doctors and surgeons who wished to assist the Paris Society for Maternal Charity in its work. They issued an _arrêté_ that decreed that the number of _médecins_ associated with the society would be twenty-four (two for each _arrondissement_), while the number of _chirugiens_ would be twelve. BN Fonds Français Mss. 11368, _Procès-verbaux de la Société de Charité Maternelle, 1810–14._

133. BMB D 11096, _Comptes rendus,_ 1805–10.

134. BMB Mss. 713/8, Pierre Bernadau, _Oeuvres complètes de Pierre Bernadau de Bordeaux,_ tome 8. Quatrième recueil es tablettes manuscrites de l'Écouteur Bordelais de Septembre 1802 à 1813 inclus (1814). I thank Jeff Horn for the references.

135. AN F¹⁵ 2565, *Compte rendu par l'administration de la Société de Charité Maternelle, dans l'assemblée générale du 18 janvier 1810.*

## Chapter 2. The Society for Maternal Charity under Napoleon

1. Bibliothèque Municipale de Bordeaux (BMB) D 11096, *Compte rendu des opérations de la Société de Charité Maternelle de Bordeaux,* 1810, 8.

2. Rachel G. Fuchs, *Abandoned Children: Foundlings and Child Welfare in Nineteenth-Century France* (Albany: State University of New York Press, 1984), 19–25. Fuchs includes the text of the "Décret du 19 janvier 1811, concernant les enfants trouvés ou abandonnés et les orphelins pauvres" in appendix A (282–85).

3. Yvonne Knibiehler and Catherine Fouquet, *Histoire des mères du moyen âge à nos jours* (Paris: Montalba, 1977), 164. In fact, article 9 of Napoleon's 1811 decree on foundlings, abandoned children, and poor orphans explicitly indicated that these boys, once they reached the age of twelve, would be placed at the disposition of the minister of the navy. Fuchs, *Abandoned Children,* 24.

4. F. Gille, *La Société de Charité Maternelle de Paris* (Paris: V. Goupy et Jourdan, 1887), 19; for the figures on Bordeaux, see "Tableau faisant connaître le nombre des mères secourues par la Société depuis l'année 1805, époque de sa fondation, et les sommes qui leur ont été distribuées, chaque année, depuis 1805 à 1840," Archives Départementales de la Gironde (ADG), 4J 727; *Compte rendu de la Société de Charité Maternelle de Bordeaux pour l'année 1840* (Bordeaux : Deliège Aîné,1841), 4.

5. Léon de Lanzac de Laborie, *Paris sous Napoléon,* 8 vols. Vol. 5, *Assistance et bienfaisance approvisionnement* (Paris: Libraire Plon, 1908), 148–49.

6. Gabriel Vauthier, "La Société Maternelle sous l'empire," *Revue des Études Napoléoniennes* 2 (1914): 71.

7. The text of the decree, "Décret impérial, au Palais d'Anvers, 5 mai 1810," can be found in the *fonds* of the Société de Charité Maternelle in a number of departmental archives. It is reproduced in full in A. Cornereau's *Notice sur la Société de Charité Maternelle de Dijon* (Dijon: Darantière, 1900), 44–48. Also see Christine Adams, "Constructing Mothers and Families: The Society for Maternal Charity of Bordeaux, 1805–1860," *French Historical Studies* 22:1 (Winter 1999): 80.

8. In the words of Lanzac de Laborie, *Paris sous Napoléon,* 5:148.

9. However, as Catherine Duprat notes, this never actually happened. Subscriptions brought in 270,000 francs in 1811 and fell to 63,000 francs in 1812. *Usage et pratiques de la philanthropie: pauvreté, action sociale et lien social, à Paris, au cours du premier XIXe siècle,* 2 vols. (Paris: Association pour l'Étude de l'Histoire de la Sécurité Sociale, 1996–97), 2:617.

10. Colin Jones suggests that the Society for Maternal Charity was being groomed to become the female equivalent of the Légion d'honneur. *Charity and Bienfaisance: The Treatment of the Poor in the Montpellier Region, 1740–1815* (Cambridge: Cambridge University Press, 1982), 237.

11. Philip Mansel analyzes Napoleon's efforts to aggrandize and formalize the life of the court in *The Court of France, 1789–1830* (Cambridge: Cambridge University Press, 1988), chaps. 3 and 4.

12. Bibliothèque Nationale (BN), Fonds Français Mss. 11369, *Société maternelle, correspondance: 1810–1814,* letter from the comtesse de Ségur to Cardinal Fesch, August 23, 1811. Philip Mansel stresses Napoleon's increasing attention to ritual and symbolism in the life of his court in *The Eagle in Splendour: Napoleon I and His Court* (London: George Philip, 1987), and *The Court of France,* especially chap. 4. Entrepreneurs were ready to benefit from this attention to the details of prestige associated with the new Imperial Society. The artist David sent out a prospectus recruiting subscribers to purchase an engraving celebrating the Society for Maternal Charity. See Archives Départementales de la Côte-d'Or (ADCO) 22 X G, article 1, Prospectus by David.

13. This letter can be found in most of the provincial archives examined for this project, including ADG 3X 18 and Archives Départementales de la Seine-Maritime (ADSM) 3XP 217, correspondence to the prefect accompanying "Note: pour servir d'instruction aux dames qui veulent former, dans les villes de l'empire, des conseils d'administration de la Société Maternelle," June 28, 1810.

14. Archives Nationales (AN) F$^{15}$ <2>, Registre, Société de Charité Maternelle, n.d.

15. Ibid. For more on the contents of this register, see Jean-Pierre Chaline, "Sociabilité féminine et 'maternalisme,' les Sociétés de Charité Maternelle au XIXe siècle," in *Femmes dans la Cité, 1815–1871,* ed. Alain Corbin, Jacqueline Lalouette, and Michèle Riot-Sarcey (Grâne: Créaphis, 1997), 73.

16. ADCO 22 X G, article 1, letter from the prefect to the minister of the interior, August 4, 1810.

17. Vauthier, "La Société Maternelle sous l'empire," 77. Vauthier suggests that perhaps the bishop penned these lines.

18. Ibid., 74.

19. On Fesch and Dejean, see Nicole Gotteri, *Grands dignitaires, ministres et grands officiers du Premier Empire: autographes et notices biographiques* (Paris: Nouvelles Éditions Latines, 1990), 109–10 and 122–23.

20. BN Fonds Français Mss. 11368, *Procès-verbaux de la Société de Charité Maternelle, 1810–1814,* February 22, 1811, 7–8; Duprat, *Usage et pratiques,* 2:616.

21. "Note: pour servir d'instruction aux dames." *Brevets* were certificates signed by the empress and given to the members of the *conseil général* of the society.

22. Knibiehler and Fouquet, *L'histoire des mères,* 165.

23. Duprat, *Usage et pratiques,* 2:632.

24. This account of Montalivet's difficulties, including the text of the *circulaire,* is taken from Lanzac de Laborie, *Paris sous Napoléon,* 5:150–53.

25. For the text of letters that Montalivet sent to the provincial bishops and archbishops as well as prefects, urging them to solicit memberships to the society, see Vauthier, "La Société Maternelle sous l'Empire," 72–73. Examples can also be found in many of the provincial archives—for example, Archives Départementales de la Haute-Vienne (ADHV) 3X 15, dated June 28, 1810.

26. The personal letters to the wealthiest provincial *dames,* and the frequent *circulaires* to subprefects, local clergy, and municipal officials amply demonstrate the efforts that the prefect made to find subscribers to the society. The prefect of the Rhône kept track of his efforts to attract subscribers, including placards and letters to the subprefects and the president of the *bureaux de bienfaisance.* See the notes scribbled in the margin of the

*circulaire* sent out by the minister of the interior on June 28, 1810, Archives Départemen-tales de la Rhône (ADR) 4M 523.

27. Paul Delaunay, *La société de charité maternelle du Mans et ses origines* (Le Mans: Imprimerie Monnoyer, 1911), 10–12.

28. John M. Merriman's *The Red City: Limoges and the French Nineteenth Century* (New York: Oxford University Press, 1985) focuses on the period after the Restoration. However, for a discussion of the poverty of Limoges, and the relatively small size of its elite, see chapter 1.

29. See ADHV 3X 15, *lettre circulaire* to the *curés* of the diocese of Limoges, dated 1810; rough drafts of letters from the prefect to the *sous*-prefects and mayors of the Haute-Vienne, July 2, 1810; rough draft of letter from the prefect of the Haute-Vienne to the minister of the interior, August 4, 1810; letters from Dejean, *trésorier général* of the Société Impériale de Charité Maternelle, August 31 and December 24, 1811. Limoges did eventually establish a Society for Maternal Charity in 1817.

30. Chaline, "Sociabilité féminine et 'maternalisme,'" 71.

31. Vauthier, "La Société Maternelle sous l'empire," 75.

32. Knibiehler and Fouquet, *Histoire des mères,* 165; Vauthier, "La Société Maternelle sous l'empire," 75–76. Thibaudeau, a prefect considered "dur et autoritaire" (hard and au-thoritarian), was not popular in Marseille, where he was nicknamed "Barre de fer" (iron bar). Raoul Busquet and Joseph Fournier, *La vie politique et administrative,* volume 5 of *Les Bouches-du-Rhône, Encyclopédie départementale,* gen. ed. Paul Masson, part 2: *Le Bilan du XIXe siècle* (Paris: Librairie Honoré Champion/Marseille: Archives Départementales des Bouches-du-Rhône, 1929), 91.

33. Susan Grogan, "Philanthropic Women and the State: The Société de Charité Mater-nelle in Avignon, 1802–1917," *French History* 14:3 (2000): 300.

34. Chaline, "Sociabilité féminine et 'maternalisme,'" 71.

35. Mansel, *The Eagle in Splendour,* 169.

36. ADCO 22 X G, article 1.

37. ADHV 3X 15, letter from the subprefect of the arrondissement of Saint-Yrieix to the prefect, le baron Texier, August 5, 1810.

38. ADG 3X 18, letter from the prefect Gary to the minister of the interior, July 26, 1810. Steven M. Beaudouin illustrates that the Revolutionary and subsequent Napoleonic wars had a devastating effect on the commercial life of this port city. "'A Neutral Terrain': Public Assistance, Private Charity, and the State in Third Republic Bordeaux, 1870–1814," PhD diss., Carnegie Mellon University, 1996.

39. ADSM 3XP 217, letters to the prefect written in July 1810.

40. ADSM 3XP 217, letter from the prefect to the minister of the interior, July 19, 1810.

41. "Décret impérial, au Palais d'Anvers," May 5, 1810.

42. For further analysis of these issues, see Christine Adams, "The Provinces Versus Paris? The Case of the Society for Maternal Charity of Bordeaux," *Proceedings of the Western Society for French History* 23 (Fall 1996): 420–27.

43. ADSM 3XP 217, letter from the prefect to the minister of the interior, July 19, 1810.

44. ADG 3X 18, letter from the prefect Gary to the minister of the interior, July 19, 1810.

45. As Stuart Woolf notes, "personal visitations were soon to be theorized by Gérando, and adopted as the standard mould of nineteenth-century voluntary charity." "The Société de Charité Maternelle, 1788–1815," *Medicine and Charity before the Welfare State,* ed. Jonathan Barry and Colin Jones (London: Routledge, 1991), 104. He is referring to Gérando's *Le visiteur du pauvre,* translated into English as *The Visitor of the Poor* (London, 1833).

46. BN Fonds Français Mss. 11368, séance of December 22, 1810.

47. These concerns were passed on to Napoleon in a letter from Cardinal Fesch titled "Projet à Rapport à S.M. l'Empereur," BN Fonds Français Mss. 11369, letter of December 10, 1810.

48. For the text of the "Décret relatif à l'organisation de la charité maternelle," finally published in 1811, see Ad. de Watteville, ed., *Législation charitable et recueil des lois, arrêtés, décrets, ordonnances royales, circulaires, décisions et instructions des Ministres de l'Intérieur et des finances, arrêtés de la Cour des Comptes, etc., etc., qui régissent les établissements de bienfaisance, mise en ordre et annotée* (Paris: Alexandre Heois, 1843), 165–67. Copies also exist in most departmental archives.

49. Sent out on August 15, 1811. Dejean had sent a letter earlier, in April 1811, to notify the prefects that "You may, M. le Préfet, reassure the individuals who have subscribed in your city concerning the use of the amount of their subscriptions. The bylaws of the society, which have not yet received the approval of Her Majesty the Empress, state positively that 'The product [sum?] from the subscriptions of each *arrondissement* of the Empire will be used exclusively in that *arrondissement* unless the donors have ordered otherwise.'" See ADG 3X 18, letter from Dejean, trésorier général, to the baron Gary, prefect of the Gironde, April 6, 1811.

50. Cornereau, *Notice sur la Société de Charité Maternelle de Dijon,* 22. For the minutes of their first and second séances, held on December 8 and December 18, 1811, see ADCO 22 X G, Article 1.

51. Bibliothèque municipale de Lyon (BML) Ms. Coste 948, *Compte rendu au Comité Central par la Société Maternelle de Lyon,* October 7, 1812. A letter from the prefect to the mayor of Lyon, written on August 17, 1811, noted that "it seems that the number of subscriptions in this Department offers little latitude for the choice of the Comité Central." Archives Municipales de Lyon, 744 WP 074.

52. On June 14, 1811, Ségur and Pastoret wrote a letter to Napoleon, stressing that it was urgent that he approve the règlement of the Imperial Society. BN Fonds Français Mss. 11369, *Société Maternelle: correspondance.*

53. ADG 3X 18, letter from the comité d'adminsitration of the Société de Charité Maternelle of Bordeaux to the baron Gary, prefect of the Gironde, December 15, 1810.

54. In letters written on January 11 and January 17, 1811, Cardinal Fesch and the prefect Gary urged the society to continue its operations until the new organization was put into place. ADG 3X 18.

55. ADG 3X 18, letter from the comité d'administration of the Société de Charité Maternelle of Bordeaux to the baron Gary, prefect of the Gironde, March 5 (?), 1811.

56. ADG 3X 18, letters of April 6, 13, and 16, 1811.

57. See ADG 3X 18, correspondence from the fall of 1811.

58. ADG 3X 18, printed document addressed to the prefects, dated August 25, 1811.

59. This was true, for example, of maternal societies in Carcassonne, Châlons, Rennes,

and Tours, among others; see AN F$^{15}$ 2565, *Compte rendu à S.M. l'Impératrice-Reine et Régente, Protectrice et Présidente de la Société de la Charité Maternelle, par S.A. Em. le secrétaire général et S.Ex. le trésorier général de la situation de la Société dans tout l'empire, et de l'emploi de ses fonds; et par les dames du conseil d'administration de Paris, des opérations de ce conseil* (Paris: Imprimerie Impériale, 1813), 64–66.

60. BN Fonds Français Mss. 11368, Procès-verbal, Comité Central, November 23, 1811.

61. *Règlement pour la Société de la Charité Maternelle* (Paris: De l'Imprimerie Impériale, 1811), Titre 1er.

62. BN Fonds Français Mss. 11368, séance of December 22, 1810.

63. Ibid., séance of February 28, 1811.

64. Ibid., Procès-verbal, Comité Central, August 14, 1811.

65. Bordeaux, however, maintained a parallel administrative council staffed by men throughout the nineteenth century.

66. BN Fonds Français Mss. 11368, Procès-verbal, Comité Central, November 23, 1811.

67. Ibid., Procès-verbal, Comité Central, March 19, 1812. During a meeting of the Comité Central on July 30, 1812, the Comité approved the budget of the Society of Marseille, "always manifesting hope that this council will eventually find a way to reduce its administrative costs further, following the example of Paris, where they are almost nonexistent." In correspondence with the conseil d'administration of Marseille, Pastoret and Ségur urged them to try to bring about further reductions in their expenses. BN Fonds Français Mss. 11369, letter of May 1, 1812.

68. BN Fonds Français Mss. 11368, Procès-verbal, Comité Central, December 12, 1812.

69. Ibid., Procès-verbal, Comité Central, May 18 (?), 1813. Although the document was dated May 18, given its order and its content, that date was clearly incorrect.

70. There are a number of letters offering assistance in the register BN Fonds Français 11369, *Société Maternelle: correspondance.*

71. BN Fonds Français Mss. 11368, séance of September 3, 1811.

72. BN 4 R 164, *Compte rendu par le conseil d'administration de la Société de Charité Maternelle de Paris à S.M. l'Impératrice-Reine et Régente, exercice de 1811, présenté le 17 juillet 1813* (Paris: l'Imprimerie Impériale, 1813), 15, n.

73. BN Fonds Français Mss. 11368, Procès-verbal, Comité Central, November 23, 1811.

74. Ibid., séances of August 14, September 3, and September 27, 1811.

75. Ibid., Procès-verbal, Comité Central, November 23, 1811.

76. Ibid., séance of December 5, 1811.

77. The 150,000 FF was eventually increased to provide additional food supplies for the poor of Paris. Ibid., séances of February 4 and 8, March 2, 16, and 19, and April 1, 13, and 27, 1812; Lanzac de Laborie, *Paris sous Napoléon*, 5:154.

78. Ibid., Procès-verbal, Comité Central, February 4, 1812.

79. Ibid., Procès-verbal, Comité Central, July 30, 1812.

80. Ibid.

81. See Charles Simond (pseud.), *La vie parisienne à travers le XIXe siècle: Paris de 1800*

*à 1900 d'après les estampes et les mémoires du temps,* tome 1, 1800–1830: Le Consulat–Le Premier Empire–La Restauration (Paris: Plon, 1900), 233–38.

82. BN Fonds Français Mss. 11368, séance of April 13, 1812. The empress heard their request sympathetically and attributed another 100,000 FF to the society to use for bread and *soupes économiques.* Ibid., séance of April 27, 1812.

83. ADSM 3XP 217, letter from Madame Brémontier Fouquet to the prefect of the Seine-Inférieure, June 22, 1812.

84. ADCO 22X G, article 2, letter to the prefect from M. Gelot, *curé* of Auxonne, March 22, 1812.

85. BMB D 11096, *Compte rendu des opérations de la Société de Charité Maternelle, à Bordeaux,* 1812, 4.

86. One detailed account of this disaster can be found in Alan Schom, *Napoleon Bonaparte* (New York: HarperCollins, 1997), chap. 35.

87. BN Fonds Français Mss. 11368, Procès-verbal, Comité Central, December 12, 1812.

88. Ibid.

89. This account also covers expenses and information from 1812. See BN 4 R 164, *Compte rendu par le conseil d'administration de la Société de Charité Maternelle de Paris,* 1813.

90. AN F$^{15}$ 2565, *Compte rendu à S.M. l'Impératrice-Reine et Régente,* 1813. See p. 3.

91. BN Fonds Français Mss. 11368, Procès-verbal, Comité Central, May 18 (?), 1813.

92. BN Fonds Français Mss. 11369, letter from le comte Daru to Madame Pastoret, December 17, 1813. There is no evidence of a response from the society.

93. BN Fonds Français Mss. 11368, séance of January 10, 1814.

94. Ibid., séance of March 14, 1814.

95. Ibid., séance of April 18, 1814.

96. Gille, *La Société de Charité Maternelle de Paris,* 35.

97. AN F$^{15}$ 2565, letter sent by the minister of the interior to the prefects, December 11, 1814.

98. On the return to power of Louis XVIII and the Bourbons, see André Jardin and André-Jean Tudesq, *Restoration and Reaction, 1814–1848,* trans. Elborg Forster (Cambridge: Cambridge University Press/Paris: Éditions de la Maison des Sciences de l'Homme, 1983), 3–17; Philip Mansel, *Paris between Empires: Monarchy and Revolution, 1814–1852* (New York: St. Martin's Press, 2001), chap. 1.

99. BN Fonds Français Mss. 11368, séance of May 21, 1814.

100. Ibid., séance of May 25, 1814. The princess was already well known for her charitable works. Philip Mansel notes, "In other cities like Warsaw, where she had lived in 1801–5, and Bordeaux, which she visited in 1815, her dignity, simplicity and charity made her beloved." *Paris between Empires,* 66.

101. AN F$^{15}$ 2565, letter from the *conseil d'administration* of the Society for Maternal Charity of Paris to the baron de Vitrolles, secrétaire général du Conseil d'État, June 16, 1814.

102. ADCO 22X G, article 1, *Extrait des registres des délibérations de la Société de Charité Maternelle pour la ville de Dijon,* May,21 1814.

103. BMB D 11096, *Compte rendu des opérations de la Société de Charité Maternelle de Bordeaux,* 1815.

104. Watteville, *Législation charitable,* "Ordonnance portant réorganisation de la Société Maternelle," 178–79. F. Gilles discusses both the chaos created by the fall of the imperial government and the reorganization under the Bourbons in *La Société de Charité Maternelle de Paris,* 34–36 and 39–41.

105. AN F[15] 2565, "Note sur la Société de charité maternelle," inserted by order of Madame [the Duchess of Angoulême] in *Le Moniteur,* November 23, 1814.

106. For an example of this letter, dated December 19, 1814, see ADG 3X 18.

107. ADG 3X 18, letter from the baronne de Valsuzenai and M. Capelle, January 9, 1815.

108. ADG 3X 18, letter from the Bureau Central de Charité de la Ville de Bordeaux to the prefect, February 1, 1815. However, the letter does not explicitly support the need for a maternal society; rather, the administrators of the Bureau Central de Charité suggested that the administration of assistance was too dispersed and that it might be better to centralize distribution.

109. ADBR X[2] 26, letter from the conseil d'administration of the Société Maternelle of Marseille to the prefect, the marquis d'Albertas, January 3, 1815.

110. ADBR X[2] 26, letter from the Administration Centrale des Secours Publics de la Ville de Marseille to the prefect, the marquis d'Albertas, January 3, 1815. The prefect sent a letter to the Interior Ministry on January 7, 1815, strongly supporting the need for a maternal society but noted that he would work with the conseil d'administration to see if they could reduce the amount of assistance per mother.

111. ADR 4M 523, letter from the minister of the interior to the prefect of the Rhône, May 16, 1815; the prefect passed this information on to the members of the conseil d'administration on June 13, 1815. The prefect had been forced to send a note to the mayor prodding him to submit the necessary information to the minister of the interior after making the original request on January 2, 1815. Archives Municipales de Lyon, 744 WP 074, letters of January 2 and 19, 1815.

112. ADCO 22 X G, article 1, "Réponses aux questions contenues dans le lettre de Monsieur le Préfet," December 29, 1814, and letter from the mayor of Dijon to the prefect of the Côte-d'Or, January 3, 1815.

113. Charles Des Alleurs, *Histoire de la Société de Charité Maternelle de Rouen* (Rouen: Imprimerie Alfred Péron, 1854), 44.

114. AN F[15] 2565, letter from the Interior Ministry to Madame Pastoret, May 21, 1816.

115. The correspondence of the society for the year 1815 clearly indicates the confusion over the levels of funding to be extended by the central government. BN Fonds Français Mss. 11369, letter from Minister of the Interior Carnot to Madame Ségur, April 15, 1815; ADBR X[2] 26, correspondence from May 1815; ADG 3X 18, correspondence of March–June 1815; ADR 4M 523, correspondence of May–June 1815.

116. AN F[15] 2565, correspondence between the Interior Ministry and the prefects of the various departments, April–May 1815.

117. ADG 3X 18, letter of January 18, 1816.

118. The "États des recettes et des dépenses" of the provincial branches of the maternal societies, along with some correspondence, are located at AN F[15] 2564.

119. See Delaunay, *La Société de Charité Maternelle du Mans,* 13–14; and ADHV 3X 15, letter from the minister of the interior to the prefect of the Haute-Vienne, May 6, 1815.

120. AN F¹⁵ 2565, Société de la Charité Maternelle de la ville de Limoges, séance of February 6, 1817; *Règlement pour la Société de la Charité Maternelle de la Ville de Limoges, Département de la Haute-Vienne* (Limoges: J. B. et H. Dalesme, 1817).

121. AN F¹⁵ 1939, "Précis sur la Société de Charité Maternelle de Paris," June 2, 1814.

122. ADG 3X 18, *Règlement de la Société de la Charité Maternelle* (Bordeaux: Chez Pinard, 1815), 1.

123. See, for example, ADBR X² 26 and ADG 3X 18, February 10, 1816.

124. ADG 3X 16, letters of April 19, 1817, and May 9, 1818; ADG 3X 17, letters of June 19, 1817, and May 27, 1819; ADG 3X 18, letters of February 7 and June 18, 1816.

125. For example, in 1816 the minister of the interior drafted a letter to the prefects of the Gironde, the Bouches-du-Rhône, and Moselle, suggesting that one of the members of the organization should fill the role of secretary rather than paying a man to do so. AN F¹⁵ 2565, letter of September 18, 1815.

126. Duprat, *Usage et pratiques,* 2:618.

## Chapter 3. *Relations between the* Dames Visiteuses *and the* Pauvres Mères Indigentes

1. Bibliothèque nationale (BN) 4 R 164, *Compte rendu par le conseil d'administration de la Société de Charité Maternelle de Paris à S.M. l'Impératrice, Reine et Régente, Exercice de 1811, présenté le 17 juillet 1813* (Paris: L'Imprimerie Impériale, 1813), 5n.

2. Catherine Duprat notes that the Paris society included women of various political persuasions. *Usage et pratiques de la philanthropie: pauvreté, action sociale et lien social, à Paris, au cours du premier XIXe siècle,* 2 vols. (Paris: Association pour l'Étude de l'Histoire de la Sécurité Sociale, 1996–97), 2:632.

3. Joan Wallach Scott, *Gender and the Politics of History* (New York: Columbia University Press, 1988), 153.

4. See Yvonne Knibiehler and Catherine Fouquet, *Histoire des mères du moyen âge à nos jours* (Paris: Montalba, 1977), 163–68. Some historians have traced this image of women to the influence of Rousseau and the discourse of the French revolutionaries. See, e.g., Joan B. Landes, *Women and the Public Sphere in the Age of the French Revolution* (Ithaca, N.Y.: Cornell University Press, 1988); and Stuart Woolf, "The Société de Charité Maternelle, 1788–1815," in *Medicine and Charity before the Welfare State,* ed. Jonathan Barry and Colin Jones (London: Routledge, 1991), 101–2. Karen M. Offen notes that *philosophes* and others vigorously debated the appropriate role and rights of women, in "Reclaiming the Enlightenment for Feminism; or, Prolegomena to Any Future History of Eighteenth-Century Europe," in *Perspectives on Feminist Political Thought in European History from the Middle Ages to the Present,* ed. Tijitske Akkerman and Siep Stuurman (London: Routledge, 1998), 85–103.

5. Jennifer J. Popiel, *Rousseau's Daughters: Domesticity, Education, and Autonomy in Modern France* (Durham: University of New Hampshire Press, 2008), 89–92.

6. Denise Z. Davidson, *France After Revolution: Urban Life, Gender, and the New Social Order* (Cambridge, Mass.: Harvard University Press, 2007), 3.

7. Ibid., 187.

8. Bonnie G. Smith, *Ladies of the Leisure Class: The Bourgeoises of Northern France in the Nineteenth Century* (Princeton, N.J.: Princeton University Press, 1981).

9. Rachel G. Fuchs, *Poor and Pregnant in Paris: Strategies for Survival in Nineteenth-Century France* (New Brunswick, N.J.: Rutgers University Press, 1992).

10. Jennifer Popiel notes, "Women, unlike men, were seen as uniquely capable of giving young children the love and care that they would need to become moral adults, but women themselves also needed to develop the qualities enabling them to be nurturing and self-controlled from a relatively young age." *Rousseau's Daughters,* 10.

11. Knibiehler and Fouquet, *Histoire des mères,* "Le temps de l'exaltation"; introduction to *Mothers of a New World: Maternalist Politics and the Origins of Welfare States,* ed. Seth Koven and Sonya Michel (New York: Routledge, 1993), 10; Popiel, *Rousseau's Daughters,* especially chap. 3.

12. Archives Nationales (AN) AD XIV 12, *Compte rendu par la Société de la Charité Maternelle pour l'année 1790,* 3.

13. Knibiehler and Fouquet, *Histoire des mères,* 138–39, 145. In fact, some went so far as to argue that replacing the real mother's milk with that of a "stranger" to the family could corrupt that loving relationship. See Mary Jacobus, "Incorruptible Milk: Breast-feeding and the French Revolution," in *Rebel Daughters: Women and the French Revolution,* ed. Sara E. Melzer and Leslie W. Rabine (New York: Oxford University Press, 1992), 60–61.

14. Knibiehler and Fouquet, *Histoire des mères,* 135.

15. For Rousseau's views on motherhood, see Mary Seidman Trouille, *Sexual Politics in the Enlightenment: Women Writers Read Rousseau* (Albany: State University of New York Press, 1997), chap. 1, esp. 22–30.

16. Archives Départementales du Rhône (ADR) 3X 1850, *Rapport présenté aux dames composant la Société de Charité Maternelle au nom du conseil d'administration* par M. Mottet-Degérando, secrétaire-trésorier, February 21, 1827.

17. The celebration of pity, sympathy, and empathy is a theme prevalent in eighteenth-century literature. See Anne Vincent-Buffault, *The History of Tears: Sensibility and Sentimentality in France,* trans. Teresa Bridgeman (New York: St. Martin's Press, 1991); William Reddy, *The Navigation of Feeling: A Framework for the History of Emotions* (New York: Cambridge University Press, 2001), 155–56, 159, 164; G. J. Barker-Benfield, *The Culture of Sensibility: Sex and Society in Eighteenth-Century Britain* (Chicago: University of Chicago Press, 1992.), esp. chap. 5; and Sarah Maza, "Luxury, Morality, and Social Change: Why There Was No Middle-Class Consciousness in Prerevolutionary France, *Journal of Modern History* 69 (June 1997): 222.

18. Archives Départementales des Bouches-du-Rhône (ADBR) $X^2$ 26, Société de Charité Maternelle de Marseille, "Rapport au Conseil d'Administration de la Société Maternelle par M. le Trésorier honoraire, lû dans le séance du 5 janvier 1816."

19. Sarah Maza, *Private Lives and Public Affairs: The Causes Célèbres of Prerevolutionary France* (Berkeley: University of California Press, 1993). See esp. 98–104, 218–20, and 226–29.

20. AN $F^{15}$ 2565, "Rapport fait à Mesdames composant la Société de charité maternelle [of Marseille] par Monsieur le trésorier honoraire dans la séance du 18 février 1817."

21. Archives de l'Assistance Publique (AAP) B-832[17], *Réglemens de la Société de la charité*

*maternelle,* arrêté à l'Assemblée du 13 Février 1789 (Paris: De l'Imprimerie de Seguy-Thiboust, 1789), 4.

22. Ibid., 9.

23. Reddy, *The Navigation of Feelings,* chap. 7.

24. ADR 3X 1850, *Société de charité maternelle de Lyon, Compte-rendu de 1858* (Lyon: Imprimerie de Ve. Mougin-Rusand, 1859), n.p.

25. A *Notice historique* issued by the society in 1831 and cited by Frances Gouda underlined the effects of this personal contact: "By showering poor mothers with 'wholesome advice, guiding them with sweet exhortations, evoking sentiments of piety, and by giving them new hope, the members of the Société engender in the souls of these unfortunate women a greater sense of peace. Through the virtue of constancy, the rich align themselves with the poor, who forge emotional bonds with the rich by recognizing the Société maternelle ladies' goodwill.'" *Poverty and Political Culture: The Rhetoric of Social Welfare in the Netherlands and France, 1815–1854* (Lanham, Md.: Rowman and Littlefield, 1995), 216.

26. Vicomte de Pelleport-Burète, *Études municipales sur la charité bordelaise,* vol. 1 (Paris: P. Chaumas,1869), 7.

27. AAP B-832[17], *Réglemens de la Société de la charité maternelle,* 1789, 11–12.

28. Ibid., 4.

29. Claude-François-Étienne Dupin, *Histoire de l'administration des secours publics* (Paris: Alexis-Eymery, 1821), 333–34.

30. A. Cornereau, *Notice sur la société de charité maternelle de Dijon* (Dijon: Darantière, 1900), 12.

31. Bibliothèque municipale de Bordeaux (BMB) D 11096, letter from the Comité d'Administration aux Dames Distributrices des Secours de la Société, et Surveillantes de Leur Emploi (20 *thermidor* year XIII), 4.

32. This was for practical as well as moral reasons. Janet Ruth Potash notes, "For many centuries, mothers and nurses had been able to dispose of unwanted children by a semi-accidental suffocation known as overlaying." Potash, "The Foundling Problem in France, 1800–1869: Child Abandonment in Lille and Lyon," PhD diss., Yale University, 1979, 299.

33. Archives Municipales de Bordeaux (AMB) 312 Q 1, letter from the Conseil d'Administration de Bordeaux à Mesdames les Distributrices des Secours de la Société, September 7, 1813.

34. ADR 3X 1849, *Société de charité maternelle de Lyon, compte rendu de 1856* (Lyon: Gerente Fils, 1857), n.p.

35. BMB D 11096, letter from the Comité d'Administration aux Dames Distributrices des Secours de la Société, et Surveillantes de Leur Emploi (20 *thermidor* An XIII), 4.

36. ADR 3X 1850, *Société de Charité Maternelle de Lyon, compte rendu de 1865* (Lyon: Imprimerie de P. Mougin-Rusand, 1866), n.p.

37. Rousseau and others had made this link as early as the 1760s; George D. Sussman, *Selling Mothers' Milk: The Wet-Nursing Business in France, 1715–1914* (Urbana: University of Illinois Press, 1982), 27–29. In 1858, Louis-Adolphe Bertillon presented a paper in which he provided the statistical evidence, indicating that babies sent to wet nurses died at a much higher rate than those nursed at home by their mothers. However, Joshua Cole notes

that the accuracy of infant mortality statistics in nineteenth-century France is difficult to gauge. *The Power of Large Numbers: Population, Politics, and Gender in Nineteenth-Century France* (Ithaca, N.Y.: Cornell University Press, 2000), 149–60.

38. Ellen Ross, "Good and Bad Mothers: Lady Philanthropists and London Housewives Before the First World War," in *Lady Bountiful Revisited: Women, Philanthropy, and Power,* ed. Kathleen D. McCarthy (New Brunswick, N.J.: Rutgers University Press, 1990), 179.

39. Ferdinand Béchard, *De l'état du paupérisme en France et des moyens d'y remédier* (Paris: Librairie de Charles Douniol, 1853), 14; Honoré-Antoine Frégier, *Des classes dangereuses de la population dans les grandes villes et des moyens de les rendre meilleures,* 2 vols. (Paris: Chez J.-B. Baillières, 1840), 1:7; see also Fuchs, *Poor and Pregnant in Paris,* chap. 2.

40. AAP, Fonds Fosseyeux, 791 FOSS 14, n. 2, *Compte rendu par l'administration de la Société de Charité Maternelle dans l'Assemblée Générale du 29 décembre 1806,* 1.

41. Fuchs analyzes the ways in which their perceived morality influenced nineteenth-century views on poor mothers in *Poor and Pregnant in Paris,* esp. chaps. 2 and 4. See also Annie Flacassier, "La Société de Charité Maternelle de Bordeaux de 1805–1815," *105e Congrès, Comité d'Histoire de la Sécurité Sociale* (Caen: Comité d'Histoire de la Sécurité Sociale, 1980), 40–42.

42. BN Fonds Français Mss. 11368, *Procès verbaux de la Société de Charité Maternelle, 1810–14,* séance of March 14, 1811.

43. The division of labor within the maternal society could differ, depending on the locale. For example, in its 1869 *compte rendu,* the *présidente* and secretary of Bordeaux's society described the process as follows: "aux Messieurs les inspections à domicile pour constater l'état de misère, à eux également l'administration et la comptabilité, à Messieurs les Docteurs de la Société les appréciations médicales, aux Dames l'administration partagée avec ces Messieurs, la surveillance de la confection des layettes, la distribution exclusive des secours, les quêtes et le bal de charité" (The gentlemen [are in charge of] home inspections to determine the state of poverty, and also [in charge of] the administration and keeping accounts; the doctors [are in charge of] medical assessments; the ladies [are in charge of] administration, shared with these gentlemen, [and] the supervision of the preparation of the layettes, the exclusive distribution of assistance, collections, and the charitable ball). Archives Départmentales de la Gironde (ADG) 4J 710, *Assemblée générale annuelle des bienfaiteurs de la Société de Charité Maternelle de Bordeaux, rapport sur l'exercice 1869* (Bordeaux: Imprimerie Administrative Ragot, 1870), 4.

44. The documents are sometimes vague about how this process took place. In her statement to the queen on January 4, 1790, Madame la Marquise de Montagu reported, "A few days ago, I went to the dwelling of a woman who had been recommended to me as very poor, very honest, and of great interest." Bibliothèque Historique de la Ville de Paris (BHVP) Mss. 996, rés. 34, *2ème Registre des Délibérations de la Société de Charité Maternelle,* January 7, 1790.

45. ADR 3X 1850, *Société de Charité Maternelle de Lyon, compte-rendu de 1865* (Lyon: Imprimerie de P. Mougin-Rusand, 1866), n.p.

46. Isser Woloch, *The New Regime: Transformations of the French Civic Order, 1789–1820s* (New York: Norton, 1994), 279.

47. This was the case in Bordeaux, Marseille, and Paris. In Marseille, the original Society

for Maternal Charity was an offshoot of the Société de Bienfaisance de Marseille, while in Bordeaux, the society was created by the administration of the Société des Soupes Économiques. See Bibliothèque Municipale de Marseille, 50.079, Société de Bienfaisance de Marseille, *Charité maternelle: arrêté du Comité Administratif de la Société de Bienfaisance de Marseille pour l'institution de la Charité Maternelle*, arrêté au Bureau de Direction, 28 *floréal* and 15 *messidor* year XII; ADG 4J 727, text of arrêté creating the Société de Charité Maternelle de Bordeaux, handwritten extract from *L'écho du commerce de Bordeaux*, n. 2623, n.d. In Paris, the maternal society was subsidized by the Société Philanthropique; see BHVP Mss. 996, rés. 34, séance of February 5, 1790.

48. ADR 4M 523. Printed in Lyon: De l'Imprimerie de la Préfecture aux Halles de la Grenette, 1812.

49. Bibliothèque Municipale de Dijon, Br. IV-1150, Société de Charité Maternelle de Dijon, Poster, n.d.

50. BN Fonds Français Mss. 11369, *Correspondance: Société Maternelle, 1810–14*, letter from vice presidents Ségur and Pastoret to the twelve mayors of Paris, February 9, 1812.

51. BN Fonds Français Mss.11368, Procès-verbal, Comité Central, March 19, 1812. These collaborations could sometimes lead to tensions; Madame de Ségur complained to the minister of the interior on one occasion that "some *bureaux de bienfaisance*, unaware of the rules of our institution and the liberty of choice that they leave to us, have tried many times to prescribe the conditions of admission and to demand that we admit to the assistance of the society women carrying their certificates; this pretension, which we have rightly rejected, often inflamed and emboldened the complaints of the poor whom we could not admit and to whom we preferred other women who, according to our wisdom and our particular information, seemed to us to merit that preference." Procès-verbal, Comité Central, December 12, 1812. The Inspection du Service des Enfants-Trouvés et des Établissements de Bienfaisance of the Gironde sometimes recommended women it chose not to assist to Bordeaux's maternal society. ADG 3X 18, letter from the Département de la Gironde, Inspection du Service des Enfants-Trouvés et des Établissements de Bienfaisance to the prefect, January 26, 1853, and undated letter from the prefect to Madame Guestier.

52. BN Fonds Français Mss. 11368, séance of March 2, 1812. The Conseil d'Administration declined to assist the woman, because she did not live in Paris, and "our assistance does not extend beyond the walls of this city."

53. ADG 3X 18, letters of August 12 and August 17, 1812.

54. Madame Guestier regretfully declined to assist Gallet and her child, noting the "renseignements . . . tellement défavorable" she had uncovered, and that furthermore, "This woman could not produce the certificate of religious marriage required by our bylaws." ADG 3X 18, letter from the prefect of the Gironde to Madame Guestier, January 29, 1853; response from Madame Guestier to the prefect, February 20, 1853.

55. ADG 3X 18, letter from the prefect to Madame Guestier, September 14, 1858. There is no follow-up to this particular request.

56. ADR 3X 1848, letters of June 20 and July 1, 1861.

57. See Archives Départementales de la Seine-Maritime (ADSM) 3XP 213, correspondence between the prefect and the baronne Le Mire, letters dated October 4, 5, and 9, 1870.

58. ADR 3X 1848, letter from the prefect of the Rhône to the minister of the interior, March 24, 1864.

59. BHVP Mss. 996, rés. 34; BN Fonds Français Mss. 11368, *Procès verbaux de la Société de Charité Maternelle, 1810–14.*

60. BHVP Mss. 996, rés. 34.

61. ADR 3X 1848, *Règlement intérieur de la Société de Charité Maternelle de Lyon* (1846), 9.

62. See for example, ADG 3X 18, *Règlement de la Société de Charité Maternelle de Bordeaux* (Bordeaux, 1810), 10.

63. Dupin, *Histoire de l'administration des secours publics,* 331.

64. This emphasis on the feminine and maternal qualities that made women a desirable choice not only for charitable work, but for employment in the "caring professions," continued into the nineteenth and twentieth centuries. See, for example, Smith, *Ladies of the Leisure Class,* 139–40; Linda A. Clark, "Bringing Feminine Qualities into the Public Sphere: The Third Republic's Appointment of Women Inspectors," in *Gender and the Politics of Social Reform in France, 1870–1914,* ed. Elinor A. Accampo, Rachel G. Fuchs, and Mary Lynn Stewart (Baltimore: Johns Hopkins University Press, 1995), 128–56; and F. K. Prochaska, *Women and Philanthropy in Nineteenth-Century England* (Oxford: Clarendon Press, 1980), especially the introduction, 1–17.

65. AAP B-832[17], *Réglemens de la Société de la Charité Maternelle,* 28.

66. Bibliothèque Municipale de Lyon (BML), Fonds Coste 113287, *Compte présenté aux dames composant la Société de Charité Maternelle de Lyon, pour l'année 1834* (Lyon: Louis Perrin, 1835), 7.

67. Sarah A. Curtis argues that women's charitable organizations were on the front lines not only in the war against poverty, but in the war against social revolution. "Charitable Ladies: Gender, Class and Religion in Nineteenth-Century Paris," *Past and Present* 177 (November 2002): 124.

68. Robert Bezucha, *The Lyon Uprising of 1834: Social and Political Conflict in the Early July Monarchy* (Cambridge, Mass.: Harvard University Press, 1974).

69. ADR 3X 1849, *Société de Charité Maternelle de Lyon, compte-rendu de 1849* (Lyon: Chanoine, 1850), n.p.

70. Ibid.

71. ADR 3X 1850, *Société de Charité Maternelle de Lyon, compte-rendu de 1858* (Lyon: Imprimerie de Ve. Mougin-Rusand, 1859), n.p.

72. Alisa Klaus, *Every Child a Lion: The Origins of Maternal and Infant Health Policy in the United States and France* (Ithaca, N.Y.: Cornell University Press, 1993), 111. Jean-Pierre Chaline also cites evidence that indicates this perception on the part of several maternal societies, in "Sociabilité féminine et 'maternalisme,' les Sociétés de Charité Maternelle au XIXe siécle," in *Femmes dans la cité, 1815–1871,* ed. A. Corbin, J. Lalouette, and M. Riot-Sarcey (Grâne: Créaphis, 1997), 75–76.

73. Charles Des Alleurs, *Histoire de la Société de Charité Maternelle de Rouen* (Rouen: Imprimerie de Alfred Péron, 1854), 30–31.

74. AN F[15] 2565, November 22, 1815. A subsequent letter dated April 23, 1817, noted that the population of Lyon was 120,000, with 60,000 workers. Timothy B. Smith argues that public assistance—and thus, perhaps, charitable assistance—in nineteenth-century

Lyon was influenced by a desire to regulate that city's labor supply. "Public Assistance and Labor Supply in Nineteenth-Century Lyon," *Journal of Modern History* 68:1 (March 1996): 1–30.

75. AN F[15] 3806–3811, *Société de Charité Maternelle de Lyon, compte rendu de 1866* (Lyon: P. Mougin-Rusand, 1867).

76. Archives Départementales de la Haute-Vienne (ADHV) 3X 15, *comptes moraux* of the Society for Maternal Charity of Limoges. This seems to be boilerplate language, repeated in most of the accounts.

77. Flacassier, "La Société de Charité Maternelle de Bordeaux," 57–58.

78. On the vulnerability of single women, see Fuchs, *Poor and Pregnant in Paris,* chap. 1, esp. 34.

79. BMB D 11096, letter from the Comité d'Administration aux Dames Distributrices des Secours de la Société, et Surveillantes de leur Emploi (20 *thermidor* year XIII), 4–5.

80. ADG 3X 18, letters of May 19, 22, and 24, 1815.

81. ADG 3X 18, letters of May 23 and 24, 1815.

82. ADG 3X 18, letters of January 26 and 29, 1853, as well as an undated letter from the prefect of the Gironde to Madame Guestier, president of the Société de Charité Maternelle de Bordeaux.

83. ADG 3X 18, letters of November 26 and December 3, 22, and 28, 1812.

84. BN Fonds Français Mss. 11368, séance of February 28, 1811.

85. BHVP Mss. 996, rès. 34, February 20, 1790.

86. BMB D 11096, *Compte rendu,* Bordeaux (1817), 5.

87. BMB D 11096, *Compte rendu,* Bordeaux (1819), 5, (1821), 5.

88. ADSM 3XP 215, *Compte moral,* 1857, presented February 4, 1858.

89. BN Fonds français Mss. 11368, séances of November 9 and December 12, 1812, and March 8, 1813.

90. BMB D 11096, from the Conseil d'Administration aux Dames Distributices des Secours, May 28, 1816.

91. ADSM 3XP 215, *Compte moral,* 1857, presented February 4, 1858; *Compte moral,* 1856, January 31, 1857.

92. Fuchs, *Poor and Pregnant in Paris,* chap. 2.

93. Quoted in Flacassier, "La Société de Charité Maternelle de Bordeaux," 40. Fuchs stresses the prevalence of this attitude in the first half of the nineteenth century in *Poor and Pregnant in Paris,* 39–49.

94. ADBR X² 26, copy of letter written to Madame la comtesse de Pastoret, vice-présidente de la Société de Charité Maternelle de Paris, September 18, 1816.

95. ADG 3X 18, *Règlement de la Société de Charité Maternelle de Bordeaux* (Bordeaux, 1810).

96. ADG 3X 18, *Règlement de la Société de Charité Maternelle de Bordeaux* (Bordeaux, 1815).

97. ADR 3X 1850, *Société de Charité Maternelle de Lyon, compte rendu de 1865,* n.p.

98. See, for example, BHVP Mss. 996, rés. 34, meeting of February 5, 1790, 11; and meeting of March 5, 1790, 15.

99. BHVP Mss 996, rés. 34, General Assembly of January 4, 1790, 2.

100. ADG 3X 18, correspondence of January 11, 16, 18, 23, and 24, 1860.

101. BMB D 11096, *Compte rendu,* Bordeaux (1810), 6.

102. BN Fonds français 11368, procès-verbal, Comité Central, May 18, 1813.

103. Ellen Ross, "Good and Bad Mothers," 178.

104. ADSM 3XP 215, "Compte moral pour 1861," presented (?) February 1862, attached to an undated letter to the prefect of the Seine-Inférieure.

105. BMB D 11096, *Compte rendu,* Bordeaux (1830), 8.

106. BMB D 11096, *Compte rendu,* Bordeaux (1838), 10.

107. ADR 3X 1849, *Compte rendu présenté aux Dames composant la Société de Charité Maternelle, année 1846* (Lyon: H. Brunet, Fonville et Cie, 1847), 3–4.

108. See Carol Blum, *Strength in Numbers: Population, Reproduction, and Power in Eighteenth-Century France* (Baltimore: Johns Hopkins University Press, 2002).

109. BHVP Mss 996, rés 34, séance of February 20, 1790, 12. Each meeting lists the names of the women proposed for assistance, the number of children living, and the number of pregnancies the woman had already experienced.

110. AN F$^{15}$ 2565, *Compte rendu à S. M. l'Impératrice-Reine et Régente,* 1813, 3.

111. Angus McLaren notes that while the fact that lactating women enjoy some contraceptive protection was proven only in the twentieth century, it was popularly believed in the eighteenth and nineteenth centuries. Taboos against intercourse while nursing also would have had the effect of reducing the fertility of nursing mothers. *Sexuality and Social Order: The Debate over the Fertility of Women and Workers in France, 1770–1920* (New York: Holmes and Meier, 1983), 18–19.

112. Stuart Woolf, "The Société de Charité Maternelle," 104. Catherine Duprat even suggests that the somewhat limited participation in Paris's society during the nineteenth century might have been due to the perception that it encouraged fecundity among the poor. However, she offers no evidence making this link. *Usage et pratiques,* 2:622.

113. BMB D 11096, *Compte rendu* (1820), 7.

114. Blum, *Strength in Numbers,* 179–92.

115. See Karen M. Offen, "Depopulation, Nationalism, and Feminism in Fin-de-Siècle France, *American Historical Review* 89:3 (June 1984): 648–76; Joshua H. Cole, "'There Are Only Good Mothers': The Ideological Work of Women's Fertility in France Before World War I," *French Historical Studies* 19:3 (Spring 1996): 639–72.

116. Stansell quoted in Kathleen D. McCarthy, "Parallel Power Structures: Women and the Voluntary Sphere," in *Lady Bountiful Revisited,* 10.

117. Ibid.

118. ADG 3X 16, *Compte rendu* (1824), 6.

119. Louis-Sébastien Mercier, *Tableau de Paris,* vol. 1 (Amsterdam, 1783), 112–14, cited in *Liberty, Equality, Fraternity: Exploring the French Revolution,* accessed July 26, 2007, at http://chnm.gmu.edu/revolution/

120. Vicomte de Falloux, "Variétés: Biographie de Madame de Pastoret," *Annales de la charité* (1846): 243.

121. From the *Journal des Débats,* 1er *floréal* (April 21, 1801), printed in *Paris sous le consulat: recueil des documents pour l'histoire de l'esprit public à Paris,* ed. A. Aulard, 4 vols. (Paris: Cerf, Noblet et Quantin, 1903–9), 2:258.

122. In large cities, each *dame administrante* was assigned to a particular *arrondissement* where she was expected to get to know and administer to the families of that area. Susan

Grogan sees these *femmes de charité* as the precursors of the state-employed *inspectrice* of the twentieth century. "Philanthropic Women and the State: The Société de Charité Maternelle in Avignon, 1802–1917," *French History* 14 (2000): 319–21. The volunteer and paid *dames visiteuses* encouraged by Paul Strauss also reflect this model. Rachel G. Fuchs, "The Right to Life: Paul Strauss and the Politics of Motherhood," in *Gender and the Politics of Social Reform in France*, 100.

123. ADBR X² 26, letter from the *présidente* to the prefect des Bouches-du-Rhône, December 27, 1854.

124. BML Fonds Coste 113287, *Compte présenté aux dames composant la Société de charité maternelle de Lyon*, 1831, 8.

125. ADR 3X 1850, *Société de charité maternelle de Lyon, Compte rendu de 1865*, n.p.

126. Dupin, *Histoire de l'administration des secours publics*, 333–34.

127. ADBR X² 26, Société de Charité Maternelle de Marseille, rapport au Conseil d'Administration de la Société Maternelle par M. le Trésorier honoraire, lû dans le séance du 5 janvier 1816.

128. The vicomte de Falloux, in his *éloge* of Madame de Pastoret, one of the vice presidents of the Society for Maternal Charity of Paris, cites this article of the bylaws to stress that charity "must not happen by proxy." "Biographie de Madame de Pastoret," 224–50.

129. This was common among female charitable associations of this nature. In the case of the Society for the Relief of Poor Widows with small children, one of the first female relief organizations founded in the United States, Kathleen D. McCarthy notes that "Despite the stern tone of their warning, these women envisioned forming personal relationships with those they sought to service; transferring applicants from one manager to another was roundly discouraged." "Parallel Power Structures," 2.

130. ADG 3X 18, letter from the Conseil d'Administration to the prefect of the Gironde, December 1822. The prefect transmitted this information to the Interior Ministry on December 13, 1822.

131. ADSM 3XP 215, "Compte moral pour 1862, présenté à l'Assemblée générale du 11 février 1863," recounted in an undated letter to the prefect; also see other *comptes moraux*.

132. ADHV 3X 15, "Noms des dames composant le bureau de la Société de Charité Maternelle de Limoges," n.d. Limoges's *comptes moraux* regularly note that "The Sisters of Charity assigned by the *bureau de bienfaisance* are very willing to lend their support to the Société de Charité Maternelle and to come to its assistance to distribute aid and oversight that [the society] must exercise over small children."

133. ADHV 3X 15, *Compte moral*, 1867.

134. Alisa Klaus suggests that this ecclesiastical patronage may have decreased the maternal society's popularity with authorities under the Third Republic. *Every Child a Lion*, 114.

135. Sylvie Fayet-Scribe discusses the charitable "*devoir social*" of women in *Associations féminines et catholicisme: XIXe–XXe siècle* (Paris: Les Éditions Ouvrières, 1990), 39–41.

136. *Almanach national pour l'année 1790* (Paris: Chez Cuchet, 1790), 85.

137. ADSM 3XP 215, *Compte moral*, 1859, Rouen, March 11, 1860.

138. Archives Départementales de la Côte d'Or (ADCO) 22 X G, article 1, "Extrait des

registres des délibérations de la Société de Charité Maternelle pour la ville de Dijon," May 21, 1814.

139. ADR 3X 1849, *Rapport et compte rendu présenté aux dames composant la Société de Charité Maternelle, année 1836* (Lyon: Perrin, 1837), 6–7.

140. See BMB D 11096, *comptes rendus*; ADG 3X 18, *Règlement de la Société de Charité Maternelle de Bordeaux* (1810 and 1815).

141. Jean-Pierre Chaline notes that a number of Protestant and Jewish women were among the members of the Parisian society, including Mesdames Louis Cahen, Furtado-Heine, and Isaac Pereire, among others. "Sociabilité féminine et 'maternalisme,'" 71n4.

142. The year 1846 was the first in which the *comptes rendus* for the Society for Maternal Charity of Lyon indicated that the *dames administrantes* operated in the various *arrondissements* of the city based on religious affiliation. See ADR 3X 1849, *Compte rendu présenté aux dames composant la Société de Charité, année 1846* (Lyon: H. Brunet, Fonville et Cie, 1847).

143. See, for example, ADBR X² 26, *Règlement pour la Société de Charité Maternelle de Marseille* (Marseille: Typographie des Hoirs Feissat ainé et Demonchy, 1844), 9 (originally approved in 1816); AN F¹⁵ 2565, *Règlement pour la Société de Charité Maternelle de la ville de Limoges, département de la Haute-Vienne* (Limoges: Chez J. B. et H. Dalesme, 1817), 12; ADCO 22 X G, article 1, *Règlemens de la Société de Charité Maternelle de Dijon* (Paris: De l'Imprimerie Royale, 1822), 13.

144. ADSM 3XP 217, *Société Maternelle de Rouen: règlement* (Rouen: P. Périaux, Père, 1844), 13; see also Des Alleurs, *Histoire de la Société de Charité Maternelle de Rouen,* 107–13.

145. Duprat, *Usage et pratique,* 2:619, fn.

146. ADG 4J 727, Société de Charité Maternelle de Bordeaux, reconnue d'utilité publique par décret du 25 juillet 1811. Nouveaux Statuts approuvés par décret du 9 janvier 1867. *Statuts et règlement* (Bordeaux: Imprimerie Ragot, 1909), *Règlement*, Article 14; ADBR X² 26, *Règlement de la Société de Charité Maternelle de Marseille,* approved May 13, 1851 (manuscript); ADCO *Statuts et règlement de la Société de Charité Maternelle de Dijon* (Dijon: Imprimerie Loireau-Feuchot, 1852), 12.

147. Rachel G. Fuchs, *Abandoned Children: Foundlings and Child Welfare in Nineteenth-Century France* (Albany: State University of New York Press, 1984), 6–16.

148. Reddy, *The Navigation of Feeling,* 324–30.

149. ADG 4J 710, *Assemblée générale annuelle des bienfaiteurs de la Société de Charité Maternelle de Bordeaux, rapport sur l'exercise 1870* (Bordeaux: Rabot, 1871), 6.

150. Michel Foucault offered the classic formulation of the escalating intervention of the state into private matters with the increasing "tutelage" of the family in *An Introduction,* vol. 1 of *A History of Sexuality,* trans. Robert Hurley (New York: Random House/Vintage Books, 1978). Jacques Donzelot keyed in on the alliance between the state and the family, and the different repercussions for rich and poor, in *The Policing of Families,* trans. Robert Hurley (New York: Random House/Pantheon Books, 1979).

151. ADG 3X 18, Société de Charité Maternelle de Bordeaux, Ordonnance du Roi, October 1822; the Conseil d'Administration of Bordeaux found this highly objectionable, arguing that it would "remove from our administrative functions very charitable and very

active ladies who, having no protectors at Court, would not want to risk being refused by Her Royal Highness." In 1855, Rouen's maternal society changed its bylaws to accommodate the empress's desire to name the president and vice president of all maternal societies. ADSM 3XP 217, letter from Elie Lefébure, president, to the prefect of the Seine-Inférieure, May 24, 1855.

152. For a discussion of domesticity in the French context, see Smith, *Ladies of the Leisure Class;* and Elizabeth Fox-Genovese and Eugene D. Genovese, *Fruits of Merchant Capital: Slavery and Bourgeois Property in the Rise and Expansion of Capitalism* (Oxford: Oxford University Press, 1983), chap. 11. On civic motherhood, see Offen, "Reclaiming the Enlightenment for Feminism."

153. Catherine Hall, "The Sweet Delights of Home," in *From the Fires of Revolution to the Great War,* ed. Michelle Perrot, vol. 4 of *A History of Private Life,* gen. ed. Philippe Ariès and Georges Duby, trans. Arthur Goldhammer (Cambridge, Mass.: Belknap Press of Harvard University Press, 1990), 77–78.

154. Smith, *Ladies of the Leisure Class,* 138.

## Chapter 4. Charitable Associations and Public-utility Status

1. See A. de Faget de Casteljau, *Histoire du droit d'association de 1789 à 1901* (Paris: Libraire Nouvelle de Droit et de Jurisprudence, Arthur Rousseau, Éditeur, 1905), 154.

2. Paul Nourrisson, *Histoire de la liberté d'association en France depuis 1789,* 2 vols. (Paris: Librairie de la Société du Recueil Sirey, 1920), introduction, 1:16.

3. Archives Départementales de la Gironde (ADG) 4J 727, copy of legal opinion rendered by Lacoste, St. Marc, and Vaucher, June 4, 1850, attached to *Compte rendu des opérations de la conseil d'adminstration de la Société de Charité Maternelle de Bordeaux pour l'année 1853.* Several other copies exist in the same dossier containing the correspondence dealing with the issue of the Bordeaux society's legal status and its efforts to obtain the appellation of *utilité publique.*

4. See, for example, Carol E. Harrison, *The Bourgeois Citizen in Nineteenth-Century France: Gender, Sociability, and the Uses of Emulation* (Oxford: Oxford University Press, 1999), 22–23. The chief exception would be associations that called into question the existing social structure—for example, Saint-Simonian or workers' organizations. See Evelyne Lejeune-Resnick, *Femmes et associations (1830/1880): vraies démocrates ou dames patronnesses?* (Paris: Publisud, 1991), 15–19.

5. In her study of associational life in Villefranche-sur-Saône, Grange found that approximately 1.5 percent of the associations were exclusively female. *L'apprentissage de l'association, 1850–1914: naissance du secteur volontaire non lucrative dans l'arrondissement de Villefranche-sur-Saône* (Paris: Mutualité Française, 1993), 67, 94. See also 92–93.

6. Catherine Duprat, "Le silence des femmes: associations féminines du premier XIXe siècle," in *Femmes dans la cité, 1815–1871,* ed. A. Corbin, J. Lalouette, and M. Riot-Sarcey (Grâne: Éditions Créaphis, 1997), 79–100, especially 96–97. Annie Grange also suggests that it was difficult for women to exercise public responsibility, which restricted the visibility of their associational activities. *L'apprentissage de l'association,* 94. It is worth noting that most provincial maternal societies did hold general assemblies of subscribers and

benefactors each year, unlike the Paris society, which Duprat examined. Sarah A. Curtis suggests that this lack of interest in the political role of female charitable associations extends to historians, who have done much more research on men's Catholic charity associations, which were more explicitly political and which left more abundant records. "Charitable Ladies: Gender, Class and Religion in Nineteenth-Century Paris," *Past and Present* 177 (November 2002): 122.

7. David H. Pinkney, *Decisive Years in France, 1840–1847* (Princeton, N.J.: Princeton University Press, 1986), 64.

8. Stéphane Gerson, *The Pride of Place: Local Memories and Political Culture in Nineteenth-Century France* (Ithaca, N.Y.: Cornell University Press, 2003), 67.

9. Patrick Joyce, *The Rule of Freedom: Liberalism and the Modern City* (London: Verso, 2003), 1–3.

10. For a more detailed theoretical discussion of strategies of liberal rule, see Nikolas Rose, "Governing 'Advanced' Liberal Democracies," in *Foucault and Political Reason: Liberalism, Neo-liberalism and Rationalities of Government,* ed. Andrew Barry, Thomas Osborne, and Nikolas Rose (Chicago: University of Chicago Press, 1996), 37–64.

11. Gerson cites numerous examples of this resistance in *The Pride of Place;* see especially chap. 6. See also Timothy B. Smith, *Creating the Welfare State in France, 1880–1940* (Montreal: McGill–Queen's University Press, 2003), 33–36.

12. Religion had long played a political role in France, in particular since the time of the Revolution. Women, possessing few political outlets, frequently used religious ritual to signal and justify political resistance. For one example of this, see Suzanne Desan, *Reclaiming the Sacred: Lay Religion and Popular Politics in Revolutionary France* (Ithaca, N.Y.: Cornell University Press, 1990), chap. 5. On tensions between the ministers of Louis-Philippe and the Catholic church, see H. A. C. Collingham, *The July Monarchy: A Political History of France, 1830–1848* (London: Longman, 1988), chap. 22; on relations between Legitimists and the regime of Napoleon III, see Roger Price, *The French Second Empire: An Anatomy of Political Power* (Cambridge: Cambridge University Press, 2001), chap. 9.

13. Catherine Duprat outlines the affiliations of the members of the Paris society in *Usage et pratiques de la philanthropie: pauvreté, action sociale et lien social, à Paris, au cours du premier XIXe siècle,* 2 vols. (Paris: Association pour l'Étude de l'Histoire de la Sécurité Sociale, 1996–97), 2:616–35.

14. Pétronille-Marie Baudot, Madame Ranfer de Bretenières, was the first president of the Dijon maternal society. Her grandson, Edmond de Bretenières, was well known for his political activity on behalf of Legitimists and for the intensely religious nature of his family life; his wife, Anne-Jeanne-Baptiste-Marie Lantin de Montcoy, Madame de Bretenières, served as a *dame administrante,* in addition to many other charitable ventures. A. Cornereau, *Notice sur la Société de Charité Maternelle de Dijon* (Dijon: Darantière, 1900), 22, 32n35, 34n87; Pierre Lévêque, *La Bourgogne de Lamartine à nos jours* (Dijon: Éditions Universitaires de Dijon, 2006), 305–13.

15. Fernande Bassan, *Politique et haute société à l'époque romantique: la famille Pastoret d'après sa correspondance (1788–1856)* (Paris: Lettres Modernes Minard, 1969), 22.

16. Mary P. Ryan, *Cradle of the Middle Class: The Family in Oneida County, New York, 1790–1865* (Cambridge: Cambridge University Press, 1981), 123.

17. See, for example, M. Grégoire Raymond's legacy of 20,000 FF in 1821. F. Gille, *La Société de Charité Maternelle de Paris* (Paris: Imprimerie de V. Goupy et Jourdan, 1887), 57.

18. Archives Départmentales du Rhône (ADR) 3X 1848, letter from the Interior Ministry to the prefect of the Rhône, October 10, 1855 (this was a *circulaire* sent out to all prefects). The Interior Ministry carefully tracked the excess funds of maternal societies to make sure that they were not left *"improductifs."* See letter from the minister of the interior to the prefect of the Rhône, December 15, 1855.

19. The *comptes rendus* record *dons* and *legs* (gifts and legacies) as well as the interest from any invested funds under *recettes*. Beginning in 1868, Bordeaux's annual report listed its *"principaux bienfaiteurs"* (those contributing at least 500 francs) from 1817 onward.

20. Archives Départementales des Bouches-du-Rhône (ADBR) X² 26, Société de Charité Maternelle de Marseille, "Legs fait à la Société."

21. Archives Départementales de la Côte d'Or (ADCO) 22 X G, article 3; documents relating to legacies and donations.

22. H. Drouin, A. Gory, and F. Worms, *Traité théorique et pratique l'assistance publique*, 2 vols. (Paris: Librairie de la Société de Recueil Général des Lois et des Arrêts, 1900), 1:4n1.

23. Jean-Luc Marais, *Histoire du don en France de 1800 à 1939: dons et legs charitables, pieux et philanthropiques* (Rennes: Presses Universitaires de Rennes, 1999), 55.

24. Duprat, "Le silence des femmes," 83; Evelyne Lejeune-Resnick notes that authorities were more comfortable when women's associations pursued strictly philanthropic goals and did not stray into policy. *Femmes et associations*, 15.

25. Christiane Douyère-Demeulenaere, "Femmes et associations dans les archives publiques," in *Un siècle de vie associative: quelles opportunités pour les femmes?*, ed. Evelyne Diebolt and Christiane Douyère-Demeulenaere (Paris: Colloque International Tenu à l'Assemblée Nationale et au Centre Historique des Archives Nationales et au Centre Historique des Archives Nationales, le 14–15 mai 2001 pour la Commémoration du Centenaire de la Loi 1901), 180. I thank Karen Offen for the reference.

26. Léon Béquet, *Régime et législation de l'assistance publique et privée en France* (Paris: Société d'Imprimerie et Librairies Administratives et des Chemins de Fer, Paul Dupon, Éditeur, 1885), 300.

27. See Lucien Jaume, "Une liberté en souffrance: l'association au XIXe siècle," in *Associations et champ politique: la loi de 1901 à l'épreuve du siècle*, ed. Claire Andrieu, Gilles Le Béguec, and Danielle Tartakowsky (Paris: Publications de la Sorbonne, 2001), 79.

28. Nourrisson, *Histoire de la liberté d'association*, 1:176; Charles Beaumont, *Extension de la capacité civile des associations privées de bienfaisance* (Avesnes-sur-Helpe: Éditions de l'Observateur, 1936), 52. Articles 910 and 938 of the *Code civil* regulated associational activity; subsequent to Napoleon, the laws of January 2, 1817; May 24, 1825; and April 10, 1834, also governed associations. Béquet, *Régime et législation de l'assistance publique et privée en France*, 300.

29. Maurice Agulhon, *Le cercle dans la France bourgeoise, 1810–1848: étude d'une mutation de sociabilité* (Paris: Armand Colin, 1977), 21. Article 294 required municipal permission prior to meetings. Faget de Casteljau, *Histoire du droit d'association*, 173–81, 207; Nourrisson, *Histoire de la liberté d'association*, 1:184.

30. Articles 292–94 enumerated sanctions to be imposed in case of infractions of article 291. For the text of the law, see *Répertoire du droit administratif,* 28 vols., ed. Léon Bequet et al. (Paris: Société d'Imprimerie et des Chemins de Fer, 1884–1911), 2:490.

31. Béquet, *Régime et législation,* 304. Evelyne Lejeune-Resnick notes that in the nineteenth century, women became active in a wide variety of associations that focused specifically on women's needs and issues "in favor of children, popular education, prisoners, but also, quite simply, in defense of their interests." See *Femmes et associations,* 15.

32. Catherine Duprat suggests that the government preferred this quasi-legal regime of "tolerance." "If societies were not authorized, the government could suspend them, when it wanted to, without the need to provide a reason other than the infraction of article 291 of the penal code." *Usage et pratiques,* 2:1,100.

33. Nourrisson, *Histoire de la liberté d'association,* 1:24.

34. Béquet, *Régime et législation,* 307–8.

35. Barthélemy Terrat, *Quelques considérations sur les biens de mainmorte* (Lille: Imprimerie Victor Ducoulumbier, 1897), 13.

36. On the concept of "police," see Christopher L. Tomlins, "Law, Police, and the Pursuit of Happiness in the New American Republic," *Studies in American Political Development* 4 (1990): 3–34.

37. Félix Garcin, *La mainmorte, le pouvoir, l'opinion de 1749 à 1901* (Paris: Librairie de la Société du Recueil Général des Lois et des Arrêts, and Librairie A. Cote, 1903), 194–95.

38. Charles Amédée Vuillefroy and Léon Monnier, *Principes d'administration, extraits des avis du Conseil d'État et du Comité de l'Intérieur, des circulaires ministérielles, etc., etc.* (Paris: Joubert, Librairie-Éditeur, 1837), 443.

39. Archives nationales (AN) AD XIV 12, *Rapport sur l'établissement de la Charité-Maternelle de Paris par le Comité de Mendicité* (Paris: De l'Imprimerie Nationale, 1790), 4.

40. AN F15 3894, "Notes pour le budget, 1836," and "Notes pour le budget du Ministère de l'Intérieur."

41. Ad. de Watteville, ed., *Législation charitable, ou recueil des lois, arrêtés, décrets, ordonnances royales, avis du Conseil d'État, circulaires, décisions et instructions des ministres de l'intérieur et des finances, arrêts de la Cour des Comptes, etc., etc., qui régissent des établissements de bienfaisance, mise en ordre et annotée, avec une préface par Ad. de Watteville* (Paris: Alexandre Heois, 1843), 178–79.

42. Archives de l'Assistance Publique (AAP) 4771. The legal opinion requested by the Society for Maternal Charity of Bordeaux in 1850 noted, "However, it was never questioned that the Société de Charité Maternelle of Paris possessed that capacity, and it has constantly conducted all civil acts without the least impediment." ADG 4J 727, legal opinion rendered by Lacoste, St. Marc, and Vaucher, June 4, 1850. Catherine Duprat verifies this point. See *Usage et pratiques,* 2:1,094–95.

43. For example, the *comptes rendus* of Bordeaux's society list each year's returns from *rentes* and any extraordinary legacy or donation. In 1832, M. Verneuilh bequeathed a building to the society; see ADG 4J 710, *Compte rendu des opérations du conseil d'administration de la Société de Charité Maternelle de Bordeaux pour l'année 1832* (1833), 9. Various prefects of the Bouches-du-Rhône authorized Marseille's maternal society to accept at least five legacies between 1825 and 1844—it wasn't until 1844 that the minister of the interior objected to the prefect's recommendation to accept the donation, because the Marseille so-

ciety lacked public-utility status. ADBR X² 26, Société de Charité Maternelle de Marseille, "Legs fait à la Société." Lyon also received a number of gifts and bequests prior to 1842, including a legacy of 600 francs from Mesdames Vitton et Cost-Bethenod. Bibliothèque Municipale de Lyon (BML), Fonds Coste 113287, *Compte présenté aux dames composant la Société de Charité Maternelle de Lyon, 1831,* 4. Various *comptes rendus* note the investments of Lyon's maternal society in *rentes.* Charles Des Alleurs's account of the Society for Maternal Charity of Rouen makes note of the legacies it received prior to 1844, including 1,500 FF in 1830 and another 1,000 in 1836. *Histoire de la Société de Charité Maternelle de Rouen* (Rouen: Imprimerie de Alfred Péron, 1854).

44. Bibliothèque Municipale de Bordeaux (BMB) D 11096, *Compte rendu des opérations du conseil d'administration de la Société de Charité Maternelle de Bordeaux à Mmes et Mrs. Les bienfaiteurs de l'année 1818,* 10.

45. This was in accordance with articles 910 and 937 of the *Code civil.* See *Code civil des français: édition originale et seule officielle* (Paris: De l'Imprimerie de la République, 1804), 221 and 228. This authorization was necessary to ensure "the tutelage of the state over institutions, governmental authorization, and the protection of families." Marais, *Histoire du don,* 27.

46. The Interior Ministry was responsible for the surveillance of associations. Douyère-Demeulenaere, "Femmes et associations dans les archives publiques," 181.

47. A letter signed by the *sous-secrétaire d'état* for the minister of the interior to the prefect of the Gironde dated May 25, 1842, summarizes the previous correspondence between the minister and the prefect and outlines the arguments on both sides. See ADG 3X 16, "Société de Charité Maternelle de Bordeaux, demande de déclaration d'utilité publique," 1842–54.

48. The heated three-way correspondence concerning these issues can be found in ADG 3X 16, "Société de Charité Maternelle de Bordeaux, demande de déclaration d'utilité publique, 1842–54," and 4J 727, "Société de Charité Maternelle de Bordeaux, correspondance, 1847–74." The emphasis on the "particular circumstances" and customs of the Bordeaux region reflects the heightened awareness of regional particularism at a time of growing Parisian centralization that Stéphane Gerson discusses in *The Pride of Place,* 95–97. Timothy Smith also highlights this point in his analysis of the Lyon Municipal Council's resistance to prefectoral interference in the operation of local charity and public assistance. See *Creating the Welfare State,* 31–40.

49. ADG 3X 16, letter of March 8, 1851.

50. Catherine Duprat cites the case of the Infirmerie Marie-Thérèse, a diocesan establishment with royal patrons. In 1846 the *infirmerie*—which had already received several legacies—requested permission to receive another. According to Duprat, "a fussy bureaucrat, responsible for preparing the authorization to approve acceptance [of the legacy], thought to research whether the foundation had ever been endowed with the authorization that would allow it to receive donations and legacies." Finding no mention of the *infirmerie*'s legal status in the *Bulletin des Lois,* he refused approval, which resulted in two years of correspondence among the archbishopric, the Ministry of Religion, the Prefecture of the Seine, and the mayor of Paris. A compromise was reached after June 1848 with the new ministry. *Usage et pratiques,* 2:1,097.

51. AN F15 3894, draft of a letter from the Interior Ministry, n.d.

52. ADBR X² 26, letter of January 31, 1844.

53. ADBR X² 26, *Règlement pour la Société de la Charité Maternelle de Marseille* (Marseille, 1844). See especially 10–11.

54. Vaublanc had responded, "Private charitable donations are all the more abundant when their use is left unfettered and the sentiments that have brought together the Ladies who make up the [membership of] the maternal societies to come to the aid of indigent mothers must be considered a sufficient guarantee of the care that they will bring to regulate their expenses in an economical fashion & to make the most useful employ of the funds at their disposal. For these reasons, M. le Préfet, I am willing to excuse the Société de Charité Maternelle of Marseille from submitting its bylaws & annual accounts for my approval & they will be drawn up in the form that the Société considers the most suitable." See ADBR X2 26, letters of April 17 and May 10, 1844.

55. AN F15 2564, letter from the minister of the interior, June 21, 1816: "Instructions sur la comptabilité des hospices et établissements de charité." Correspondence between the Interior Ministry and the prefects of both the Gironde and the Bouches-du-Rhône demonstrates that the Interior Ministry required detailed accounts from the various branches of the maternal societies in exchange for yearly subsidies. See ADG 3X 17 and 3X 18, 1814–39 and 1822–60; ADBR X2 26, "Secours et dépenses, 1817–1825 and 1824–1831."

56. ADBR X² 26, letter of August 28, 1847.

57. ADBR X² 26, letter of December 11, 1847. The prefect transmitted the request to the minister of the interior, but without offering any words of support on the society's behalf. Letter of December 20, 1847.

58. ADBR X² 26, letter of January 15, 1848.

59. ADR 4M 523, "Extrait du registre de délibérations de la Société de Charité Maternelle de Lyon," séance of April 29, 1842. On June 11, 1842, the prefect forwarded various documents to the mayor of Lyon, along with the maternal society's request for recognition as *utilité publique.* Archives Municipales de Lyon, 744 WP 074, letter of June 11, 1842.

60. Des Alleurs, *Histoire de la Société de Charité Maternelle de Rouen,* 77.

61. ADCO 22 X G, article 3, letter from the president of the Société de Charité Maternelle de Dijon to the prefect, January 28, 1849; A. Cornereau, *Notice sur la Société de Charité Maternelle de Dijon,* 27–28.

62. Archives Départementales de la Haute-Vienne (ADHV) 3X 15, letter from the Interior Ministry to the prefect of the Haute-Vienne, January 21, 1844. Présidente Louise Alluaud sent two copies of the bylaws to the prefect on April 16, 1844; he sent them on to the Interior Ministry on April 20, 1844.

63. Collingham, *The July Monarchy,* chap. 10.

64. Paul Thureau-Dangin, *Histoire de la Monarchie de Juillet,* 6 vols., 5th ed. (Paris: Plon, 1914), 2:217.

65. See Pamela Pilbeam, *Republicanism in Nineteenth-Century France, 1814–1871* (New York: St. Martin's Press, 1995), 97–100; Thureau-Dangin, *Histoire de la Monarchie de Juillet,* 2:220–21.

66. Edwin De T. Bechtel, *Freedom of the Press and l'Association Mensuelle: Philipon versus Louis-Philippe* (New York: The Grolier Club, 1952), 31.

67. Thureau-Dangin, *Histoire de la Monarchie de Juillet,* 2:228–29.

68. The uprising of 1834 was the largest urban disturbance in France between the

Revolutions of 1830 and 1848. The Law on Associations was signed into being on April 10, 1834, the second day of the Lyon uprising. See Robert J. Bezucha, *The Lyon Uprising of 1834: Social and Political Conflict in the Early July Monarchy* (Cambridge, Mass.: Harvard University Press, 1974), especially 135. On the law of 1834, see Faget de Casteljau, *Histoire du droit d'association*, 226–61; and Thureau-Dangin, *Histoire de la Monarchie de Juillet*, 2:235.

69. Thureau-Dangin, *Histoire de la Monarchie de Juillet*, 2: 236; Faget de Casteljau, *Histoire du droit d'association*, 277.

70. Faget de Casteljau, *Histoire du droit d'association*, 285–87, 301. Paul Nourrisson sees this legislation as "un recul dans l'histoire de la liberté d'association" (a step backward in the history of the freedom of association). *Histoire de la liberté d'association*, 1:286. See Bequet, *Répertoire du droit administratif*, 486 and 490 for the text and explanation of the Law on Associations of 1834.

71. Roger L. Williams, *The World of Napoleon III, 1851–1870* (New York: The Free Press, 1957), 40–41; Harrison, *The Bourgeois Citizen*, 30–31; Thureau-Dangin, *Histoire de la Monarchie de Juillet*, 2: 236–37.

72. Duprat, *Usage et pratiques*, 2:1,095–97. On the Société Philanthropique, see Catherine Duprat, *"Pour l'amour de l'humanité": le temps des philanthropes: la philanthropie parisien des Lumières à la monarchie de Juillet* (Paris: Éditions de C.T.H.S., 1993), 65–75.

73. Ferdinand-Dreyfus, *L'assistance sous la Second République (1848–1851)* (Paris: Édouard Cornély et Cie., Éditeurs, 1907), 14.

74. See Chapter 5 this volume.

75. Duprat, in *Usage et pratiques*, discusses both the background of misery in the nineteenth century and the ongoing response through the creation of voluntary associations. See also Gerson, *The Pride of Place*, 124.

76. According to Vuillefroy and Monnier, "On doit chercher à prévoir toutes les difficultés qui pourraient amener de fâcheuses collisions entre ces sociétés et les fonctionnaires publics chargés de la direction ou de la surveillance des services analogues" (One must try to anticipate any difficulties that could lead to unfortunate clashes between these organizations and the public functionaries responsible for the direction or the oversight of similar services). Vuillefroy and Monnier, *Principes d'administration*, 444.

77. Terrat, *Quelques considérations sur les biens de mainmorte*, 13–14; Garcin, *La mainmorte, le pouvoir, l'opinion*, 131–83.

78. See Terrat, *Quelques considérations sur les biens de mainmorte*, 4.

79. This was part of the justification for requiring that the Council of State approve charitable legacies of more than 300 francs to hospitals. Isser Woloch notes that "According to a report on 'legal charity' in the early nineteenth century, 'the action of the Council of State tends to moderate the exaggerated zeal of the benefactors and to restore to the dispossessed family the portion which seems beneficial for its needs.'" See *The New Regime: Transformations of the French Civic Order, 1789–1820s* (New York: Norton, 1994), 276.

80. In the case of Bordeaux, more men than women left money to the Society for Maternal Charity. However, some of the most generous legacies—including 25,000 FF from the Widow Strekeysen in 1819, subsequently invested in a *rente*—came from women. Archives Municipales de Bordeaux (AMB) 312 Q 1, "Assemblée générale annuelle des bienfaiteurs

de la Société de Charité Maternelle de Bordeaux, preside par S.G. Mgr, l'Archevêque de Bordeaux, rapport sur l'exercice 1883."

81. See Suzanne Desan, *The Family on Trial in Revolutionary France* (Berkeley: University of California Press, 2004), chap. 4.

82. Marais, *Histoire du don,* 28 ; Ferdinand-Dreyfus, *L'assistance sous la Second République,* 138.

83. On the disputed Guiraut succession, see ADG 3X 17, "Dons et legs, M. Guiraut à la Société de Charité Maternelle, 1867–1870"; ADG 4J 710, *Comptes rendus,* 1866 and 1867.

84. Quoted in Marais, whose analysis of this issue influenced my interpretation. *Histoire du don,* 28–29.

85. Terrat, *Quelques considérations sur les biens de mainmorte,* 4.

86. Smith, *Creating the Welfare State in France,* 15–16.

87. Collingham, *The July Monarchy,* 304; Anne-Martin Fugier, *La vie quotidienne de Louis-Philippe et de sa famille* (Paris: Hachette, 1992), 206.

88. As Lucien Jaume points out, liberals were often as suspicious of associations as were conservatives—although for different reasons. See "Une liberté en souffrance," 82–84. Catherine Duprat agrees that the July Monarchy was less favorable toward Catholic associations than the Restoration government had been. *Usage et pratiques,* 1:473–83.

89. Marais, *Histoire du don,* 38.

90. See Terrat, *Quelques considérations sur les biens de mainmorte,* 19.

91. Duprat, *Usage et pratiques,* 2:632.

92. Alisa Klaus, *Every Child a Lion: The Origins of Maternal and Infant Health Policy in the United States and France* (Ithaca, N.Y.: Cornell University Press, 1993), 114–16; Catherine Rollet-Echalier, *La politique à l'égard de la petite enfance sous la IIIe République* (Paris: Presses Universitaires de France, 1990), 378. Also see Chapter 5 and Epilogue of this volume.

93. Duprat, *Usage et pratiques,* 2:1217.

94. Marais, *Histoire du don,* 38–43.

95. Maréchal Soult was the official head of government, as the *président du conseil* and minister of war, but Guizot, as foreign minister, effectively controlled the government. Collingham, *The July Monarchy,* 289–302.

96. However, it is worth noting that Charles Des Alleurs complained that the government "répugnait à ces sortes de reconnaissance" (was reluctant to offer these types of recognition) and he believed that this was part of the reason for the slow movement regarding the application for public-utility status on the part of the Rouen maternal society. *Histoire de la Société de Charité Maternelle de Rouen,* 81.

97. This translation was accessed at http://www.readprint.com/chapter-574/Honore-de-Balzac, April 30, 2006. The original reads as follows: "On compte environ quarante mille employés en France . . . pour ce prix, la France obtient la plus fureteuse, la plus méticuleuse, la plus écrivassière, paperassière, inventorière, contrôleuse, vérifiante, soigneuse, enfin la plus femme de ménage des Administrations connues! Il ne se dépense pas, il ne s'encaisse pas un centime en France qui ne soit ordonné par une lettre, prouvé par une pièce, produit et reproduit sur des états de situation, payé sur quittance; puis la demande et la quittance sont enregistrées, contrôlées, vérifiées par des gens à lunettes." See Honoré de Balzac, *Études de moeurs. 3e livres. Scènes de la vie parisienne, T. XI* [sic]:

*les employés ou la femme supérieure.* Document fourni par les editions Acamedia, http://www.acamedia.fr, accessed at http://www.gallica.fr, April 30, 2006. I thank the anonymous reviewer at the *Law and History Review* for this reference.

98. ADBR X² 26, letter of June 6, 1848; ADG 3X 16, letter of June 16, 1848.

99. ADG 3X 16, letters of June 22 and July 1, 1848.

100. See Ferdinand-Dreyfus, *L'assistance sous la Second République,* especially chap. 5.

101. ADG 3X 16, letters of December 8 and 28, 1848; January 29, February 8, 12 and 24, March 12 and 16, July 28, August 1 and 25, and November 7, 1849; and March 27, 1850.

102. For a list of donations made to the Society for Maternal Charity of Bordeaux between 1843 and 1853 (and whose acceptance was delayed by its disputed legal status), see AMB 312 Q 1, "Conseil d'administration, assemblée générale des bienfaiteurs de la Société de Charité Maternelle de Bordeaux, présidée par S.G. Mgr, l'Archevêque de Bordeaux, rapport sur l'exercice 1883," 13.

103. Faget de Casteljau, *Histoire du droit d'association,* 319–44.

104. Jaume, "La liberté en souffrance," 85–86.

105. The prefect supported the society in its resistance; he believed that it would be possible to establish an annual budget "comme une mesure de comptabilité qui peut être imposée à la Société de Bordeaux sans qu'il soit nécessaire de l'inscrire dans le règlement" (as an accounting step that could be imposed on the Société of Bordeaux without the need to put it in the bylaws). As for the "receveur salarié & soumis à une cautionnement" (salaried officer who will provide a [financial] guarantee), he argued that the society "ne pouvant jamais manquer de trouver parmi ses membres quelqu'un d'honnête et de soluable qui se chargera gratuitement des fonctions de trésorier" (can never fail to find among its members someone honest and solvent who will take on the functions of treasurer *gratis*) and that a paid treasurer would add nothing to the security of the society's funds. However, the permanent secretary for the Interior disagreed and ordered the society to bring itself into conformity with the models provided. Until then, he would not authorize acceptance of the legacies left to the society by Madame Arnozan and le sieur Fayolle. The prefect passed the secretary's message on to Madame Guestier. ADG 3X 16, "Société de Charité Maternelle de Bordeaux, demande de déclaration d'utilité publique, 1842–1854," letters of March 12 and 16, 1849.

106. ADG 3X 16, letter of July 28, 1849.

107. The assets were listed as follows: "This Société has 2,873 francs in *rentes* at five percent coming from the sum that has been left to it for that purpose; in addition, a house which was also passed on to it in a will. The acceptance of these various donations was authorized by royal ordinances." According to the notes attached to the legal opinion, the society had been authorized to accept a bequest from Verneuilh on December 31, 1831, and from Capelle on May 20, 1834. ADG 4J 727, Correspondance, 1847–74.

108. The relevant section, quoted in the legal opinion of Lacoste, St. Marc, and Vaucher, reads: " . . . these establishments must be regulated and supervised, and consequently the Minister of the Interior, after having accounted for these establishments, must, through a report to His Majesty, submit to him their bylaws and put him in a position to decide, in his Conseil d'État, which ones he must get rid of, which ones can be maintained, and what means are suitable to put into place for the regulation and the administration of the latter."

109. ADG 4J 727, legal opinion rendered by Lacoste, St. Marc, and Vaucher, June 4, 1850.

110. Madame Guestier had forwarded the *mémoire* to the prefect, noting that the consultation was prepared by "three eminent members of our bar," who were in complete agreement with the contention of the administrative council that their society "is regularly and legally organized and that it is qualified to collect donations, as it is to perform all other acts of civil life, without being first reorganized and recognized as an *établissement d'utilité publique.*" ADG 3X 16, letters of August 3, 1850, and February 20, 1851.

111. ADG 3X 16, letter of March 8, 1851.

112. ADG 3X 16, letter of March 11, 1851.

113. ADG 3X 16, letter of September 20, 1853.

114. Howard C. Payne, *The Police State of Louis-Napoleon Bonaparte, 1851–1860* (Seattle: University of Washington Press, 1966), 153.

115. Marais, *Histoire du don,* 44; Nourrisson, *Histoire de la liberté d'association,* 2:62 and 102.

116. Harrison, *The Bourgeois Citizen,* 32–33.

117. Victoire Bidegain, "L'origine d'une réputation: l'image de l'impératrice Eugénie dans la société française du Second Empire (1853–1870)," in *Femmes dans la cité,* 61.

118. ADG 3X 16, letters of April 12 and October 20, 1854.

119. See Paul Delaunay, *La Société de Charité Maternelle du Mans et ses origines* (Le Mans: Imprimerie Monnoyer, 1911), 20.

120. ADG 3X 16, letter of April 16, 1853.

121. ADG 3X 16, Société de Charité Maternelle de Bordeaux, decree signed by Napoleon February 24, 1855. A modification was made to article 10 of the statutes: the empress wanted to retain the right to name the president and vice president of the society herself. ADG 3X 16, letter of March 5, 1855. See also ADG 4J 727, *Société de Charité Maternelle de Bordeaux, statuts et règlement* (Bordeaux, 1909), 9–10. The bylaws were adopted by the administrative council on March 28, 1854. See page 13. The minister of the interior had informed the prefect in a letter sent on May 27, 1853, that only the statutes needed imperial approval. When the prefect forwarded approval of the statutes to Madame Guestier on March 8, 1855, he noted that he would now need to approve the bylaws that had been adopted by the conseil d'administration on March 28, 1854. However, the minister noted on May 8, 1855, that he had found a couple of problems with the bylaws as submitted and they needed to be brought into conformity with article 18 of the statutes. ADG 3X 16, "Correspondance, statuts et règlements."

122. ADBR X[2] 26, letter of November 5, 1848.

123. ADBR X[2] 26, letter from the conseil d'administration of the Société de Charité Maternelle de Marseille to the prefect of the Bouches-du-Rhône, January 10, 1815; letter from the Interior Ministry to the prefect of the Bouches-du-Rhône, September 18, 1816.

124. ADBR X[2] 26, letter of December 23, 1848.

125. ADBR X[2] 26, letter of January 15, 1849.

126. See ADBR X[2] 26, letters of March 16 and 31, April 18, 27, and 28, May 12 and 19, June 18, July 4, and August 8, 1849; and February 9, 1850.

127. ADBR X[2] 26, Société de Charité Maternelle de Marseille, decree issued by Louis Napoleon Bonaparte, president of the republic, January 2, 1851.

128. ADBR X² 26, *Statuts de la Société de Charité Maternelle de Marseille*, articles 9, 12, and 13; *Règlement de la Société de Charité Maternelle de Marseille*, articles 12 and 14.

129. ADCO 22 X G, article 3, correspondence and other documents on public-utility status, 1847–52; Cornereau, *Notice sur la Société de Charité Maternelle de Dijon*, 27–28.

130. ADR 4M 523, letter from the Interior Ministry to the prefect of the Rhône, February 9, 1846.

131. ADR 4M 523, "Extrait du registre de délibérations de la Société de Charité Maternelle de Lyon," séance of April 29, 1842; ADR 3X 1849, *Compte rendu présenté aux dames composant la Société de Charité Maternelle de Lyon au nom du conseil d'administration, année 1846* (Lyon: Imprimerie d'H. Brunet, Fonvielle et Cie., 1847), 4.

132. Archives Départementales de la Seine-Maritime (ADSM) 3XP 213, note drafted by the prefect, no date.

133. Des Alleurs, *La Société de Charité Maternelle de Rouen*, 79.

134. Ibid., 81–85.

135. ADSM 3XP 217, letter from Charles Des Alleurs to the prefect of the Seine-Inférieure, March 18, 1849.

136. ADHV 3X 15, letters of August 28, 1847; April 19 and 23, 1849; May 2, 14, and 21, 1849; June 11 and 25, 1849; and July 3 and 20, 1849. In the late 1850s, the president of Limoges's Society for Maternal Charity, along with the prefect, began to look into the process of obtaining public-utility status for the society. However, I found no evidence that this status was ever granted. See letters of March 20, 1856, and February 25 and March 3, 1858.

137. ADSM 3XP 217, letter of May 24, 1855.

138. ADSM 3XP 217, letter of August 8, 1855.

139. John Merriman's *Police Stories: Building the French State, 1815–1851* (Oxford: Oxford University Press, 2006), looks at this process of centralization, in this case examining the evolution of the provincial *commissaires de police*.

140. This was not true only in the case of "strong" or highly centralized states, like France. William Novak argues that there was also a strong connection between purportedly independent voluntary associations and the machinery of the government in the United States. See "The American Law of Association: The Legal-Political Construction of Civil Society," *Studies in American Political Development* 15 (Fall 2001): 171–72.

141. See Gerson, *The Pride of Place*, chap. 8.

142. Smith, *Creating the Welfare State in France*, 40–41.

143. Christine Adams, "Maternal Societies in France: Private Charity before the Welfare State," *Journal of Women's History* 17:1 (Spring 2005): 87–88.

144. Marais, *Histoire du don*, 29.

145. Nourrisson, *Histoire de la liberté d'association*.

146. Harrison, *The Bourgeois Citizen*, 233. Peter Mandler notes that, over the course of the nineteenth century, "Not only the receiving but also the giving of charity was recast as a domestic function," and that by the second half of the century, "the organization (and, increasingly, the funding) of charity was largely a private and female function." See "Poverty and Charity in the Nineteenth-Century Metropolis: An Introduction," in *The Uses of Charity: The Poor on Relief in the Nineteenth-Century Metropolis*, ed. Peter Mandler (Philadelphia: University of Philadelphia Press, 1990), 20.

147. Duprat, "Le silence des femmes," 90.

148. See Bonnie G. Smith, *Ladies of the Leisure Class: The Bourgeoises of Northern France in the Nineteenth Century* (Princeton, N.J.: Princeton University Press, 1981), 134–35.

## Chapter 5. Maternal Societies and the State

1. Archives de l'Assistance Publique (AAP), B-832¹⁷, *Réglemens de la Société de la Charité Maternelle*, arrêté à l'assemblée du 13 Février 1789 (Paris, 1789), 5–6.

2. See Linda L. Clark's essay "Bringing Feminine Qualities into the Public Sphere: The Third Republic's Appointment of Women Inspectors," in *Gender and the Politics of Social Reform in France, 1870–1914,* ed. Elinor Accampo, Rachel G. Fuchs, and Mary Lynn Stewart (Baltimore: Johns Hopkins University Press, 1995), 128–56.

3. Kathleen D. McCarthy notes, "The enduring caricature of Lady Bountiful has served to stigmatize women's philanthropy, often trivializing its presence on the American scene. "Parallel Power Structures: Women and the Voluntary Sphere," in *Lady Bountiful Revisited: Women, Philanthropy and Power,* ed. Kathleen D. McCarthy (New Brunswick, N.J.: Rutgers University Press, 1990), 1. In her introduction to *Women and the Work of Benevolence: Morality, Politics, and Class in the Nineteenth-Century United States* (New Haven, Conn.: Yale University Press, 1990), Lori D. Ginzburg discusses the various ways in which historians have approached the complicated question of women's benevolent work.

4. "Sociabilité féminine et 'maternalisme,' les Sociétés de Charité Maternelle au XIXe siècle," in *Femmes dans la Cité, 1815–1871,* ed. Alain Corbin, Jacqueline Lalouette, and Michèle Riot-Sarcey (Grâne: Créaphis, 1997), 77. Sarah A. Curtis also emphasizes the important role of charitable women in "Charitable Ladies: Gender, Class and Religion in Nineteenth-Century Paris," *Past and Present* 177 (November 2002): 121–56.

5. Different maternal societies gave various titles to their female members.

6. Adélaïde-Anne-Louise Piscatory, marquise de Pastoret, was the wife of Claude-Emmanuel, the marquis de Pastoret, a man well known for both his political and charitable activities. Madame de Pastoret served as secretary, then vice president, of the Society for Maternal Charity until 1830. See her *éloge* by the Vicomte de Falloux, "Biographie de Madame de Pastoret," *Annales de la charité* (1846): 224–50; and Fernande Bassan, *Politique et haute société à l'époque romantique: la famille Pastoret d'après sa correspondance (1788–1856)* (Paris: Lettres Modernes Minard, 1969), 3–27.

7. Bordeaux's *compte rendu* of 1873 makes reference to Madame Guestier's forty years of service. Archives Départementales de la Gironde (ADG) 4J 710, *Conseil d'administration: assemblée générale annuelle des bienfaiteurs de la Société de Charité Maternelle de Bordeaux, rapport sur l'exercice 1873* (Bordeaux: Imprimerie Administrative Ragot, 1874).

8. Annie Flacassier, "La Société de Charité Maternelle de Bordeaux de 1805 à 1815," in *105e Congrès, Comité d'Histoire de la Sécurité Sociale* (Caen: Comité d'Histoire de la Sécurité Sociale, 1980), 44–45.

9. On the Delahante family, see M. Adrien Delahante, *Une famille de finance au XVIIIe siècle: mémoire, correspondances et papiers de famille réunis et mis en ordre par M. Adrien Delahante,* 2 vols. (Paris: J. Hetzel et Cie, 1881).

10. Jean-Pierre Chaline, *Les bourgeois de Rouen: une élite urbaine au XIXe siècle* (Paris: Presses de la Fondation Nationale des Sciences Politiques, 1982), 307.

11. A. Cornereau, *Notice sur la Société de Charité Maternelle de Dijon* (Dijon: Darantière, 1900), 32.

12. Both Catherine Duprat (*Usage et pratiques de la philanthropie: pauvreté, action sociale et lien social, à Paris, au cours du premier XIXe siècle*, 2 vols. (Paris: Association pour l'Étude de l'Histoire de la Sécurité Sociale, 1996–97), 2:634–35; and Chaline, *Les bourgeois de Rouen*, 307, make note of this phenomenon. The repetition of the same names on the membership lists of other cities also suggests how common it was for daughters, daughters-in-law, and granddaughters to join maternal societies.

13. Sarah A. Curtis notes that "organizing, soliciting funds, visiting: all took assertive, self-confident individuals." "Charitable Ladies," 144.

14. Cornereau, *Notice sur la Société de Charité Maternelle de Dijon*, 27; ADG 3X 18, letters of November 14, December (n.d.), and December 13, 1822; Archives Départementales des Bouches-du-Rhône (ADBR) X² 26, letters of November 12, 1822, and January 29 and April 14, 1823, and "Correspondence, 1844–58."

15. Bibliothèque nationale (BN) Fonds Français Mss. 11368, *Procès-verbaux de la Société de Charité Maternelle, 1810–1814*; séances of November 9, 1812, and March 8, 1813; Christine Adams, "Constructing Mothers and Families: The Society for Maternal Charity of Bordeaux, 1805–1860," *French Historical Studies* 22:1 (Winter 1999): 77.

16. Maria Luddy points out that women's involvement in philanthropy provided them with personal and group authority and power. Kathleen D. McCarthy and Anne Summers make similar arguments. See Luddy, *Women and Philanthropy in Nineteenth-Century Ireland* (Cambridge: Cambridge University Press, 1995), 3; McCarthy, "Parallel Power Structures"; and Anne Summers, "A Home from Home—Women's Philanthropic Work in the Nineteenth Century," in *Fit Work for Women*, ed. Sandra Burman (New York: St. Martin's Press, 1979), 33–63.

17. Katherine A. Lynch, "The Family and the History of Public Life," *Journal of Interdisciplinary History* 24:4 (Spring 1994): 676.

18. Duprat, "Le silence des femmes: associations féminines du premier XIXe siècle," in *Femmes dans la cité*, 79.

19. Archives Municipales de Bordeaux (AMB) 312 Q 1, letter to Mesdames les Distributrices des Secours de la Société de Charité Maternelle, September 7, 1813, 3.

20. Duprat, "Le silence des femmes," 86.

21. See, for example, Bibliothèque Municipale de Lyon (BML) Fonds Coste 113287, *Compte présenté aux dames composant la Société de Charité Maternelle de Lyon, 1834* (Lyon: Louis Perrin, 1835), 7–8. These *éloges* can be found throughout the *comptes rendus*, as well as in the records of the *2ème Registre des délibérations de la Société de Charité Maternelle*, Bibliothèque Historique de la Ville de Paris (BHVP) Mss. 996, rés. 34.

22. Denise Z. Davidson, *France after Revolution: Urban Life, Gender, and the New Social Order* (Cambridge, Mass.: Harvard University Press, 2007), 146; Christine Adams, "Maternal Societies in France: Private Charity Before the Welfare State," *Journal of Women's History* 17:1 (2005): 87–111.

23. Adams, "Constructing Mothers and Families," 83.

24. Catherine Duprat gives particular weight to the stability and longevity of the membership of the Parisian members of the Société de Charité Maternelle. See *Usage et pratiques,* 2:633–34.

25. Chaline, "Sociabilité féminine et 'maternalisme,'" 74–75. See also Curtis, "Charitable Ladies."

26. ADG 3X 18, *Règlement de la Société de Charité Maternelle de Bordeaux* (1815).

27. Chaline, "Sociabilité féminine et 'maternalisme,'" 74.

28. BML Fonds Coste 113287, *Compte présenté au dames composant la Société de Charité Maternelle de Lyon,* 1830, 17–20.

29. Catherine Duprat, "*Pour l'amour de l'humanité*": le temps des philanthropes, la philanthropie parisienne des Lumières à la monarchie de Juillet (Paris: Éditions du C.T.H.S., 1993).

30. Suzanne Desan, "What's After Political Culture? Recent French Revolutionary Historiography," *French Historical Studies* 23:1 (2000): 170.

31. See Roger Chartier, *The Cultural Origins of the French Revolution,* trans. Lydia G. Cochrane (Durham, N.C.: Duke University Press, 1991), 16, 162–67; Desan, "What's After Political Culture?," 171. Some historians, of course, see this "practice" in a negative light.

32. BHVP, Mss. 996, rès. 34.

33. BN Fonds Français Mss. 11368–69.

34. BML, Fonds Coste 113287, *Compte présenté au dames composant la Société de Charité Maternelle de Lyon, 1831,* 8.

35. In some cases, although not all, the position of president was honorary, and the real authority lay with the vice presidents.

36. Between 1816 and 1912, the Society for Maternal Charity of Le Mans had only four presidents. Paul Delaunay, *La Société de Charité Maternelle du Mans et ses origines* (Le Mans: Imprimerie Monnoyer, 1911), 16. Madame Guestier served as president of the Bordelais society for over thirty years. See Bibliothèque Municipale de Bordeaux (BMB) D 11096, ADG 3X 16 and 4J 727, *comptes rendus* of the Society for Maternal Charity of Bordeaux. Charles des Alleurs writes warmly of the efficacy of Madame de Vanssay, wife of the prefect of the Seine-Inférieure, who served as president of the Society of Rouen in the 1820s; *Histoire de la Société de Charité Maternelle de Rouen* (Rouen: Imprimerie de Alfred Péron, 1854), 66.

37. Des Alleurs, *La Société de Charité Maternelle de Rouen,* 129.

38. Archives Nationales (AN) F[15] 2565, letter of October 11, 1817.

39. ADBR X[2] 26, letters of January 7 and 10, 1815.

40. ADG 3X 18, letters of September 24 and October 8, 1816.

41. In certain cities, men played administrative roles in the organization. In 1822 the Duchess of Angoulême asked that the provincial societies come into conformity with the regulations of Paris's maternal society, excluding all men from the organization. BMB D 11096, *Compte rendu des opérations du Conseil d'Administration de la Société de Charité Maternelle de Bordeaux,* 1822. Both Bordeaux and Marseille, however, did retain men in the positions of secretary and treasurer, and Bordeaux, alone among the societies I have studied, maintained a male *conseil d'administration* as a counterpart to the female one. This movement of men out of the Society for Maternal Charity parallels Peter Mandler's

argument that increasingly, over the course of the nineteenth century, the organization and funding of charity became a private and female function. "Poverty and Charity in the Nineteenth-Century Metropolis: An Introduction," in *The Uses of Charity: The Poor on Relief in the Nineteenth-Century Metropolis,* ed. Peter Mandler (Philadelphia: University of Pennsylvania Press, 1990), 20.

42. Luddy, *Women and Philanthropy,* 3. Michela De Giorgio suggests that charitable activity was an important field of action for women, as they were excluded from the political scene. "The Catholic Model," in *A History of Women in the West,* Georges Duby and Michelle Perrot, gen. eds., vol. 4: *Emerging Feminism from Revolution to World War,* ed. Geneviève Fraisse and Michelle Perrot (Cambridge, Mass.: Belknap Press of Harvard University Press, 1994), 177.

43. Seth Koven and Sonya Michel, "Womanly Duties: Maternalist Politics and the Origins of the Welfare States in France, Germany, Great Britain, and the United States, 1880–1920," *American Historical Review* 95:4 (Oct. 1990): 1,079, 1,085.

44. McCarthy, "Parallel Power Structures," 6.

45. Mandler, "Poverty and Charity in the Nineteenth-Century Metropolis," 20.

46. Jean-Pierre Chaline suggests that we may, in fact, underestimate the influence and the power of "dames patronnesses." "Sociabilité féminine et 'maternalisme,'" 77.

47. AAP B-832[17], *Réglemens de la Société de la Charité Maternelle,* 8–11.

48. Duprat, *Usage et pratiques,* 2:617–18.

49. The correspondence located in the Archives Nationales (AN) F[15] 3806–11 details the distribution of funds among the various maternal societies during these years.

50. In 1860 the prefect of the Haute-Vienne announced triumphantly to the Interior Ministry that the *conseil général* of his department had been convinced to provide a 500 FF subvention to Limoges's maternal society the previous year, and that the *conseil municipal* had agreed to a *secours annuel* of 500 FF, as well. Archives Départementales de la Haute-Vienne (ADHV) 3X 15, draft of letter from the prefect of the Haute-Vienne to the Interior Ministry, August 2, 1860. Also see letters of November 21 and December 12, 1860. The Interior Ministry pressured prefects to persuade local governments to provide resources to maternal societies. In a letter to the prefect of the Côte-d'Or, written in 1857, the *secrétaire-général* noted that "The Society of Dijon is among the very small number of those who receive a subvention from neither the department nor the Commune. However, it provides assistance to families who, without this aid, would be the responsibility of the *bureau de bienfaisance;* it frees the department from certain expenses by turning poor parents away from the thought of abandoning their children. The department and the city should thus support [the society] through annual subsidies. It is up to you to bring about this result." Archives Départementales de la Côte-d'Or (ADCO) 22 X G article 3, letter of June 5, 1857. However, the prefect was unable to persuade either council to provide a subvention.

51. Anne Martin-Fugier, *La vie élégante, ou, la formation du Tout-Paris, 1815–1848* (Paris: Librairie Arthème Fayard, 1990), 155–56.

52. Ibid., 156.

53. Kathleen McCarthy notes the important role that women played in fund-raising campaigns for American charitable associations, as well. "Parallel Power Structures,"

15–16. See also Suzanne Lebsock, *The Free Women of Petersburg: Status and Culture in a Southern Town, 1784–1860* (New York: Norton, 1985), 211.

54. These amounts are recorded in the annual *comptes rendus*.

55. Davidson, *France after Revolution*, 144–52.

56. Archives Départementales de la Seine-Maritime (ADSM) 3XP 217, letter from Elie Lefébure, president of the Société de Charité Maternelle de Rouen to le baron Dupont Delporte, prefect of the Seine-Inférieure, November 5, 1838.

57. These figures were calculated from the *comptes rendus* of the three cities.

58. In response to a letter from the cabinet of Queen Marie-Amélie, the prefect of the Seine-Inférieure noted that the duchesse de Berry had always contributed a few objects to Rouen's yearly exposition and sale. ADSM 3XP 217, letter from the prefect to the queen's secretary, March 9, 1831. Lyon's *compte rendu* of 1839 noted that "The queen wished to participate in our lottery, sending us charming prizes; Madame the duchesse d'Orléans and Madame Adélaïde also had the extreme goodness to take part." Archives Départementales du Rhône (ADR) 3X 1849, *Compte rendu présenté aux dames composant la Société de Charité Maternelle, année 1839* (Lyon: Imprimerie Typographique et Lithographique de Louis Perrin, 1840), 1.

59. F. Gille, *La Société de Charité Maternelle de Paris* (Paris: Goupy et Jourdan, 1887), 172–73.

60. AAP 791 FOSS 17n2, *Compte rendu pour l'année 1823 par le Conseil d'Administration de la Société de Charité Maternelle de Paris.*

61. ADG 4J 727, *Compte rendu pour l'année 1841 par le Conseil d'Administration de la Société de charité maternelle de Paris.*

62. ADG 3X 16, *Compte rendu des opérations de la Société de Charité Maternelle de Bordeaux,* 1828.

63. AN F[15] 3806–3811, *Société de Charité Maternelle de Lyon, Compte rendu de 1868.*

64. At least, this was the case for the government and the ladies themselves, if not on the part of the poor women seeking financial assistance.

65. In large cities, each *dame députée* was assigned to a particular *arrondissement* where she was expected to get to know and administer to the families of that area. Susan Grogan sees these *femmes de charité* as the precursors of the state-employed *inspectrice* of the twentieth century. "Philanthropic Women and the State: The Société de Charité Maternelle in Avignon, 1802–1917," *French History* 14 (2000): 319–21. The volunteer and paid *dames visiteuses* encouraged by Paul Strauss also reflect this model. Rachel G. Fuchs, "The Right to Life: Paul Strauss and the Politics of Motherhood," in *Gender and the Politics of Social Reform in France,* 100.

66. Duprat also notes that the heavy workload of the *dames administrantes* may explain why the society was never able to recruit enough volunteers to fully staff all the *quartiers* of Paris. See *Usage et pratiques,* 2:634, and "Le silence des femmes," 86.

67. For the meetings of the Paris society, see BHVP Mss. 996, rés. 34 and BN Fonds Français Mss. 11368, *Procès-verbaux.* Evelyne Lejeune-Resnick notes that in the case of the Society of Strasbourg, the *dames administrantes* had the right to admit a mother if she met all of the conditions set out in article 2 of the bylaws. However, if she met only some of the conditions, the conseil d'administration was required to make the final deci-

sion. *Femmes et associations (1830/1880): vraies démocrates ou dames patronnesses?* (Paris: Publisud, 1991), 179.

68. Catherine Duprat notes that at least until the 1840s, the Society for Maternal Charity was second only to the Philanthropic Society in its resources and the numbers it assisted—and it was far ahead of all other charitable associations. *Usage et pratiques,* 2:621–22.

69. AN F¹⁵ 3806–3811, *Société de Charité Maternelle de Lyon, compte rendu de 1866* (Lyon: Mougin-Rusand, 1867).

70. Des Alleurs, *Histoire de la Société de Charité Maternelle de Rouen,* 94–95.

71. ADG 4J 727, *Compte rendu des opérations de la Société de Charité Maternelle de Bordeaux pour l'année 1840.*

72. ADG 4J 710, *Compte rendu des opérations de la Société de Charité Maternelle de Bordeaux pour l'année 1866.* In that particular year, the society assisted 1,034 families, 860 of whom had been admitted in 1866, while assistance was continued for 174 mothers admitted in 1865.

73. Timothy B. Smith, "Public Assistance and Labor Supply in Nineteenth-Century Lyon," *Journal of Modern History* 68:1 (March 1996): 1–30; and his *Creating the Welfare State in France, 1880–1940* (Montreal: McGill–Queen's University Press, 2003), 6, 25–26. At the turn of the century, Lyon had at least 245 private charities. Ibid., 18. Also see introduction, fn. 59.

74. Rachel G. Fuchs, *Abandoned Children: Foundlings and Child Welfare in Nineteenth-Century France* (Albany: State University of New York Press, 1984), 81. The amounts of assistance available to both single and married women from public assistance varied enormously over the course of the century, and from city to city, as well. On aid to mothers and their children in Paris over the course of the century, see Fuchs, *Poor and Pregnant in Paris,* chap. 6.

75. *Règlement pour la Société de la Charité Maternelle* (Paris: De l'Imprimerie Impériale, 1811).

76. ADBR X² 26, *Règlement pour la Société de Charité Maternelle de Marseille* (Marseille: Typographie des Hoirs Feissat Ainé et Demonchy, 1844), 6.

77. ADG 3X 18, *Règlement de la Société de charité Maternelle de Bordeaux,* 1815, 5.

78. ADR 4M 523, *Règlement du détail de la Société de Charité Maternelle de Lyon,* May 20, 1847.

79. AN F¹⁵ 2565, *Règlement pour la Société de Charité Maternelle de la Ville de Limoges, Département de la Haute-Vienne* (Limoges: Chez J. B. Dalesme, 1817), 9.

80. ADCO 22 X G, article 3, *Statuts et règlement de la Société de Charité Maternelle de Dijon* (Dijon: Imprimerie Loireau-Feuchot, 1852), 9.

81. ADSM 3XP 217, letter from Elie Lefébure, *présidente* of the Société de Charité Maternelle de Rouen to baron Dupont Delporte, prefect of the Seine-Inférieure, November 5, 1838.

82. ADG 4J 727, *Compte rendu des opérations de la Société de Charité Maternelle de Bordeaux pour l'année 1840.*

83. Des Alleurs, *Histoire de la Société de Charité Maternelle de Rouen.* This figure did vary from year to year, depending on the resources of the organization.

84. Cornereau, *Notice sur la Société de Charité Maternelle de Dijon,* 83–84.

85. ADSM 3XP 217, *Société de Charité Maternelle de Rouen, reconnue comme établisse-*

*ment d'utilité publique par un arrêté du président de la République en date du 26 février 1849*
(Rouen: Imprimerie de Alfred Péron, 1849), 23–24. In 1869, however, Rouen's maternal
society decided to add a cradle and straw mattress (*paillasse*) to their regular assistance.
3XP 213, extrait, séance of November 13, 1869.

86. ADR 3X 1849, letter from the minister of the interior to the prefect of the Rhône,
December 15, 1855.

87. ADR 3X 1850, letter from S. Delphin, *secrétaire-trésorier* de la Charité Maternelle
de Lyon, to the prefect of the Rhône, January 30, 1861.

88. Rachel G. Fuchs, *Poor and Pregnant in Paris: Strategies for Survival in the Nineteenth Century* (New Brunswick, N.J.: Rutgers University Press, 1992), which examines
the resources available to single pregnant women, is one of the most effective texts in
highlighting the fragmentary nature of French assistance to mothers and children.

89. Smith, *Creating the Welfare State in France,* 33.

90. Frances Gouda, *Poverty and Political Culture: The Rhetoric of Social Welfare in the
Netherlands and France, 1815–1854* (Lanham, Md.: Rowman and Littlefield, 1995), 210.

91. Duprat, *Usage et pratiques,* 2:619.

92. ADBR X² 80, correspondence of the Société de Charité Maternelle d'Arles, February
14, 1852; February 21, 1853; July 14, 1853.

93. ADHV 3X 15, *Compte moral,* February 26, 1862.

94. Hazel Mills, "'La Charité est une mère': Catholic Women and Poor Relief in France,
1690–1850," in *Charity, Philanthropy and Reform: From the 1690s to the 1850s,* ed. Hugh
Cunningham and Joanna Innes (London: St. Martin's Press, 1998), 172.

95. ADHV 3X 15, *Compte moral,* March 30, 1864.

96. Despite the assurances of the new minister of the interior in 1815, Vauban, that the
societies would now regain their independence, this was not, in fact, the case. Christine
Adams, "The Provinces Versus Paris? The Case of the Society for Maternal Charity of
Bordeaux," *Proceedings of the Western Society for French History* 23 (Fall 1996): 424.

97. For example, at the end of 1838 la baronne Pasquier, vice president of the Society
for Maternal Charity of Paris, acting on behalf of the queen, requested a complete list of
the personnel of the provincial societies, along with detailed information on the situation
of the husbands of all the ladies of the administration. Des Alleurs, *Histoire de la Société
de Charité Maternelle de Rouen,* 73.

98. BMB D 11096, *Compte rendu des opérations du comité d'administration de la Société
de Charité Maternelle de Bordeaux,* 1808, 7. Victor Lamothe, physician at Bordeaux's
Hospice des Enfants Trouvés, and one of the founders of the Society for Maternal Charity
of Bordeaux, was also the *conservateur du vaccin* and head vaccinator at the foundling
hospice and an avid promoter of vaccination against smallpox. See Christine Adams, *A
Taste for Comfort and Status: A Bourgeois Family in Eighteenth-Century France* (University
Park: Pennsylvania State University Press, 2000), 180–86.

99. See AN F¹⁵ 2564, "États des recettes et des dépenses des Sociétés de Charité Maternelle."

100. ADR 3X 1850, *Société de Charité Maternelle de Lyon, compte rendu de 1861* (Lyon:
Imprimerie de Ve. Mougin-Rusand, 1862), n.p.

101. On the official campaign to promote vaccination, see Evelyn Ackerman, *Health Care
in the Parisian Countryside, 1800–1914* (New Brunswick, N.J.: Rutgers University Press,

1990), 67–76. On the spread of vaccination in France and the rest of Europe, see Pierre Darmon, *La longue traque de la variole: les pionniers de la médecine préventive* (Paris: Librairie Académique Perrin, 1986), and Yves-Marie Bercé, *La chaudron et la lancette: croyances populaires et médecine préventive (1798–1830)* (Paris: Presses de la Renaissance, 1984).

102. ADR 3X 1850, letter from M. Delphin, *secrétaire-trésorier* of the Société de Charité Maternelle to the prefect of the Rhône, February 10, 1859; letter from the prefect of the Rhône to the minister of the interior, February 21, 1859; letter from the minister of the interior to the prefect of the Rhône, June 25, 1864.

103. The 150,000 FF was eventually increased to provide additional food supplies for the poor of Paris. BN Fonds Français Mss.11368, séances of February 4 and 8; March 2, 16, and 19; and April 1, 13, and 27, 1812; L. de Lanzac de Laborie, *Paris sous Napoléon,* 8 vols. Vol. 5: *Assistance et bienfaisance approvisionnement* (Paris: Librairie Plon, 1908), 5:154.

104. ADG 3X 16, *Compte rendu des opérations de la Société de Charité Maternelle de Bordeaux,* 1824, 6.

105. BN Fonds Français Mss.11368, séance of August 14, 1811.

106. ADBR X² 26, letter of December 12, 1837, from Dudemaine, secretary of the Société de Charité Maternelle de Marseille, to DeLaCoste, prefect of the Bouches-du-Rhône; response from the prefect, December 18, 1812; *avis* dated December 18, 1837.

107. BN Fonds Français Mss. 11368, séance of November 23, 1811.

108. Ibid., séance of August 2, 1812.

109. Ibid., séance of March 22, 1813.

110. Ibid., séance of July 17, 1813.

111. BMB D 11096, *Compte rendu des opérations du comité d'administration de la Société de Charité Maternelle de Bordeaux,* 1805.

112. Adams, *A Taste for Comfort and Status,* 181–86.

113. The last year that Bordeaux's *compte rendu* listed the medical personnel associated with the organization was 1846, according to my records. However, it seems likely that this is related to the fact that financial constraints meant that the society had to write its accounts by hand from at least 1843 to 1867. There is no evidence that medical personnel suddenly abandoned the society.

114. Des Alleurs, *Histoire de la Société de Charité Maternelle de Rouen,* 57–58.

115. Ibid., 72n. He was nominated to this position in 1837 by the prefect, M. Dupont Delporte. ADSM 3XP 217, nomination of M. Weille as *chirurgien-dentiste.* It appears that this association was not entirely happy; in 1854, M. Weille complained to the prefect that he was not being invited to the assemblies of the Society for Maternal Charity; Elie Lefébure, *présidente,* informed the prefect that the conseil d'administration "does not believe that his presence could be useful at these meetings" and that he could not be considered an officer of the society, whose bylaws authorized only a *médecin* and *chirurgien.* ADSM 3XP 213, letter from Elie Lefébure to the prefect of the Seine-Inférieure, December 30, 1854.

116. ADR 3X 1849, *Société de la Charité Maternelle de Lyon, compte rendu de 1852* (Lyon: Gerente Fils, 1853).

117. The *compte rendu* of 1858 indicated that the society had *médecins* in only three of their *arrondissements.* ADR 3X 1850, *Société de la Charité Maternelle de Lyon, compte rendu de 1858* (Lyon: Imprimerie de Ve. Mougin-Rusand, 1859).

118. BMB D67.630, *Compte rendu des opérations de la Société de Charité Maternelle de Bordeaux pour l'année 1836,* 8.

119. ADHV 3X 15, *Compte moral,* 1864.

120. ADSM 3XP 213, letter from A. Ballin, *secrétaire-archiviste* of the Société de Charité Maternelle de Rouen to the prefect of the Seine-Inférieure, June 2, 1862; two "extraits du procès verbal de l'Assemblée," May 28, 1862. This *secours extraordinaire* was extended in 1863. See "Extraits du Procès-verbal de l'Assemblée générale," October 30, 1862, and March 28, 1863. On the actions of the Municipal Council, see ADSM 3XP 215, "Conseil Municipal de la ville de Rouen, extrait du registre des délibérations," séance of April 8, 1864. The entire 1,200 FF shows up in the accounts for 1864. See 3XP 215, "Compte général des recettes et dépenses de 1869," séance of March 10, 1870. A table on the back of the *compte général* included in the notes lists the receipts and expenses from 1864 to 1869.

121. ADR 3X 1849, *Société de Charité Maternelle de Lyon, compte rendu de 1849* (Lyon: Chanoine, Imprimeur, 1850), n.p.

122. Some prefects, such as those of the departments of Gers and Calvados, sent out letters asking for advice on how best to form a maternal society in their department. ADSM 3XP 217, letter from the prefect of the Calvados to the prefect of the Seine-Inférieure, November 14, 1838, with follow-up letters dated November 17, November 24, and November 27, 1838; ADHV 3X 15, letter from the prefect of Gers in Auch to the prefect of the Haute-Vienne, January 14, 1857. In some cases, mayors also expressed an interest in creating a maternal society in their cities. See Des Alleurs, *Histoire de la Société de Charité Maternelle de Rouen,* 73.

123. See Delaunay, *La Société de Charité Maternelle du Mans,* 13–14; and ADHV 3X 15, correspondence, 1815–17.

124. The "États des recettes et des dépenses" of the provincial branches of the maternal societies, along with some correspondence, are located at AN F$^{15}$ 2564 and document the subsidies provided by the Interior Ministry. Just a few examples: in 1817 the society of Rouen received 5,125 FF of its 10,049.84 FF receipt total from the central government; in 1816, Dijon received 4,500 FF of its 9,423.38 FF total from the government. On March 4, 1819, the prefect of the Rhône noted in a letter to the minister of the interior that the city's Society for Maternal Charity had raised only 1,500 FF the previous year, the same amount it had received from the government. To provide a later example, the Society for Maternal Charity of Limoges raised a total of 5,480 FF in 1859, 2,950 FF of which came from the imperial government, and 500 FF of which was provided by the city. ADHV 3X 15, *Compte rendu,* 1859. Catherine Duprat notes that the Paris branch's subvention of 40,000 francs made it the most generously subsidized charity of its era. *Usage et pratiques,* 2:618.

125. Fuchs, *Abandoned Children,* 157.

126. Ibid., chap. 2 carefully traces the shifts in French social-welfare policies that made it more or less difficult to abandon children.

127. AN F$^{15}$ 3896, "Enfants trouvés. Département du Rhône, conseil général, session de 1841, budget de 1842, 1er Section, chap. 10, Dépenses ordinaires, Enfans trouvés et abandonnés, rapport du préfet." Janet Ruth Potash found that, on the average, Lyon's Hospice de la Charité admitted 1,000–2,000 children per year and supported a foundling population of 6,000–10,000 between 1800 and 1869. See "The Foundling Problem in

France, 1800–1869: Child Abandonment in Lille and Lyon," PhD diss., Yale University, 1979, 156.

128. AN F$^{15}$ 3896, "Enfants trouvés, extrait du régistre des délibérations du Conseil Général," séance of September 15, 1842. Janet Potash found that Lyon's foundling service cost the city about 400,000 FF per year over time. "The Foundling Problem in France," 157.

129. At a meeting held in 1839, the conseil général du Rhône requested "Monsieur the prefect to provide advice on the means to increase the resources of the Maternal Society, and to put it in a position to assist legitimate abandoned children who had been sent back to their parents." AN F$^{15}$ 3898, Département du Rhône, "Enfants trouvés, extrait du régistre des délibérations du Conseil général du Département du Rhône, Session du 1839."

130. See Fuchs, *Abandoned Children,* 34–43; and Potash, "The Foundling Problem in France," chap. 2, for a close analysis of these issues.

131. The complaint was part of the Croix-Rousse's efforts to avoid contributing 3,637 FF to defray the cost of abandoned children in the Department of the Rhône. Archives Municipales de Lyon 3 WP 218 2, *Rapport de la Commission du Conseil municipal de la Croix-Rousse au sujet de la somme de 3,637 francs imposée par M. le Préfet au budget de cette ville, à titre de part contributive dans la Dépense des Enfans trouvés ou abandonnés* (Lyon: Imp. et Lith. de Veuve Ayné, Neveu, 1835).

132. For example, in a meeting held on August 28, 1838, the *conseil général* of the Haute-Vienne reported that the policy of *déplacement* had had few good effects in the department. "It has not produced the hoped-for result in our department; the advantages taken away have been almost nonexistent. Many wet nurses had broken hearts when it was necessary to separate them from their babies; some made enormous sacrifices to keep them; others were obliged to give way before poverty. The use of such a measure would no longer allow us to find wet nurses." AN F$^{15}$ 3896, "Enfants trouvés, Extrait du procès verbal des délibérations du Conseil général de la Haute-Vienne, Session du 1839, tenue en 1838," séance of August 28, 1838. The prefect of the Gironde noted that the policy of *déplacement* had reduced expenses but had also been severely criticized. Letter from the Conseiller de Préfecture de la Gironde (préfet par interim) to the minister of the interior, October 24, 1838. The closing of the *tours,* which made anonymous abandonment impossible, could lead to higher rates of infanticide, abortion, or exposure of infants. Fuchs, *Abandoned Children,* 42–43. Série F$^{15}$ 3896–98 in the Archives Nationales holds correspondence and other documents related to these debates over policies dealing with *enfants trouvés* in the 1830s and 1840s. See also Anatole Lemercier, "Exposé de la question des enfants trouvés, orphelins et abandonnés," *Annales de la Charité* (1855): 201–29.

133. Fuchs, *Abandoned Children,* 193. Fuchs points out, however, that "More specific generalizations . . . cannot easily be made, because it is impossible to obtain consistent data and to fix accurate ratios year by year."

134. Claude-François-Étienne Dupin, *Histoire de l'administration des secours publics* (Paris: Alexis-Eymery, 1821), 313 and 335.

135. BMB D 11096, *Compte rendu des opérations du comité d'administration de la Société de Charité Maternelle de Bordeaux,* 1810, 8.

136. Duprat, *Usage et pratiques,* 2:621.

137. Commission d'enquête sur le service des enfants assistés, *Enfants assistés: enquête*

*générale ouverte en 1860, dans les 86 départements de l'Empire.* Rapport de la commission instituée le 10 octobre 1861, par arrêté de S. Exc. le ministre de l'intérieur (Paris, 1862), 186–90. These reports put out by the French government were not without problems; Joan Wallach Scott, among others, has dissected "the problematic and contingent nature" of the immense statistic reports of the nineteenth century. See *Gender and the Politics of History* (New York: Columbia University Press, 1988), chap. 6; see also Joshua Cole, *The Power of Large Numbers: Population, Politics and Gender in Nineteenth-Century France* (Ithaca, N.Y.: Cornell University Press, 2000).

138. ADR 3X 1850, letter from the Interior Ministry to the prefect of the Rhône, January 7, 1859.

139. ADR 3X 1850, letter from M. Delphin to the prefect of the Rhône, February 10, 1850.

140. Dominique Banquey, "La Société de Charité Maternelle de Bordeaux: un organisme de protection maternelle et infantile aux XIXe siècle?" Thèse pour le doctorat en médecin, thèse no. 282 (Bordeaux: A.C.E.M.B., 1976), 17.

141. *Histoire de l'administration des secours publics,* 334.

142. *Enfants assistés: enquête générale,* 184–85.

143. In 1821, Dupin noted that the state paid out more than seven million francs per annum, in *Histoire de l'administration des secours publics,* 313. Over the course of the nineteenth century, the financial responsibility for abandoned children was highly decentralized, which makes it difficult to determine precisely how much the central government paid specifically for *enfants assistés.* The 1860 report, *Enfants assistés: enquête générale,* offers no yearly figure paid by the state. The central government refused to (or was incapable of) bearing the entire cost, which meant that departments were responsible for the care of children abandoned within their borders. See Fuchs, *Abandoned Children,* 157.

144. This could, in fact, be a problem. Lyon put a temporary aid program for single mothers into effect after the Revolution of 1848 but discovered that one year's aid was often insufficient; the hospital administration received regular requests for the renewal of assistance, and if refused, these mothers often abandoned their children. Potash, "The Foundling Problem in France," 218–19.

145. ADG 4J 727, *Société de Charité Maternelle de Bordeaux, reconnue d'utilité publique par décret du 25 juillet 1811. Nouveaux statuts approuvés par décret du 9 janvier 1867. Statuts et règlement* (Bordeaux: Imprimerie Ragot, 1909), 15–16.

146. ADG 3X 18, letter of October 5, 1852. As it turned out, the father, Pascal Pradeau, had died, and his widow had gone to claim a small property in Bruges that he had left to her. The inspector of the Service des Enfants-Trouvés et des Établissements de Bienfaisance du Département de la Gironde suggested to the prefect that the baby be sent to its mother (presumably at the expense of the Society for Maternal Charity), and the prefect passed this information to Madame Guestier, *présidente* of Bordeaux's maternal society. See letters of October 16 and November 13, 1852.

147. See, for example, ADR 3X 1849, *Rapport et compte rendu présentés aux dames composant la Société de Charité Maternelle, année 1836* (Lyon: Imprimerie Typographique et Lithographique de Louis Perrin, 1837), 7; and *Société de Charité Maternelle de Lyon, compte rendu de 1856* (Lyon: Gerente Fils, 1857), n.p.; BMB D 67.630, *Compte rendu des opérations du Conseil d'administration de la Société de Charité Maternelle de Bordeaux*

*pour l'année 1836* (Bordeaux: Imprimerie de Deliège Aîné, 1838), 10; ADG 4J 727, Société de Charité Maternelle de Bordeaux, *compte rendu,* 1852, n.p.

148. For more on the Société de Saint-François-Régis, see Barrie M. Ratcliffe, "Popular Classes and Cohabitation in Mid-Nineteenth-Century Paris," *Journal of Family History* 21:3 (July 1996): 316–50; Michael Frey, "Du mariage et du concubinage dans les classes populaires à Paris (1846–1847)," *Annales, E.S.C.* 33:4 (July–August 1978): 803–19; and Fuchs, *Poor and Pregnant in Paris,* 103–5. Katherine A. Lynch notes that the provincial branches frequently grew out of the work of local conferences of the Société de Saint Vincent de Paul. See *Family, Class and Ideology in Early Industrial France: Social Policy and the Working-Class Family, 1825–1848* (Madison: University of Wisconsin Press, 1988), 88–100.

149. Ratcliffe, "Popular Classes and Cohabitation," 327.

150. BMB D 67.630, *Compte rendu des opérations du conseil d'administration de la Société de Charité Maternelle de Bordeaux pour l'année 1836,* 10. In its *compte rendu* of 1875, Bordeaux's society specifically mentioned its ties to the Société de Saint-François-Régis. ADG 4J 710, *Assemblée générale annuelle des bienfaiteurs de la Société de Charité Maternelle de Bordeaux, rapport sur l'exercice 1875* (Bordeaux: Imprimerie Administrative Ragot, 1876), 5–6.

151. *The Power of Large Numbers,* 156. See *comptes rendus,* ADG 4J 410, beginning in 1868.

152. See AAP 4771 for some of the twentieth-century *comptes rendus,* which list some of the added services sponsored by the Paris Society for Maternal Charity.

153. Catherine Rollet-Echalier, in *La politique à l'égard de la petite enfance sous la IIIe République* (Paris: Presses Universitaires de France, 1990), 378–79.

154. Fuchs, *Abandoned Children,* 46–48.

155. AN F¹⁵ 3897, "Enfants trouvés," *circulaire,* Ministre de l'Intérieur, May 27, 1856, with responses from the prefects.

156. Gille, *La Société de Charité Maternelle de Paris,* 109–10.

157. Fuchs, *Poor and Pregnant in Paris,* 116–24.

158. See, for example, AAP 827 FOSS 118, *Compte rendu de la Société de Charité Maternelle,* 1873, 4.

159. La baronne de LeMire, Rouen's president, discussed this in a letter to the prefect of the Seine-Inférieure in 1868. ADSM 3XP 213, November 25, 1868.

160. See Roller-Echalier, *La politique à l'égard de la petite enfance,* 378.

161. ADR 3X 1850, *Société de Charité Maternelle de Lyon: compte rendu de 1863* (Lyon: Imprimerie de Ve. Mougin Rusand, 1864), n.p. Timothy Smith argues that Lyon's public-assistance policies were relatively generous until late in the nineteenth century, when the regional economy began to suffer and the Lyonnais elite became less interested in maintaining an expansible workforce. "Public Assistance and Labor Supply."

162. *Hospices civils de Lyon, compte moral administratif, pour l'exercice 1863 présenté au Conseil Général des Établissements par la Commission Exécutive le 6 juillet 1864* (Lyon: Imprimerie Administratif de Chanoine, 1865), 30. Janet Potash suggests that this shift had another purpose: to discourage married workers from relying too heavily on public assistance when private charities were available to assist married mothers. "The Foundling Problem in France," 219–20.

163. ADR 3X 1850, *Société de Charité Maternelle de Lyon, compte-rendu de 1863,* n.p.

164. ADR 3X 1850, *Société de Charité Maternelle de Lyon, comptes rendus.*

165. ADR 3X 1848, Conseil Municipal de Lyon, "Session extraordinaire de Juillet 1873," séance of July 11, n.p.

166. This decision was reaffirmed at a meeting held on July 17, 1873. ADR 3X 1848, "Session extraordinaire de Juillet 1873," séance of July 17.

167. ADR 3X 1848, extract from a meeting of the Conseil Général du Rhône, September 10, 1873.

168. ADR 3X 1848, "Extrait du registre des delibérations de la Commission Municipale," *séance ordinaire* of November 21, 1873; "Rapport de M. le Prefet, Commission Municipale," n.d.

169. A report from the Section d'Économie Sociale et d'Assistance from the Exposition Universelle of 1889 reported that "The department and the city of Lyon also used to provide large subsidies [to the Society of Maternal Charity] which increased to 30,000 and 10,000 francs per year, but since 1874 and 1876, these subventions have been discontinued." Comité Départemental du Rhône, Exposition Universelle de 1889, *Rapports: Notes et Documents de la Section d'Économie Sociale et d'Assistance* (Lyon: Mougin-Rusand, 1889), 353.

170. ADR 3X 1848, letter from the *trésorier* of the Société de Charité Maternelle of Lyon to the prefect of the Rhône, November 6, 1873.

171. ADR 3X 1846, Crèches et Sociétés de Charité Maternelle, letter of December 13. 1894. It was this insistence that led the Interior Ministry to discontinue its yearly grant of 3,000 FF per year, as well. See letter from the Président du Conseil, Ministre de l'Intérieur, Direction de l'Assistance & de l'Hygiène publique, 2e Bureau, to the prefect of the Rhône, April 17, 1895.

172. Hazel Mills, "La Charité est une mère," 176–78.

173. BMB D 11096, *Compte rendu des opérations du comité d'administration de la Société de Charité Maternelle de Bordeaux,* 1810. Annie Flacassier suggests that the various religious communities in Bordeaux cohabited peacefully and that this facilitated their cooperation within the Society for Maternal Charity. See "La Société de Charité Maternelle de Bordeaux," 51.

174. AN F[15] 3806–3811, Société de Charité Maternelle de Lyon, *comptes rendus,* 1866 and 1868.

175. Grogan, "Philanthropic Women and the State," 317. And certainly the French government itself, as well as male politicians, demographers, and doctors, continued to differentiate between "deserving" and "nondeserving" poor mothers who requested assistance from the state. See Joshua H. Cole, "'There are only Good Mothers': The Ideological Work of Women's Fertility in France before World War I," *French Historical Studies* 19:3 (Spring 1996): 639–72; Jean Elizabeth Pedersen, "Regulating Abortion and Birth Control: Gender, Medicine, and Republican Politics in France, 1870–1920," *French Historical Studies* 19:3 (Spring 1996): 673–98. Rachel G. Fuchs suggests that while there was a "shift away from a moral policy towards the single mother, to an alternative favouring subsidies for her child," the state still had a clearly defined image of the "good mother," who was a nurturing mother along the lines of Rouuseau's ideal. "Morality and Poverty: Public Welfare for Mothers in Paris, 1870–1900," *French History* 2:3 (1988): 288–311.

## Epilogue: Toward a Welfare State

1. For a general overview of the French political scene in the 1870s, see Charles Sowerwine, *France Since 1870: Culture, Politics and Society* (New York: Palgrave, 2001), chaps. 2–4; and Gordon Wright, *France in Modern Times: From the Enlightenment to the Present*, 4th ed. (New York: Norton, 1987), chaps. 18–19.

2. F. Gille, *La Société de Charité Maternelle de Paris, considérée aux divers points de vue humanitaire, économique, et moralisateur* (Paris: Goupy et Jourdan, 1883), 21.

3. F. Gille, *La Société de Charité Maternelle de Paris* (Paris: V. Goupy et Jourdan, 1887), 178–79.

4. Archives Nationales (AN) F[15] 3799–3805, *Société de Charité Maternelle, compte rendu, 1876* (Paris: Paul Dupont, 1877), 6.

5. Archives de l'Assistance Publique (AAP) C 2390, Conseil Supérieur de l'Assistance Publique, *comptes rendus,* 18 vols., Fascicule no. 6. n. 1, Crèches, Sociétés de Charité Maternelle, 1888, 3–4.

6. Ibid., Fascicule no. 6, n. 2, 15, 22.

7. Ibid., Fascicule no. 6, n. 3, March 12, 1888, 26.

8. Alisa Klaus asserts that there were at least eighty-one maternal societies in France by the end of the nineteenth century. See "Women's Organizations and the Infant Health Movement in France and the United States, 1890–1920," in *Lady Bountiful Revisited: Women, Philanthropy, and Power,* ed. Kathleen D. McCarthy (New Brunswick. N.J.: Rutgers University Press, 1990), 167.

9. Alisa Klaus, *Every Child a Lion: The Origins of Maternal and Infant Health Policy in the United States and France* (Ithaca, N.Y.: Cornell University Press, 1993), 114.

10. Bonnie G. Smith notes that the members of Lille's maternal society also refused to change their ways in order to keep public subsidies in the 1880s and 1890s. *Ladies of the Leisure Class: The Bourgeoises of Northern France in the Nineteenth Century* (Princeton, N.J.: Princeton University Press, 1981), 154–55.

11. Archives Départementales de la Haute-Vienne (ADHV) 3X 15, letter from the president of the Society for Maternal Charity of Limoges, Amélie Basset, to the prefect of the Haute-Vienne, April 9, 1888. However, it appears that Limoges's society eventually reconsidered, since they received a subvention of 2,100 FF from the government in 1896, along with a departmental subsidy of 560 FF.

12. Archives Départementales de la Côte d'Or (ADCO) 22 X G, article 5, letter from the mayor of Dijon to the prefect of the Côte d'Or, May 4, 1888.

13. ADCO 22 X G, articles 4 and 5, "Comptes rendus de la Société de Charité Maternelle de Dijon, 1869–1885," and Bibliothèque Municipale de Dijon, Br. IV-1150, Société de Charité Maternelle de Dijon, "Statuts, listes de membres, comptes rendus financiers, etc., 1849–1900."

14. ADCO 22 X G, article 5, letters from the mayor of Dijon to the prefect, February 2, 1893, and February 24, 1894. This does not appear to have been strictly true. In reports to the Prefecture of the Côte-d'Or in 1908 and 1911, the *commissaire central de police,* Dreyfus, reported that "From the information gathered, it seems, after all, that several mothers of families whose husbands professed very advanced opinions were assisted for the same reasons as other women who consistently observed the practices of the Catholic faith."

But he also noted that "all [the members of the maternal society] are of good conduct and morality and considered to belong to the reactionary party." ADCO 22 X G, article 5, Préfecture de la Côte-d'Or, Cabinet du Préfet, Confidential, April 11, 1908, and March 9, 1911.

15. ADCO 22 X G, article 5, letter from the Interior Ministry, Direction de l'Assistance et de l'Hygiène Publique, March 13, 1896; response from the prefect of the Côte-d'Or, February 22, 1897.

16. ADCO 22 X G, article 5, letter from the Interior Ministry, Direction de l'Assistance et de l'Hygiène Publique, June 20, 1907; response from the prefect of the Côte-d'Or, July 13, 1907.

17. Archives Départementales du Rhône (ADR) 3X 1846, draft of letter from the prefect of the Rhône to the Interior Ministry, December 21, 1894. This letter was in response to a letter from the *président* du Conseil, Ministre de l'Intérieur et des cultes, Direction de l'Assistance & de l'Hygiène Publique, 2e bureau, to the prefect of the Rhône, November 10, 1894.

18. ADR 3X 1846, letter from the président du Conseil, Interior Ministry, Direction de l'Assistance & de l'Hygiène publique, 2e bureau, to the prefect of the Rhône, 17 April 1895.

19. Annie Flacassier, "Rapport sur l'état des recherches menées avec pour theme: aide et assistance à l'enfant et à la famille à Bordeaux du XVIIIe siècle à nos jours," *Comité d'Histoire de la Sécurité Sociale, Association pour l'Étude de la Sécurité Sociale: bulletin de liaison* 9 (March 1981): 57; Dominique Banquey, "La Société de Charité Maternelle de Bordeaux: un organisme de protection maternelle et infantile aux XIXe siècle?" Thèse pour le doctorat en médecin, thèse no. 282 (Bordeaux: A.C.E.M.B., 1976), 6.

20. Archives Départementales de la Gironde (ADG) 4J 710, *Assemblée générale annuelle des bienfaiteurs de la Société de Charité Maternelle de Bordeaux, rapport sur l'exercice 1875* (Bordeaux: Imprimerie Administrative Ragot, 1876), 5–6. Catherine Rollet-Echalier notes that in most departments, legitimate children received a derisory amount of assistance compared to illegitimate children, if they were admitted at all. *La politique à l'égard de la petite enfance sous la IIIe République* (Paris: Presses Universitaires de France, 1990), 246. Rachel G. Fuchs notes that aid to single mothers tripled between 1875 and 1910. *Contesting Paternity: Constructing Families in Modern France* (Baltimore: Johns Hopkins University Press, 2008), 153.

21. Fuchs, *Contesting Paternity,* 138.

22. See AAP, Fonds Fosseyeux, 827 FOSS 118, *Compte rendu de la Société de Charité Maternelle, 1873* (Paris: Imprimerie Administrative de Paul Dupont, 1874), 4; and AN F[15] 3799–3805, *Compte rendu de la Société de Charité Maternelle, 1876* (Paris: Imprimerie Administrative de Paul Dupont, 1877), 4.

23. Gilles, *La Société de Charité Maternelle de Paris* (1883), 1–2.

24. Ibid., 26; Ad. de Watteville, ed., *Législation charitable et recueil des lois, arrêtés, décrets, ordonnances royales, circulaires, décisions et instructions des Ministres de l'Intérieur et des finances, arrêtés de la Cour des Comptes, etc., etc., qui régissent les établissements de bienfaisance, mise en ordre et annotée* (Paris: Alexandre Heois, 1843), "Ordonnance portant réorganisation de la Société maternelle," 178–79.

25. Gille, *La Société de Charité maternelle de Paris* (1887), 228–38.

26. ADR 3X 1846, letter from the Département du Rhône, Inspection des Services des Enfants Assistés des Établissements de Bienfaisance et de la Protection du Premier âge to the prefect, February 11, 1892.

27. Gille, *La Société de Charité Maternelle de Paris* (1887), 199, 221. In 1933 the Paris Society for Maternal Charity spent a total of 1,972,106 FF. AAP 4771², *Société de Charité Maternelle de Paris, compte rendu pour 1933* (1934).

28. Catherine Duprat notes that even in the first half of the nineteenth century, the Society for Maternal Charity of Paris was unique in the longevity of its members. The same appears true in the provincial societies. Duprat, *Usage et pratiques,* 2:634–35.

29. Maternal societies outside of Paris provided similar services; Bordeaux's society, beginning in 1920, provided support to a *consultation du nourrisson* in Caudéran (a suburb of Bordeaux) and to a Société de Secours aux Blessés Militaires. ADG 4J 727, typed document from 1938.

30. AAP 4771⁵, *Société de Charité Maternelle de Paris, compte rendu pour 1925* (1926); AAP 4771², *Société de Charité Maternelle de Paris, compte rendu pour 1933* (1934).

31. Janet Ruth Potash, "The Foundling Problem in France, 1800–1869: Child Abandonment in Lille and Lyon," PhD diss., Yale University, 1979, 294.

32. Banquey, "La Société de Charité Maternelle de Bordeaux," 65.

33. Gille, *La Société de Charité Maternelle de Paris* (1887).

34. See especially the conclusion to Rachel G. Fuchs, *Poor and Pregnant in Paris: Strategies for Survival in the Nineteenth Century* (Brunswick, N.J.: Rutgers University Press, 1992); and Jacques Donzelot, *The Policing of Families,* trans. Robert Hurley (New York: Random House/Pantheon Books, 1979).

35. Paul Delaunay's account of the Society of Le Mans also notes this shift in emphasis. *La Société de Charité Maternelle du Mans* (Le Mans: Imprimerie Monnoyer, 1911), 26–27.

36. AAP 4771⁴, *Société de Charité Maternelle de Paris, compte rendu pour 1926* (1927), 26.

37. AAP 4771⁵, *Société de Charité Maternelle de Paris, compte rendu pour 1925* (1926) and AAP 4771⁴, *Société de Charité Maternelle de Paris, compte rendu pour 1926* (1927).

38. See Joshua Cole, *The Power of Large Numbers: Population, Politics and Gender in Nineteenth-Century France* (Ithaca, N.Y.: Cornell University Press, 2000), especially chaps. 5–6; and Karen M. Offen, "Depopulation, Nationalism, and Feminism in Fin-de-Siècle France," *American Historical Review* 89 (June 1984): 648–76.

39. This redundancy eventually led some maternal societies to fold; in 1969 the Society for Maternal Charity of Bordeaux decided to disband "because, with the development of family benefits and aid to families, its existence was no longer necessary." Annie Flacassier, "Rapport sur l'état des recherches menées avec pour theme: aide et assistance," 57. The Society for Maternal Charity of Paris continues to exist today in greatly changed form: providing assistance to babies with AIDS, and continuing to raise money for a pediatric center that it founded in 1952. See http://www.centredescotes.com, accessed on November 7, 2009; and http://www.charitybenefits.com/BalDesBerceaux2005a.htm, accessed on July 29, 2008.

40. Rollet-Echalier, *La politique à l'égard de la petite enfance,* 245–46.

41. Grogan, "Philanthropic Women and the State: The Société de Charité Maternelle in Avignon, 1802–1917," *French History* 14 (2000): 319–21; Clark, *The Rise of Professional Women in France: Gender and Public Administration Since 1830* (Cambridge: Cambridge University Press, 2000), as well as "Bringing Feminine Qualities into the Public Sphere: The Third Republic's Appointment of Women Inspectors," in *Gender and the Politics of Social Reform in France, 1870–1914*, ed. Elinor A. Accampo, Rachel G. Fuchs, and Mary Lynn Stewart (Baltimore: Johns Hopkins University Press, 1995), 128–56.

42. Klaus, *Every Child a Lion*, 118–21; Clark, *The Rise of Professional Women*, 86, 91–92.

43. Banquey, "La Société de Charité Maternelle de Bordeaux," 96.

44. Ibid.

45. Lisa DiCaprio also treats this question in *The Origins of the Welfare State: Women, Work, and the French Revolution* (Urbana: University of Illinois Press, 2007).

46. Sarah A. Curtis, "Charitable Ladies: Gender, Class and Religion in Nineteenth-Century Paris," *Past and Present* 177 (November 2002): 121–56.

47. Klaus, *Every Child a Lion*, 134; Rollet-Echalier, *La politique à l'égard de la petite enfance*, 246.

48. Jane Jenson, "Representations of Gender: Policies to 'Protect' Women Workers and Infants in France and the United States Before 1914," in *Women, the State, and Welfare*, ed. Linda Gordon (Madison: University of Wisconsin Press, 1991), 170.

49. Susan Lebsock offers interesting analysis relevant to this point. She writes that while the short-term benefits of benevolent activities for women are clear—a sense of purpose, development of skills, participation in democratic activities—"The debate centers on what all of this had to do with the origins of organized feminism and the growth of feminist consciousness. It has been contended on the one hand that the women's rights movement was a direct outgrowth of organized benevolence. It can also be argued that organized benevolence inhibited the development of feminism, first by perpetuating the image of woman as possessed of a special mission (as opposed to equal capacities) and second by encouraging women to engage in projects that gave them the semblance but not the substance of power. The compromise position is that benevolent activity helped women to become conscious of themselves as a group, a necessary precondition for feminist protest, though not in itself a sufficient cause." *The Free Women of Petersburg: Status and Culture in a Southern Town, 1784–1860* (New York: Norton, 1985), 196–97. See also Offen, "Depopulation, Nationalism, and Feminism," 672–76.

50. For a discussion of infant/maternity legislation passed under the Third Republic, see Rachel G. Fuchs, "The Right to Life: Paul Strauss and the Politics of Motherhood," in *Gender and the Politics of History*, 96–99, and Rollet-Echalier, *La politique à l'égard de la petite enfance*. Lisa Di Caprio sees the Third Republic as an important phase in the development of modern, secular social welfare and notes that "across the political spectrum, the status of women and children emerged as a central concern and an object of governmental intervention." *The Origins of the Welfare State*, 199. She traces the social legislation passed under the Third Republic in the epilogue, 199–204.

51. Fuchs, "The Right to Life," 82.

52. Ibid., 90.

# Index

July Revolution. *See* July Monarchy

June Days, 128

Klaus, Alisa, 9, 25, 97, 179

Knibiehler, Yvonne, 30, 62

Koven, Seth, 5, 25, 26

Laborie, Lanzac de, 59, 63

Lambert, Jacques, 40

Law on Associations, 117

leadership, 140–41. *See also* social class factors

*le droit à la subsistence. See* right to subsistence

legacies, 224–25n79. *See also* private donations

legal status, 123–39. *See also* public utility designation

Legitimists. *See* Royalists

Lejeune-Resnick, Evelyne, 25

Limoges: administrative problems, 64; demographics, 20–21; government funding, 80, 232n50, 237n124; government relationship, 159; medical affiliations, 159; overview, 20–21; public utility designation, 123, 135; service statistics, 151, 154; Sisters of Charity assistance, 142–43, 155; Third Republic, 155

lottery, 42, 43–44

Louis-Philippe (king of France), 110, 115, 118, 136

Louis XVI (king of France), 43

Louis XVIII (king of France), 76

Lynch, Katherine, 141

Lyon: administrative work, 143; affiliated organization, 151; Bourbon restoration, 79; breast feeding, 87; charitable institutions list, 187n61; complaints to government, 146; decline, 171; demographics, 12–14; emotional style, 88, 95–96; government funding, 80; government relationship, 165–68; infant mortality rates, 161; leadership, 140; medical affiliations, 158; membership, 187–88n66; moral restrictions on aid, 91–92, 104; Napoleonic era, 54, 64, 67; nineteenth century case study, 1–3; overview, 13–14; private donations, 149, 150; public utility designation, 122–23; religious influence, 109; service statistics, 151, 152, 154; social class reconciliation, 95–98; Third Republic, 172, 174; vaccinations, 156

Maison de la Couche, 29

management structure, 35–36

Marais, Jean-Luc, 128, 136

Marie-Amélie (queen of France), 127, 140, 233n58

Marie-Louise (empress of France), 59, 60, 140, 156–57

marriage requirement, 172–73. *See also* religiosity

Marseille: administrative work, 143; Bourbon restoration, 143; breast feeding, 87; complaints to government, 146; demographics, 16–17; moral restrictions on aid, 101; Napoleonic era, 55, 64, 71; overview, 17; private donations, 128–29, 221–22n43, 223n54; public utility designation, 121–22, 128–29, 132–34; service statistics, 151, 152, 154

Martin-Fugier, Anne, 149

maternalism: breast feeding, 86–87; as critical to female identity, 27; membership policies, 111–12; moral restrictions on aid, 91–92; as "natural," 87, 88, 91; practical skills, 89; social vision, 84–86; solidarity between women, 85–86, 106–7; support, 83–84; teachable skills, 89–91; women's roles, 84. *See also* domestic ideology

maternal love, 7–8, 209n10, 213n64. *See also* breast feeding; maternalism

Maza, Sarah, 87

McCarthy, Kathleen D., 105, 146

medical affiliations, 157–58, 159

membership policies, 111–12. *See also* social class factors

membership statistics, 68–69, 70

*Memoirs d'un ouvrier rouennais* (Noiret), 18–19

mendicancy, 42

Mercier, Louis-Sebastien, 31

Merriman, John, 20

Michel, Sonya, 5, 25, 26

Mills, Hazel, 155

*Le Moniteur*, 25

Montalivet. *See* Bachasson, Jean Pierre

moral restrictions on aid: Bordeaux, 98–99, 101; "deserving" v. "undeserving" mothers, 241n175; in general, 94–95, 102–4; Lyon, 94, 101–2, 104, 165; Marseille, 101; mortality statistics (abandoned children), 161; Paris, 94, 99; Rouen, 99, 100. *See also* religiosity

mortmain, 118, 125

CHRISTINE ADAMS is a
professor of history
at St Mary's College of
Maryland.

The University of Illinois Press
is a founding member of the
Association of American University Presses.

―――――――――――――――――

Composed in 10.5/13 Adobe Minion
by Jim Proefrock
at the University of Illinois Press
Manufactured by Sheridan Books, Inc.

University of Illinois Press
1325 South Oak Street
Champaign, IL 61820-6903
www.press.uillinois.edu